SPIRIT RISING

The Coming Light, photograph, Kathleen Burckhardt, 18, Saanich Peninsula
Monthly Meeting, Canadian Yearly Meeting (FGC-FUM), Canada

Spirit Rising

YOUNG QUAKER VOICES

EDITED BY

Angelina Conti, Cara Curtis, C. Wess Daniels, Harriet Hart,
Sarah Katreen Hoggatt, Evelyn Jadin, John Epur Lomuria,
Emma Condori Mamani, Katrina McQuail, Rachel Anne Miller

A PROJECT OF
QUAKERS UNITING IN
PUBLICATIONS (QUIP)

QUAKER PRESS
OF FRIENDS GENERAL CONFERENCE
PHILADELPHIA, PENNSYLVANIA

Copyright © 2010 by Quakers Uniting in Publications

Published by Quaker Press of Friends General Conference
1216 Arch Street, 2B, Philadelphia, PA 19107

Cover design by Alice Rutherford and David Botwinik

Cover art components: Abraham Quispe Ticona, David Botwinik, and Sadie Forsythe

Cover concept: Betsy Blake, Angelina Conti, Carly Frintner, Sadie Forsythe, and Alice Rutherford

Interior design by David Botwinik

Translations from Spanish to English by Emma Condori Mamani

For more information about Quakers Uniting in Publications (QUIP) and this book, contact QUIP at www.quakerquip.org

Library of Congress Cataloging-in-Publication Data
    Spirit rising : young Quaker voices / edited by Angelina Conti . . . [et al.].
       p. cm.
    ISBN 978-1-888305-86-9 (alk. paper)
       1. Spiritual life—Society of Friends. 2. Christian life—Quaker authors.
I. Conti, Angelina, 1982–

BX7738.S65 2010
248.8'30882896—dc22

                                        2010005924

For additional copies, contact QuakerBooks of FGC at www.quakerbooks.org
or bookstore@fgcquaker.org

Contents

Practicing Faithfulness: Seeking, Callings, Leadings, Ministry

One Source, Many Streams: Friendship, Convergence, Ecumenism, and Intervisitation

Kingdom Life: Witness and Engagement in the World

Deep Oceans of Darkness and Light: Sufferings

Stories of Convincement, Conversion, Salvation, and Personal Transformation

Breaking Bread: Fellowship with God and Others

Troubling the Water: Calls for Transformation and Renewal

List of Images and Illustrations

Acknowledgments

As is usually the case with a project like this one, this book would not have been possible without the work and support of many people. To recognize the circles of Friends whose work and faith have shaped this book, the editorial board would like to thank:

Our elders, spiritual Friends, and support committees (official and unofficial): Marge Abbott, Zachary Moon, Bainito Wamalwa, Eden Grace, Robin Mohr, Claire Reddy, Stephen Dotson, Gil and Chris Skidmore, Elizabeth Cave, Trish Carn, Ben Hustis, Stuart Breyer, Deborah Shaw, Kody Hersh, and Elaine Emily.

We would especially like to thank Lucy Duncan for her strong support and accompaniment as an elder to us as individuals and to the project as a whole. She offered us considerable wisdom from her work on *Whispers of Faith* and has walked with us from the beginning.

Barbara Mays, former Publications Manager at Quaker Press of Friends General Conference (FGC), drew upon her experience on *Whispers*, long history with Quakers Uniting in Publications (QUIP), and Friends publishing. She was a joyful, tender, and supportive editor.

All those f/Friends who helped with initial translations into English: Kori Heavner, Louise Salinas, Vicki Hain Poorman, Max Rennebohm, W. Geoffrey Black, Kat Griffith, Kathryn Lum, Michael Lemon, Madeline Kreider Carlson, Inez Steigerwald, and Eden Grace.

We are indebted to our Friend and colleague, Emma Condori Mamani, for translating a Spanish edition of this book.

Staff and Friends involved with the Friends World Committee for Consultation (FWCC) for their help with outreach to Friends worldwide, particularly Valerie Joy for her help with contacting Friends in Asia, and Louise Salinas for her support and enthusiasm from the beginning, and her support in contacting Friends in Latin America. Louise also worked as a copy editor on the Spanish manuscript, and we are grateful for her time and energy. Margaret Fraser provided invaluable assistance with the names and affiliations of yearly meetings and enthusiastic support throughout the project. FWCC has done profound work to cultivate connections among Friends around the world, and this project would have been impossible without those connections.

The Friends General Conference staff, the Pendle Hill resident community, the home of Chris Gradel and Rich Conti, and the Sierra Friends

Center community all supported this project by allowing it to find fertile ground and a logistical "home base."

The Youth Ministries Committee of FGC and the Children and Young People's program of Britain Yearly Meeting, and specifically Emily Stewart and Howard Nurden, respectively, for their early and lasting support of this project.

Those Friends who offered hospitality for editorial board members during our meetings outside Greensboro, North Carolina, in 2008 and in Portland, Oregon, and Seattle, Washington, in 2009, and while we traveled to conduct workshops and collect submissions. Your hospitality was a profound and gracious gift.

QUIP Friends and officers have been steadfast in their trust and support of us and unwavering in their belief and enthusiasm for this project since its beginning. They are truly good youth allies—offering strong support, resources and accompaniment, but also trusting us to do the work ourselves. Those QUIP Friends not already mentioned here include: Charles Martin, Liz Yeats, Terry Sorelle, and Betsy Muench.

The following monthly meetings, churches, yearly meetings, Quaker granting bodies and other funders gave generously to this project: the Joyce Green Association of Finchley Quaker Meeting and the Children and Young People's Program, both of Britain Yearly Meeting; North Carolina Yearly Meeting (Conservative); the Publications Services Committee, Friends Institute, Jonathan Rhoads Trust and Bequests Fund of Philadelphia Yearly Meeting; the Obadiah Brown Benevolent Fund of New England Yearly Meeting; individual Friends in Canadian Yearly Meeting; the Hurford Humanities Center of Haverford College; QUIP's Sowle Fund; and monthly meetings including San Francisco Friends Meeting, Jamestown Friends Meeting, Delta Monthly Meeting, and Vancouver Monthly Meeting.

The Tyson Memorial Fund of Philadelphia challenged us, with their generous matching grant, to increase the support of individual Friends. Subsequently, many individual Friends, including many younger Friends, supported this project financially. We would like to break with tradition and name all of those Friends: Brigitte Alexander, Claire Bateman, Lauren Baumann, J. Brent and Nancy Bill, Deborah Block and Bill Harley, John Burdick, Elizabeth Cave, Anne Collins and Bruce Crauder, Lucy Duncan and Graham Garner, Christopher Hanning, Bruce Hawkins, Kody Gabriel Hersh, Andrea and John Kintree, Linda Lawson, John C. Lawson-Meyers, Judith Lumb, Charles Martin, Donna McDaniel, Ann Marie Moriarty, Elizabeth Muench, Tom Mullen, George Owen, Helene Pollock, Judy

Rangnes, Johanna Rioardan, Maggie Simmons, Rebecca Sullivan, Erika Tarabini, Nancy Wallace, Susanne Ratcliffe Wilson, Warren Wilson-Reiner, Greg Woods, and all those Friends who gave after the manuscript was finished.

To all those teenage and young adult Friends who submitted their visual art and creative writing to this Project, both those whose work is included here and those whose work is not, *Thank you*. Your stories and creative expression are important. You are heard. You are seen. Keep writing. Keep creating. Keep speaking. Keep ministering to us. The Religious Society of Friends *needs* you.

Finally, and most importantly, we thank that force and power that brought us together, guided and inspired our work, and was tender, challenging, and awesome. We have many names for the Divine—Spirit, God, Heavenly Father, Universe, Papa, Mother, Light—and we know that without it this work would not have been possible.

Faithfully,

Angelina Conti
Cara Curtis
C. Wess Daniels
Harriet Hart
Sarah Katreen Hoggatt
Evelyn Jadin
John Epur Lomuria
Emma Condori Mamani
Katrina McQuail
Rachel Anne Miller

Introduction

Where the Words Come From

In 1763, John Woolman, an American Quaker from the state of New Jersey, set out to travel and visit among the indigenous people in Wyalusing, who were called the Delaware or Lenape Indians. At that time in American history, during the French and Indian War, relations between European colonists and indigenous people in the Americas were often violent and antagonistic. It would have been considered unusual, if not radical, for John Woolman to visit them as a friend. (John Woolman was no stranger to radical witness, however, and was also a passionate opponent of slavery.)

The Lenape graciously received him and another visitor and welcomed their speaking at a community meeting. John Woolman noted in his *Journal*: "The interpreters, endeavouring to acquaint the people with what I said, in short sentences, found some difficulty." Noting their struggle, he released them from interpreting and expressed his faith that if he prayed well, God would hear him and he would be understood.

He then prayed aloud for all to hear, even though he knew that his language was different from that of the Delaware, and that his words would not be fully translated or understood.

After he had finished praying, John Papunehang, a Lenape who was recognized as a leader and prophet among his people, turned to an interpreter and said, *"I love to feel where the words come from."*

When the editorial board of the Quaker Youth Book Project gathered on the Oregon Coast in April 2009 to make selections for the book you now hold, we took this story as inspiration. Our editorial team of ten young adult Friends represents all of the major theological branches of the Religious Society of Friends and five countries: Bolivia, Canada, Kenya, the United Kingdom, and the United States of America. Our work together has necessitated considerable explaining of our lives, faith, experiences and language as Friends. We have done a lot of sharing and a lot of listening. It has been joyful and occasionally quite hard.

Our work together began in April 2008 in Greensboro, North Carolina, and the editorial board spent over a year gathering submissions of writing and art through the summer of 2009. We each worked in our home regions and countries (and occasionally those foreign to us) to solicit work for the book—often traveling long distances, and on more than one occasion risking bodily harm. We have sat with young Friends while they wrote, and worked with them in writing workshops and through correspondence as they refined their pieces. We received many, many pieces via e-mail (indeed, this project would have been considerably more difficult without the Internet) and we also received many handwritten pieces as well as original paintings and drawings. In all, we received nearly three hundred pieces from Australia, Bolivia, Burundi, Canada, Cuba, El Salvador, Guatemala, Italy, Kenya, Korea, New Zealand, Nepal, Norway, Peru, Sweden, the United Kingdom, and the United States.

Whenever possible, we have worked closely with writers on the editing of their pieces and have endeavored to include explanations of topics, cultural practices, language, and theology. In an effort to include and preserve the diverse voices of Friends, pieces originally written in Spanish appear here in both Spanish and English, and we have preserved the British spellings of certain words in pieces from the United Kingdom, Kenya, Canada, and Australia. A full Spanish translation of this book will also be available. In some instances we have titled pieces that either did not have a title or whose original title was the query to which it was a response. Whenever the editors have picked a title, we have used language directly from the piece in an effort to further support the author's voice. Because we did not have contact information for all of our contributors, particularly from Latin America and Africa, we have edited some pieces especially gently and used brackets to show where we changed or added something for clarity.

We endeavored to do all of our editorial work with integrity, care, and tenderness.

If we have done our job well—if we have successfully gathered the voices of teenage and young adult Friends from around the world and across the theological branches of Friends—there will be language and content in this book that both profoundly resonate with you *and* that are not at all consistent with your tradition of Quakerism or your cultural experiences. Some pieces may surprise, confuse, alarm or even offend you. We recognize that, and we trust you to hold this book, *all of it*, as a testimony and gift of the Spirit.

In his *Journal*, John Woolman noted that while struggling with language, the interpreters "helped one another and we labored along together, divine love attending." That has been our experience; we have labored together and we have felt the presence of Divine love.

So as you begin to read, we invite you to remember John Woolman and to read with an open heart, to listen fully, and to *feel where the words come from*. It may be a source you recognize.

May this book be a journey for you. It has been a journey for us.

Faithfully,

Angelina Conti
Cara Curtis
C. Wess Daniels
Harriet Hart
Sarah Katreen Hoggatt
Evelyn Jadin
John Epur Lomuria
Emma Condori Mamani
Katrina McQuail
Rachel Anne Miller

August 2009

Front row from left: Rachel Miller, Katrina McQuail, Cara Curtis, Angelina Conti. Back row from left: Emma Condori, Evelyn Jadin, C. Wess Daniels with Lillian Daniels, John Epur Lomuria, Sarah Katreen Hoggatt, Harriet Hart.

The Quaker Tapestry is a modern embroidery of 77 fascinating panels. Made by 4,000 men, women and children, this international community project explores three centuries of social history. The Exhibition Centre in Kendal, Cumbria UK is open to the public from early spring to late autumn each year. For more information visit their website www.quaker-tapestry.co.uk

> Editor's note: For information about the history of the branches of Friends, go to www.quakerinfo.org/quakerism/brancheshistory.html

List of Abbreviations

AFSC The American Friends Service Committee is a Quaker organization which carries out service, development, social justice, and peace programs throughout the world. Founded by Quakers in 1917 to provide conscientious objectors with an opportunity to aid civilian war victims, AFSC's work attracts the support and partnership of people of many races, religions, and cultures.

EFCI The Evangelical Friends Church International (formerly known as EFI) is a branch of Religious Society of Friends (Quaker) yearly meetings (regional associations) around the world that profess evangelical Christian beliefs. The mission of EFCI is "to help local Friends churches around the world meet the spiritual needs of their communities." Over 1,100 Evangelical Friends churches representing more than 140,000 Friends in 24 countries are currently associated with EFCI.

FGC Friends General Conference is a Quaker organization in the unprogrammed tradition of the Religious Society of Friends which primarily serves its affiliated yearly and monthly meetings. There are fifteen affiliated yearly meetings in the United States and Canada, and ten directly affiliated monthly meetings. FGC's statement of purpose reads: "Friends General Conference, with Divine guidance, nurtures the spiritual vitality of the Religious Society of Friends (Quakers) by providing programs and services for Friends, meetings, and seekers."

FUM Friends United Meeting is an association of twenty-six yearly meetings of the Religious Society of Friends (Quakers) in North America, Africa, and the Caribbean. In addition, there are several individual monthly meetings and organizations that are members of FUM. FUM's headquarters is in Richmond, Indiana, and has offices in Kisumu, Kenya. FUM's statement of purpose reads: Our purpose is "to energize and equip Friends through the power of the Holy Spirit to gather people into fellowships where Jesus Christ is known, loved and obeyed as Teacher and Lord."

FWCC Friends World Committee for Consultation is an international organization whose purpose is to encourage fellowship among all the branches of the Religious Society of Friends.

Country Door, photograph, Susanna Corson-Finnerty, Germantown Monthly Meeting, Philadelphia Yearly Meeting (FGC), United States

Ways of Worship,
Forms of Faith

The Opening

As I open myself, God flows into every vein of my body.
When God flows in, I become more loving, kind and hopeful.
I'm smiling, sunny and holding onto hope,
Like a baby holds on to her pacifier.

God's love is such a gift to me,
It is pure, radical and unquestioning.
He also gives me great love and joy
Through the friends and family that touch my life.

I no longer continuously ask things of God,
I know He has given me the circumstances,
It is up to me to decide what to do with them.
He has given me life, what will I make of it?

With each breath I take I have the opportunity
To make a difference, to do great things.
There are a whole twenty-four hours in a day,
How many can I use to glorify Him?

How much love can I show to others,
Like He has shown to me?
What can I do to thank Him for
Every little thing He has done for me?

I can make my life meaningful and devoted to Him.
He does not need presents, tied with a pretty bow.
All He wants is my heart, soul
And my servitude throughout my days.

Liz Wine, 27
University Friends Church, dually affiliated with EFC—Mid-America and Great Plains Yearly Meeting (FUM)
United States

La Adoración

Alguna vez te has preguntado ¿Qué es la adoración? Y ¿por qué adoras? Bueno en mi surgieron esas preguntas y muchas mas, antes lo hacia porque si y ya, cantar y nada mas, pero ahora la adoración cumple un rol muy importante en mi vida diaria. Para mi es una experiencia muy importante, es una forma de comunicarme con Dios cantando.

Dirigir una oración en cántico es algo que surge de lo más profundo de tu corazón, como buscar la perla de gran precio en el fondo del mar, el mar eres tú y la perla tu corazón dirigido a Dios. ¿Cuándo adoras como lo haces? ¿Realmente sientes lo que sale de tu boca cuando alabas? Muchas veces adoramos con voz en cuello y realmente no vemos la verdadera manera de alabar ya que es una experiencia inolvidable y edificable. Les comparto una pequeña experiencia cuando participé en un encuentro de UJESA (Unión de Jóvenes Santidad Amigos) que se llevó en el pueblo de Patamanta, todas las hermanas y los hermanos jóvenes adoraban y alababan a Dios, pero cuando lo hacíamos sentíamos en nuestro corazón ¡Que hermoso fue! Venía nantos jóvenes que perseguían lo mismo que yo, lo que yo buscaba con tanto afán.

Es así que como todos nosotros tenemos experiencias y nos edificamos y regresamos con mas fuerza de seguir adelante sin desmayar, es como cuando un león persigue a su presa, este cae pero se levanta con mas fuerza es así como cada Amigo debe levantarse cuando siente caer. También la adoración te da consuelo en momentos de angustia y felicidad cuando está alegre, funciona como algo complementario en nuestra fe, algo así como la arena al mar así como dice la palabra de Dios "¿Está alguno alegre? Cante alabanzas, ¿está alguno afligido? haga oración."

Entonces lo único que podríamos hacer es que cuando estemos dando adoración no lo hagamos con voz en cuello, sino de todo nuestro corazón, no caigamos sigamos adelante, perseveremos, y sigamos las pisadas del maestro hasta el fin de nuestras vidas.

Fanny Mamani
Iglesia Evangélica Misión, Boliviana de Santidad Amigos (EFCI)
Bolivia

Worship

Have you ever asked yourself, *What is worship? And why do you worship?* These and many other questions have arisen for me. Before I used to just do it—sing, and that was all, but now worship plays a really important role in my daily life. For me it is a very important experience. It is a way of communicating with God through song.

To pray in song is something that wells up from the depths of your heart, like looking for the pearl of great price in the bottom of the sea. You are the sea and the pearl is your heart directed to God. When you worship, what do you do? Do you really feel what comes out of your mouth when you praise? Often we worship when our hearts are not really in it, and we don't see the true way of worshipping, which is unforgettable and edifying. I share with you a little experience when I participated in a gathering of UJESA (Santidad Friends Youth Gathering) that took place in the town of Patamanta. All the young brothers and sisters worshipped and praised God, and when we did it we felt it in our hearts! How beautiful it was! Lots of young people came who were seeking the same thing I was looking for with such devotion.

It is in this way that we all have experiences and we learn and return with more strength to carry on and not grow weary. It is like when a lion pursues its prey, the prey falls but gets up with more strength than before. This is how a Friend should get up when she/he falls. Also, worship gives consolation in moments of anguish, and happiness when one is cheerful. It functions as a complement to our faith, something like the sand is to the sea. As the word of God says, "Is someone happy? Sing praises. Is someone afflicted? Pray."

So, the only thing we can do when we are giving praise or adoration, let's not do it half-heartedly, but rather with our whole heart. Let's not fall away, but press on, persevere, and continue to follow the footsteps of the Master until the end of our lives.

Fanny Mamani
Bolivian Holiness Mission of EFCI
Bolivia

Silence

Silence
Gives me peace
So I can breathe
In this chaotic world

Silence
Is more than the absence of speech
It is a free moment
When we clean the air
Have time to think
to clear our soul
And go deep into our selves,
into our minds

Silence
Is my friend
I want to go there again and again

Tonje Smidt Hundevadt, 21
Oslo Meeting, Norway Yearly Meeting
Norway

Quaker Haiku

Silence envelops
Hearts gathering together
Waiting to be led

Kathleen Burckhardt, 18
Saanich Peninsula Monthly Meeting, Canadian Yearly Meeting
(FGC-FUM)
Canada

Cultural Activities

The founders who established the Quaker church held their rules and beliefs, which they followed from that time until now. The leaders of the Quaker church still follow the ways and rules of those who established the church a long time ago, e.g., they say that George Fox used to conduct the church slowly and there was no clapping of hands in the church. So they have remembered such steps, thus making the church be like a cult. They [aren't] to be led by the Holy Spirit, but they follow the culture, thus the church is not growing.

The Quaker church is among the first churches that were established in the country [of Kenya], but when it comes to development and growth it is really behind as compared to other churches. This is just because they don't want changes in the church. Also because of the culture of the church, which does not allow use of musical instruments such as keyboards, *kayambei*, and others. This has really made the church to be boring when it comes to worship and praising, thus it ends up losing many youth who go to fellowship in other denominations, thus leaving the Quaker church because of the culture of the church. And remember, it does not even attract people or Christians from other denominations to join them, but it always loses more Christians to other churches.

Liani Phylis
Kwanza Secondary School
Kenya

Worship

From an outside perspective, my relationship with worship must seem tense and sporadic at best. I am always incredibly busy, packing my life full of commitments and projects. Movement, noise, and chaos flow with me, almost inextricably linked to my core being. In the last few years I have rarely made it to Quaker meeting on a regular basis and though I have formalized my membership with Kitchener Area Monthly Meeting, I am still searching for a meeting community that I am physically near and also meets my spiritual and community needs.

I think it is the constant chaos and busyness of my life that makes my relationship with worship that much more important to me. I attempt to find ways to commune and connect with the divine every day, not just waiting for meeting or a Sunday to build that relationship. I shy away from labeling my actions and interactions as worship, because that feels too limiting. But the moments when I find myself most at peace and closest to God are boringly ordinary and everyday.

Worship, when I am by myself, looks like baking, cooking, or going for a walk outside. It is quiet, with a purpose, but not one that distracts from my ability to be open to the Spirit and centered. External noises add to, instead of distract from, the experience. I believe that my creativity and relationship with God are bound together, that I would not have one without the other.

My worship community is spread across the globe. This is something that is incredibly frustrating at times, but it also creates very special bonds and intense relationships because you really have to work to maintain them. I choose to worship with people I trust and feel safe with. This does not mean that I have to know them before I worship with them. That would make attending a new meeting almost impossible. Instead, it is simply a gut feeling that I get. If I were to attend a meeting and feel uncomfortable or unsafe, I would be unable to worship. I cannot open myself up to the inner light and that of God if I feel my safety could be compromised.

Worship and my relationship to God are very personal things, which is why I love the Quaker style of worship I grew up in. I think it is so incredible to meet with a group of people and settle into silent worship together. The energy that is created by a diverse group of individuals seeking the Divine together, knowing that God speaks to each person and that on occasion the messages you receive are meant to be shared, because they are for others, just awes me.

I wish more of my group experiences of worship included singing or music. Not that I am a talented musical individual, but I feel like music and dancing are ways of celebrating God and the miraculousness of our existence and that we don't always need to be serious and quiet to show our reverence and deep connectedness to the Divine.

Being in such a transient and transitional phase of my life has made it hard for me to find a meeting and feel really connected to my faith community that way. I love visiting other meetings, but do not find them to be a calming and centering experience. Too often I am distracted by meeting new people, seeing what the meeting house or space looks like, experiencing the little ways in which different Quaker groups worship differently or similarly. I find it difficult to start attending a meeting when I know that I will only be there for a short or set amount of time. I am afraid of becoming attached and involved and then having to leave it when I move and then going through it all again in the next place.

I have long-term relationships with the Friends General Conference Gathering, Camp NeeKauNis, and Canadian Yearly Meeting, as well as with the worship groups and meetings I attended as a child, so that when I go back to visit them or attend yearly sessions I can slip back in without a hitch. It doesn't feel like I have been away from those communities, sometimes for over a year.

Worship brings me closer to the people I am with because, despite our different beliefs, lifestyles, and personalities, we obviously all have the desire to strengthen our relationships with the Divine, to create community, and to continue seeking together. I think that the various ways that Quakers worship together celebrate individuality and similarities. It is an incredible gift for me to be able to pray with Friends in their style of worship and then be able to share with them my preferred way of prayer. I give thanks every day for the bounty of my life.

Katrina McQuail, 26
Kitchener Area Monthly Meeting, Canadian Yearly Meeting
(FGC-FUM)
Canada

Untitled Portrait, photograph, Joe Oram, 22, Warwick Friends Meeting, Britain Yearly Meeting, United Kingdom

Un Minuto Especial

De todos los momentos que tengo en mi vida, solo uno me cambia el día por completo, es un momento de tranquilidad que me fortalece y me anima a enfrentar el día con todos sus problemas y dificultades con alegría; para alegría mía no es la única vez y nunca es la misma, sino que cada momento que ocurre no dura mas de un minuto.

Todo se resume en una palabra o frase que sólo en ese momento tiene sentido en mi vida y lo único que existe es Dios y yo; que me encuentro a solas con El y que quisiera que durara mas y sea eterno y sin final.

Al igual que todos los jóvenes de mi Iglesia tengo muchos gustos, pero el que me gusta mas es ese minuto especial en mi vida.

¿Quién como tú? No hay nadie
¿Cómo yo? Hay muchos
Pero para mi vida
Solo existes Tú.

Si lo lees desearía que tú también lo vivieras.

Henry Loza Diaz
Congregación Cristiana Amigos, Iglesia Nacional Evangélica "Los
Amigos" de Bolivia (EFCI)
Bolivia

A Special Moment

Of all the moments that I have in my life, only one changes me so completely this day. It's a moment of peacefulness that strengthens me and encourages me to face the day and all its problems and difficulties with joy, for my joy comes often and is never the same, instead every moment in which joy happens does not last more than a minute.

Everything can be summed up in one word or phrase that only in that moment has meaning in my life and the only things that exist are God and me; that I find myself alone with Him and that I would like it to last longer, maybe eternally and without end.

Like all the young people in my church I have many pleasures, but that which I like the most is that special minute in my life.

Who is like you? There is no one.
Like me? There are many.

But for my life
Only you exist

If you read this I would hope that you also will experience it.

Henry Loza Diaz
Christian Friends Church, INELA—Bolivia
Bolivia

Incantation

Shhhhh.

It will come to you
unexplained
without pretension
or expectation.

The addiction
from a past
no longer yours
or
never yours
but for your
blood

Will
wane with the moon,
never subsiding
but becoming
full then half to the
crescent smile of the
Cheshire Cat
laughing at you
from above.

But

Remember
the eclipse
and your moment
of redemption,

the Sun,
in your blackest
hour of replanting.

Shhhhhh.

Rest your black heart,
your weary mind,
your cramped hand
for a moment
in the space
between.

Rest for a moment
beside the candle
of your hand and

Pause

to see—

if blind
with your
ears—

if deaf
with your heart —

if dead

with the life
that surrounds you
with eyes
and ears
and hearts
Open
to images
captured
repainted
replanted
relived
in the

Silence
of the
space between.

Shhhhhh.

It will come to you
unexplained
without pretension
or expectation.

The muse you
crave is there
not here
in hand.

She is you.

Sara Waxman, 27
Chestnut Hill Monthly Meeting, Philadelphia Yearly Meeting (FGC)
United States

Editor's note: This piece previously appeared on Sara's blog
at www.grummelot.blogspot.com.

¿Cuan Importante Es la Oración en Su Vida?

La oración es algo que te fortalece, alienta, reconforta y te da confianza ¿Sabes como orar? ¿Sabes porque lo haces? De algún modo cada ser humano elevó alguna oración, corta o tal vez larga o unas simples gracias. Por ejemplo, lo que yo encuentro en la oración, es una comunicación con nuestro Padre Celestial, que, aún a pesar de todo sabe lo que me pasa durante el día, pero espera que se lo cuente, que le hable. Es tan importante de una u otra manera hacer una oración ¿Cómo lo haces tú?

Cada persona sabe que la fortaleza es un valor, muchas veces inalcanzable, ¿Lo alcanzaste tú? De que manera puede uno demostrar fortaleza a lo largo de su vida, acaso es tan simple como decir "Lo siento" o "Me equivoqué." No es algo que está tan dentro de ti que en vez de demostrarlo lo actúas. Oramos cuando estamos tristes, cantamos y adoramos cuando estamos alegres. Y te fortaleces espiritualmente cuando te comunicas con tu Dios Padre y te sientes con nuevas fuerzas para continuar. Bueno, ora constantemente y comunícate con Aquel que te entiende.

Has sentido alguna vez que desfalleces y nada te alienta, pero otras veces tienes tal animo para seguir que tienes un corazón que nada ni nadie lo contamina? Yo si lo he sentido tambien, y muchas veces no tengo fuerzas para continuar. Pero cuando me acerco en oración a Dios tengo tal animo y fuerza. Y nada me puede hacere decaer. Entonces si quieres seguir adelante, como Dios dice en sus escrituras: "Esfuérzate y se valiente."

¿En ocasiones sientes que no vales nada, que andas sin rumbo lejos vagando sin saber a donde ir y sin saber a quien acudir? Se que en esos momentos oraste tal vez sin conocer a quien te dirigías pero te reconfortaste y sentiste nuevas fuerzas que jamás antes sentiste. Y entendiste que alguien te guarda y que esta ahí sin importar donde tú estés. Recuerda que El es tu amparo y fortaleza, tu pronto auxilio en las tribulaciones.

Cuando pierdes la confianza en alguien y no sabes a quien acudir ¿a quien te diriges? ¿En quien confías? Muchos de nosotros involuntariamente como jóvenes confiamos en seres humanos que a la larga nos fallan. Yo al final de todo me di cuenta que eso no era necesario; sino simplemente comprendí que he tenido un fiel amigo, mi Dios, en quien confiar, y en quien agachar mi cabeza en su hombro y decirle cuanto lo necesito. Si, ¡eso es!. Ahora tú confías en el Dios eterno que creó los cielos y la tierra, quien te escogió a ti de entre muchos.

Entonces qué más queda decir. Sabemos que la vida está llena de obstáculos y si no como triunfamos. Orar a Dios no nos cuesta tiempo; además a El le encanta escucharnos y ayudaros. Recuerda que el Señor nos espera con los brazos abiertos; lo cual no deberíamos olvidarlo.

Fanny Mamani
Iglesia Evangélica Misión Boliviana de Santidad Amigos (MBSA)
(EFCI)
Bolivia

How Important Is Prayer in Your Life?

Prayer is something that strengthens you, encourages, comforts, and gives you confidence. Do you know how to pray? Do you know why you do it? One way or another, every human being has raised his or her voice in some prayer, short or perhaps long, or some simple thanks. For example, what I encounter in prayer is communication with our Celestial Father, who, in spite of everything, knows what happens to me during the day, yet waits for me to tell it, waits for me to talk to Him. It is so important, in one way or another, to say a prayer. How do you do it?

Everyone knows that fortitude is a value, many times unattainable. Have you attained it? In what way can one demonstrate fortitude throughout one's life? Maybe it is as simple, perhaps, as saying "I'm sorry" or "I was wrong." Is it not something that is so deep inside you that in place of demonstrating it you simply pretend? We pray when we are sad, we sing and worship when we are joyful. And you strengthen yourself spiritually when you communicate with God your Father, and you feel new strength to continue. Well, pray constantly and communicate with the One who understands you.

You have sometimes felt that you lost heart and nothing encouraged you. Other times you have such spirit to continue, you have a heart that nothing and no one can corrupt. I have felt it too, and many times I don't have strength to continue. But when I approach God in prayer I have such encouragement and strength. And nothing can make me fail. Therefore, if you want to continue forward, as God says in his scriptures: "Be strong and courageous."

On some occasions you feel that you are worth nothing; that you walk without direction, wandering far without knowing where you are going and without knowing whom to turn to. I know that in those moments you prayed, perhaps without knowing whom you addressed, but you were comforted and felt new strength that you had never felt before. And you understood that someone protects you and that He is there no matter where you are. Remember that He is your refuge and fortress, your immediate help in tribulations.

When you lose confidence in someone and you don't know to whom to turn, to whom do you address yourself? In whom do you trust? Many of us as young people involuntarily trust in human beings who let us down in the long run. At the end of it all I realized that was not necessary; instead I simply understood that I have had a faithful friend, my God, in whom to trust, on whose shoulder to lay my head while telling Him how much I need him. Yes, that's how it is! Now you trust in the eternal God who created the heavens and the earth, who chose you from among many.

Then what remains to be said? We know that life is full of obstacles, if not how to overcome them. Praying to God does not cost us time. Besides, God loves to listen to us and help us. Remember that the Lord awaits us with open arms; we shouldn't forget that.

Fanny Mamani
Bolivian Holiness Mission (EFCI)
Bolivia

Phish Food

"Why are we so quiet?"

Those are the first words I ever spoke in Quaker meeting. I was twelve years old and my dad had bet me an entire pint of Ben & Jerry's Phish Food ice cream to stand up and ask that in the middle of meeting.

As a member of the family assigned to read the Psalm, I was seated on the facing bench, looking out at the hundred or so people who would soon witness my embarrassing début. "The wrinklies" (as my Aunt Esther calls them) were hunched over, their gnarled hands clutching each other, their eyes squinched shut. The middle-aged crowd sat straight, their eyes peacefully closed. The youngest of the congregation did not sit straight. They twisted fuzzy pipe cleaners into animal and flower shapes and surreptitiously poked each other until their parents stopped them with a look. The only sounds that interrupted the silence were the occasional loud cough or a muffled giggle.

At the fifteen-minute mark, all the other children stood up and left for Sunday School downstairs. I was left alone on the top bench. I glanced around a bit desperately. "Why didn't I speak up earlier?" I berated myself. "I could've asked my question, escaped, and gotten that pint."

But I had not spoken up. I was now trapped there for the next hour, with nothing to do but fret over my upcoming speech. After ten minutes, I finally got up the nerve to speak. I took a deep breath, and had started to rise to my feet when Ellen Hallowell's voice broke the silence: "On Tuesday morning I went to visit my mother, who is dying of cancer. . . ."

I sat back down. By the time she finished I was a wreck. How could my one, short, childish phrase compare with that moving message? But I wanted that Phish Food. So I gathered my wavering courage and stood up. The bench creaked. All those eyes flicked open and swiveled to me. Their interest was engaged. Rebecca Gilbert had never, ever spoken in meeting.

"Why are we so quiet?" I quickly sat back down. The eyes still watched me, the speculation in them crystal clear. Then they closed and resumed their quiet contemplation. Whew, that wasn't so bad, I thought. Phish Food, here I come.

The silence was broken by Jeff Franklin: "I believe that silence is the foundation of the Quaker belief. . . ." For the next hour, I listened, stunned, as six different people spoke about the importance of silence. Some saw silence as the chance to reflect on the events of their week.

Others used silence to contemplate how God affects their lives. All of them saw silence as an opportunity to worship God in their own way. When meeting ended, many people came up to me to thank me for asking my question. On that Sunday, I discovered that sitting in silence for an hour is not just something Quakers do when they go to meeting. Rather, it is the outward expression of our deep faith in God. I did not realize at the time that my innocent question would have a greater result than a simple pint of Phish Food.

Rebecca Brinton Gilbert, 22
Willistown Meeting, Philadelphia Yearly Meeting (FGC)
United States

Amazing Things

When I go to church I always sit in the same pew.
I sit in front of Mandy and Linda and a couple of other people too.
We sing and take time to praise the Lord,
and when Jack starts talking I get a little bored.
Sometimes I get upset and I start to cry.
Everyone cares so they turn and ask why.
During greeting time we all
shake hands,
and when we pray and sing we stand.
We all love each other very much.
Jack and I always do a knuckle touch.
Audrey always pokes me and pulls my hair,
but she's the cutest and I love her mom so I don't care.
Sarah is always joking around with me,
but there are times when we have a conversation
seriously.
No matter what mood I come in,
I can't wait until next Sunday so I can come again.

Alissa LeMond, 17
Anderson First Friends Church, Indiana Yearly Meeting (FUM)
United States

Bench, photograph, Sarah Katreen Hoggatt, Freedom Friends Church, United States

When I Attend Quaker Meeting

When I attend Quaker meeting with my family and I see all the other people sitting in what seems like a deep sense of peace, I find myself experiencing envy. I cannot seem to find my peace during meeting. I find myself in a more peaceful state of mind late at night when I am beginning to drift off to sleep. I believe that a more controlled sense of peace will come with age, and I hope that someday I won't feel as restless during meeting so I can participate in the stillness and peaceful mood.

Max Dixon-Murdock, 12
Vancouver Monthly Meeting, Canadian Yearly Meeting (FGC-FUM)
Canada

Dot-to-Dot

I used to ride to "quiet meeting" on the back of my Dad's bike. I would sit in the corner with felt-tips and Dot-to-Dot books trying to colour between the lines and not make too much noise. Later, I remember wriggling and fidgeting on the laps of friendly strangers, studying the facial expressions in the practically silent circle.

I wonder how much time I spent in that circle over the following years, in the ten minutes before creeping out to read, shout, sing, and draw in Children's Programme. I spent that time making faces at the other kids, watching the ducks out the window, counting different types of shoes, reading books from the library trolley, asking forgiveness for having snuck a spoonful of Nutella, listening really hard to see if God would talk to me. . . .

I still remember the pride I felt the first time that I sat through a whole meeting, how nervous I was the first time that I gave a reading.

Now, after ten years of meetings, I realise how much I've changed. I still know how many beams there are across the meeting house ceiling and how many bars on the window, but I could no longer tell you the ratio of shoes to sandals or how many people had their eyes shut last Sunday.

I've been to quite a few discussions about how different people spend their time in meeting for worship, been given suggestions and things to try, but those ten minutes I have twice a month are different every time. I listen to and reflect on the readings and ministry. I breathe deeply. I admire the beautiful world out the window. I give thanks for the people who are present and think of those who are not. I try to clear my mind of daily worries. I try to focus on my feelings. Sometimes I just stare at the ticking clock waiting for it to be over. I've felt enlightened, relaxed, happy. I've made resolutions. I've come to feel a sense of peace. But I wouldn't claim to ever have cleared my mind completely or to have heard the Inner Voice.

Watching the younger children in the meeting as they wriggle and whisper, I'm reminded of how far I've come . . . and how far I have to go.

Keava McKeogh, 16
Waikato-Hauraki Meeting, Yearly Meeting of Aotearoa/New Zealand
New Zealand

Song of an Iona Pilgrimage*

Listen!
God sings
sausage-sizzle of surf-shifted sand
ah of the sea's vast sighs
wild goose wing-strokes.

Here!
our sandcastle
society suffers and grows each ferry
love enmeshes and embraces
this many-layered parcel.

See!
the Trinity
in scented sisterhood: yeast creating
aluminum conveying, cumin uplifting
scrubbing and swearing side-by-side.

Feel!
Laces of faith
firm on my booted feet
I step open-eyed into swamps
theological, metaphorical, literal, littoral.

Rhiannon Grant, 24

Nottingham and Derby Area Meeting, Britain Yearly Meeting

United Kingdom

*Editor's note: Iona is an ecumenical Christian community focused on
peace and social justice, the rebuilding of community, and the renewal
of worship. It has several locations in the United Kingdom, with the
primary location on the isle of Iona, off the west coast of Scotland.
This piece was written during a residence at the MacLeod Centre.

The Bread Testimony

Of the several deaths that struck my extended family lately, I find myself most reflective upon that of my cousin John Jay, who died unexpectedly early. What I know of him I learned almost entirely after his death. He was what you'd call a troubled soul, I guess (didn't fit in, didn't find a calling, though he had many interests). One of the pursuits John took up before his death was baking bread, an activity that may in some way have contributed to the increased peace of mind noted by those who were in contact with him. Though I play better with others than he ever learned to, and though I do not chain-smoke the unfiltered cigarettes that probably contributed to his early death, I feel some kinship with my cousin. I too have been slow to find a guiding course in life. I too sometimes have a hard time dealing with other people. I, like he, have a restless mind, acquiring new hobbies and interests, swiftly absorbing available information and throwing myself into my new subject with abandon. Cooking, music, bicycle repair, knitting, and many other subjects have become passions of mine, and there are sure to be more.

I have recently been turning my attention to baking bread like my cousin did. It's a perverse art, perhaps, in the supermarket era where bread, even bread that simulates very well the homemade, can simply be bought. Is it not hopelessly old fashioned to do the baker's work yourself? To mix, knead, let rise, divide, let rise again, finally bake, and (you hope) produce a beautiful loaf, brown and crackling. Put that way, the appeal may be more obvious. Baking fresh bread in the modern age, like access to fresh, local, and organic foods, nudges against the line of privilege. Only the well off have the leisure to make their own bread as a hobby, or conversely the very poor must bake their own bread out of dire necessity. This may be an oversimplification, but the fact is that the bulk of Americans do not bake bread, or even seek out fresh-baked bread. Most can afford a loaf of bread, and few may believe they can afford to take time to bake as they struggle with meeting their other daily needs. But as stress and exhaustion continue to plague the American psyche, taking the time to thoughtfully prepare the daily bread might be of some help to us harried souls, as I believe it was to John Jay. Think of that lump of dough as a big stress ball.

Baking bread is a great joy. The smell of baking bread is a smell of home, even perhaps for those who did not grow up with that smell as a regular part of their childhoods. The reaction may be ingrained, or culturally programmed. That yeasty, warm scent is the signifier for kitchen in many food cultures. Cooking from scratch and eating fresh and local food are slowly catching on in America, where food science has taken the place of food culture over the last several decades. Though the scientists are absent from the advertising and the image of our foods, they are present more than ever in the food itself. People are starting to take notice, and to push back. Look at the ingredient list on an average loaf of bread in the grocery store. How many of these ingredients can you pronounce on the first attempt? Compare this list to the basic necessaries of home-baked bread: flour, water, yeast. Why is such a simple food as bread now filled with so many things that, for thousands of years, bakers had never heard of, or even imagined? Is that not reason enough to consider starting over from the beginning and rediscovering the basic essence of what we make our toast and sandwiches from?

In kneading dough, the baker's hands reach deep into the bread, touching every interior surface, becoming intimately acquainted with the food. This closeness to the source of nourishment enriches us. This intimacy is impossible with that which comes from bag, box, or can. Such food can only provide a vicarious connection to the sources of our nourishment. It is a convenient assistant, but not a close companion, and enriches only the agribusinesses that have insinuated themselves into our kitchens. I've only made this home baking attempt a half dozen or so times as yet and have so far managed edibility but not perfection. I still eat a lot of bread from the grocery store shelves and am not on the verge of giving up that resource, nor declaring complete self sufficiency. After all, someone else grew the wheat and milled the flour I bake with. What I am declaring is that I recognize the difference between the food I own and the food I've only bought. The bread I've baked myself is food that I own. As Thoreau said of wild fruit, and could equally be said of home-made, whole foods:

> It is a grand fact that you cannot make the fairer fruits or parts of fruits matter of commerce; that is, you cannot buy the highest use and enjoyment of them. You cannot buy that pleasure which it yields to him who truly plucks it. You cannot buy a good appetite, even. In short, you may buy a servant or slave, but you cannot buy a friend.
>
> — Henry David Thoreau, *Faith in a Seed: The Dispersion of Seeds & Other Late Natural History Writings*, Bradley P. Dean, ed., Island Press, 1993.

Though I don't expect to die at forty-nine like John Jay did (and who does?), I'd like to bake some beautiful loaves before I go, so I will continue to bake in order to fuel my body and soul as I engage with life through many avenues. I will make friends with bread. As nourishing others nourishes my spirit, I will give bread to family and friends—to feed them when they are hungry, to comfort them when they grieve, and to give pleasure when they celebrate. Even if they have not reached into the heart of that bread, they can hold the hand that did. The author of that famous prayer, "Give us this day our daily bread," wasn't thinking of something pre-sliced and plastic-wrapped, but something made by hand, and with love. Surely if one can proclaim that bread is life, one should look to treat it with respect, and to take pleasure in it as you take pleasure in life.

> Keith Lepinski, 31
> Madison Friends Meeting, Northern Yearly Meeting (FGC)
> United States

Practical Experimenting with Light and Marveling

For a few years, three aspects of my life (my Quaker spirituality, poetry, and photography) have been deeply intertwined and sustaining of each other. In 2000, I started compiling a short series of haikus around the theme of daily little joys and metaphors to explore, to help me grow spiritually. As I was doing this I started to illustrate the metaphors visually by taking pictures.

Light got in the equation with one of the first pictures I found inspiring. This was a picture I saw in France where a woman was standing laughing in the sun surrounded by a copper-orange mass. Looking more closely I realised that the mass was her hair waving in the sunshine. It really struck me, as in other photos her long platted hair didn't look like this at all. Letting the light shine through her hair dramatically changed it, just as we expect—in a more permanent way—to change, be changed, grow, and progress in the Light of our Quaker worship and discipline.

In photography the light and its quality are very important, as it can tremendously change a picture. I found myself experimenting with the light in a very practical way through my photos. I enjoyed discovering how different things interact with light; to what extent and how dramatically letting the light through can change their aspect, how more vivid and vibrant dull-coloured leaves, petals, glass…became. And this echoed as a spiritual metaphor showing how much more vibrant people can become after meeting. It also echoed the phrase about holding things or people in the light.

My photography nourishes my spirituality and is also nourished by it as I explore reflections, night shadows, and how objects can change the colours of light. Taking pictures tends to reinforce my belief that the Light can be found absolutely anywhere, even in my darkest hours. There is always some light to be found, however small it may be.

Being in a Quaker context tends to give me more chances to take very strong pictures. As my soul settles, my pace slows down and I look at the world differently. I enjoy the practical aspect of taking pictures as a spiritual discipline. Some of my pictures exemplify my search for light and my curiosity for what it does; some other pictures work metaphorically on me. I then tend to have several pictures exploring the same theme.

The pictures often allude to things unseen or feelings that would be hard to put into words. They capture all these funny, surreal, magic-like moments of life where the contradictions presented can actually reveal something deeper. I love to have some humour in those pictures, pictures that remind you of something more than what they are: like the patterns on a worn threshold stone can remind us of a shore, for instance. I like multilayered pictures that can be held in different ways and still bring something to the viewer; these nourish my soul.

I'll exemplify this with two pictures I like. One (see p. 214) shows some cherry blossom petals on a path. I always found something cheerful about falling cherry blossom petals as they remind me of party confetti scattered, or swirling along the pavement in the street. This is the image and feeling of happiness and merriment I was trying to capture in this picture: some remains of happiness.

One picture I like (see p. 289) is called *Green Ripple*. It was taken at Woodbrooke, the Quaker study centre in Birmingham, England. A part of the lawn has been mowed in labyrinth shape as a meditative, reflective path to follow. Looked at sideways, it resembles ripples in water and also conveys the quietness of the exercise and of the place. I just placed myself in such a way that it looks like the bent branch of the tree in front of it is dipping in the grass, creating the ripple. It feels like ministry within silent worship, creating a ripple like that. You have different branches brushing the surface of the silence and the new and unexpected patterns are created, that go beyond just the ripples.

There is a deliberate choice on my part as well, to look for the light, for beauty and the daily marvels of life; this is the viewpoint I choose to take, others can look at things differently. I was reminded of this perspective on things by a Sufi story about Isa—Jesus in the Muslim tradition. Isa comes across a group of people around a street corner, all huddled together, commenting noisily and showing their disgust for the rotting body of a dead dog. Isa just says, "Look at its wonderful shiny teeth!" and walks on. My point here is not to ignore what is painful and negative; this is still there and present, but so are the beautiful teeth. As Quakers, it feels to me we are not looking in fascination at the depth of wickedness and suffering to scare ourselves into being good. We are building on the positive in ourselves, in our souls and in the world, looking for that of God in everyone and in my pictures of everything. This is the standpoint I can start from to address the injustice and the pain.

The camera allows me to look at the world and take the time to marvel, to rejoice in its beauty and quirkiness. Sometimes, as I said before, this is from a fairly bleak place, from the darkness finding some light; sometimes it isn't. What is permanent is the joy it brings to me and hopefully the smile it puts on other people's faces.

> Marie-Helene Drouin, 35
> Derby Local Meeting, Britain Yearly Meeting
> United Kingdom

> Editor's note: This piece first appeared in the May 2009 edition of *The Friend*.

This Prayer Has No Words

This prayer has no words.
It has no request, no plea,
no expectation of fulfillment,
nor does it belong entirely to me.

This prayer has no words.
Its connection is direct, uncluttered.
Peripheral thoughts slip softly out of focus.
A mind, a heart, a whole being
reaches out to its spiritual source.

This prayer has no words.
It is an intensity in the chest, a free tightness of breath
at the same time excited and nervous
A boundless feeling, an energy finding direction.

This prayer has no words.
It was not planned or written before

but caught me in a burst
as I looked to the sky.

> Joanna Waters, 20
> Portsmouth and Cambridge Meeting, Britain Yearly Meeting
> United Kingdom

I Think I Have a Crush on Jesus

I think I have a crush on Jesus. That dark and dusty auburn hair, the long white robe, those sensible yet fashion forward cloth sandals that just scream "itinerant messiah, generous ascetic." They really do me in. And when he comes over, there's something about the way he rests joyfully and happily expectant, waiting on my couch and turning his head to take in the scenery even though he's seen it a dozen times before that brings out the glee in me. Turns me back into the kid: architect of piano and blanket forts and the inventor of suspicious kitchen creations that were never so much palatable as intriguing in their color and viscosity. He invites my own joy and creativity out to play with a gilded and bubble-gum-smelling, sticky-sweet Spider Man Valentine. And heavens, I can't ever figure out how he gets it under my door. His timing is acute and his sweetness surprising even as it confuses me. What did I do to deserve this? Someone said the other day (and I'm still trying it on to see if I believe it) that he's crazy about me. You can be crazy about a lot of things: good Thai food, size-ten black boots at the Goodwill, or a Smashing Pumpkins song on the radio that you haven't heard since sixth grade. But me? I'm still trying to get used to that. And wait: Can I just talk about how funny he is for a minute? That man has jokes about nuns, giraffes, and ice cream cones that confuse the hell out of you 'cause you don't know whether to laugh or blush first.

Of course, I really appreciate a lot of things now that I didn't at first. We grew up together, Jesus and I, and now it's hard to tell if my memories are extravagantly colored or if he really was the terror I remember. My grandma first mentioned this kid she knew, and JC's old man, bless her heart, but all the things she told me made me more pissed off than pleased to meet him. The two of them together, Father and Son, sounded like the pair you'd never stop long enough to talk to 'cause they might laughingly bring up the time Jr. won the derby car race by pushing all the other cars off the road. The younger one especially sounded like he had some anger control issues. I remember one of Grandma's friends talking about how Jesus could hold you lovingly in his hand and then either comfort you like a baby or crush you in his fist if you messed up. Maybe just like a Barbie® doll your head would pop right off. Now I don't know where you'd learn how to do that growing up in Nazareth, but it sounded like some pretty messed-up version of kung fu or tai chi to me. And then there were all the stories about what would happen to you if you weren't on this Jesus' team, like he was some neurotic megalomaniac or something. The way I heard it, he was kinda caring. He liked the Jews, tolerated the Hindus, the Buddhists, and maybe the Muslims too (but definitely a little less). But if you didn't bat for him, you'd be sitting on the bench for not just nine whole innings, but the rest of frickin' eternity. And you definitely didn't get any cherry Pepsi® down there.

Try as she might, Grandma just couldn't sell him to me. I had had enough of control freaks. My family churns them out them like poor vision and a tendency toward halitosis, and I wasn't going to go looking for another one. I'll tell you, though, I was a tiny bit curious to catch a glimpse of him. Was he eight feet tall with a flushed and furious face, mashing his teeth and his hands together because everyone was playing dodge ball and he wanted to play tiddlywinks? Or did he look like the other JC that sometimes showed up along with the apple juice and graham cracker crumbs?

We sang "Jesus loves the little children, all the children of the world" in Sunday School. And all over the walls, along with our cotton-ball sheep, were pictures of a glossy-haired, white-robed angel-man smiling in a portrait that reminded me of the Vaseline® smiles of Glamour Shots girls. I thought, singing those bouncy songs and seeing this pretty man with other kids leaning into his sides, that he was ours. He loved the same jump-rope games and summer forts that we did. He probably hid his buttons, foreign coins, and Muppet temporary tattoos in a box under the crumbly sycamore roots just like we did. He was on my side and would let me stand between his knees and gasp and cry while he listened to how unfair it was that dad made me leave the table because I wouldn't wash my hands for a second time.

He was a refuge too in those loud, cymbal-crashing church services. The adults would use their outside voices and hold their hands, palms up to the sky, and pray and pray and chant "thankyoujesus" without pause, like believing in Christ meant you never had to take a regular human breath anymore. They forgot that they looked ridiculous and that they were just letting all their weirdness hang out right where everyone could see. I wondered if it was Jesus who made you free like these people seemed to be. I'd felt the Holy Spirit move in me—Hallelujah!—and I, too, wanted to cry and clap and be held by the fervent-prayer ladies at the front of the church. Then, instead of stories of judgment and exclusion told to me about the man, it was the stories I told myself about what I couldn't be—soft and vulnerable—that kept me separate from him.

Growing older, I heard more stories, enough to drown out my own sweet sensitivity and the Sunday School record player. Any curiosity I had about exploring a different tale wasn't enough to get close to the man. There was something else called prostrate, which for a long time I thought was a part of the male anatomy, so I was a little confused when folks said I needed to do that at Jesus' feet. I was wondering just how that might look until someone told me it meant to get down low and admit how my life, at age twelve, was a damned mess without Jesus. Well, my hard, adolescent self would never submit to that. And I knew I loved my dad, my cat, and my lesbian aunts, and none of them were "saved" except the cat. (Just kidding, he's a heathen named Hercules.) And all that love inside me made me feel good. Like I was good. My life wasn't a mess and even if I did join the Jesus club, I'd never be able to stand on the same side of the pearly gates as my family. And that was enough. I gave up finding any middle ground with Jesus. The man eventually lost any significance for me except his complicity with exclusion, and—as I grew older and gained a liberal lexicon—with bigots, racists, and homophobes.

The warmth of my home church still held me, though, as long as they didn't say "Christ" too often and talked more about the gifts of the Buddha than the Holy Spirit. Anything that had nothing to do with a messiah was what I wanted. So I learned about energy and sage smoke for purification, creative visualization, chanting "om," and speaking with spirits that had passed on. I became bilingual as I learned to translate funda-speak: words like "prayer" and "blessing" became "meditation" and "juju."

It surprises me now that the things that kept me an eager youth group attender back then were the ties that eventually brought me back into relation with JC. Even in the middle of my rebellion against my church family—instead of dyeing my hair, I was studying Wicca—I showed up for workdays in food pantries and week-long service trips to rebuild houses in the Appalachians. While I refused the Lord's Prayer and Apostles' Creed, I knew, experientially, the value of buying the smelly rambling man a Wendy's sandwich and coffee and then having a conversation with him. I learned in Honduras after Hurricane Mitch that we work with others not to build them new schools and irrigation systems, but to remind them that they're not forgotten by the rest of the world.

It makes me angry now that I was in my early twenties before I learned that Jesus understood these things also. That there was sweet redemption for those who were broken, rest and new life for the weary and oppressed, and a spotlight of grace for those who just felt so over-looked and lonely. Growing up, I had a sense of what was required of me to be in relation with the poor and the examples of a few lovely ladies who I envisioned walked with me occasionally to tell me what they knew—Mother Teresa, Dorothy Day, and the daughter of my minister who left for Kenya with three large suitcases of medicine for a hospi-tal there and only a small backpack for herself. But my discovery of this man Jesus felt so different from all of that. This was the being who had flown into the hearts of the justice-filled women I adored to feed and wash them in courage and faith. He was their sustenance and cloak for the tired, hopeless days. Good Lord, it was like he was their savior.

The story of how I became reintroduced to this man is not important. It was just that gradually other people's stories of a damning Christ were replaced with my own experiences of slowly finding a friend and confidant. My mother acted as bridge at times, helping me link the spiritual educa-tion I had been seeking with his mystical and Divine acts. She introduced me to his gentle presence in visualizations where her prompting would lead me to seek out beautiful settings in which to sit and seek comfort from him. And I was entranced by folks in the Catholic Worker movement who seemed liberated by following Christ's example, but never bound up.

But becoming friends with this "new" vision of Jesus was so slow. First, walking in a world of young, smart, and cynical warriors for Truth that had long ago left their own marginalizing messiah on the side of the road, I felt as if I were breaking union vows by inviting mine to the party. I kept him in my pocket for a while before I finally felt comfortable introducing him, like a bad boyfriend, to a few friends and family members. And then there were starts and stops where I would wonder if he was the same old red-eyed avenger with a different face. I'm still angry that he was for centuries the Church's Great Tool, brandished over the heads of nonbelievers in a play for power and domination. Was he still bringing oppression into my life or the life of others? Was I being duped just like all the other sheep?

I turn to what little I know about our Friend, George Fox, when I have these doubts. In my most private spaces, in the dark hallways of my mind and squeezing recesses of my heart, I know Him to be a sweet comfort to me. This I know is true, experientially. And the ecstasy of this bond does indeed save me when it seems that shame and ego will swallow me up.

Do I need Jesus? He and other teachers have taught me to know that the Divine saving grace I seek is found within. One thing I really appreci-ate about this guy: He knows I'm spotty with commitment, and he's not looking to be a superlative in my life. For this I'm grateful because rather than a crutch or a ticket into everlasting life, this man can be the runway that starts my journey home. Hallelujah.

Stephanie Speicher, 26
Unaffiliated and unprogrammed (but loves a rollicking church service)
United States

La Benedición de la Oración en Mi Vida

Desde el momento de mi conversión aprendí cuán importante es la oración. Veía como la oración cambiaba vidas en la Iglesia, las formas de actuar que ocasionaba, de ahí en adelante fui practicando la oración. Recuerdo en una ocasión en mi familia pasamos una crisis espiritual y material tremenda.

Los problemas se acumularon, parecía que no tenia salida, era extremadamente doloroso ver a mi padre y a mi madre que como la preocupación los consumía. Mi refugio y en el único lugar en el que me sentía confortable y sin preocupaciones era en la Iglesia; escuchar las prédicas, las alabanzas me daban esperanzas de que el problema era temporal y que todo pasaría. Y recuerdo ese domingo la prédica del pastor sobre un caso similar al mío, me di cuenta que como el caso mío habían miles; pero en ese entonces el pastor hablaba de cuán importante es la oración en la vida de cada persona, ya sea en momentos de felicidad, de tristeza y dolor. Entonces fue cuando tomé muy enserio la oración, lo cual practicaba en las noches antes de dormir, antes de consumir cualquier alimento, y al salir de mi hogar; y era increíble como los resultados eran instantáneos. Fue entonces que mi familia y yo decidimos tener un tiempo de oración como es un culto devocional para hablar con Dios.

La verdad es que veía la alegría en los rostros de mi familia después de concluir la oración. Y poco a poco los problemas disminuyeron hasta que al final salimos de esa situación incómoda. Es por eso que la oración es bendición en mi vida. El mismo hecho de hablar con Dios es muy importante. Hoy en día no hay un día que no le de gracias a Dios por lo que hace en mi vida. Y este versículo de la Biblia me inspira y me ayuda a seguir practicando la oración: "Clama a mí y yo te responderé y te enseñare cosas grandes y ocultas que tú no conoces" (Jer. 33:3, New King James).

José Luis Cuellar Avalos, 21
Congregación Cristiana Amigos, Iglesia Nacional Evangélica "Los Amigos" de Bolivia (EFCI)
Bolivia

The Blessing of Prayer in My Life

From the moment of my conversion, I learned the importance of prayer. I saw how prayer changed lives in church, the ways that prayer caused people to act, and from this moment I practiced prayer. I remember one occasion when my family encountered a tremendous spiritual and material crisis.

The problems accumulated, and it seemed as if there was no escape; it was extremely painful to see my father and mother being consumed with worry. My refuge (and the only place where I felt comfortable and without worry) was the church: Listening to the preaching and the praises gave me hope that the problems were temporary and that all this would pass. And I remember one Sunday, when the pastor's sermon was about a situation similar to mine, I realized that there were thousands of situations like mine; but in his sermon, the pastor then spoke of how important prayer is in the life of every person, whether in moments of happiness, of sadness, or of pain. That was when I began to take prayer seriously, practicing prayer every night before I went to sleep, before eating any meal, and each time I left my house; and it was incredible how instantaneously I felt the results. It was then that my family and I decided to have a time of prayer together as a devotional worship when we could talk to God.

The truth is that I saw the joy in the faces of my family after finishing our prayer. And little by little the problems lessened, until finally we found a way out of our uncomfortable situation. It is because of this that prayer is a blessing in my life. The very act of speaking with God is extremely important. Today, there is not a day that I don't give thanks to God for what he has done in my life. And this Bible verse inspires me and helps me to continue practicing prayer: "Call to me and I will respond and tell you great and mighty things that you do not know" (Jer. 33:3, New King James).

José Luis Cuellar Avalos, 21
Christian Friends Church, INELA—Bolivia
Bolivia

Invite Your Body to Worship

Let us be ready for worship.

One of my blessed elders here in my new community at Stillwater Meeting (Ohio Yearly Meeting, Conservative) told me about her resentment of the admonition to "come with heart and mind prepared": "When I attended Olney Friends School I had cows to milk Sunday mornings—you must run to worship!" she said. "But milking cows really puts you in a rhythm. You're attentive to the task, just being there with the udders, one squirt, two squirts, the sound on the metal bucket, that had to be preparation enough—and I think it was."

We are so often busy in the body; there are places to be, people to see, tasks that require our attention at every moment we try to set aside. Making the space to "come with heart and mind prepared" does not always look like stillness as I once imagined.

As a child, I was silent through meeting for worship. Unlike my brother, who seemed to want to wrestle every surface or hand extended to him, I sat in my parent's lap, on the floor, or on a friend's lap. Was I prepared? Had I contemplated a query or centered my thoughts? The intellectual definition we assign this activity does not allow for a child, or perhaps any nonintellectual, to prepare. I trust in my wise child self—that I indeed had "heart and mind prepared," as did my brother. Or perhaps I had body prepared? A child's body is always prepared for its journey of worshipful discovery.

Children's first gestures have joy and wonderment in movement before they have will. As the individuated self develops, baby bodies read and define space. Body-mind centering is one method used in dance therapy and other disciplines to recall the development of physical sensation. As you lie on the floor, one directs her attention to the different locations from which early movement originates. It is not until an advanced stage that the child reaches for an object. This shift from discovery-movement to willful movement is dramatic. In preparation for this desire-guided stage, the neck must strengthen so the head lifts easily, and the hand follows the eye's gaze. The whole body falls into line with what the eye sees. There is a loss of wonder, in a way. Instead: reaching, acquiring, holding, owning.

Our bodies have so much to teach us. When we listen, they are offering us a constant commentary on our thoughts and actions. Nay, the body has a mind of its own. It is not just the obedient servant of the mind. Too often we treat the sacred vessel of our lives like a support system for the head. Injury and illness are reminders of the importance of caring for, maintaining, and spending loving time with our bodies. When we pretend the body is just the high-maintenance support system for the brain, we commit that sin Descartes introduced (dividing mind from body, Cartesian dualism) and, thankfully, revoked.

Let our worship affirm the unity of mind, body, and spirit. Indeed, Friends owe their name to this mystical and life-affirming connection. Did we not tremble in the presence of the Lord? And now? That would be a little embarrassing, I guess? Are we ashamed of what moving in the Spirit looks like? We say "moved by the Spirit," but this rarely errs from the seated or standing position, chairs in a circle or lines facing one another. Were there chairs on Pendle Hill?

We are not a seated people, Friends.

Jaya Karsemeyer, 29
Toronto Monthly Meeting, Canadian Yearly Meeting (FGC-FUM)
Canada

Yearn for the Word of God

The Quaker culture early had opposed the use of musical instruments and hands clapping in praising the name of God. This resulted in a reluctance to participate fully in activities. Currently, Quakers—through the reformation of churches and reviewing of the Quaker constitution— have improved greatly, thus making me yearn for the word of God, and I can now praise him through claps and dance to him for good deeds done to me.

Through the innovations of Internet services, I can easily receive God's message by downloading information. This has also been made easier through hearing of fellowship programmes conducted by other Quakers across the world.

Mobile phones and radios have contributed greatly to growth of my faith because I can hear and see the experiences faced by other youth and how I can overcome them. I have learned a lot how to persevere and how to forgive those who have done wrong to me. Through this I am in a position to explore my spiritual gifts that I had never understood.

Mathew Amoyi Lanogwa
Kitale Village Meeting, East Africa Yearly Meeting (North) (FUM)
Kenya

Testifying for Peace

There are some questions Quakers get used to answering over and over—about Friends schools, about silence, about our perceived relationship to the Amish or Mennonites. Outside those topics, which constitute the vast majority of conversations I've had about my faith, I'm not used to having to explain all that much. But last year, at a conference for youth in the interfaith community, I found myself challenged to clarify the deepest questions about Quakerism, especially by a girl with an impressive and inspiring record of interfaith work around the country. I had just finished the Testimony of Peace portion of my little Quakerism 101 lecture, and she broke in to remark politely, "You know, that's interesting, because to me it seems so antithetical to what Hillel said: 'If I am not for myself, who will be for me?' I can't understand that, standing idly by."

Right then, in a little plastic chair in an over-air-conditioned conference room with six other people and her waiting respectfully for a response, I froze. I fumbled for words and managed to get out something about Jesus' turning the other cheek in Golgotha and how peace is supposed to be radical. But said in front of a room full of people from Israel, from Palestine, from Pakistan, with brothers in bombed-out yeshivas and sisters in the army, cousins who pass by soldiers with guns on their hips on their way to school—in that room, it sounded feeble even to me. It's a lot harder to explain that pacifism doesn't mean inaction to people for whom doing nothing means losing a way of life and life itself. Somewhere inside me this part of my faith makes sense, but when I was suddenly asked to explain it in real terms to people who genuinely wanted to understand, I just didn't know what to say.

I guess it makes sense that, to a large extent, I don't experience my faith in words. It's about an inimitable insight that ebbs and flows, a sense of something moving and growing in the silence, a feeling of huge presence much greater than just the twelve people sitting quietly in a circle on Sunday morning. Even when we do speak in meeting, it tends to be in parable form, in metaphor—at least, in the one I've attended since childhood. Within the Quaker community I've grown up in, there's rarely any need to distinctly articulate matters of our faith. But I'm beginning to realize that I'm not able to talk about things like peace and truth in the way that I talk about the rest of the world, and that inability is crippling when it comes time to live out these testimonies in a way that will help heal the world and help the people around us. I didn't know how to answer the question that day of how pacifism is different than inaction, and I am finding it harder and harder to answer the questions now of how pacifism is able to be an effective answer to violence on an individual and systemic scale.

At the time of this writing, people in Gaza have been without water for ten days; a woman was brutally gang raped outside a bar in San Francisco because she was a lesbian; Oscar Grant was shot in plain sight by the police meant to be maintaining peace. I'm having trouble moving on from these stories; I'm turning them over in my head over and over again. In their powerful poetic duet "Black Irish," Eamon Mahone and Paul Graham address the reality of English oppression and gang violence by saying "I am not committed to non-violence. I am committed to staying alive." For millions of people all over the world, it's overwhelmingly difficult to have both. I'm not pointing fingers, but large portions of the Quaker community (myself included) are middle-class, American, well-educated, affluent, and white. For many of us (myself included), pacifism is an issue of registering as a conscientious objector, holding peace vigils in local churches, and demonstrating against the war. For many of us, the stakes aren't that high. I believe, and I venture to guess that others do also, that as the stakes get higher the importance of nonviolence only gets greater. We are called as a species to make peace not just a priority, but our highest priority. But I've never had to make the decision between an ideal of peace and my family's safety, and so it seems pretty presumptuous of me to ask it of someone else.

It's this, and more, that's had me feeling helpless lately. It's not just the comment made by my fellow conference participant, but a feeling of terrible momentum that leaves me asking what I am supposed to do with pacifism. How to explain that nonviolence is different than just standing idly by; that it is urgently necessary instead of idealistic. I am intensely grateful that I have never had to try to explain to someone like Oscar Grant's daughter, or Sean Bell's parents, or Duanna Johnson's sister, or Lawrence King's grandparents, that peace is going to prevail, that hurting someone else or allowing the state to do it for them will only make this much, much worse. So far, the closest I've come is another little parable, the kind of thing that someone from my meeting at home would rise to share in the sleepy quiet of Sunday meeting for worship.

I'm told that this is the original account, or at least an alternative one, of the Hebrews' exodus out of Egypt. The beginning part is the same: the bush, the staff, the lamb's blood, and the long walk toward the sea, with Pharaoh's army behind them, furious and bitter with grief. Except that in this version of the story, when Moses raises his arms toward the waters of the Red Sea, nothing happens. And he tries again, and still there is nothing. And now the children are crying, the people are shouting, and you can practically hear the hooves of Pharaoh's horses in the distance. Moses stands with his staff in his hand, frozen on the shore, not knowing what else to do. In the middle of all the chaos, one of the Hebrews takes a deep breath and begins to wade into the sea. The waves crash over his thighs and his waist, and soon the water is up to his shoulders. There's no miracle in sight, and the water is freezing, but he keeps going—even though by now his toes can barely touch the bottom. Moses has lowered his staff in defeat, and terror and confusion reign on the shore. And just as the water closes over his head and he's totally engulfed in the brine, the seas divide themselves and he is standing on dry land.

As is the case with parables, it's not all that instructional in terms of how exactly we should approach, say, the attacks on Mumbai that left all of India in shock and grief—as Quakers or just as people. To be honest, I still don't really have anything concrete to tell people if they ask how being a "pacifist" is different from being a "coward," or how being a conscientious objector is different from neglecting my duties as a citizen. I still don't have words for that. But I have this ridiculous, mulish belief that if we keep going, if we keep doing this even though it is stupid and irrational and right now it is just making us cold and wet, something incredible will happen. I guess where I am at is that I really can't explain to myself or anyone else why this thing I believe is not absurd. All I can do is agree that yes, it is, and isn't it amazing how the most important things are like that sometimes.

Rachel Kincaid, 21
North Shore Friends Meeting, New England Yearly Meeting
(FGC-FUM)
United States

My Relationship with God in Terms of Prayer

I am an inborn Quaker. "Success is just a matter of attitude." I was born and raised up as a Friends churchgoer, and I am now a true Quaker believer.

I will discuss my relationship with God in terms of prayer, which has led me into tremendous success experiences and amended my social life

as a Christian. Through prayers I am able to cross into mighty worlds of
different people, for example this opportunity I am given to write and to
contribute in a publication, which was also my dream.

As a Quaker church believer I learned and appreciated the value of
truthfulness and commitment in prayer practice. Education and success in it is through the prayer that I was involved in and hence a strong
strength grew in me that there is actually Jesus Christ around each and
every struggle that I underwent.

I remember at one time I cried to God during a prayer session, just
wanting Him to bless my life, parents and, above all, not to deny me an
exam success. I passed my KOSE exemplarily and was able to enroll in
an important program provided by the successful financial institution
where I currently work before I join the university for further studies. So
it dawned on me that I had to go back again and down on my knees to
thank God for inclining to my prayers.

As for technology, it's a great impact on the Quaker faith, especially
the young Quaker faith, which is a great draw on youth. We've been given a
great chance to explore our Christian faith through [instilling] our innermost talent in singing, dancing, and praising God, since young people have
a great liking for music. Some of us have this great opportunity of realizing our dream faith "that God, I will serve you to the end of my life."

Through this marvelous combination of technology, culture, and
prayer, I have become a wonderful product of a committed and self-driven
young Quaker. I believe the Quaker church is not only rising at gigantic
speed to the top but also it will last to the age of brighter years to come.
And as we fellowship together in prayer, worship, [and] of traversing
cultures from different people worldwide, an even greater Quaker Group
might just emerge.

We as Quakers believe in faith and that we must be the best church in
the world, hence embrace the values of striving for the best through good
attitudes and hard work in our faith life. Our actions must also contribute to our faith [and] are also important factors, which will in the end
demystify the Quaker church and hence help us achieve the much-needed
success. Good planning and influential skill must be developed through
prayer and determination as we realize that without Jesus Christ, the son
of God in our souls, there is no important step we are going to make.

God is truly great, and let's work together in unity, power, and strength
to keep the fire of Quakers burning and its light shining day and night.

Elyne Juma Namuma, 19
Kenya

The Subtle Power of Meeting for Worship

Quaker worship carries a subtle and transformative power. The work of Christ in the worship service is often accomplished over the course of time. My spiritual journey has had truly powerful experiences, but upon reflection I realize that God was transforming me into Christ-likeness over years, not moments. This idea is seen in the Creation account of Genesis, chapter one. God did not form the universe with one motion; rather, it was a process by which land and life were formed over time. The same is true for Paul, who experienced the Risen Christ on the road to Damascus, but continued to grow and mature in faith until the end of Acts when he proclaimed, *"I have had God's help to this very day"* (Acts 26:22, NIV). Spending my formative years attending meeting for worship was instrumental in developing my image of God.

As a boy I remember the unwavering consistency of the First Day worship. Before service, I would walk the same aisle of our meeting room toward my favorite pew and see the same faces. Because nearly everyone sat in their specific places, I knew who was absent with a glance. After getting a bulletin from the friendly usher, I would get a mint from the church candy man and I would find my seat in the back. After getting settled I would say a little prayer that the regular entourage of elderly ladies would *not* come by, pinch my cheeks, and tell me how cute I was! My prayer was rarely answered. The service began at eleven a.m. sharp, and not a moment later. Huffs and groans were heard if the service went more than a few minutes after noon.

My meeting lacked the jumbo-tron, smoke, and mirrors that are considered essential in many of today's Christian congregations. There were no altar calls or dancing in the aisles. I am told that the sermons were always very good, but I rarely pulled myself away from my games of tic-tac-toe on the back of the bulletin to hear a word. The worship would be considered by many to be tedious and unexciting, but those services shaped my spiritual journey, even though I did not sense it at the time.

Each time I gathered with Friends for worship I was being transformed by the perpetual work of the Spirit. The quiet, consistent service was steadily shaping my idea of God. My image of God and the powerful ministry of Christ was developed by the Friends who sat in the same places each week with a Godly consistency. As I grew into adulthood, I developed a view of God that reflects my meeting's worship. The God I believe in is consistent in Grace and Truth, unwavering in Mercy, and dependable in Providence. God is not a shifting force that changes each week with the tides. Rather, my God mirrors the meeting I call home: steady, dependable, peaceful, and reliable. I appropriate God as One who brings good order to the chaos, just as my home meeting brought peace and stability to my life during many chaotic times.

It is a rare and sacred task to gather as Friends. Sometimes we are tempted to latch onto every contemporary trend and keep up with the mega-Church down the street. Often, ministers feel that they must create some sort of "feeling" or "experience" so that congregants believe the service was meaningful. In a culture that demands our senses to be heightened during every activity, meeting for worship should be the one place where we do not need to be entertained by trivial antics. We let the soap operas and politicians have their emotive pandering. As Friends we realize that worship does not need to be a dramatic, overly emotional experience. Fads come and go, and vain sentiment is fleeting, but the consistent, loving, and nurturing Presence of Christ continues to draw Friends to True, transformative worship. The Presence in the Midst can work when the same people sit in the same spot week after week. Growing up in meeting, there was a certain comfort in staring at the back of the same heads every week. In a world that seems increasingly chaotic, God can work through the subtle and consistent language of meeting for worship.

David R. Mercadante, 29
Archdale Friends Meeting, North Carolina Yearly Meeting (FUM)
United States

How I Experience the Holy Spirit

Most churches claim that our church has no Holy Spirit, but I would like to prove they are wrong by saying that Holy Spirit comes on its own way that God decided. It quakes in you and you start seeing God's power filled in you. I usually experience [it] when praying. What makes me believe that it is Holy Spirit is that I usually become strong and lifted to a different place where I have never been, and then I start seeing what is going to happen. And what is happening is that, after praying for some days, my prayers get answered. Let glory be to God.

Wycliffe M. Musera
East Africa Yearly Meeting of Friends (North) (FUM)
Kenya

I Am

I am the light and the dark
I am life and death
I am hope when there is no hope
I am solitude and a great crowd
I am joy and sorrow
I am a friendly word and look
I am a kiss and a touch
I am first love and love after many years
I am the wind that touches your face
I am the thunder and the lightning
I am the bird in the sky and the fish in the sea
I am spring summer autumn winter
I am the sun on a cloudy day
I am the seas and the rivers
I am the land and the creatures
I am the beginning and the end

I am

Gayle Yeomans, 30
Stafford Meeting, Britain Yearly Meeting
United Kingdom

Eye on the Cross, etching, Erin McKibben, 18, Portland Friends Church, Indiana Yearly Meeting (FUM), United States

Practicing Faithfulness
Seeking, Callings, Leadings, Ministry

Leadings

I have been trying something new when I ask for things in prayer. My prayers start the same way they have in the past; I think about the problem I am facing and then I ask for help. I usually have something in mind, a sort of instruction for God. The difference now is I try to end with, "Or whatever you think would be better."

When I told my mom that I was interested in reading the Bible again, she went out and bought a new one and sent it to me. It is *The Message* translation, which is good because I read the New International Version so much when I was growing up that I have a hard time even seeing the words anymore. Seeing familiar verses stated differently helps me read with new eyes. One thing that has surprised me is how short all the stories are. They loomed so large in my childhood that I have a hard time believing they are only a few pages long.

The first biblical character I really connected with this time around was Moses. God knew that Moses was going to need something spectacular, so he sent an angel in the form of a burning bush. But even after God explicitly told Moses what to do, Moses tried to talk God out of it. Moses pointed out all of the reasons he was a poor choice: He lacked confidence, he was not a good speaker, and no one was going to listen to him. Even after Moses eventually came around, he was not exactly saint-like. He was impatient with the Israelites and repeatedly reminded God he was not interested in leading them.

I have never encountered God in a burning bush, but I have experienced unmistakable leadings. The most forceful is like a kick in the stomach. I can't breathe and I know I will not be able to breathe easily again until I do whatever it is that I am led to do. With this kind of leading, the leading usually happens first and I have to figure out why afterward. Sometimes a leading is more of a growing conviction. One thing leads to the next, and I can see each step I am supposed to take. Most often, leadings are more like a whisper, a quiet sense of what I should do and a strong feeling that I need to follow and trust.

Every once in a while I get leadings for other people. Fortunately, this does not happen very often. Usually these are more of the kick-in-the-stomach sort of leadings. Otherwise, I would never have the guts to approach the person and say, "I feel led to tell you . . ." When this happens, I try to say that I could be wrong. I also try to remember that like any other leading, it may not turn out the way I want it to or think it will. But usually, I get some reassurance it was the right thing to do.

The most dramatic example of a leading I have had for another person happened shortly after I met my friend Sarah Peterson. We were both at the Pacific Northwest Quaker Women's Theology Conference for the first time and had barely spoken to each other when I approached her and said, "I feel led to be on the epistle committee, and I feel led to tell you that you should be too." I was sure she was going to think I was crazy. Instead, she thought for a minute and then nodded. I don't think either of us could have imagined the friendship that would result or that we would together co-clerk the planning committee for the next conference, but I am glad that I followed the leading and that she said yes.

One of the hardest parts for me is to not let fear interfere with leadings. It is easy to convince myself something is not a good idea, and leadings usually take me in directions that make my life more difficult. I am afraid of a lot of things that can keep me from following leadings, including public speaking, ridicule, not having the right words, and never being good enough. But I am more afraid of what I will miss or fail to do by not being faithful.

I know that trying to discern leadings is not something I can or should do alone, so I am constantly checking in with others about my leadings. I go to people I trust, usually friends and family. They probably don't know this is what I am doing most of the time; they just know me well and know whether something is right for me. I also ask weightier Friends for more formal counsel. I am grateful they have been elders to me in the best sense, providing nurturing support and guidance.

In the inside cover of the Bible my mom gave me, she included a reference to Jeremiah 29:11, which in this translation says, "I know what I'm doing. I have it all planned out—plans to take care of you, not abandon you, plans to give you the future you hope for." It is scary to trust God and follow leadings without knowing where they are going. But God made me and knows everything I am capable of and the best ways to use my gifts. Even if I can't always see the pattern, I need to have faith God's plans are better than my plans.

The verses that follow are a comforting reminder: "When you call on me, when you come and pray to me, I'll listen. When you come looking for me, you'll find me. Yes, when you get serious about finding me and want it more than anything else, I'll make sure you won't be disappointed." Amen.

Ashley M. Wilcox, 28
Freedom Friends Church (Independent) and University Friends
Meeting, North Pacific Yearly Meeting (sojourning member)
United States

Procuro Vivir Mi Día en la Presencia de Dios

Personalmente, pienso que no es sencillo vivir fielmente en una sociedad sin valores; pero le digo a los jóvenes tampoco es imposible solo debemos procurar vivir con la mente de Cristo las 24 horas del día tratando de revisar paso a paso cada una de nuestras actividades y decisiones diarias. Mi meta es no ofender a mi Dios con nada de lo que hago: como humanos fallamos muchas veces por los impulsos que en ocasiones no controlamos y cuando menos sentimos hemos caído en un error; pero tenemos un Dios muy grande que si le suplicamos Su perdón olvida nuestra falta. Recordemos y nunca olvidemos que somos de Cristo pues El pagó con su vida por nosotros y por eso debemos procurar no ofenderle en nada.

Somos jóvenes y todos con diferentes temperamentos, esto nos lleva a dificultades pues en ocasiones no logramos ponernos de acuerdo, la mayoría de las veces cuando ofendo lo hago con palabras. Los jóvenes somos muy arrebatados esto significa que cuando estamos enojados se nos olvida muchas veces que la blanda respuesta aplaca la ira y que también en todo tiempo debemos conectar nuestra lengua con el cerebro y no permitirle que ella obre sola porque dañamos al ofender con nuestras respuestas ásperas y miradas fulminantes que actualmente los jóvenes en su mayoría hemos acostumbrado practicar. A quienes más ofendemos con estas actitudes son a nuestros padres y a nuestros amigos porque son con ellos con quienes pasamos más tiempo, pero en ocasiones hasta nuestros líderes ganan un poco de nuestras ofensas.

Personalmente las veces que otros me han ofendido han sido de la misma forma una mirada con desprecio, un gesto de desinterés, o palabras ásperas bastan para ocasionar grandes raíces de amargura que solo Dios puede curar. Así que es mejor tener cuidando, ¡no ofendamos! Porque la mayoría de los jóvenes a la primera ofensa quieren alejarse del grupo y no volver más. Pidamos a Dios sabiduría y dirección, entréguelos a El nuestra lengua y ojos . . . y todo nuestro cuerpo, solo así podremos soportar ofensas de otros y velar por no ofender nosotros a nadie. Recordemos esto es difícil más no imposible. Porque para nuestro Dios no hay nada imposible.

La oración es una de las mejores herramientas para buscar la dirección de Dios. Al orar trato de orar de rodillas en un lugar apartado para no tener interrupciones, aunque en mi hogar no hay un lugar determinado para orar procuro esperar la madrugada y que mi alarma me avise que es la hora y es en ese momento cuando todo está en quietud y por fin hay silencio sin la interrupción de mis 10 hermanos y mis papás llamándome.

Así es tengo una familia donde somos 12 hijos: 9 chicas y 3 chicos más papá y mamá. Aunque ya 3 de mis hermanos se casaron y no viven en casa; el resto hacemos 11 y si que hacemos mucho ruido por las noches al volver de nuestro trabajo.

Procuro vivir mi día en la presencia de Dios pues cuando salgo de casa desde que pongo mi primer pie fuera de casa empiezo a platicar con Jesús como mi compañero de viaje, de estudio, de trabajo y de diversión. Claro como humana que soy en mas de algún momento de mi día el afán me trata de separar de mi compañero de vida que es Dios y olvido que El está a mi lado; es allí cuando me estreso y vivo momentos difíciles que solo son aliviados cuando recuerdo que no estoy sola, que hay Uno que me conoce y aunque yo lo olvide por un momento El sigue estando a mi, lado para amarme y apoyarme.

Esto es adoración para mi vivir al lado de Cristo siempre de forma programada nunca he elegido con quien adorar, solo lo hago y ya. Pero cuando estamos en la Iglesia con todos los Amigos se siente hermoso adorar a Dios juntos y lo hacemos de diversas formas a veces sirviendo en ministerios como la música, el evangelismo, siendo maestros de niños/as, vendiendo comida, dirigiendo, orando, y muchos más tiempos de comunión con Dios que en su mayoría son programados. En todo momento Dios puede hablar a nuestra necesidad. Personalmente, Dios me habla por medio de Su palabra, de Su creación y de Sus hijos: muchas veces cuando oro Él pone en mi corazón las respuestas que anhelo o las respuestas que no anhelo pero que Él desea. Realmente es difícil pero no imposible lograr obedecer el pacto de Dios frente a la vida moderna. En mi experiencia con el divino Salvador me ha encomendado muchos proyectos de los cuales ya he desarrollado varios pero hay otros que no lo he logrado a causa de la vida moderna que nos pone a prueba por dificultades económicas o temores personales. Mi anhelo es que la vida moderna no me aleje de la visión de Cristo para mi vida.

Y sobre todo que ningún joven se aleje de la visión de Cristo para su vida; quisiera poder verlos a todos sonreír y nunca llorar o ver depresión en su rostro; los últimos días he tenido la oportunidad de ayudar a muchas muchachas con diferentes problemas personales y hemos orado mucho pidiendo solución divina para su condición. Después de hablar con ellas al regresar a casa he sentido mucho dolor por sus problemas y a veces hasta el sueño se me va pero eso es bueno porque aprovecho y oro mas. En fin quiero animar a los jóvenes a no rendirse ante nada ni nadie que no sea Jesucristo. Ante todo tenemos Su fiel promesa en Josué 1:5.

Dios me encuentra sobretodo en mis momentos de debilidad cuando Le rindo todo mi ser y Le digo que sola no me es posible hacer nada, cuando reconozco Su majestad en mi vida y en todo el mundo. Es allí cuando El toca mi corazón y me hace sentir nuevas fuerzas y que en El todo lo puedo. Jesús es mi luz interior, la luz que me guía, me salva y me transforma de mi condición de pecadora. El me ha transformado y está transformando poco a poco en mí hasta las áreas que por años habían atado mi comunión con El y me mantenían separada de Su perfecto amor. Hoy gracias a su perfecto amor he decidido cuidar mi mente, mis ojos y mis manos del mundo.

Nuestra Fe influye en todo desde ¿Que haré cuando me levante? hasta la toma de las decisiones más grande en la vida como joven que somos ¿A quién serviré?, ¿A que me dedicaré? y ¿con quien me casaré? La voz interior del Espíritu Santo de Cristo nos puede guiar y hasta hoy como joven cristiana puedo compartir que a mí no me ha fallado y dejo claro que no todo ha sido hermoso en mi vida; ni creo que haya un joven en todo el mundo que pueda afirmar eso, como humanos fallamos y las malas decisiones nos traen dolor y consecuencias por eso suplico a todos busca a Dios cuanto antes para que sea Él quien dirija nuestras vidas y con El todo irá mejor. Lo digo por experiencia. Personalmente nunca he escuchado la voz de Dios audiblemente pero estoy segura que habla a mi vida por medio de mi mente y mi corazón. Anhelo nunca alejarme de Él y ser cada día más obediente hasta que El me llame a Su presencia.

Termino, alabando el nombre de Dios por Su amor, fidelidad, comprensión y dirección a mi vida, por la preciosa familia en la que me colocó, por los retos que Él ha puesto y sigue poniendo en mi vida; y oro por todos los jóvenes que sufren sin conocer que hay Uno que le entiende y le ama con todo y sus malos hábitos. El solo quiere que nos purifiquemos de todo pecado acercándonos a Él y alejándonos del mundo actual que no nos ofrece nada bueno. Para esto solo es necesario un sincero arrepentimiento de pecados y disposición de entregar nuestras vidas en sus manos. Jóvenes les animo a arriesgarse y probar a Dios porque nunca falla. Recuerda quien es amigo del mundo; esta contra Dios.

Damaris Mercedes Guardado Lemus, 29
Junta Anual de la Iglesia de los Amigos en El Salvador (ILAES)
(EFCI)
El Salvador

I Try to Live My Daily Life in the Presence of God

Personally, I think it is not easy to live faithfully in a society that lacks values. But I tell young people that it isn't impossible either. We should live with the mind of Christ twenty-four hours a day, trying to review step by step each one of our daily activities and decisions. My goal is to not offend my God with anything I do. As humans we fail often because of the impulses we sometimes do not control. When we least feel it we have fallen into error. But our God is great and if we ask His pardon He forgets our failings. We remember and we never forget that we are of Christ and that He paid for us with His life and for that reason we should try never to offend our God.

We are young and we have different temperaments and this leads us into difficulties and sometimes we do not manage to come to agreement. Most of the time when I offend I do it with words. We youth get very carried away. This means that when we are angry we often forget that a gentle response calms anger. We also forget that at all times we should connect our tongue with our brain and not let it work alone because we cause harm with our sharp replies and our angry looks that these days most young people have become accustomed to making. Those we most offend in this way are our parents and our friends because we spend the most time with them. But at times even our leaders experience a little of our offenses.

Personally, the times that others have offended me it has been in the form of a disdainful look, a gesture of disinterest, or rough words that have been enough to cause great roots of bitterness that only God can heal. Thus it is best to *Take Care Not to Offend*! Because the majority of youth will distance themselves from the group at the first offense and not return. We ask that God bring wisdom and direction and that we dedicate our tongues and our eyes . . . and our whole body. Only in this way can we bear the offenses of others and be careful to avoid offending them. Let's remember that this is difficult but not impossible. For our God nothing is impossible.

Prayer is one of the best tools for seeking direction from God. I try to pray on my knees in a place removed from distractions so as to not have interruptions. Although in my house there isn't a specific place to pray, I try to await the dawn and my alarm telling me that it's time. It is at that time that all is in quiet and finally there is silence without interruption from my 10 siblings and my parents calling me. I have a family where we are 12 children: 9 girls and 3 boys plus mother and father. Although 3 of my siblings are already married and do not live at home, the rest of us make 11 and we make a lot of noise at night when we return from work.

I try to live my daily life in the presence of God. When I leave the house from my first step out the door I begin to talk with Jesus as my companion in travel, study, work, and play. Of course, as I am human, in more than one moment of my day my obligations try to separate me from my life companion who is God, and I forget that He is at my side. It is then that I experience stress and I live difficult moments that are only relieved when I remember I am not alone, that there is One who knows me, and that even though I forget it for a moment, He continues at my side to love me and support me.

This is worship for me, to live at the side of Christ. Worship for me is always programmed; I have never chosen with whom to worship, I just do it and that's how it is. But when we are in church with all the Friends it feels wonderful to worship together and we do it in various ways, sometimes serving in ministries of music, evangelism, being teachers of children, selling food, directing, praying, and many more ways. Time of communion with God is generally programmed. In all moments God can hear our need. Personally, God has spoken to me through His word, His creation, and His children. Frequently when I pray He puts answers in my heart that I yearn for, or answers that I don't desire but He does. Really, it is difficult but not impossible to achieve obedience to our covenant with God in the face of modern life. In my experience with the divine Savior, He has burdened me with many projects, some of which I have started to develop but others that I haven't managed on account of modern life that puts us to the test by economic difficulties or personal fears. My yearning is that modern life does not distance me from the vision Christ has for my life.

And above all it is my desire that no young person stray from the vision of Christ for his or her life. I wish I could see all youth smiling and never crying or seeing depression on their faces. In recent days I have had the opportunity to help many girls with different personal problems and we have prayed a lot, asking for divine help for their condition. After talking with them, upon returning to my house I have felt a great deal of pain for their problems and at times I am unable to sleep, but that is good because I take advantage of being awake and pray more. Finally, I would like to encourage young people never to yield to one who is not Jesus Christ. Before all we have His faithful promise in Joshua 1:5.

God finds me above all in my moments of weakness when I yield my whole being to Him and I say to Him that I can't do anything alone, when I recognize His majesty in my life and in all the world. It is there at those times when He touches my heart and makes me feel new strength, and that in Him I can do anything. Jesus is my inner light, the light that guides me, saves me, and transforms me from my condition as a sinner. He has transformed me and is transforming me little by little, even the things that for years have interfered with my communion with Him and kept me apart from His perfect love. Today thanks to His perfect love I have decided to protect my mind, my eyes, and my hands from the world.

Our faith influences everything from "What will I do when I get up?" to the biggest decisions in our lives as young people. "Whom will I serve? To what will I dedicate myself? Whom will I marry?" The inner voice of the Holy Spirit of Christ can guide us. Up until today as a young Christian I can share that the Holy Spirit has never failed me, and I want to make clear that not everything in my life has been wonderful; I don't think there is a young person in all the world who cannot say this. As human beings we make mistakes and bad decisions bring pain and consequences. For that reason I beg you all to seek for God as soon as possible so it is He who directs your life and with whom everything will go better. I say this from experience. Personally I have never heard the voice of God audibly, but I'm sure that He talks to me through my mind and my heart. I yearn never to be apart from Him and to grow in obedience until He calls me into His presence.

I finish, praising the name of God for His love, faithfulness, understanding, and direction in my life, for the precious family in which He placed me, for the challenges He has put to me and continues putting in my life. I also pray for all the young people who suffer without knowing that there is One who understands them and loves them even with all their bad habits. He only wants us to purify ourselves of all sin, getting closer to Him and distancing ourselves from the current world that doesn't offer us anything good. For this all that is necessary is sincere repentance of our sins and a willingness to place our lives in His hands. Youth, I encourage you to take a risk and try God because he never lets you down. Remember that whoever is a friend of the world is against God.

Damaris Mercedes Guardado Lemus, 29
The Yearly Meeting of the Evangelical Friends Chruch in El Salvador (EFCI)
El Salvador

Burning: A Reflection on
One Morning's Message

I live in that life and power which takes away the occasion of war.

I live in that life and power which creates the Kingdom of God beneath my feet as I walk.

There is no worldly power with such potential for transformation.

I hate seeing vocal ministry written down. It seems so dry without the context of worship, the resonance of the human voice, filled with God's power, filling the container of the worshipping space. Not so much breaking the silence, but emerging from it. Written out, they are just words.

When I spoke them, I was burning. The first person to speak in meeting that morning had given a speed-of-light declaration about Friends and wealth, a lecture on Quaker history combined with a call to accumulate monetary resources for the defense of progressive values. It felt to me like a denial of Jesus' teaching and a denunciation of God's power. Must we rely on *mammon* to achieve transformation?

So I burned. And rose, after a few moments' pause, to repeat Fox's words, to speak that there is no power greater than a faithful life. I took my seat again and sat, shaking, for the remainder of the worship. I felt clear that I had spoken faithfully, but had to remind myself to release ego attachment to the message. If I was faithful, then the message was not mine.

This is the ministry I have been given so far in my life: to sit with Friends in waiting worship, to speak as led my best understanding of what Quakerism is called to do and be, to bear the power of that. Then, to keep an eye on my sneaky ego, to stay as low as I can in the Truth that is God's alone.

It is not easy work. I am so imperfect, and the challenges are great. I fail more often than not, and Friends resist the messages even (especially?) at the times I manage to be mostly faithful. I have found some incredible mentors, but they are geographically scattered. I am often overwhelmed by despair at the gap between my vision (God's vision, I hope) and the reality of the meetings I worship in. Other Quakers, it seems, are as imperfect as I am.

I stay and labor—not without whining, complaining, and threatening to defect—because I have no choice. Because God has given me a clear leading to ministry within the Religious Society of Friends;

because Quaker belief and practice are embedded in me at a molecular level; because I am deeply in love with a vision of what Quakerism has the potential to be, what it is as a sweet, pure, totally butt-kicking concept.

The concept is about the unfiltered relationship between humanity and the creator God. About deconstructing spiritual hierarchy and reconstructing God's kingdom of justice. It is human beings submitting to the guidance of an awesome, benevolent, and tenderly present God because they believe with all their hearts in a transformed world.

> When we speak, dear God,
> May it be for your glory, and not for our own.
> May it be for Truth, out of love.
> May our practice of Truth create Truth.
> Teach us who and what we are to be,
> As teachers and ministers, as writers and prophets,
> As lovers, above all.

> Kody Gabriel Hersh, 22
> Miami Monthly Meeting, Southeastern Yearly Meeting (FGC-FUM)
> United States

God Is Calling, Will Liz Please Pick Up?

In early March of 2008, I received an e-mail from Evangelical Friends Missions regarding the need for a short-term missionary (to be a teacher of missionaries' children). When I read this e-mail, I had a physical reaction: My body almost shuddered (I am still not sure what word to describe the reaction my body had). I argued with myself about it saying it would be so impractical: I just got a new job, have student loan payments, etc. The lights in the room dimmed for a second. My interpretation of this was that God wanted me to stop my negativity.

A week later, I had a dream about Rwanda. In my dream I was on the way to the house I would be living in. Along the way I encountered exotic looking huge lizards—everyone kept telling me to watch out for their heads (which was odd to me). Then while traveling through the country (by foot) to get to my house, I had to sleep in an open field. I was terrified of large bugs and lions. I sought comfort and guidance from the women in the group that was escorting me. As I have come further along this journey, I have begun to see these are symbolic for the obstacles I will need to overcome to get to Rwanda.

Three nights later I had a dream. I saw the face of Debby Thomas (a missionary in Rwanda with Evangelical Friends Missions). She was saying something to me, but I woke myself up as I wasn't ready to listen. Two nights after that, I had a dream that a lady was talking to a group about missions. She had encyclopedias about different countries and I asked to read one on Rwanda. In my dream I heard God say "I need you to go." I think I woke myself up at this point, still not ready to listen!

I decided, much as two-year-old might, to put my fingers in my ears and pretend I couldn't hear anything. It was full on resistance. Why would I want to leave my family and friends, my job—life as I knew it? Was I strong enough to move across the world? What about finances? What about . . . what about what about? My head was filled with so many questions.

So God gave me space. Three months of space! Looking back now I see I needed that time to be prepared to accept this call and for it to be seasoned within me. Would it have been a lot easier to say yes right then, right there? Of course! I am only human and I thank God for being patient with me.

In June, I was in Nebraska at Great Plains Yearly Meeting having a good old time worshipping and fellowshipping. While we sang the hymn "Here I Am Lord," God gave a little nudge to remind me of what he was calling me to do. I don't remember having much of a reaction to that moment. I think I was still trying to absorb that the calling had *resurfaced*.

When I returned from Nebraska, I began talking to a few people from my church and let it be known I was ready for a clearness committee for discernment to help reach clarity, in this instance, on where God is leading.

I met with my clearness committee, and after meeting for over an hour they felt released that I should submit my application to Evangelical Friends Missions for the two-year teaching position to Rwanda. Since that time it has been a whirlwind of paperwork, phone calls, an interview with the person who just returned from this position, some testing . . . and on September 5th I was accepted! I am so very humbled to have received this calling and I pray daily to be able to live up to what God is calling me to do.

Liz Wine, 27
University Friends Church, dually affiliated with EFC-Mid America
and Great Plains Yearly Meeting (FUM)
United States

La Mano de Dios en la Naturaleza

A mediados del mes de marzo del 2008 realice un viaje de trabajo a la provincia San Ignacio de Velasco de Santa Cruz.

El día domingo después de almorzar el grupo de trabajo decidimos ir a la represa, la cual estaba cerca a unos 800 metros aproximadamente del lugar de donde estábamos hospedados. Cuando llegamos a la represa los chicos estaban emocionados por entrar a la represa. En un inicio yo no quería entrar allí por que no había llevado ropa para entrar, uno de ellos me presto el short e ingrese con un poco de incomodidad porque no me quedaba bien esto. Cuando paso unos cinco minutos, Pablo uno de los compañeros dijo: "Algo me mordió." Pero no le dimos importancia porque el siempre hacia bromas, al pasar algunos segundos, volvió a decir: "Algo me mordió." Pensé que el había pisado alguna piedra filosa o algo asi, pero cuando salía hacia la orilla alzo su pie y estaba sangrando. También de pronto Micaela dijo: "algo me mordió." En esta represa había pirañas, entonces salimos rápidamente de la represa. Ambos sangraban mucho e inmediatamente lo llevamos a un hospital.

Al retornar al hotel conservamos con Gabriela, quien es nuestra coordinadora de trabajo. Ella me decía: "Dios nos cuida a sus hijos," pues yo me encontraba a unos metros de Pablo en la represa, pero es como si las pirañas no me hubieran visto. Ahora puedo ver la mano de Dios en la naturaleza puesto que El cuida de nosotros, nuestra entrada y salida en el lugar que nos encontramos. Dios siempre nos cuida por lo tanto encomendemos nuestra vida a El cada día cuando salgamos de casa.

Efraín Cuellar Avalos, 25
Iglesia Nacional Evangélica "Los Amigos" de Bolivia (EFCI)
Bolivia

God's Hand in Nature

In the middle of March 2008, I took a service trip to San Ignacio de Velasco in the province of Santa Cruz.

After eating lunch on Sunday, the entire service group decided to go to a nearby dam, which was only about eight hundred meters from the place where we were staying. When we got to the dam, the whole group was excited to get into the water. At first I didn't want to get in because I hadn't brought any clothes to go swimming. One of them lent me a pair of swim trunks and I got into the water although I was a little uncomfortable because they didn't fit me well. After about five minutes had gone by, Pablo, one of the guys in our group, said: "Something bit me." But we didn't pay any attention to him because he is always making jokes. After just a couple more seconds, he said that something bit him again. I thought that he had just stepped on a sharp rock or something like that, but when he got out of the water, he lifted his foot and it was bleeding. Suddenly, Micaela also said: "Something bit me." There were piranhas at the dam, and we all got out of the water as quick as we could. They were both bleeding a lot and immediately we took them to the hospital.

When we got back to the hotel, I talked to Gabriela, who is our service coordinator. She told me: "God takes care of his children." I was standing just a few meters from Pablo, but it was as if the piranhas hadn't even seen me. Now I can see how God's hands take care of us in our comings and our goings wherever we are, even in nature. God always takes care of us so that it is necessary to put our lives in His hands when we go out everyday.

> *Efraín Cuellar Avalos, 25*
> *INELA (EFCI)*
> *Bolivia*

So, About Leadings

I guess leadings are just one of the many ways to look at our relationship with God. To be open to what you can bring, in a divine spirit, and to be open to the fact that these things can be from God, that Spirit of love, in whom all things are made. I wonder if focusing on where God might be leading us can help us be who we want to be, where we want to be. Is the idea of leadings one that can help us live our lives as we want to live them? Is it an idea that can bring us closer to God?

Maybe it's the spirit of God, or a divine spirit of love, that leads you to care for your body and mind, for your health, cleanliness, and for that joy in little things that sustains you. Maybe it's a divine spirit that tells you to open your ears and your mind to new ideas, to the voice of the friend, or to something perfect and wonderful within yourself. Maybe it's the voice of God who speaks through you when you share your passion for stepping lightly on the earth, in your ways of eating, traveling, living, and recreation.

Callister Boots, Jacob Johansen, Bend, Oregon. Photo by Alan Brandt, Bend, OR. "God calls me to be a boot maker. This is what I do to make the world a better place."

I ask myself, is God some whimsical person who is interested in you only if your contribution is grandiose or is God down-to-earth, a spirit of joy, who's there in every tiny bit of love you share, the love for the little things and the doing of little loving things? Does God concern herself only with the showy displays of important people, not the day-to-day work done by the normal people who plant the seed, cut the wheat, grind the flour, bake the . . .

But wait. Maybe God's actually interested in you. Maybe you're already going about some of God's work in your daily life. Would it make a difference if you stopped to think about what might be "the work of God" that you accomplish each day?

Do you need to be clear on what God is or what comes from God to do God's work? Do you have to believe you're doing "God's work" for it to be something God asks of you?

Maybe it's God that makes us take care of each other, in the little ways and in the big ways: when you respond with help for someone in a tough situation, for a stranger, or a friend, when you listen or give someone a hug. Maybe God is truly leading us to strengthen the beautiful, the perfect, and the wonderful within ourselves.

Julian Brelsford, 27

Central Philadelphia Monthly Meeting, Philadelphia Yearly Meeting (FGC)

United States

Editor's note: This piece uses female pronouns to describe the Divine, an identification that is familiar and comfortable to some Friends while shocking and offensive to others. How do the words we use to describe the Divine, and our various vocabularies of faith, influence how we engage each other?

The Support of Experience

My meeting has no formal structure for supporting its transitioning youths, perhaps because there aren't very many of them. Recently I have been asked to help cater to this growing need. But I too am in transition and I too need Friends to encourage me and help me as I discern my path through the overwhelming hum and responsibility of adult life. Thankfully, I find that this support hangs in the silence on a Sunday. It clings to my elders; they have the air of wisdom, the aura of experience.

The Truth I find in the silent room is comforting and tenderly familiar. It feeds the seed of silence within me, this little space beyond the comprehension of the human mind, this little space that cannot be touched through words alone. And as I sit in our ancient meeting house I feel the years rising up around me. The spirit is in the stone work, the wonky windows with their glass rippling, the stooped door, and the stained wooden panels. Years of worship have infused this house with spirit. Walking in, I step into the silence like entering the shadow of a forest, from the roots to the branches it surrounds me and, with a sigh, I breathe once more the deepest peace. Standing amongst the tree trunks, in the thickening hush I sense the life of the place, the soft and soggy floor with its leaf mould festering, and each tree spreading its roots far, holding its rings inside, growing up and up, leaves and twigs mingling against the burning blue sky. I am held in the silence woven by this meeting, by the long life and experience of every member present. It is strong and almost tangible in the air. It is something that I can lean back into, supported and safe.

Within that silence and after it, in the community, there always seem to be chance meetings that foster deeper, unspoken connections. There are individuals who have walked along similar paths, who have reached for similar goals, whose ideas, experiences, and values are in sympathy with mine. Our branches meet whilst our roots may reach to different sources. It is their encouragement that I value above all the formal support structures that Friends may initiate. It is an organic support that grows naturally, with all the grace and truth of the Silence.

> *Harriet Hart, 22*
> *Settle Local Meeting, Britain Yearly Meeting*
> *United Kingdom*

Trabajando en el Ministerio del Señor

Mi nombre es Ruth Calle y vivo en la ciudad de El Alto del departamento de La Paz, Bolivia, con mis padres y mi hermana; además vivía con mi abuelo quien falleció hace 25 días, lo que nos genera un ambiente de tristeza y vacío, pero tenemos la esperanza de que un día nos reuniremos otra vez cuando Jesucristo vuelva por nosotros a medio cielo, sé que su promesa es fiel a los que le aman (Deuteronomio 7:9).

Mi familia y yo asistimos en la Iglesia "Ballivián 2" de la Misión Boliviana de Santidad "Amigos" gracias a que mi abuelo conoció y aceptó a Dios en el año 1955 por la llegada del evangelio a las comunidades de Achacachi a través de los misioneros que llegaron del Norte América, por lo que yo prácticamente nací y crecí en el evangelio o en el camino del Señor, y estoy decidida a seguir en el camino del Señor a pesar de todos los obstáculos que se me presenten, mi alma, cuerpo y espíritu están consagrados a El.

Desde el año 1999 al 2006 estuve trabajando como maestra dominical de niñas, fue una experiencia muy linda poder compartir de la palabra de Dios con hermanas más pequeñas que yo y que ellas recibían con mucho agrado. Desde antes de trabajar como maestra, se presentaron varias oportunidades donde estuve trabajando en el campo de la evangelización impartiendo la palabra de Dios, haciendo conocer de El a las personas que no conocían de El y que el Señor podía ser la esperanza y solución a sus problemas; casa por casa, con cultos al aire libre en plazas, mercados de barrios periféricos donde no se podían acceder fácilmente llegamos con la palabra de Dios; también estuve impartiendo la palabra de Dios en mi escuela, en el colegio, en la universidad y en el trabajo. Ahora estoy trabajando como superintendente dirigiendo con himnos de alabanza al empezar el culto, y seguiré trabajando en su obra hasta que El me de vida.

Para mi el trabajar en el ministerio del Señor es muy grande porque dice su palabra "La mies es mucha, los campos ya están maduros faltan obreros para el trabajo" (San Lucas 10:2), debemos trabajar no por la comida que perece, sino por la comida que da vida eterna permanece, (San Juan 6:27), porque cualquier trabajo que hagas en el Señor no es en vano (Ira Corintios 15:58). El Señor nos recompensará a cada uno según sean nuestras obras (Apocalipsis 22:12).

Quiero contarle que he tenido la oportunidad de trabajar en el Hospital durante 1 año después que terminé mi estudio en medicina, donde cada día se ven casos que conmueven los sentimientos mas profundos que uno tiene, al ver como varios niños, jóvenes, adultos y ancianos enfermos quienes mueren sin esperanza, al no haber conocido ni aceptado a Dios, por no poder solucionar sus problemas de salud, en accidentes de tránsito, por enfermedades incurables y terminales y uno se siente imponente sin poder hacer nada en ese momento ante este problema, qué hermoso hubiera sido haber contribuido en que esa persona *muriera con esperanza*, aceptando a Dios; aquí me doy cuenta que hay mucho por trabajar haciendo conocer el Evangelio que es la verdad de Dios a todos aquellos que no lo conocen.

Estos versículos y hechos que vi me hacen reflexionar y me dan más aliento y fuerza para seguir trabajando en la obra del Señor y también saber que mi trabajo será recompensado en aquel día cuando ya esté junto con el Señor. Si tu todavía no sabes en qué trabajar para el Señor puedes también dedicar parte de tu tiempo en trabajar en el campo de la evangelización hablando ya sea en tu trabajo, en tu casa, en tu escuela, en tu universidad y en tu barrio, sobre las maravillas que hizo el Señor Jesucristo cuando estaba en la tierra y que ese mismo Jesús está ahora con nosotros para ayudarnos y hacer el milagro que queremos en nuestras vidas. Pienso que no sólo el evangelizar es ir casa por casa o saliendo con campañas al aire libre en las plazas y mercados, sino que uno puede hacerlo en su diario vivir dentro de su comunidad y además estas cosas pequeñas le hacen a uno más grande delante del Señor.

Dios para mi lo es todo, sé que mi vida sin El no sería igual, me ha mostrado que siempre está conmigo, ayudándome en momentos de pruebas, aflicciones y dificultades como un gran Padre y Amigo fiel sin desampararme, en todo mi diario vivir, desde mi niñez hasta ahora que hace poco terminé mis estudios superiores en la universidad, le agradezco por la vida que me da y sé que seguiré en el camino del Señor, trabajando en su ministerio, El guiará mis pasos por el bien y yo estoy dispuesta a seguir sus huellas, aunque sufra desprecios, hambre y persecuciones.

Ruth Calle, 24
Iglesia Evangélica Misión Boliviana de Santidad Amigos (EFCI)
Bolivia

Untitled, watercolor, Abraham Quispe Ticona, Bolivia

Working in the Lord's Ministry

My name is Ruth Calle, and I live in the city of El Alto, in the Department of La Paz, Bolivia, with my parents and my sister. I also used to live with my grandfather, who passed away twenty-five days ago; this has left us feeling sad and empty, but we have the hope that one day we shall meet again when Jesus returns for us in the air. I know that His promise is faithful to those who love Him (Deut. 7:9).

My family and I attend the "Ballivián 2" Church of the Bolivian Mission of Holiness Friends Church. We owe this to my grandfather, who met and accepted God in 1955 with the arrival of the Gospel to the communities in Achacachi through missionaries who came from North America. Thus, I practically was born and grew up in the Gospel, or in the way of the Lord, and I have decided to follow in the path of the Lord despite all the obstacles that I may face; my soul, body, and spirit are consecrated to Him.

From 1999 until 2006 I was working as a Sunday school teacher for girls. It was a lovely experience to be able to share from the word of God with sisters who were younger than I, and they received it gratefully. Even before working as a teacher, I found several opportunities where I was working in the field of evangelism; teaching the word of God, making Him known to people who did not know about Him and that the Lord could be the hope and the solution to their problems. House by house, with open-air worship services in plazas and markets of outlying neighborhoods where access was not easy, we arrived with the word of God. I was also teaching God's word in my school, in my high school, at the university and at work. Now I work as a superintendent, leading the beginning of worship with hymns of praise, and I will continue working on His labors as long as He gives me life.

For me, working in the Lord's ministry is very great because His word says, "The harvest is plentiful, but the laborers are few" (Luke 10:2, NRSV) and that we must work not for the food which perishes, but rather for the food which endures to eternal life (John 6:27), because whatever work you do for the Lord is not in vain (1 Cor. 15:58). God will compensate each of us according to our works (Rev. 22:12).

I want to tell you that I have had the opportunity to work in the hospital for one year since I finished my studies in medicine. There, each day you see cases that move the deepest feelings you have, seeing sick children, youth, adults, and elderly people who die without hope, never having known or accepted God, because they could not solve their health problems, or in traffic accidents, or from incurable and terminal illnesses, and you feel helpless and unable to do anything at that moment about that problem. How beautiful it would have been to have contributed to that person *dying with hope*, accepting God. Now I realize there is much work to do to make known the Gospel, which is the truth of God, to all those who do not know it.

These verses and the things I saw make me reflect and give me more inspiration and strength to continue working in God's labors, and also to know that my work will be compensated on that day when I am together with the Lord. If you still do not know what work to do for the Lord, you can also dedicate part of your time to working in the field of evangelism, whether by speaking at your job, in your house, in your school, in your university, and in your neighborhood, about the wonders that Jesus Christ performed when he was on the earth, and that same Jesus is with us now to help us and work the miracle that we want in our lives. I think that evangelizing is not only going from house to house or going out with companions to the open air in the plazas and marketplaces, but is also something that you can do in your daily life within your community, and besides, these small things make you greater before the Lord.

God, to me, is everything; I know that my life would not be the same without Him; he has shown me that he is always with me, helping me in moments of trials, afflictions, and difficulties, like a great Father and faithful Friend, not leaving me unprotected. In all my daily living, from my childhood until now, since I recently finished my higher university studies, I thank Him for the life He gives me and I know that I will follow in the path of the Lord, working in His ministry. He will guide my steps for good and I am willing to follow in His footsteps, even though I may suffer insults, hunger and persecution.

Ruth Calle, 24
Bolivian Holiness Mission of Evangelical Friends Church (EFCI)
Bolivia

Faithfully Dancing*

Have you ever been led to dance in meeting for worship? I was, once, but I was not faithful to the leading, because I was afraid of what others might think. A few years ago I did watch someone rise in the silence, walk into the circle of gathered Friends, and begin to dance. She moved slowly and with intention, listening for God to guide her body. At first, I felt uncomfortable, as if I was an intruder, secretly watching an intimate dance between lovers. But I realized that in her act of faithfulness, her willingness to walk into the center of the room, she was inviting us all to feel the connection that flowed through her body and steadied her feet. Through her movement we were all dancing together, for God, with God.

I believe that I too am called to dance, to surrender to what is being asked of me in the moment, to listen deeply, and to move with intention in the dance of the Spirit.

I experience my spiritual journey as a continuous dance throughout the land. I see it in images of hard, painful treks over mountains, into valleys of forgiveness, of deep-sea dives into the depths of unknowing, through deserts of harsh, hot anger, into jungles thick with misunderstanding, and to landscapes of breathtaking clarity. This journey is a dance of love and loss, of anger and forgiveness, of unimaginable joy, of mystery and wonder. I'm constantly trying to keep my feet grounded on the earth, while also jumping toward the stars, of wanting to understand where I am being led, and slowing down so I don't out-dance my guide.

I'm learning how to share this journey with others. As a child, I don't remember hearing Friends talk in meeting about what they believed. As a young adult, I yearn to hear what Friends believe, to listen to their spiritual experiences, and to understand how their faith has grown or weakened throughout their life.

In the last few years, my life dance has changed, as I began to listen to the choreographer within. After graduating from college, I realized there was a spiritual void in my life. That realization helped me begin a new dance, one of going inward, seeking Truth, learning to experience God through loving others, and wrestling with what it means to live a faithful life. There are moments in the last few years that really stand out, when I knew clearly what God was asking of me. Those are the ones I return to, hoping to understand what helped me be open to the message. I'm coming to believe that life is not so coincidental, but that when I listen to the still, small voice within, there is more meaning and purpose in each step.

So now in hopes of sharing my journey of faith, I stand and walk to the center of the circle of gathered Friends. This is my dance.

The Message of Love
Young Adult Friends Conference, Burlington, New Jersey, Winter, 2007

I sit in the Burlington Meeting House with over one hundred other young adult Friends. It's late in the evening, so I'm fidgeting and counting down the minutes before I can go to bed. I'm too overwhelmed to be present to God. The vocal ministry seems distant and disconnected as Friends try to address the theme, *What are we called to as Friends?* Then one Friend stands. He invites Friends to join him in a song that many of us grew up singing. He suggests that even though we are all coming from different places, geographically and theologically, the simple, oversung "This Little Light of Mine" is something that connects us. I sort of roll my eyes, but as I begin to sing, the words touch me in a way they never have. "This little Light of mine, I'm gonna let it shine" feels like we are pronouncing to the world our intention to let our lives speak in different ways, but together as Friends. In that moment, I am overcome with a feeling of deep love for everyone in the room. We are all trying to shine, seeking that of God within ourselves and in others. As I sit there shaking, I realize that it is in loving these Friends in all of their differences and similarities, that I am able to know God.

Trusting God

Intergenerational Quaker Camp, Barnesville, Ohio, Summer 2007

I sit still and silent on an old wooden bench in the Stillwater Meeting House in Barnesville, Ohio. There are many new faces here on this Sunday morning. Friends of all ages have gathered for a week-long Quaker Camp. Elders of the meeting sit on the facing bench welcoming us into their spiritual community. I feel my heart begin to pound, faster and faster. My body begins to tremble and tears roll down my cheeks. I know this feeling, and I know the awful feeling that comes when I'm not faithful to the message or song I am given to share. But this time is different. No message comes. My body continues to shake, so I take some deep breaths and reach for a friend's hand to steady myself. "What would you have me say?" I ask without speaking. I've never been led to speak without knowing what I am supposed to share. I'm aware that although it's a room full of new faces, I do not feel afraid to speak. There is an overwhelming sense of peace in the air. I take a deep breath and stand, "What would you have me say?" I ask aloud.

Was I being asked to be a vessel for Truth? I don't remember the message I spoke that day, but when I sat down, I felt a deep peace within. I'm not sure if it was a leading, but I know that sitting in Stillwater Meeting that day, I surrendered to something greater than myself and trusted in God to provide the message. It's been my experience that being faithful is not always easy, and sometimes the messages we are given are really hard to hear. I keep listening, hoping that when the time comes, I will surrender again.

Speaking Truth

Young Adult Friends Conference, Richmond, Indiana, Spring 2008

I sit in silence in the Clear Creek Meeting House. A hundred young adult Friends from all branches of Quakerism have come together to build relationships and to explore how we experience, name, and worship the Divine. We are not trying to discern who is Quaker and who is not, or to heal theological divides, but to come together to listen, laugh, play, and worship as Friends.

In the calm of the moment, I wrestle with whether I have listened hard enough, spoken up enough, and if I have truly been faithful. I feel upset for not sharing what I believe and publicly naming my support for gay and lesbian Friends. In trying to create a space where everyone feels welcome, I have held back from sharing my own beliefs.

Out of the silence a woman stands. She shares with us her internal struggle about whether to water down the message she was given for fear that Friends would disagree or be angry with her for what she believed. Yet, she stands and delivers the message. She asks us, "What are you waiting for?" Over and over again she asks. "I'm sorry that anyone has ever hurt you in the name of Jesus Christ. That was so wrong and I'm so sorry. It should not have happened. But you can't throw the baby out with the bathwater. There is that of Jesus Christ who can speak to thy condition and he lives in each one of us, right now. He loves you. He is speaking through us even today. Why aren't you listening? There is so much going wrong in this world. When will you act? What are you waiting for? What are you waiting for?"

Another Friend stands, thanking her for speaking her truth, for not watering it down so that it was easier for others to hear. In sharing the message, she was not threatening other Friends' experience of the Divine, but giving different words for the same love.

The air is charged, some Friends are crying, others are smiling. Another young woman stands. She speaks softly and with hesitance. She had heard others speak of God or Jesus loving them, and how amazing that felt, but she had never experienced it herself. She believed the things that had happened to her in this life were an indication that God actually did not love her. But, over the weekend she experienced such acceptance and in this moment, for the first time, she heard God say, "I love you."

God's love for us and through us, heals us and unites us. We are all wounded. We must hold one another in love, listening to our different beliefs and experiences without judgment or attack. We must come together in Divine love, embracing all of our diversity. Heart pounding, I begin to sing the song that has finally come.

How could anyone ever tell you that you are anything less than beautiful?
How could anyone ever tell you that you are less than whole?
How could anyone fail to notice that your loving is a miracle?
How deeply you're connected to my soul?

Awakening

Last spring I started a group to explore intentional living. One night someone asked us to imagine where we wanted to be in five to ten years. I closed my eyes and had a startlingly clear vision. I was alone in a dark room joyfully dancing with God, twirling white streamers. All of a sudden a bright light shone down on me. My head snapped up, I dropped the streamers, and I was miles away watching myself. I saw that the dark room was part of a lush, green mountain range. In the distance an erupting volcano was destroying the land. The following poem came to me.

Let go my angel, let go of what you hold dear
For it can be taken away in a moment
And you left alone
Oh, then where will you turn, but upward
Neck wrenched back, chest exposed to the sky
The light shines through, penetrating deep into your depths.
Your soul revealed

You who danced with streamers in your hands
Twirling in the darkness,
You who knew the joy of movement, alone
Then the spotlight comes on, the dancing stops
The streamers drop to the ground, your head falls back.

In silence you stand. Unconscious to the world around you.
You are exposed in the Light,
As the lava flows from the volcano,
As darkness takes over the forest,
As death and decay leave the landscape dry, bare, and scorched.

You who dance in darkness, are exposed in the Light
What are you doing? Why are you here?
Why aren't you listening?
What are you afraid of?

Learning to dance, listening and understanding what God asks of me, may only be the first step. I am now being called to act, step out of my comfort zone, take risks to follow where God leads.

I know that being faithful is not easy. God asks me to speak at times when I just want to sit and listen. God asks me to love someone when all I want to do is walk away. God asks me to stand when my legs won't stop shaking. But it is in that moment when I finally give myself over, that my breath slows, my heart pounds, and I feel overcome by love.

This dance is much larger than the gathered body of Friends. There are many others faithfully dancing, communities of people around the world listening for God's guidance. I believe that we are being called to come together, to share our stories, to listen, and to act in love.

> Emily Stewart, 28
> Durham Monthly Meeting, North Carolina Yearly Meeting
> (Conservative) and Piedmont Friends Fellowship (FGC)
> United States
>
> *Editors' note: Social dancing has a long and complicated history among Friends. Historic Friends abstained from dancing for many generations, and many Friends today still do, including many Friends in Latin America. We invite you to consider how this Friend uses dancing as a metaphor for her faithful and joyful walk with God, even if the act of dancing itself is unfamiliar or disturbing to you.

The *Really* Reluctant Leader

At a recent business meeting I was on the agenda to present a request to the meeting. When the clerk called me up front to share, he introduced me by saying that he and the co-clerk thought I was a leader and so they wanted to make sure I got up in front of the meeting and in front of the microphone.

Ack! I think I rolled my eyes and frowned a bit. *I'm not a leader! What gives people that idea!?* But actually, I didn't balk at the title as much as I have in the past.

People have been assigning me that label since I was thirteen and I have been eager to avoid, deny, and otherwise run away from the idea. I can't be a leader! I don't like public speaking and I tend to be shy; I'm an introvert; I really don't like being in the spotlight. Do I really want to be responsible for making big, important decisions? Am I capable of being someone you can come to for advice or wisdom? I was never the popular "school body president" type of person who knew everyone—don't I have to be like that to be a leader?

Perhaps that is what the problem was: I had no idea what it meant to be a leader. I assumed leaders were presidents and meeting clerks and pastors, CEOs and managers—the top person. The person giving speeches and standing on a stage in front of everyone. No matter what it meant to be a leader, I felt very inadequate for the job.

Life was difficult growing up. I came from a broken family and we were very poor. I had a lot of anger, fought with my sister all the time, was really frustrated with God. God didn't seem to be looking out for my family and I sometimes doubted if God was even there at all. I might make a fine president or CEO, but surely I couldn't be a pastor or clerk with thoughts like that!

I went to Quaker leadership camps and to YouthQuake not to be a leader or learn how to be a leader, but in hopes that I would discover God or at least learn how to be a better person (sort of an outrageous expectation, I later realized). As I grew up, matured, and grew in my relationship with God, I still wouldn't answer to being a leader!

But I was clearly on that path. I had met a lot of interesting folks at YouthQuake and had learned about the wider world of Quakers. I knew I wanted to be more involved. I became part of the Friends Youth Executive Committee of Northwest Yearly Meeting when I got to college. But it's not leadership I told myself; I'm just the person that puts the calendar together. Later I got an application to apply for the Quaker Leadership Program, which I fought against. The word leadership again, right there in the title! But I did apply and was accepted into the program, and it wasn't so bad.

After college I found myself trying out teaching Sunday School for a year, I joined the planning group for our church's "alternative" Saturday night worship, and I joined the Nominating Committee. I somehow found myself on the planning committee for a regional FWCC gathering. And, most unbelievably, I found myself part of the planning committee for the World Gathering of Young Friends. How did it get to this!?

It happened because I had friends and elders around me encouraging me all the time. It happened because at some point I realized I liked being involved and I had gifts to share. Perhaps that is what leadership is: getting involved, recognizing your gifts and skills, and offering them to the group. For me, leadership also means listening, humility, and discernment. It is important for me to discern my leadings and callings and to be aware of my limits.

This new idea of leadership has helped me not to be scared of leadership opportunities but to be excited about them. I was recently asked to be on the new FWCC Young Adult Friends Committee. I agreed to this, and then I was asked to be co-clerk! I am feeling a bit daunted, but also excited. I do not know what the future holds for me, but I don't doubt there will be more leadership opportunities.

Aimee McAdams, 31
North Seattle Friends Church, Northwest Yearly Meeting (EFCI),
regular attender of Twin Cities Friends Meeting, Northern Yearly
Meeting (FGC)
United States

Way Opens

When I was a counselor at Catoctin Quaker Camp, we would often go on hiking trips, setting a destination several days away, but without planning our route or where we would stay along the way. It was an adventure! We had to figure things out as we went along and rely on the kindness of strangers. As evening approached on the first day after walking many miles of road, dark clouds started rolling in. We knew we had to find a place to camp soon, but no obvious opportunities had presented themselves. I was in step with one of my co-counselors as we hiked up a long hill, an occasional car whizzing by. It had been a long day and there was no end in sight, but she had a big smile on her face when she turned to me and said, "You know what I'd like to be saying at the end of the day?" "What?" I replied, "Way opens." As we crested the hill and could see our whole unit of campers stretched before us, a car pulled over and the driver spoke briefly with our third co-counselor at the front of our group. He put down his pack and waited for us to catch up. The driver owned a farm just up the road and she had offered to let us sleep on her front porch out of the rain. She even insisted upon cooking our dinner for us. It's amazing how people will help you if you give them the opportunity. The hard part is to put yourself in a position of vulnerability, open to receiving the help of others. That night, lying on the wide farmhouse porch dry and with a full belly, I said "Way opens," and it had.

To proceed "as the way opens" is an old Quaker saying. It means trusting that if we put one foot in front of the other and start toward something that the next steps will become clear, the way will open. These days (privileged) young people often grow up without much opportunity to step into that uncertainty, to put themselves in a vulnerable position. There is too much at stake to take the road less traveled, much less the road never traveled. From a very young age everything has been set out in front of us. If we follow the path that has been laid out for us we have a "reasonable expectation" of where it will lead: a job, a car, a house, maybe a spouse, some kids, and two weeks of vacation a year.

It is nice to have some measure of security, but it is also valuable to become comfortable with a certain level of uncertainty. After all, even if we do everything "right" there is still no guarantee that we will get what we "reasonably" expect. If we don't allow ourselves the opportunity to sit with uncertainty and proceed as the way opens on occasion, we will find that when uncertainty does strike we may not be prepared to handle it.

Right now, there is a great deal of uncertainty. The global economic system is in crisis. Tens of millions in the United States are unemployed. Young people are graduating from college, many with significant debt, and they are finding few opportunities to pursue what were, a short time ago, "reasonable expectations." The well-traveled paths are jammed with people waiting patiently for their opportunity. If the conventional systems are not providing the security that they once promised, we may be more inclined to try something different. Now more than ever may be the time to embrace uncertainty and proceed as the way opens. We need new paths with different destinations in mind and markers of success that give more weight to the well-being of people and the planet than to dollars and luxury cars.

To this end, when I finished graduate school in May, I decided not to get a job. I've thrown myself into the work of growing a local food system in the Triangle region of North Carolina. I've lived rent free in my tent, house sitting, in a bunk house, and now in a yurt. I'm living simply and sipping on my savings while I build a new kind of capital. I don't measure my success by the amount of money I earn, which is virtually none, but by the relationships I'm building, the community that is forming, and by the good local food that I eat. This provides me with a different kind of security—security in community. I trust that if I am an active and contributing member of my community that the community will provide for or help me to provide for my needs. It's hard sometimes in this culture of independence and self-reliance for me to be open to receiving help, much less asking for it. I live with quite a bit of uncertainty right now, but, as the economic system unravels around us, I'm not worried about my investments losing value. I'm invested in people, relationships, and community, not Citigroup, Goldman Sachs, and Bear Stearns.

I'm really thankful that I had the opportunity to proceed as the way opened in a relatively safe space at camp, where I knew that if I really needed to I could always call camp and have them whisk us to safety in a bus. My experiences taught me to trust that what needed to happen would happen and that often all it took to get what you needed was to ask. As I continue along my path, I'm at peace with the uncertainty I know I will face. All I want to be saying at the end of the day is "Way opens," and it will.

> Rob Jones, 28
> Chapel Hill Monthly Meeting, Baltimore Yearly Meeting (FGC-FUM)
> United States

In the Midst of Iniquity

In the midst of iniquity
I can rejoice;
When the dark fog of atonement
Rolls down from the hills
I carry the Light of the Lord within me;
With this lantern to guide me
I shall not stumble
And shall come to dwell in
The palace of righteousness.

> Heather C. Meehan, 16
> Westbury Meeting, New York Yearly Meeting (FGC-FUM)
> United States

Isaiah

In days to come the mountain of the Lord's house shall be established as the highest of the mountains, and shall be raised above the hills; all the nations shall stream to it. Many peoples shall come and say, "Come, let us go up to the mountain of the LORD, to the house of the God of Jacob; that he may teach us his ways and that we may walk in his paths." For out of Zion shall go forth instruction, and the word of the LORD from Jerusalem. He shall judge between the nations, and shall arbitrate for many peoples; they shall beat their swords into plowshares, and their spears into pruning hooks; nation shall not lift up sword against nation, neither shall they learn war any more. O house of Jacob, come, let us walk in the light of the LORD!

— *Isaiah 2:2-5, NRSV*

I want to offer some reflections on a particular passage of Isaiah. Isaiah is not one of the more cheerful books of the Bible. It contains verses like "The earth will be completely laid waste and totally plundered. God has spoken this word." This text is rampant with messages of an impending apocalypse. However, this message makes more sense when you consider it in the time and culture of its composition. I want to take a minute to examine the genre known as the apocalypse.

An apocalypse is a specific genre of biblical literature, generally written when followers of Yahweh were in great distress. Obviously, apocalypses always feature a prediction of divine retribution, but interestingly enough, it is always prophesied to happen later in time. This makes a lot of sense if you look at the time when the apocalypses were generally written. Apocalypses are almost always written in times in which there seems to be no hope. Whether it be the occupation of the Assyrians in the case of Isaiah, the horrendous reign of Antiochus IV Epiphanes, or the occupation by the Romans in the case of the Second Testament, there seems to be no human solution. And so the apocalypticist gives both hope for the future and a reason to continue to live by the law. The point of the apocalypse is to take the attention away from present suffering and turn it to a time in which all is well.

And Isaiah is no different. Isaiah was probably prophesying from about 742 BCE until 700 BCE. This was a time in which the Assyrian empire had annexed the Northern Kingdom of what had been Israel. The Southern Kingdom was basically serving as an annex to the annex of the Northern Kingdom, functioning mainly to supply it with resources. In other words, Israel had no national identity, and its people functioned mainly as slaves for the Assyrians. In the verses above, Isaiah gives a view of what he sees the Kingdom of God to be. He speaks of the Lord's reign coming and all the nations coming to learn from his hill. The use of the word "hill" here is somewhat unclear. But it is clear that it is a place of ruling, that it is from here that Christ can see the nations and teach them, much like the Sermon on the Mount. But the verses I really want to focus on are Isaiah verses 4 and 5. Let me restate them for you again:

He shall judge between the nations,
and shall arbitrate for many peoples;
They shall beat their swords into plowshares
and their spears into pruning hooks;

Nation shall not lift up sword against nation,
neither shall they learn war anymore. O House of Jacob,
come, let us walk
in the light of God.

Now since this is clearly a vision of the Kingdom of God, it would be easy for us to say that this is just impossible. That line I have heard so many times when defending my pacifism comes to mind. "Sure it would be great if we didn't have any war, but until Christ comes again, we are merely fallen beings, and I am gonna look out for myself and my country." And so I guess it really comes down to how you think about the Kingdom of God. The view of the other person in that conversation seems to coincide with the *Left Behind* series. This is a popular series of books (and movies) in which the rapture has taken place. Those who are righteous are swept away to live in Heaven, and those who are not are forced to live here in the anarchy that ensues. The basic tenet of this belief is that one day, when things get really, really bad, Christ will come again and fix everything. We have merely to be loyal, and to be ready. To put it in Christ's own words, he will come like a thief in the night. Though this is the theme of many apocalypses, I think that Isaiah calls us to something else in that last verse. "O House of Jacob, come, let us walk in the light of God."

Here I must insert my own belief about the coming of the Kingdom of God. I believe in an inaugurated Kingdom. In other words, I believe that when Christ came and taught, and died, and was resurrected, he marked the beginning of a new way of life in this world. He himself said that he brought us new laws. These are new laws for a new Kingdom, initiated by Christ's death and resurrection; in fact, these are the laws which will bring about the Kingdom of God here on earth. The basic tenet of this belief is that Christ (and those who have come before him, like Isaiah) has shown us the way to bring about the Kingdom of God now. We just haven't done a good job of obeying the rules of the Kingdom. This is a pretty common belief among Quakers, and I think that it really colors the way I approach this passage of scripture. When we believe this, it requires us to look at the scripture as a book of instructions—not for how to get into heaven, but rather for how we should live in relation to each other and God so as to realize the Kingdom which has already come to earth. I think that this is what Isaiah is offering us here. A way to live out the idea of the Peaceable Kingdom, which has always been so dear to the hearts of Quakers.

And so let us look at what he is calling us to in more detail. Here I offer a brief summary of what I see the call to be. In the time when God judges between nations and arbitrates on their behalf, those nations will beat their swords into plowshares and their spears into pruning hooks. If we are to live out the radical message that Christ taught, when he taught us not to judge, then we are to quite literally live in the time that Isaiah speaks about. Christ says that judgment is for God alone. Therefore, when we turn over this work to God, it is our responsibility to fulfill his prophecy. This is our first job: We must hand over our disputes to God. We are not to judge ourselves, but rather every day, in every way, to let Christ be the Judge. We have simply to love. And by allowing Christ/God to arbitrate between the nations and to offer judgment for them, we have completed the when part of the prophecy.

It is now our responsibility to beat our swords into plowshares.

So what are our swords? If we read this literally, then we are to take the weapons that we have and destroy them, right? I really love the old spiritual that says, "I'm gonna lay down my sword and shield down by the riverside, and study war no more." However, I think Isaiah calls us to more than that. I have a great love for musical theater and think that perhaps this verse is summed up best in a line from the musical *Rent*. One of the lead characters, Mark, states in a song that "The opposite of war isn't peace, it's creation." Now I doubt that Jonathan Larson was thinking much about Palestine and the annexation of Assyria when he wrote this modern rock opera, but I think he is onto something. In Isaiah's prophecy, the people do not simply lay their weapons down, but instead they turn them into tools for creation. The sword's use has been reversed, but it is still useful.

To limit our reading to literalism fails to do justice to what we could learn from these words. The words also call me to look at oppressive systems of which I am a part. In a world full of "isms," God knows that there are plenty of those. These are my swords. It is not enough for me to feel bad about them and then to try to ignore them. Destruction of the systems that create and perpetuate these isms is not the goal; rather we must work to transform them. We must beat our swords into plowshares.

As a white, straight, middle-class, Christian American male in this world, I have many swords. Let me give one example of when I think I might have been on the right track. For whatever reason, most likely in part due to some of these inherited swords, I was given the opportunity to attend Guilford College. There are oppressive systems in the world that make it easier for "people like me" to pursue higher education. To simply lay down these swords would have been for me to refuse to take part in that system, and refuse the education. But that didn't feel quite right.

Part of what made my education affordable was a service-based scholarship called the Bonner Scholars Program. I chose to do my service at the Pathways Family Homeless Shelter. Pathways (in general) is not filled with people who lack motivation to improve their situation. In fact, there are rules in place that state that residents must have a job and be looking for permanent residence. Many of the people are not there for lack of trying. By that I mean that many of those people are there because of the color of their skin, or their family history, or simply a housing system that has little sympathy for the poor. These were not struggles of mine, and by accepting the ease that was granted to me, this became my sword. But I believe that by tutoring the children at the shelter, I began to transform it.

I don't want to imply that I have created a plow that will allow all of those children to go to college. I don't pretend that I have. But this is an example of the work to which I hear Isaiah calling us. And if we all begin to work together toward this, to find our swords, whether they be white privilege, the protection of the largest military in the world, cheap consumer products made in countries where laborers are not paid fair wages, or a bank account that offers us comfort when so many go hungry. We must find these swords and transform them.

It would be easier if Isaiah had simply said, "They shall bury all their swords and spears, and they will never be used again." And yet, that peace would be empty. With what would we fill the time previously used for war? Would we simply slip back into our warring ways? I don't know, but I don't want to find out. Isaiah calls us to look within, find our swords, and to beat them into tools of creation. To beat them into weapons against the oppression and violence they had once represented.

Nathan Sebens, 25

Mt. Airy Friends Meeting, North Carolina Yearly Meeting (FUM)
United States

Editor's note: Versions of this piece were originally delivered as sermons for the author's course work at Earlham School of Religion, and subsequently for First Friends Meeting, North Carolina Yearly Meeting (FUM).

Martha

I am the practical one.
Not the mystic, I make the bread, for the day instead.
Carry the water, wash the dishes, and watch over the goats.

I am not my sister.
I cannot sit at the teacher's feet
For there is always, work to do,
Food to cook, and something always needs mending.

I am the rebel.
When the soldiers came I did not turn the believers away from my house.
All those who come to my door I feed.
There is always a courtyard to sleep in
And a fire in winter.
I turn none away.

I am the believer.
When He came to our house, it was I who let Him in,
I who first believed His words.
When my brother was dying it was Him I turned to
In His name I prayed.
I saw my brother rise.
I saw Him die.
I saw the Spirit come in tongues of fire and the Angels sing.

I remember,
When all his followers
His so-called disciples
Doubted Him.
But I never did.

Anna Obermayer, 23
Binghamton Community Friends, New York Yearly Meeting
(FGC-FUM)
United States

Author's note: Martha has long been an important biblical figure. For me, I have long seen Martha representing a kind of acts-based approach to faith. While Mary is the mystical part of our relationship with God, Martha represents God's work within the world.

Un Amigo Evangélico en el Mundo Actual

Nací y crecí como un Amigo, pero eso no me obligaba a ser parte de este grupo de Amigos. Para muchos jóvenes podemos ver que nuestros padres nos lleven a las reuniones de la Iglesia como una obligación. Personalmente así lo creía hasta que por elección personal decidí rendir mi vida a Cristo gracias a un encuentro personal que Dios mismo preparó como un proceso. Primero, enfermé mucho y no asistí a la Iglesia con mi familia por esa razón estando sola en casa recostada en un sillón estando muy triste y débil: escuche en la radio (tecnología moderna: ese día le di un buen uso) un canto que hablaba de la importancia de decidir a quién le pertenecerá nuestra vida si a Cristo que solo tienen deseos de bien para nosotros o Satanás que sus deseos son de mal y luego menciono que Dios aun si estuviéramos enfermeros el nos sanaría y que aceptar estar de su lado nos llevaría a Dios; esta fue una experiencia sublime y preciosa yo pude verme como una adolescente rebelde y necesitada de Dios. Unos pocos meses después de ese encuentro hice publica mi entrega a Jesús en una reunión de amigos adolescentes donde nos hicieron la invitación a recibir a Jesucristo como nuestro salvador personal. Yo di un paso al frente para testificar mi deseo de recibir a Cristo teniendo a penas 12 años de edad. Hoy tengo 28 y he recorrido muchos momentos difíciles que sin Cristo me hubiera sido imposible salir adelante.

Mi experiencia para con los dones espirituales, llamamiento o vocación la viví por medio de la capacitación en el instituto bíblico de mi Iglesia estudiando la palabra de Dios, escuchando los retos de Dios a mi vida en cada clase y acompañando a servir de interprete en brigadas medicas evangelísticas en diversas zonas rurales de mi país así: me he comprometido con Dios a responder a su llamado poco a poco. Es importante mencionar que como joven esto del llamamiento nos da mucho temor porque no nos sentimos preparados y sobre todo no queremos dejar la vida secular como sacrificar los lindos momentos en familia, el salario que nos genera nuestro empleo o la misma comodidad de tener tiempo para no hacer nada. Esto es asunto de decisiones y como jóvenes solo podemos tomar buenas decisiones bajo la dirección de nuestro Señor La Fe cumple el rol de seguridad a la hora de tomar decisiones.

Ser un amigo evangélico en el mundo actual, es ser un buscador de Cristo por medio de la Fe, su paz, su amor y su aprobación. Personalmente mi Fe me ha impulsado a dar pasos en la búsqueda del Dios Todopoderoso por medio del voluntariado como intérprete en brigadas medicas. Así también, impulsando un esfuerzo de ayuda social hacia los niños y niñas desfavorecidos de las comunidades alrededor de mi congregación. Aunque lo difícil es mantener el ideal sin que se te pierda la mirada de un rumbo fijo a causa de la crisis económica que se está viviendo. Pues hoy todas las personas en su mayoría desean ser ayudados y para mí y mis compañeros en su mayoría todos jóvenes con quienes me he unido para levantar esta iniciativa de amor a Cristo y a quienes Dios puso a mi lado para trabajar juntos.

Como jóvenes salvadoreños nuestras preocupaciones no son la protección de nuestro medio ambiente, la política; más bien tristemente somos muy desinteresados en las preocupaciones de la sociedad. Aunque esto no debería ser así, como jóvenes amigos debemos impactar en todas las áreas donde nos movilizamos y velar por generar pequeños cambios en la sociedad: uno de los principales problemas a los que como juventud estamos viviendo son los altos índices de delincuencia: esta es una palabra o problema social que sin lugar a dudas todos los jóvenes enfrentamos a diario al salir de nuestras casas. Lamentablemente como juventud solo hay dos opciones: ser las víctimas o ser los verdugos. Este problema nos persigue y a la vez nos invita a que en el nombre de Jesucristo nuestro único y suficiente salvador busquemos lograr mejores condiciones de vida para nosotros y nuestras próximas generaciones.

Frente a la violencia e injusticia muchas veces nos defendemos y otras sencillamente soportamos con dolor lo que viene; con tal de no incrementar los problemas al responder. Es muy común en muchas de las colonias en nuestro país que ya no podemos llegar en grupo de jóvenes porque llamamos la atención y ya las pandillas piensan que les estamos violando territorio. Esto es muy injusto porque de Dios es la tierra y su plenitud el mundo y todos los que el habitamos. Por lo tanto, es injusto que ya no podamos llegar tranquilos a cualquier parte en nuestra ciudad. Aunque la injusticia muchas veces pasa por alto en nuestras vidas; los jóvenes de hoy estamos muy distraídos y acostumbrados a los medios de la modernización como la televisión, la computadora, el radio, el ipod. Somos muy pocos los que nos acordamos de vez en cuando que vivimos en un mundo con muchas tempestades porque solo lo vivimos en nuestro ego-mundo. Como quien dice en el mundo solo existimos mi familia y yo; el resto no interesa.

Pero como jóvenes que somos estamos constantemente siendo atacados para irrespetar y ofender a nuestro Dios; considero que una de las tentaciones más fuertes que Satanás nos pone es el sexo opuesto porque como jóvenes inexpertos anhelamos el conocimiento de sensaciones desconocidas; mas del 50% de las muchachas con las que estudié mi bachillerato (high school) salieron embarazadas entre sus 14 a 18 años y en la mayoría de estos casos tanto el muchacho como la muchacha pierden el deseo de buscar a Dios. Por todo esto como Jóvenes Amigos debemos luchar a diario para no ser sorprendidos por Satanás que nos impulsa por medio de la televisión, el internet y las revistas a buscar las relaciones sexuales antes del matrimonio y muchas veces sin existir un verdadero amor. Desde este punto de vista debemos cuidarnos de la tecnología pues es un instrumento que Satanás usa para impedir nuestro crecimiento espiritual, la fidelidad, la oportunidad de ser jóvenes ejemplo de amor, palabra, fe, conducta, amor y pureza.

Aprovechemos la tecnología y no permitamos que ella se aproveche de nosotros. Actualmente, como jóvenes no estamos utilizando tecnología moderna para expresar nuestra fe. Hemos formado una comunidad de Jóvenes Amigos en un grupo en internet al cual llamamos JOVENES COMSAT que significa Jóvenes Comprometidos a Sacrificar sus Vidas Trabajando en la obra de Dios; algunos muchachos de la Iglesia tienen muchos conocimientos de música pues ellos se han unido y han formado un grupo de música cristiana para adorar a Dios en todas las actividades de nuestra Iglesia. Por otro Lado, estamos empezando a utilizar las grabaciones como demos para incentivar a otros jóvenes a acercarse a nuestro grupo y darles a conocer a Cristo como su salvador personal y otros están diseñando afiches, y banner en los que llamemos la atención y le digamos al resto de jóvenes que Cristo es la solución a la condición de nuestro mundo.

Deseo que seamos la diferencia y por ello invito a la juventud a que procuremos mantenernos muy cerca de nuestro grupo de Amigos en la Iglesia, tratando de cuidarnos de los amigos o amigas que no nos brindan un buen ejemplo o que sencillamente nos incitan a traicionar nuestros valores cristianos. Pero a la vez les animo a saber aprovechar toda oportunidad para sacarlos de la inmensa suciedad en que viven para atraerlos a los pies de nuestro Salvador y que ellos puedan degustar lo sabroso que es ser un joven o una señorita al Servicio de Cristo.

Damaris Mercedes Guardado Lemus, 29
Junta Anual de la Iglesia de los Amigos en El Salvador (EFCI)
El Salvador

An Evangelical Friend in Today's World

I was born and raised a Friend, but this did not obligate me to be a part of this group of Friends. For many young people we can see that our parents take us to meetings at the church as an obligation. Personally that's the way I saw it until I decided by personal choice that I wanted to yield my life to Christ thanks to a personal encounter that God Himself prepared as a process for me. First, I got sick a lot and I didn't attend church with my family. For this reason I was alone at home lying on the couch feeling sad and weak. I heard on the radio (modern technology: that day I made good use of it) a song that talked of the importance of deciding to whom our life belonged: to Christ who only desired the best for us, or to Satan, whose desires are of evil. Then it mentioned that God, even if we were sick, would heal us and that accepting being at His side would bring us to God. This was a precious and sublime experience and I could see myself as a rebellious adolescent who needed God. A few months after this encounter, I made public my commitment to Jesus in a meeting of teen Friends, where they invited us to accept Jesus Christ as our personal savior. I stepped forward to testify about my desire to receive Christ when I was scarcely twelve years old. Now I am twenty-eight and I have lived through many difficult moments that without Christ I would not have been able to get through.

My experience with other spiritual gifts, callings, or vocations came through the training in the biblical institute of my church, studying the word of God, listening to God's challenges for my life in each class, and accompanying as an interpreter the evangelical medical brigades in various rural areas of my country. Thus I have committed myself to God to respond to His calls little by little. It's important to mention that as a young person this business of being called causes a lot of fear because we don't feel prepared and above all we don't want to give up the secular life—as you sacrifice beautiful moments among your family, the salary that a job could generate, or the comfort and pleasantness of having time to do nothing. This is about making decisions, and as young people we can only make good decisions under the guidance of our Lord. Faith takes the place of security when it is time to make decisions.

To be an evangelical Friend in the world today is to be a seeker of Christ through faith, His peace, His love, and His approval. Personally, my faith has led me to take steps in search of Almighty God through work as a volunteer interpreter for medical brigades. My faith has also led me to social aid efforts for disadvantaged boys and girls in the communities surrounding my church congregation. The difficult thing is to maintain your ideals without losing your way, given the economic crisis in which we are living. Today most people want to be helped. My companions, mostly young people with whom I have joined to start this initiative of love of Christ, have been put at my side by God so that we may work together.

As Salvadoran youth our concerns are not the protection of our environment, or politics—rather, sadly, we are very uninterested in social concerns. It should not be this way. As young Friends we should have an impact on every place we are and work to generate small changes in society. One of the principal problems we face as youth is the high level of delinquency. This is a social problem that without any doubt we all face every day upon leaving our houses. Lamentably, as youth there are only two options: to be victims or to be tormentors. This problem pursues us and at the same time invites us in the name of Jesus Christ, our one and only savior, to look to improve the conditions of life for ourselves and future generations.

In the face of violence and injustice we often defend ourselves, and other times we simply bear, painfully, what comes, so as not to add to the problems by responding. It is very common in many of the housing settlements in our country that we cannot arrive as a group of young people because we will attract attention and the gangs will think we are violating their territory. This is very unfair because the earth and the fullness thereof and all that dwell therein are of God. It is unfair that we cannot go peacefully to any part of our city. Oftentimes the injustice goes right over our heads; young people today are very distracted and accustomed to means of modernization such as television, computers, radios, and iPods. We are very few who from time to time remember that we live in a tempestuous world, because we are just living in our egocentric world. As if in the world only my family and I exist and the rest is of no interest.

However, as young people we are being constantly pressed to disrespect and offend our God. I consider that one of the strongest temptations that Satan presents us with is the opposite sex, because as inexperienced young people we yearn for unfamiliar sensations. More than 50 percent of the girls in my high school were left pregnant between fourteen and eighteen years of age; and in the majority of these cases both the boy and the girl lose their desire to seek God. For this reason as Young Friends we should struggle daily not to be surprised by Satan, who tries to influence us through television, the Internet, and magazines to seek sexual relations before marriage and frequently to exist without true love. From this point of view we should protect ourselves from technology, since it is an instrument that Satan uses to impede our spiritual growth, fidelity, and opportunity to be young examples of love, the Word, faith, conduct, and purity.

Let's take advantage of technology and not permit it to take advantage of us. Currently, as young people we are not utilizing modern technology to express our faith. We have formed a community of Young Friends into an Internet group that we call Comsat Youth, which means Youth Committed to Sacrificing their Lives Doing the Work of God. Some youth of the church are very knowledgeable about music, and they have united and formed a Christian music group to worship God in all the activities of our church. We are also beginning to use recordings as demos to motivate other youth to approach our group and help them to know Christ as their personal savior. Others are designing posters and a banner in which we try to attract their attention and tell the rest of youth that Christ is the solution to the condition of our world.

I want us to be the difference, and for that reason I invite us as youth to stay close to our group of Friends in the church, trying to protect ourselves from the friends who do not offer a good example or who incite us to betray our Christian values. At the same time I encourage you to take advantage of every opportunity to remove them from the terrible filth in which they live, to attract them to the feet of our Savior so that they may discover the richness of being a young man or woman in the service of Christ.

Damaris Mercedes Guardado Lemus, 29
The Yearly Meeting of the Evangelical Friends Church in El Salvador (EFCI)
El Salvador

El Ministerio y los Dones Espirituales

En la gran comunidad de la Sociedad Religiosa de Amigos, en cada una de sus Iglesias hay tanto que hacer para Dios. Por esta razón todos los creyentes quienes tienen esa Luz interior o el Espíritu Santo en sus vidas necesitan trabajar para Dios como un miembro más de la Iglesia de El. Sobre todo la juventud debe cumplir un rol muy importante al ejercer sus dones espirituales en cada Iglesia ya que nosotros contamos con más energía, tiempo y aptitudes.

En una Iglesia cuando los jóvenes conocen a Dios y tienen el Espíritu Santo de Dios, ellos tienen un gran anhelo de servir a Dios. Muchas veces los jóvenes Amigos buscan trabajar en lo que encuentren de hacer en su congregación, pero entonces se le presentan los obstáculos como ser el miedo de no hacerlo bien su trabajo y como también el no estar seguro sobre el don o dones que recibió por la gracia de Dios (I Corintios 12:7). Sin embargo estas barreras negativas pueden ser vencidas puesto que Dios mismo da los dones espirituales a todos sus hijos e hijas de acuerdo a su voluntad (I Corintios 12:11–18).

Los dones espirituales son capacidades y habilidades recibidas de Dios por medio del Espíritu Santo. Hay una diversidad de dones como nos indica en la palabra de Dios (ej. Romanos 12:6–8; I Corintios 12:4, 28); los cuales nos ayudan a servir en medio de la Iglesia de acuerdo al propósito de Dios. El propósito de Dios consiste primeramente en que debamos hacer conocer sobre el Reino de los cielos y de Jesucristo a todos como está escrito en San Mateos 28:19–20. En segundo lugar Dios quiere que vivamos unidos apoyándonos unos a otros y así para poder crecer espiritualmente en nuestra congregación para la honra y gloria de Dios. La Iglesia (todos los miembros o creyentes) de Dios es como un solo cuerpo donde la cabeza es nuestro Señor Jesucristo (Efesios 4:11–16).

En el ministerio de Dios en cada congregación es tan esencial. Los diferentes ministerios vienen a ser la práctica de los dones espirituales por los creyentes. Por ejemplo si hay don de evangelista, entonces hay ministerio de evangelismo; de la misma manera funciona con los otros dones. No debemos dudar en asumir nuestros dones, porque unos pueden tener varios dones y así poder trabajar en varios ministerios. También estos ministerios pueden ser más pequeños y fáciles o grandes y difíciles. Pero Dios nos da los dones de acuerdo a nuestro alcance y capacidad. Por ejemplo, en la Santa Biblia vemos muchos hijos e hijas de Dios quienes tal vez nunca pensaron ejercer su don como administrador, evangelista, profeta, apóstol, etc, cumplieron la voluntad de Dios sin importar la edad, el sexo, la educación y la cultura.

La vida de Josué, quien fue hijo de Jacob, nos puede indicar un claro ejemplo de cómo Dios nos llama y nos da sus dones. Josué era un muchacho inocente quien llegó a ser un gobernante. En todo ese camino de la inocencia al poder de Josué, podemos analizar algunos de los dones espirituales que Dios le dió a el; en primer lugar, el tuvo que ser un profeta y evangelista cuando fue vendido a otro país por sus hermanos puesto que el dió a conocer sobre el Dios Todopoderoso y Misericordioso. Y también el tuvo que ser un buen administrador para gobernar en ese país extranjero y a su propio pueblo en Egipto.

En mi corta vida de cristiana como Cuáquera, experimenté tener algunos dones espirituales. A mis 15 años Dios me ayudó a descubrir que podía enseñar a niños en la clase dominical. Luego sentí que ir a evangelizar conjuntamente con el ministerio de evangelización, a lugares que Dios nos guiaba. Más tarde Dios me permitió predicar su palabra en su ministerio. Y también El me ha enseñado a trabajar en los ministerios de servicio, liderazgo y administración. Estos dones que Dios me las dió cada día aun para mi es algo sorprendente, ya que algunas veces me sentí que no las podía ejercer, pero siempre El me ayuda a usar mis dones en la comunidad Cuáquera de mi congregación. Si, Dios me ha preparado para que pueda ser un instrumento en su ministerio (Esdras 7:10).

Nunca olvides que Dios nos invita a trabajar en su ministerio para que podamos ser un instrumento agradable ante El. La juventud Cuáquera debe confiar en Dios; y fortalecerse y ejercer los dones que hemos recibido de El, comenzando desde la Iglesia donde asistimos. Sabemos que para Dios todo es posible como dice su palabra en Filipenses 4:13. Y si alguno de nosotros faltamos aun tener este don o dones de parte de nuestro Dios, hoy es la oportunidad de pedir a nuestro Padre Dios; y así poder ocuparse en su ministerio en la Iglesia (I Timoteo 4:14; II Timoteo 1:6-10; 2:15).

Emma Condori Mamani, 31
Iglesia Evangélica Misión Boliviana de Santidad Amigos (EFCI)
Bolivia

The Spiritual Gifts in the Ministry

In the great community of the Religious Society of Friends, in each one of its meetings, there is so much to do for God. For this reason all the believers who have that interior Light or the Holy Spirit in their lives need to work for God as one member of the church of God and of our beloved Lord Jesus Christ. Mainly youth should have a very important role when exercising their spiritual gifts in each meeting, since we have more energy, time, and skills.

In a meeting when young Friends know God and have the Holy Spirit of God, they have a great desire to serve God. Usually the young Friends look forward to work in what they find to do in their congregation, but then they face obstacles such as the fear of not doing their work well and not being sure about the gift or gifts that they received for the grace of God. However, these negative barriers can be conquered, since the same God gives the spiritual gift to all his children according to His will (I Cor. 12:7).

The spiritual gifts are capacities and abilities received of God by means of the Holy Spirit (I Cor. 12:11–18). There are diversities of gifts, as is indicated in the word of God (e.g. Rom. 12:6–8; I Cor. 12:4, 28), which help us to serve in the meeting according to God's purpose. First, the purpose of God consists in making known to everybody about the Kingdom of God, His grace, and Jesus Christ as it is written in Matthew 28:19–20. In the second place, God wants us to live in unity, supporting each other so that in this way we are able to grow spiritually in our congregation for the honor and glory of God. The church (all the members or believers) of God is as a single body where the head is our Lord Jesus Christ (Eph. 4:11–16).

God's ministry in each congregation is so essential. The different ministries come to be the practice of the spiritual gifts by the believers. For example, if there is a gift for evangelism, then there is a ministry of evangelism; it works in the same way with other gifts. We shouldn't be afraid of assuming our own gifts, because some of us can have several gifts, and in this way we are able to work in several ministries. These ministries can also be small and easy, or they can be big and difficult as well. But God gives us gifts according to our achievement and capacity. For example, in the Holy Bible we see many people as God's children, who perhaps never thought to exercise their gifts as an administrator, evangelist, prophet, apostle, etc.; they completed the will of God without taking account of age, sex, education, and culture.

The life of Joseph, who was the son of Jacob, can indicate to us a clear example of how God calls us and gives us His gifts. Joseph was an innocent kid, but he was also a governor. From innocence to power, Joseph's life can be analyzed for some of the spiritual gifts that God gave him; first he was a prophet and evangelist when he was sold to another country by his siblings, as he came to know and preach about his omnipotent and merciful God. And he had to be a good administrator in order to govern that foreign country and his own people in Egypt, who belonged to God.

In my short Christian life as a Quaker, I have experienced some spiritual gifts. When I was fifteen years old, God helped me to discover that I could teach children in Sunday School. Then I joined the evangelism ministry and went to places to which God guided us. Later God allowed me to preach his word in His ministry. And He also has taught me to work in the ministries of service, leadership, and administration. These gifts that God gave to me are something that surprise me everyday since I sometimes feel as if I can't exercise them, but He always helps me to use my gifts in the Quaker community of my congregation. Thus, God has trained me to be a tool in His ministry (Esdras 7:10).

Never forget that God invites us to work in His ministry so that we can be an important tool before His eyes. Quaker youth should trust in God and begin to strengthen and to exercise the gifts that we have received from Him, in the meeting where we attend. We know that everything is possible for God, as it says in his word (Phil. 4:13). And if some one of us still lacks gifts on behalf of our God, today we have the opportunity to request them from our God the Father God; and in this way we are able to take charge of His ministry in the meeting (I Tim. 4:14; II Tim. 1:6–10; 2:15).

Emma Condori Mamani, 31
Bolivian Holiness Mission of Evangelical Friends Church
Bolivia

Tree, photograph, Helen Sladen, 22, Britain Yearly Meeting, United Kingdom

One Source, Many Streams

Friendship, Convergence,
Ecumenism, and Intervisitation

I Have Always Felt

I have always felt that my life is split across the political border between Canada and the United States. I was born and raised a Canadian by two previously American parents. My entire extended family lives in the United States, and so I spent many a holiday sitting in the backseat of a car traveling down to visit with them. This feeling grew as I attended the FGC Gathering (usually held in the US), Camp NeeKauNis and Canadian Yearly Meeting. As a dynamic young person in a rather stifling rural community, I developed deep kindred friendships with my peers at these events that became the sustaining relationships in my life. My relationships with my Quaker friends have always been first and foremost on my list of priorities.

Attending Earlham College in Richmond, Indiana, for my undergraduate degree introduced me to even more American and international Quakers and made me aware of opportunities previously unknown to me. One of these opportunities was the World Gathering of Young Friends (2005). I was selected to be one of Canadian Yearly Meetings representatives to the WGYF. There, I met even more Young Quakers from around the world and learned about our diversity and differences when it came to practices but our similarities in Spirit.

Though it can be exhausting and frustrating to have F/friends communities at such a distance, I would not trade them for the world. In some ways it has meant that I have led a very compartmentalized life—spending this week with this group of F/friends here and then spending time with these F/friends there, none of whom knew each other but heard about the others through me. As we've grown, so have the opportunities and interest among Young Friends to attend gatherings other than their own camp or yearly meeting sessions, and so my world, though spread across the globe, grows smaller and smaller.

Having a diverse group of F/friends spread across the globe and theological perspectives has been such a gift. How lucky am I to have F/friends who respect who I am as a person but challenge my beliefs in a way that we can have open dialogue and remain open? I believe that Young Friends today are so determined to have dialogue and gather together because they recognize that it is not our differences that are important, but our similarities and common beliefs. Why does it matter if one finds connection with a Higher Spirit through silent worship and one finds that relationship to the Divine through a programmed or evangelical meeting? Shouldn't we focus on the fact that all of us are seeking that experience and believe in its value? The divide among Friends about petty issues and even really hard ones hurts my soul. How can we call ourselves Quakers and believe that there is the Light of God in everyone if we can't even see it in Quakers who practice their Quakerism in a different way or, due to their experience, believe things that are different than what we believe? How can we say that we should split from a group because of those differences of opinion, instead of staying to have continued conversation? Of course it is painful to be in discord. It wouldn't be painful if the issues were not so important to us, or if we did not care about the group/people we are in discord with, but that doesn't mean that it is better to walk away from that pain and conversation.

My relationships with Quakers outside of Canada have taught me that lesson. In meeting with a group of Young Friends in Guatemala, we discussed what made us Quaker and how we practiced our Faith. To these Young Friends with their ability to talk about God and Christ as their Lord and Saviour and their expressions of Quakerism in their daily lives, I expect that we initially seemed to be unfaithful. However, through conversation (and a translator) we were able to explain how we were taught to practice our Faith and that our referencing a Higher Spirit was how we learned to talk about God. It was only a conversation— we weren't trying to figure out how to work together or questioning each other's beliefs, and so that may seem like it isn't the same as some of the issues that committees or meetings or larger Quaker bodies are dealing with. But it is the same idea. Regardless of how we practice it, the language we use or what our opinion or belief is on homosexual relationships, the role of women in society, plain dress, or evangelizing, we are all members of the Religious Society of Friends and need to start seeing the Inner Light among Friends.

Young (Adult) Friends from around the globe are aware of the need for dialogue, creating community and learning about one another. That is why there are currently so many Young Adult Friend (YAF) weekends, conferences, lectures, and gatherings. We can't get enough of each other. I think that the larger Quaker world could learn a thing or two from this group. You have to create community first and come together with open hearts before you can start having the tough conversations. I believe that is where we are failing ourselves. We do not teach Young Friends about the various types of Quakers or our history, we don't give them options for picking what type of worship they find most meaningful in creating their relationship with God/the Spirit/the Divine. We don't give them the words to express themselves in a spiritual or religious context or teach them to have an open heart to hear how other Quakers express themselves.

My F/friendships are as strong, deep, and meaningful as they are today because we are open and willing to discuss and work through our differences regardless (or maybe because) of our Quaker affiliation.

Katrina McQuail, 26
Kitchener Area Monthly Meeting, Canadian Yearly Meeting
(FGC-FUM)
Canada

Luz

Algo hay dentro de cada cual que invita a romper cristales sucios. Ese algo no nos fue dado. Hablo de algo limpio y desconocido que juzga incluso lo que para nosotros es bueno. Algo que llega y embarga, latente en el hombre incrédulo, en el político arrogante, en el terrorista, algo puro que existe en el que pide sangre, descuartiza y luego ríe. Algo sin geografías ni razas, que reina soberanamente, trasciende liturgias y oraciones. Inexplicable eterno y absoluto.

Jorge Luis Peña Reyes
Junta Anual de la Iglesia de los Amigos (Cuaqueros) en Cuba (FUM)
Cuba

Light

There is something inside each one of us that invites you to break the dirty glasses. That something was not given to us. I talk about something that is pure and unknown, which judges even what is fair for us. It is something that comes and seizes; it is latent in the smug man, arrogant politician, and terrorist; it is something pure that there is inside the one who asks [for] blood, assassinates, and then laughs. It's something without geographies or races that reigns with sovereignty and transcends liturgies and prayers. It's something unexplained, eternal, and absolute.

Jorge Luis Peña Reyes
Friends Church in Puerto Padre, Cuba Yearly Meeting (FUM)
Cuba

Quakerism Is More than a Man and a Motorcycle

Reflection on a Pilgrimage along the East Coast

Shortly after finishing my second year at Guilford College, I set out to understand what brought me there. During the stressful process of choosing schools, I felt a strong but slightly mysterious urge to explore Quakerism in my undergraduate years. Two years later, while Guilford had excited and even irritated my thoughts about the workings of Quakerism, I knew little about the human face of the Religious Society Friends over a large area of the country. Coming from the "frontiersee," splayed-out American West, I was curious to see the established community of eastern friends. I wanted to find out how Quakers worked as a group, wondering what leadership might look like within that community.

My initial plans for this project were to purchase a motorcycle, learn to ride it, and drive from Key West in Florida to Maine, visiting Quakers along the way. I wanted to stay near the coast for no other reason than the geographical continuity of the Atlantic to ground me along my way. Once the rubber hit the road, way opened in all directions, but the practice of finding spiritual continuity within myself became just as important as finding it in my surroundings. I began in Greensboro, North Carolina, and traveled south to St. Petersburg, Florida. From St. Petersburg, I traveled all the way along the Eastern Seaboard more or less to New York City. From there, I returned to the South by way of Greensboro to finish in Nashville, Tennessee. In all, I covered over 4,200 miles and visited roughly 29 meetings and Quaker places of worship, meeting with groups from 15 of them.

The purpose of my trip as outlined by my letter of introduction to Quaker meetings was:

> the development of constructive and enriching spiritual dialogue between all branches of the Quaker community. I plan to travel from South to North, speaking with meetings about how (or whether) they feel their regional culture affects their theological beliefs with the intent of gaining a greater understanding of the "spiritual state" of individual meetings.

I hoped in the discussions I might find some aspect of regional flavor to a Quaker meeting in South Carolina versus one in New Jersey, for example. I hoped to identify what these differences might be and look for a common Quaker thread that ran beneath them I could address with all Friends. I was most interested in simply gaining a greater understanding of how Quakerism is practiced over a very large area of the United States. I wanted to know what it meant to truly own up to and understand this part of my identity.

I was presented with quite a number of challenges on my trip; those obstacles came either in the form of spiritual or practical trials along my way. Some of my practical challenges were the theft of my camera early in the trip, the matter of food and lodging, and the sheer effort of traveling over very great distances day after day. Getting to know a motorcycle and traveling outside immediately put me in an unofficial club of the road, a club largely of older folks who were of the same generation I met in most of the meetings. In general, I had a sense where I would stay city by city along my route, but it was difficult to know people only through correspondence and to rely on them so much for their generosity. I realized that this demanded quite a degree of flexibility both on my part and theirs. This, like my stolen camera, taught me to stay as adaptable and gracious as my jittered knees could allow. The physical strain and mental alertness I needed to travel long distances surprised me. In the end I abbreviated my original trip plan, knowing I could not be present enough to fulfill my "Florida to Maine" ambitions.

With the goal of creating "enriching spiritual dialogue" so prominently placed as my mission, I spent a significant amount of time figuring out what this meant and how it might be achieved. If I were able to create this dialogue on my trip, I somehow felt Quakers and Quaker institutions would feel the immediate benefit of greater vitality and unity within them. At the very least they would hear what folks down in the Carolinas served at potlucks. I began to realize how subjective unity and vitality are. A distinction I failed to recognize in my idealized conception was the difference between unity of individuals, such as a good conversation between me and my host, and unity of meetings, such as a group meeting and sharing conversation.

I had hoped Friends themselves would suggest points of unity within Quakerism, but I often just heard what they believed to the exclusion of other beliefs. This shocked me, considering especially how many Friends are so eager to tout the universal message of Quaker values. As time went on, I began to become frustrated in group discussions and found myself "arguing" my interpretation of unity and vitality in much the same way I saw other Friends doing. I found that I, like many other Quakers, instinctively turned to exclusivity and defensiveness when threatened spiritually, despite my rhetoric of common understanding.

For example, I asked many meetings what they might do as a group if someone rose in meeting and brought a very evangelical Christian message to worship. While at first many spoke about "trying to accept that message" as equal to any other, it seemed that in essence many felt threatened by the question and that I asked it at all. *How can we consider ourselves a universal faith of inclusiveness if we cannot address those who interpret faith as exclusive?* I wondered. It seemed that few meetings had any established process of "eldering" or holding individuals accountable for the group, whatever their theology.

Observing group dynamics and looking for continuity or unity within Friends meetings as a whole along my journey was very hard for me. There were several notable exceptions, but as I finished my trip I found myself terribly disheartened in general by much of the group behavior I witnessed within the meetings I visited. My spiritual discussions began to leave me struggling to be lighthearted. In meetings where I felt most successful and useful, the members appeared not only to care deeply about each other and the vitality of their individual meetings but were strong enough to work outside their own communities to engage corporately in the wider body of Quakerism and the world at large. They had clear ways of holding individuals accountable to the group as a whole and did so. I did not feel I found this sense in many of the meetings I visited.

The main cause of this disunity was the unfortunate fact that many Friends are Quaker for selfish reasons. I'm sorry to say it, but this was my impression of why so many meeting groups struggle to find an effective group process. In many of the meetings I visited, it appeared that Friends not only expected complete acceptance of their personal spiritual path, but also their political, ideological, and cultural ones as well. In the case of the evangelical message question, it appeared that an evangelical person was not simply threatening to individuals in their spiritual beliefs, but also in their inferred political leanings and culture. This showed me that the meeting was not actually for embracing people in a group atmosphere but more a cultural, ideological, and political support group for like-minded individuals.

As a group-minded thinker who often loses himself in social analysis, I was pleasantly surprised when my attention often turned to the great individuals I found along my way who spoke directly to my condition. I met so many incredibly interesting, thought-provoking, eccentric, kind, and inspired people on my trip, I could not help but be awed and impressed. I certainly found a kind of unity between them and myself that I had not anticipated in my original socially oriented goals. I found people who truly listened as I listened to them. While I cannot be sure my actions benefited Friends meetings in totality, I know that my conversations with Friends were both inspiring to me and the people I found along the way. I believe I brightened some folks' days and gave them a chance to tell their stories. I am sure that I will continue to be in contact with Friends I met along the way and will continue to think about these issues with them.

Trying to understand my personal Quaker identity and where I fit in the Religious Society of Friends was the hardest lesson. A role I saw often, worrisome in its personal familiarity, was that of the "überQuakers," as we at Guilford like to call them. In many instances, I ended up staying with members who were the "movers and shakers" of their meetings for their dogged dedication to their congregation. Sadly, in many instances these folks seemed to bear a disproportionate amount of responsibility for the affairs of their meetings: spiritually, logistically, and energetically. They did not resent this role, but it appeared to me that they were rarely consciously chosen for that ministry by the group but instead had the position thrust upon them. If this is how Quakerism works, would I be fated to become an "überQuaker" just for going out of my way? While it may not have burnt out those I stayed with, what kind of example does this set for folks like me coming up in the faith? What thanks from God or community would I receive? It is not that I begrudge selflessness by any means, but Quakerism cannot survive on the selflessness of some and dependence of many.

I wish I could say I knew this trip was God's will, but the rhetoric with which many people have invoked God's name in my life has blurred the lines between spiritual surrender and egotistical manipulation. As one particularly astute Friend put it, "As with so much else in life, implementing our intentions should allow for the possibility of being self-conceited." Much of what I found along my trip reflected Friends' struggles about the will of God or Divinity in their lives versus their personal desires.

Ironically, after so much travel, I found this question to be universally true despite geography. All the Friends I talked to were in some way struggling with the issue of how they fit into the larger group, a community of the Spirit and of Quaker business. As I sought to find parallels in my conversations with Friends, I was constantly reminded of the push and pull of the individual will versus the will of the whole. In many Friends' eyes, this struggle is fundamentally a dance between the individual and the music of the Spirit that animates our lives. This music may not always be what we are ready to hear. I may have heard it as a dull drone, vibrating all throughout and beyond me as I traveled an unknown road.

Some Queries I made up for myself along my trip were:

- How do I remain secure and nonthreatened in my own faith to be open to others?
- What are my blindnesses or biases from my Quaker roots?
- What is selflessness and is it ideal?
- How do I know what is my will and what is the will of God?

Evan Welkin, 25
Olympia Monthly Meeting, North Pacific Yearly Meeting (Independent)
United States

Editor's note: Different versions of this piece have appeared on the blog *QuakerRanter*, Evan's blog (evanwelkin.wordpress.com), the *Friends Center Bulletin* at Guilford College, and in Guilford's alumni magazine.

The Journey Worth Taking

We come from far-off lands,
cultures apart, struggling to
understand a foreign tongue,
another viewpoint, another way to live,
to see, to hear God in different words.
We listen, opening to new sights, perspectives,
ways to love as we discover
we are unique parts of a greater circle,
distinctive expressions of the Divine Life.
Yet our voices together lift up the mountains.
Our chorus pulses the river down the outward
flow into a world needing to hear the rushing tide.
We are on a journey and it may not even
matter so much where we end up,
but that we rise up to take the voyage.
We speak the truth of our lives,
hear each other and are changed.
We can love without complete understanding,
walking the light together while miles apart.
If in the tension we can find

the one light we are birthed from,
the thread through our stories,
we may discover we are brothers, sisters all
of one skin, one laughter, music, lilting, free,
if we can just find the courage to come together
and take the journey.

Sarah Katreen Hoggatt, 30
Freedom Friends Church (Independent)
United States

Magnificat

I have lived in Miami a year now, through the subtle changes of season that mask the arrival of Christmas. I take a picture of the so-called Christmas Palms, the ones with heavy branches of red berries sprouting from the smooth green crown of the trunk. This will be my Christmas card this year, a tropical memento for friends and family further north.

I've lived in Miami a year now and it still doesn't feel like home. I have been trying to make this city mine, to make a place for myself in the big urban sprawl, the broad banyan trees, the blue-green waters of Biscayne Bay, the bright beaches. One of the places I have found for myself is in a Sufi group that meets each Thursday at the house of an Israeli acupuncturist. Isaac is a teacher in the Shadduliyya order; the Sheykh, whom they affectionately call Sidi, is a wizened old man in Jerusalem.

In this circle of Jews, Christians, secularists, and Muslims, I have found a new language to love, whose sounds come from a different part of me than my Spanish heart, perhaps the depths of my belly or gurgle of my throat. The language feels older than Spanish, under yet another layer of skin, and I long to learn it.

In this circle of loving people walking (Sufis journey by walking toward Allah), whose names I don't know but I know them deeper than that—we hug, we cry, we pray, we share our desire for God—I am entirely comfortable.

In the cave of Isaac's living room, feet curled under me, eyes closed like everyone else in the circle, this past Thursday night we broke into song, a simple, dissonant Middle Eastern melody of La-ilaha-il-allah, *there is no God but God*. I found myself floating, as if God were the sea, pale and green and full of light filling my ears.

Whenever I feel this light of God, I want to curl around it, press it into my belly, and guard it, rock it gently. I want to come up for air, knowing smugly that God is love, and carry that flame inside me without anyone noticing.

Then the words of Mary in the Magnificat, which I had read that morning in a fit of "Adventiness," come to my head: "My soul magnifies the glory of God" (Luke 1:46, New Jerusalem). Magnify, not shroud. So I have to let go of this urge to crawl into caves, to hide the light under a bushel, or as I thought it was as a child, a bush. I have to open up and let this light pour from me.

I can share these things afterward, when we have opened our eyes and reentered the physical world where you cannot *see* God. I share it only after Isaac has said my name, as he says the names of others, an invitation to share after he has read their hearts, whether or not they *know* they want to say something. No one judges, no one thinks I'm *out there*. They understand.

Being Sufi is not about being Muslim, though we use the name Allah for God and chant in Arabic. It is not about being wishy-washy new-agey, either, where people dance around with scarves and sit on pillows and talk about Oneness in hushed tones (I went to a Sufi workshop like this at Oberlin). This is simply a time to remember to be in the presence of God, to know that God loves us and holds us, forgives us, even as we walk mindlessly and haughtily through our forgetful daily lives.

Today I go to the beach. There is a break in our long days of clouds and rain, and I lie in the sun for the first time in ages. I walk into the chilly water and swim through the pale green light of God. *Allahu akhbar*, God is great. This is not a shout for vengeful soldiers who have just killed their enemies halfway across the world. This is a simple truth to be magnified from my lips.

"What is Christmas to you?" I asked one of my students during art class, trying to help him come up with an image to draw. I don't want him to talk about presents and the grabbing-shouting-whooping tear of wrapping paper and grumpy jealousy of the children when they eyed each other's Secret Santa presents.

"The birth of God in the world?" he asked.

Yes! I want to shout. Yes. *Allahu akhbar*, my soul magnifies the greatness of God.

Hannah C. Logan-Morris, 29
Friendship Friends Meeting, North Carolina Yearly Meeting
(Conservative)
United States

Modern-Day Esther

I am a modern-day Esther. I was once known and recognized by my people—they understood who, understood *what*—I was. You could say I grew up in a Quaker town. Christians nodded their heads knowingly when I told them I was Quaker. No explanations were necessary. I grew up in the same home, attending the same Quaker camp each summer and the same Quaker church out of several nearby, in the same Quaker-populated community. Heck, even our town university is named after George Fox.

But then came the uprooting.

Leaving my well-known bubble of friends and family, I packed my bags and headed north, believing the Canadian Christian university would broaden my horizons. That it did. As a college senior, I am quite certain I've witnessed one too many furrowed brows, inevitably preceding the question, "Quaker? Like the oats?" Or, just as common, the musing: "Ahh, Quaker . . . aren't they like the Amish?" Someone asked me if I churned my own butter. I kid you not. I even had an ex-boyfriend once say, "Oh, I thought you said you were German." I am baffled as I divulge the fact that my Pentecostal Church pastors from the church I've joined in British Columbia asked me what a Quaker is.

Once, during my Atlantic History course, an entire class was spent in a lecture on the history of Quakers. My beloved professor was the first person I have met at three hundred miles north of "Quakertown" who is knowledgeable of the Quaker faith! Inwardly I could have yawned at hearing yet again the basic and fundamental facts of Quakerism, but at the same time I was excited. I wanted to shout, "Hey, I'm a Quaker! They still exist!" I casually mentioned this to my professor in an e-mail sent later that night. She, in turn, informed the class next period, who swiveled their heads around to look at me. I was a novelty. But I was also a little embarrassed. A classmate asked if I was allowed to wear normal clothes, and I had to laugh because on this day I happened to be wearing a long, pioneer-looking skirt and ethnic jewelry.

Like Esther, I had not a single friend in Canada know me for who I was. What they knew of my denomination came only from the facts I chose to share. I was a stranger in a foreign land, literally.

Finally, the figurative lightbulb floating above my head clicked on: this is not a reason to despair. Instead, it is an opportunity! Unlike Esther, I have every reason to relish the freedom of expressing my faith. It has been a good thing for me to discover from an outside perspective the reasons I have for actually wanting to be Quaker. I have been learning how to summarize basic differences between denominations into just a few sentences so that my friends can see how the Quaker faith is unique. I'm proud to say that the faith has become my own, and by leaving a like-minded community, it has become much more real to me. I don't preach it, but I don't hide it; I love saying that I'm Quaker.

In writing this, I hope to encourage those who find themselves in similar situations to my own. It's easy to focus on the exasperation or the humor of the moments when you find yourself among non-Quakers. And yet, what really matters is not which denomination we claim, nor the reaction we get from others in claiming it, but the way in which we are living our lives.

This line from the hymn "The Summons" by John Bell convicts me every time I hear it: *Will you risk the hostile stare? Should your life attract or scare?*

Kate Symank, 23
Newberg Friends Church, Northwest Yearly Meeting (EFCI)
United States

Presence of the Living Christ

Growing up in a large, liberal, unprogrammed, urban meeting, I never heard of the Living Christ, let alone experienced it. My home meeting taught me and the other children that peace, the inner light, and love were the core Quaker beliefs. Apart from the Christmas programming, words like God and Christ were rarely spoken to us, and when they were they often had a negative connotation, usually framing concepts of inequality and systems of oppression. So I was surprised my sophomore year of college when I actually read the Gospels and discovered that Jesus' teachings were the grounding for the Quakerism I had been taught. After this I read early Friends writings and I realized that the early Friends were Christians, who loved Christ. From these two experiences I felt an interior shift and had a new respect for Jesus and his teachings—after all, his teachings were the basis for the things I loved most about Quakerism. But I did not give Christ much thought, let alone the presence of Christ, whom early Friends described as inhabiting their hearts and surrounding their worship.

But this all shifted one Sunday when two other Guilford students and I attended West Grove Friends Meeting, a small, Conservative Friends meeting (meaning to conserve the traditional form of Quakerism) in Snow Camp, North Carolina. The West Grove Meeting House, situated within a small grove of trees, did not look like much from outside. Built in 1915, it still has a dividing wall and outdoor toilets, plus a noticeably sinking foundation. The other students and I arrived ten minutes late, but when we entered the worship, the Presence in the silence was already palpable and deep—our entrance did not disturb it. When we sat, we were enfolded by the silence and brought into deep communion with those around us and the Spirit. Throughout the worship I felt the presence of others around me and a greater presence standing over and around us all, bringing us together under it. Through this worship I felt the Presence of the Living Christ. Finally, after twenty years of worshipping with a variety of Quakers from FUM, FGC, America, and Britain, I understood what the early Quakers wrote about when describing their worship:

> The Lord of Heaven and earth we found to be near at hand, and, as we waited upon him in pure silence, our minds out of all things, his heavenly presence appeared in our assemblies, when there was no language, tongue nor speech from any creature. The Kingdom of Heaven did gather us and catch us all as in a net, and his heavenly power at one time drew many hundreds to land. We came to know a place to stand in and what to wait in; and the Lord appeared daily to us, to our astonishment, amazement, and great admiration.
>
> — Francis Howgill, 19.08, *Quaker Faith and Practice: the Book of Christian Discipline of the Yearly Meeting of the Religious Society of Friends (Quakers) in Britain*, 1999, The Yearly Meeting of the Religious Society of Friends in Britain, London

Until this Sunday I had never experienced a worship that was grounded and filled with the Presence of the Living Christ. Before this worship I had felt a connection with Jesus' teachings, but afterwards I felt a connection with the Living Christ, which has stayed ever since.

Evelyn Jadin, 25
Jamestown Friends Meeting, North Carolina Yearly Meeting (FUM)
United States

Seeking

I go to church with a friend tonight. "There's really good music," she says, and I know that means contemporary. A band. Rock. I teach my friend the word "ecumenical" because she hesitates in saying "nondenominational."

It's Saturday night. They meet in the Methodist church downtown, across from Bayside Park, across from the American Airlines Arena and all the Miami Heat fans with $150 tickets (and surrounded by the deep doorways and nooks of quiet businesses and skyscrapers where all the homeless people curl up for a warm Miami night).

They have a free dinner in the church fellowship hall. Florescent lights and bare tables scattered with young people. The median age here is about twenty, someone tells me. Chicken, tater tots, and canned green beans, and on the side, white bread with Country Crock®. Something in this meal is comforting to me, the simplicity, the cheapness, like dinner at a homeless shelter.

My friend has a crush on a guy over there. She points and says she won't talk about it because he's in rehab, so this crush can't really be happening. A young woman sitting at my table is pregnant, happy, and talkative. This is a group of eccentric misfits, socially awkward, seemingly normal, dressed in old jeans or fashionable suits, cool and uncool, broken, whole, black, white, brown.

There is a screen set up in the sanctuary, and a sound system, and six or seven musicians up on the stage (I know that's not what they are called in churches, but it's the same function). My self-outside-myself looks at all this and says, *Are you kidding?*

Who cares, I shrug. I used to play in a contemporary Christian praise band at church. What did we call ourselves, Joyful Noise? And I cut a track on a CD when I was at Koinonia, pirating some Christian rock band's beautiful tune. It's not the music itself that makes me cringe just a little; it's the theology of the lyrics. But traditional hymns are just as bad.

People wander in, talking, laughing. They introduce themselves to me, ask me questions. The service starts and the young people jump to their feet, singing with the loud music. The lyrics pop up on the screen. Some are still laughing and talking.

Is this what I need? I wonder. I sing. I sway back and forth, close my eyes sometimes, testing. Is this my home? Is this me?

I cannot shake other people's judgments on this tiny congregation. I see one girl put her hand into the air to receive the Holy Spirit, and I remember a scene from that movie *Saved*—only this is not a spoof. I imagine all of my friends who are offended by Christianity shutting their ears and turning their backs, criticizing. I picture my partner looking at me with a sinking feeling and asking with her worried eyes, "Is the woman I love really into this?"

The prayer time goes on forever. Everyone has something to pray about. Everyone here has a story. *What's my story?* I wonder. I think of all the people I could pray for, but keep silent. I know myself this well—if I begin to speak, I will cry. My friend closes our prayers with her own, sprinkled throughout with as many "Gods" as the Pentecostal Mexican women I knew in El Paso. Her words pull me, lift me, and humble me. She prays like I haven't been able to pray in weeks. I cry anyway.

When she's standing next to me, singing again, my friend opens her palms like I sometimes did in front of the cross at Taizé. Like me. She could be me. This could be *me*.

I try to close my eyes and just be. The young woman who preaches tonight is scattered, and I have a hard time picking out her point. She talks about the Bible and has us flip through it like we were all raised Baptist. She says her favorite book is Romans, and if we ever need to know how to get saved, we should read Romans. Maybe that's why I've never read it. I imagine someone asking me, "What are your favorite Bible passages?" and I'll only be able to answer vaguely, unable to pin down chapter and verse.

After the sermon, the band starts in on a jazzy version of "Amazing Grace." The singer, a black woman with an incredible voice, takes off, bent almost double, her free hand trembling with the force of the Spirit.

This is one of those hymns I've always loved, despite its lyrics. But tonight, those lyrics don't make me cringe. Mostly they are about feeling lost, about loving God, about surrender. And I find as the woman finishes singing, as the worship experience ends, my skepticism and judgment of this type of service has begun to dissipate, and I can step a little closer to God.

Hannah C. Logan-Morris, 29
Friendship Friends Meeting, North Carolina Yearly Meeting
(Conservative)
United States

We Are Struggling to Find out Who We Are

The many Quaker cultures—liberals, evangelicals, conservatives, ethical, and the like—cause confusion in the church in Africa and even elsewhere. The many missionaries who came to Africa from Quaker families gave their own individual messages as from where they came from [and their] cultures.

We are struggling to find out who are we in the meetings because in one meeting we are carrying evangelicals, FUM members, Conservative, and everybody. The flock is never one because those who were taught by Jefferson Ford are with different ideas of the Quakerism as compared to those of Edgar Hole. We are struggling to [make] our house to come to one unity in Christ Jesus.

Technology is bringing the Quaker families into one village all over the world. However, the Internet is [causing] more division since different ideas are [available]. The silent worshippers think they are on the right track and those who go verbal celebrate their track.

From the electronic media, we see our nominal Quaker [numbers] and shy from the faith because of the many confusions in the way of our messages. Distinctiveness and doctrines are challenging. I remain to be a Quaker minister of truth amidst the challenge.

Pastor Leonard Sshivage, 36

Kitale Village Meeting, East Africa Yearly Meeting of Friends (North) (FUM)*

Kenya

*East Africa Yearly Meeting North was formerly registered as a yearly meeting on June 5, 1988. Until that date (and in spite of the creation of several other yearly meetings in the mid-seventies) EAYM North remained attached to the parent body, East Africa Yearly Meeting (Kaimosi).

Editor's note: Jefferson Ford, Western Yearly Meeting, served in Kenya (1914-1948) as an evangelist, teacher, and principal of Friends Bible Institute.

I Believe

I believe under the light of the sun we are all equal
Whatever we have done, and whoever we have been
Whatever we will do, and be, and think and say
I believe under the light of the sun we are all equal

I believe the stars shine because we are all children of God
Guiding every person to their personal Bethlehem
We all carry our own candle, and bear our own cross
I believe the stars shine because we are all children of God

The soft light of the Moon says we can never be wholly evil
That we are all children of Mother Mary
And she will see good in us, even when others cannot
The soft light of the Moon says we can never be wholly evil

I believe that the glare of sodium streetlights highlights us
That humanity has come so far, and created so much
And even that which was turned to evil purposes was valued once
I believe that the glare of sodium streetlights highlights us

I believe by the light within, we are special
Each of us is different, valued, unique
We all have flaws and talents, made in God's image
I believe by the light within, we are special

> *M. Chadkirk, 18*
> *Godalming Meeting, Britain Yearly Meeting*
> *United Kingdom*

Confessions of a Quaker Trader/Traitor

I know you, and you know my blood too: dark, light, and shades of gray. My mother's, like yours, Fry (Elizabeth's) in dungeon cells, some by our own making. Our fathers held swords in weakening consciences, made soft with Light Flashes. And who can say the Pe(n)n's destruction by peaceful means? Who will sing of radical Foxes whose theology is noxious to crumbling colonies, toxic with greed? As we Fell (Margaret) like scriptures drunk with mead.

Untitled, ink drawing, Carly Beth Frintner, Moorestown Monthly Meeting, Philadelphia Yearly Meeting (FGC), United States

We tell stories, of Quaker grandmas brought through Underground Railroads, long collapsed with neglect. The fact is, we could not stay. Or at least not in the way that would have prolonged our race. Our face was not seen on oatmeal boxes. Our names, Rustin(g), buried (Bayard) in the closets of Peace. You will not hear our African hollers from your choirs. Will not bear the stomps when the Holy touches. And our young, humanized into oblivion.

So some stray far from the pack and act as if an unspoken G-d had shown them a way, to walk through decay, into that once-upon-a-day: When Light was Christ, and silence the Baptism, where the Eucharist reigns eternal, and G-d kissed our lips. We have the audacity to look forward, where meetings head-nod to a hip hop bass prod and the Eros of G-d within you and the vocal. Sometimes it seems, the world is spinning away, while our stone buildings stay firmly planted twenty years ago.

I want bruthas who chew flying bullets at night to find Light too. But why would they come? I want sistas, words heavy with womanist poems, to find a home in this sacred silence. And that Mary, who had to Die, her (Dyer) spirit sometimes flies above my head, screaming for witch retributions through pagan revolutions from Pendle Hill.

But that's dead, see, there's a gag on certain poems. Even when, "G▮d D▮n the world is getting fu▮ed up and falling to s▮t!" And,

> "Last night G▮d's Light
> was given to me
> s▮xually."

See, we go to that place where we know we can speak with our full voice.

The choice is in this: Will we rot in the spot designated at the back of the house? Or will we shatter all we think that matters with Youth Quake in our souls? Have I shared the Light that was given to me? I don't know, were you ready? Or am I too heady to start facing you? Would it be better that I stayed fettered to these remains of chains? Or would you rather with me, high as the roof is (Rufus) [Jones]ing for worship in sacred poems, watch what down on Earth Converges, and Light, Conservative, emerges, sprouting a seed beyond our imagination, where we no longer fear the sin of every piece of creation we are blind to.

> If you have heart to
> hear, do so, if you have
> not, prepare thyself.

Tai Amri Spann-Wilson, 30
Unprogrammed, Unaffiliated
United States

Editors' Note: This piece uses styles of poetry and prose that may be unfamiliar to some Friends. The writer understands this piece as "a theology in the ancient methodology of poetic prose, that some might refer to as Theopoetics, and utilizes my modern training in experimental prosetry."

Spiritual Biography of a Southern Friend

Chatham Friends Meeting stands in rural Alamance County, North Carolina, surrounded by farmland, a cemetery, and a few scattered houses—one of which is the parsonage. At the age of two, I came to call that house and the meeting home. This meeting and another local meeting had hired my mother as their pastor (one Sunday a month we went to the other meeting, Spring). I thus spent my early years in a fairly typical rural, Protestant church.

I had Sunday School classes in which the teacher taught stories from the Bible, Vacation Bible School in the summer where I painted plastic sun catchers and made things with colored macaroni and pony beads, and I practiced learning to read while singing the hymns each Sunday. I tried to listen attentively as my mother gave the prepared message. She changed when standing in the pulpit. Her voice took on a magical quality as she told about how the teachings in the Bible are useful for us in our daily lives. She especially used examples of her own struggles to be a better person, to be more Christ-like: being able to love others, especially those whom she found challenging (sometimes she herself was the most difficult object for her own love).

Under her tutelage, both when there was a pulpit between us and when there wasn't, I learned that our Quaker faith was about becoming better people, striving for wholeness and Christ-like perfection so that we can make this world a better, more loving place for all its inhabitants. Our job is to be our very best selves and help others have space to be their very best selves so that we may create God's kingdom here on earth.

Any memory recalled is revisionist history in one way or another so I cannot say how much of this I picked up on at the time. I knew that mom loved God and she wanted me to also feel God's presence and love in my life as she had come to feel it in her own. To say that she indoctrinated me would be absolutely wrong in the connotation that the phrase brings. I'd prefer to think that she invited me to join her in her faith by sharing her beliefs, understandings, and practices (as well as her struggles in faithfulness). If I was concerned, worried, upset, or scared, Mom might begin to pray out loud as though inviting God into our conversation, asking God to help or send "special angels" to be with me. By her example, I learned to petition God for help when anxious and to express gratitude for all my many blessings (even when they might not feel like such).

When I was seven, we said good-bye to Chatham and Spring Friends Meetings and moved eleven hours north to Erie, Pennsylvania. Besides the many cultural challenges I encountered with this move, we also were challenged to find a community of Quakers with whom to worship. In Erie, we managed to find a small group of Quakers that met every other Sunday in each other's homes for an hour of silent worship. My family nearly doubled the meeting's attendance. Although we'd had a small amount of silent worship at Chatham, it was just something tucked into the whole worship service as far as I was concerned. In Erie, I came to learn more about historical Quaker worship and the concept of waiting and listening for God by centering yourself in worship. I was in elementary school at the time and, while it seemed like a nice concept, I was happy to leave that to the adults. I'd sit for fifteen minutes. (I suppose I thought of it as practice for when I became an adult, but I was happy to leave with my squirmy little brother after fifteen minutes and go play.)

Half an hour of worship a month wasn't enough for us according to my parents, so our religious supplement came in the form of a United Church of Christ/Brethren congregation (also a historic peace church). This more closely resembled the worship in which I had grown up, but with more "smells and bells." We were welcomed and even as a kid I took part in the services. When I was older, ten or twelve, I would occasionally read scripture aloud and served as an acolyte (meaning I carried a long stick with an extendable wick to light candles at the beginning of a service and with a snuffer to put them out at the end). I even played in the bell choir, learning to read music to do so. Whatever structure and liturgy missing from the bimonthly Friends meeting was found doubly at the church.

Yet, all the while, I remained very conscious of the fact that I was a *Quaker*. This was my cultural and historical identity. Like others young in the faith, I took immense pride that I belonged to a religion that had past members in favor of positive relations with Native Americans, very vocal against slavery in Britain and the United States of America, and people who opposed all occasion for war and were willing to be put in jail or die for their convictions. I felt special to be a part of a group of people so committed to integrity and justice. And eventually, I came to realize that to be part of that I must continue the tradition in my own daily life, constantly striving in my own quiet way to seek justice, love mercy, and walk faithfully with my God.

Although our time in Erie served as an introduction to unprogrammed Quaker worship, I came to really appreciate this in middle school when my family returned to North Carolina, this time to the Asheville area. For three years we attended and were members at Asheville Friends Meeting, a part of FGC. First Day School took place after about fifteen minutes of the worship, and in it the children learned about various Quaker things and made artwork. I especially remember when some members of the meeting talked to us about having leadings in worship and another day when a member walked us through a guided meditation. The theology expressed was fairly diluted so as to welcome people turned off by other forms of Christianity. This was perfect for me because I began more fully questioning matters of organized religion and the hypocrisy I witnessed in many avowed Christians' lives. I felt much more comfortable using words like "God" (avoiding gendered language) and "Spirit" while not using the words "Christ" or "Christian" (at least when talking about my faith). I felt in tune at this time with what I would call my spirituality—aided by sitting in silent worship, listening for the Spirit.

After yet another move, when I was in high school, my family found itself again in one of the Quaker centers of the United States. Greensboro, North Carolina, and the surrounding area have many different flavors of Friends meetings. Greensboro hosts the North Carolina Yearly Meeting (FUM) office and the meetings in the area predominately have programmed worship with music and a prepared message, much like the average Protestant church around the corner, as far as worship style is concerned. There is a completely unprogrammed meeting, part of North Carolina Yearly Meeting Conservative. Greensboro also hosts a meeting for Evangelical Friends International (EFI).

Faced with these choices, my family was forced to evaluate where we fit within the wider body of Friends. What kind of worship most appealed to us? With what theology did we feel most comfortable?

We'd experienced different parts of the Friends spectrum at different times in our lives and had found elements that really spoke to us as well as others that we found less nurturing. Eventually, we ended up choosing different paths and, between the four of us, we belong to three different meetings (four if you count where my mother is currently serving as pastor and five if you count the meeting I have been attending while living in Washington, D.C., for graduate school).

Eventually, I ended up attending and choosing to apply for membership at a small meeting within North Carolina Yearly Meeting (FUM). While I feel most connected to God when I strive weekly (well, daily) to sit at length in silence, I also find music to be an important part of my religious experience and find comfort in the structure of a programmed worship. I managed to find a meeting that blends structure and music with intentional waiting and open worship. This works for me and, even though it's still not quite enough silent worship for my taste, the overall community and values of the meeting make it a good choice. As my mother is wont to say, everything is a compromise.

And every divergent bit of Quakerism that I have experienced has affected my faith and helped me to grow. It was when working in an environment with Quakers with very different theology than me that I most clearly saw how much the different branches of Friends have to gain from one another. I have felt the pain of divisions amongst Friends, but through the circumstances of my life, I know that we each have something to offer towards a more complete picture of Quakerism and spiritual understanding.

I thank my mother for her open invitation for me to develop my spirituality. I thank her for not pushing or judging, for being evangelical in the best possible sense of the word, for being a loving and faithful follower to the call of God, Jesus, Spirit—however you might name the great power that calls us to be our best selves in the service of one another.

Julia Hood, 25
Jamestown Friends Meeting, North Carolina Yearly Meeting (FUM)
United States

Convergent Friends as New Jazz Traditionalists

First off, I could not have come up with the title "Convergent Friends as New Jazz Traditionalists" without Martin Kelley, who posted a video interview with me on his website, QuakerQuaker.org, and titled it himself. The video captures a mashup idea—that Friends of various strains of Quakerism are coming together to revive our common bond of faith and to remind ourselves of our roots and instigate a rebirth, similar to the way jazz music had been reborn in America by reviving its traditions. I was beginning to see the new directions of Quakerism moving beyond its traditions, its fractious past, into a future where Quakers of many backgrounds were beginning to reorient themselves to one another and their shared history, faith traditions, and cultural roots in order to save the faith from demise through its divisions. We were seeing the development of Convergent Friends as new traditionalists, reaching back into the past to reconnect the present—similar to the jazz musician Wynton Marsalis, who revived the roots of jazz through his devotion to its traditions, its rich heritage, and its distinctive mark on American life by bringing it to a younger audience.

I thought this was a throwaway concept—how could Quakers understand their relationship to jazz and its own divided culture? Yet several Friends responded that the analogy is meaningful and helpful in teasing out the murmurings of convergent Friends as a reality coming to fruition. So now I'll do what all artists do and steal some titles from Wynton Marsalis' first, self-titled album back in 1981 (and one from 1986's *Standard Time, Volume 1*) to take you to the source of the insight.

Father Time

Just as the Quaker faith has undergone its own web of fissures, splits, and divergences from its beginnings, the jazz world has fractured into many splinters after only an eighty-year history. Arguments have erupted over the true meaning of the origins of jazz and what it encompasses, with its external influences from populism, subculture, Ivy League canonization, evangelism, divergences, strident supporters and rebels seeking new directions for its roots. And why not? Jazz music and Quakerism are flexible, malleable, and full of tensile strength, leaving them weather-worn but wide-ranging and inclusive with many points of entry.

Just as Quakerism has done, jazz has grown and developed throughlines that have spidered out since its beginnings in the early twentieth century. Jazz music has come to encompass a broad range of stylings and interpretations—Dixieland, orchestras, big bands, modernism, minimalists, fusion, and other variances—as it has made its way through American and, eventually, other world cultures. It has developed its own stars and purveyors of each style as well created a few who could find and create their own voice among the gaps between them (Duke Ellington and Miles Davis, most notably). Each layer of style was built upon reformation of the past, realigning of ideals measured against the medium and its audience who bought both records and drinks in the clubs that paid the musicians to continue.

Yet, as with Quakerism, its popularity had come and gone and was in constant need of care and revival among the young and restless. A traditionalist would suggest it requires mastery of past standards, a proficiency in the rudiments of the trade, constant practice and discipline, and respect and humility in the face of its esteemed past in order to reinterpret it for a modern audience. A new voice, not just a new sound, was needed; yet it had to be a voice that would echo the cherished past enough to build a bridge toward a brighter future. This, or non-practitioners cannibalize its roots to popular culture non-definition mass-appeal.

I'll Be There When the Time Is Right

Has it ever been up to one figure to lead the way for Quakers since the time of George Fox? One person who so embodies the Spirit that encapsulates Quakerism's core, where disparate groups can unite us? Who has the mastery to mine the depths of historical writings and insights of generations of Quaker leaders?

For jazz, it was Wynton Marsalis who, with his virtuosity, pedigree, and unflagging commitment to his vision of the tenets of jazz, plumbed the depths of its history and returned with its pearls. When I was growing up, I learned the names of historic jazz artists such as Art Blakey and Ron Carter as they were introduced alongside Wynton's youthful comrades (and auteurs) on his self-titled debut record. And as Wynton progressed, he brought together the young lions with the aged ones, fusing them under his leadership of the revival. I was being reeducated and I didn't even know it. On his later album, *Standard Time: Volume 1*, a common standard jazz tune like "Caravan" held the Afro-Cuban backbeat mixed with Dixieland that flowed easily into a swing cadence by a quartet. It wasn't until years later I learned it was Duke Ellington's contribution to the American Songbook back in 1936 that Marsalis' group had reinvigorated for my chaste ears. Wynton had brought about rebirth through mastery of tradition.

As Marsalis materialized everywhere at once during the 1980s, he brought jazz to the ivoried halls of Lincoln Center (shocking!), became a foil for his own brother Branford's success with pop musician Sting, and found an audience among jazz purists such as culture critic Stanley Crouch. He magnetized young aspiring jazz performers together, showcasing the roots of jazz (New Orleans) to eager crowds in rural areas using educational institutions like colleges and universities as his stage. His message was clear—jazz is educational, cultural, life-giving, and for the here-and-now young crowd, if you're able to handle its complexity and respect its deep cultural significance that I'm going to enjoin with you. Now watch this.

His abilities, however, proved integratable with another genre of an aging audience—classical music. Not as a tribute, but as a sign of virtuosity, Marsalis' classical works include his recordings of Haydn, Mozart, and Tomasi. Embracing classical performances demonstrated that, with his talents, Marsalis could speak to two audiences at once—jazz and classical—and ask them to meet each other on each other's turf, wooing them to notice each other as two yet-to-be-introduced lovers from across a dance floor.

Will Quakerism experience this ability of unification, of vitality, of reemergence? What will it take? So far, groups are developing under a term convergent Friends rather than under an individual. As Robin Mohr opined in her blog *What Canst Thou Say?* in 2006, the convergent Friends movement is made of "Friends who are seeking a deeper understanding of our Quaker heritage and a more authentic life in the kingdom of God on Earth, radically inclusive of all who seek to live this life." Blogs and other social networking tools of the Internet are bringing disparate Quakers together via online engagement and creating a place where traditionalists can meet with neo-traditionalists along with international Quakers from major (North America, Britain, Kenya, and Central America) and developing (Korea, Japan) Quaker populations.

Hesitation

Marsalis was not without detractors. Reaction to his purist vision and union with other classical music forms was naturally caustic to the prodigious innovators who had moved beyond traditional roots to produce jazz for the times they were in, such as pianists Chick Corea or Herbie Hancock, who had begun producing pop-jazz works ready-made for consumption. During the demise of jazz in the 1970s and '80s, as big bands and smaller combos were facing extinction by a marketplace looking for fresh voices beyond standards, new instrumentations and forms were emerging that hardly were recognizable as jazz. Even Marsalis' own brother, Branford, split with him early in their careers, with Branford persuing the delivery of jazz to the pop-rock world with Sting and a three-year run on *The Tonight Show* (ask any jazz musician under thirty and they'll know how they thought a career in jazz might actually become profitable). Wynton's vision was being called out—if you stick with tradition, where's your marketplace among the young?

Similarly, throughout Quaker faith, divergence from its roots has brought newer, modern audiences to Quakers and progressed with new pathways while abandoning the shared, past commonalities. Yet as a splintered tradition, Quakers have begun to suffer each other as distant relatives do when dining during the holidays; a failing coordination of growth that has led instead to disunity and a lack of understanding and respect for common roots essential to creating a mutually enhancing ecosystem of faith grounded in the Light.

Who Can I Turn To (When Nobody Needs Me)

Just as Quakers do, jazz musicians fear the irrelevancy and demise of their faith. As the audience and practitioners dwindle and devoted attenders begin to gray, as freshness becomes familiarity, as creativity and exploration fall to pandering to crowds or the dumbing down of past disciplines, and current work begins to rest on the laurels of past heroes and achievements, practitioners can become lazy and actions lifeless.

Marsalis offers Quakers a model for evangelism that is unique. He demonstrated that a revival can occur through mastering the roots of tradition with rigorous study, practice, cultivation, and showcasing new talent alongside weightier members of the community. A revival can occur by finding an audience through the channels to which they are attuned and plugging into them rather than looking toward outward trends in your audience. A revival can occur through rediscovery of the past as an alive world still speaking to us today.

Caravan (A Slight Return)

However, even a purist such as Marsalis has seen the need to join forces with other one time traditionalists such as cellist Yo-Yo Ma, country songwriter Willie Nelson, and bluegrass fiddler Mark O'Connor, in order to join himself to the musical world beyond his own. Among jazz neo-traditionalists, these cooperative projects may be seen as variances or distractions from iconic, jazz-traditionalist figures such as Duke Ellington or Louis Armstrong among other Marsalis neo-tradtionalists, but with Marsalis having demonstrated and established his bonafides, these cooperative projects are more like a council of elders practicing extending their trades to one another to show the world their correlations, how roots of various trees can rebuild a segregated ecosystem.

Convergent Friends face major obstacles, some simple and plain (world languages, geography, time zones) and others more complex (individualized concepts of God and the biblical texts). Three hundred fifty years of history is nearly impossible to master by a single practitioner of the faith.

Convergent Friends are being offered a chance to bring alive the variances of Quaker faith through correlation of the roots of its past. By knowing one another's faith traditions and seeing common roots, convergent Friends can build a web of support to nurture a future together: a Quaker ecosystem that includes all branches of Quakers and would be capable of supporting new life—a new face of Quakerism that would demonstrate Quakerism's viability as a growing faith. In today's world, with Quakerism's openness and malleability, its ability to breed concepts such as radical inclusiveness or gather a meeting through a blogging community, its open-source access to the Light, it offers roots in a faith tradition that fits into a post-modern world. As fellow Quaker, Liz Oppenheimer, says in her writings, "I continue to believe that the more firmly rooted we are in our own tradition and belief, the less threatened we will be by those who practice and believe differently from ourselves, and the more open we will be to learn from one another without fear of being assimilated, converted, or imposed upon."

Amen, as a Friend might say.

Or as a new jazz traditionalist would conclude, "Thank you, and good night."

> *Chad Stephenson, 38*
> *San Francisco Monthly Meeting, Pacific Yearly Meeting (Independent)*
> *United States*

Convergent Friendship and Playing with the Quaker "Other"

One of the biggest questions asked of convergent Friends, those seeking a renewed and remade Quakerism across many branches of our tradition, goes something like this: "Are you telling me we need to subscribe to a lowest-common-denominator faith so that we can get along with Friends of other branches?" While, on the other hand a separate concern arises: "Why would we want to dialogue with them? We've got no interest in that form of Quakerism, their beliefs, and practices." Finally, one of the most popular questions I hear time and time again is, "Should we be unequally yoked with people who don't believe what we believe?"

One can imagine schoolchildren trying to remember what mom and dad said about who they are allowed to play with and who is "off limits." A parent's justification for deeming some kids off limits can be founded on any number of reasons, some of which can even be unjust or based on misunderstandings, rumors, or prejudices. Regardless of whether we liked it or not, we grew up aware of "others" whom we were not allowed to associate (or play) with. Of course, issues of faith and belief are very complex and difficult to navigate, and generalizations are precious, but whether we are from the programmed or unprogrammed traditions of Quakers we have often "othered" the others. One of the goals of convergent Friends is to try and help break down these, sometimes imaginary, walls and ask, "What are the real reasons behind why some Quakers are off limits?"

There is some confusion around what *convergent* means, so here I will use it to signify a conservative (to the tradition) and emergent (leaning towards the postmodern) understanding of the Quaker faith. While those who call themselves convergent may seek to break down the walls, they are not simply just being ecumenical, at least not in the usual sense. But before I discuss how convergent Friends are spanning chasms, a bit of history may help.

Ecumenism in Modernity

The modern period (or modernity) has shaped the way we think, talk, and interact with the "others" of our world. The philosophical underpinning of the modern age is the Enlightenment, and the Enlightenment is built upon the foundation of individual reason, as opposed to and over against the authority of tradition. This has had tremendous, and oftentimes negative, implications for the church. One assumption that the Enlightenment carries with it is the idea that sameness, or likeness, is preferred over difference. The way we can best run a society is by eliminating as much difference as possible (this is part of the idea behind Hobbes' social contract theory). Sameness will ensure that when we all come together to make decisions, work, and build our societies, there will be little struggle. Difference is what causes our difficulties.

Thus, in our society, to be different is often to be rendered the outcast (here we could also turn to the way the media has overused and abused the word sect in recent years). For many, the idea of being ecumenical operates within this universalizing framework of modernity. For the church to be unified we must create a lowest-common-denominator vision of faith, we must get rid of difference. (For their part, Evangelicals have exacerbated this problem with the church-growth model.) This understanding of *ecumenical* is obviously very liberal in the sense that everyone is welcome. But the lurking problem with this idea, with liberalism in general, is that everyone is welcome, so long as you check your difference at the door.

Therefore, if modernity was for a universalizing of language, ethics, and religion, the contemporary postmodern culture leans the other way. In postmodernity we argue that context, subjectivity, and the particulars are of utmost importance for expressing who we are. Here we see that it is our very different cultures, faiths, upbringings, educations, and political systems that inform the way we think and act; we cannot just turn these things off. We are formed at a very deep and subconscious level by our culture and traditions with which we engage. This move towards the subjective and contextual ways of thinking has great implications for the way we think of ecumenism and convergence.

Let me now explain how convergence can be understood within the context of talking to people outside our particular Quaker circles. Just about everyone who identifies him or herself as being a convergent Friend has one thing in common: They have begun to connect with Friends from other parts of the Quaker tradition through a variety of modes, including blogs, online chatting, e-mail, inter-visitation, and through the works of groups like Friends World Committee for Consultation and Pacific Northwest Quaker Women's Theological Conference. None of these convergent Friends, at least that I know of, feel as though what they believe has to be checked at the door before entering into these conversations.

A Vision for Friends and Ecumenism

Below I offer some ideas on how we ought to interact with Quaker "others." How we interact with other Friends is a major concern among all Quakers, not just one group or the other. It is my bias that a (convergent) Friendship could enable us to maintain fidelity within our own subgroup while being open to Friendship.

The Virtue of Listening: Listening is a key virtue within the Quaker tradition and the Quaker understanding of listening has always been relational. We listen because we believe that God is a relational God wanting to speak and commune with us. In the same way that we believe that God's Spirit directly speaks to us through silence, historically speaking, we believe that God can (and often does) speak to us through others, even people who are very different from us. Woolman's ministry is but one example here. Convergent Friends seek to put listening into practice and truly hear the stories of others. We must be convinced that God can speak to us through the most unlikely of sources.

Unity as Obedience: Mennonite John Howard Yoder was a huge proponent of ecumenism, but of a particular kind. He believed that by being a faithful Mennonite, he had no choice but to work with the rest of the Church. Yoder did not think that unity came through trying to force people to believe one thing or another, but was to be sought after because Scripture calls us to be united. Yoder says, "Christian unity is not to be created, but to be obeyed." In other words, we have no choice but to continue to work for Christian unity from our particular traditions.

Peaceful and Prophetic: Speaking of particular traditions, Yoder points out that because we (those churches deeply concerned with peace) have very strong beliefs about certain issues we ought to be in conversation with the rest of the church. Mark Theissen Nation, one of Yoder's biographers, writes, "But if we believe...that the principles to which we hold are true before God, then they are also true for other Christians, and it is our responsibility to inform them of these principles. On the other hand, Yoder asks, might it not be that our unwillingness to lay these claims before other Christians is based instead on fear? Are we not sure enough of our convictions to believe that they will withstand the scrutiny of other Christians"? Especially as one of the Historic Peace Churches, all Quakers should be striving to speak and live prophetically in the way of the Gospel of peace.

A Church in Mission: There are also missional reasons for opening the dialogue up with other Quakers and the world. Here, our relating to others is done personally and corporately as a way to give away the gift of the Gospel (in all of its richness). We share the gift of love and grace with others because we have been given love and grace; we share with others in hopes that they will discover the mercy of God through the church. Convergent Friends seek out what it means for the church to be primarily missional, operating out of this mode of sharing and gift.

Living a Convergent Friendship

Finally, I think it is best to think of the convergent in terms of friendship. Friendship is based on listening, it is also committed to sticking together in spite of our differences; it is willing to stand up for what we believe is right (even if our friends go the other way); and it is always willing to give away all the good that we have for others. It might be said that we are looking to embody a redemptive-Friendship through our faith in Christ. As theologian LeRon Shultz wrote on his blog, "Both missions and ecumenism involve tending to religious others—others from different religions altogether or others from different traditions within one religion. The goal of such attention from a Christian perspective is redemptive fellowship—welcoming persons into the community of believers or facilitating more intimate communion among those who already strive to follow the way of Christ in the world."

This vision of Friendship is a much richer account of an ecumenical (if we must call it that) faith than offered to us by modernity. As peculiar as our faith can be, at times it is our differences that make us who we are and because of that we have no choice but to interact with and listen to others both inside and outside our tradition. We enter these relationships on our grounds, not through fear but love, hoping to hear God through others and share the Gospel with the world.

C. Wess Daniels, 31
Camas Friends Church, Northwest Yearly Meeting of Friends (EFCI)
United States

Aphorisms

The painting *Fierce Feathers*, by James Doyle Penrose, is an iconic Quaker painting. It is set in 1775, in the state of New York, when the Iroquois were fighting for the British. It tells this story: Friends were meeting on Sunday morning when an Iroquois war party approached. Four braves came through the door, ready for battle, followed by their chief. He recognized the Spirit that filled the room and the Friends as peaceful, devout individuals. The warriors sat and joined the Friends in worship. Later, the chief and his warriors joined the Friends for lunch, and they spoke about the incident via a translator. The natives were surprised to learn that Friends worshiped the Great Spirit in silence, as they did. The chief left a white feather and an arrow as a signal that the building and those who inhabited it were peaceful, and should be left alone. The painting captures the chief just as he comes through the door, hatchet raised for a blow and Friends looking up at him in the moment when the chief realizes why they are meeting.

What strikes me about this story is that the Native American war party, armed and psyched for killing and ignorant of the theology and methods practiced by the pioneer Friends, *correctly identified the Holy Spirit in terms of their own religion*. The Friends were waiting upon the Most High God for instruction, and the chief recognized them as followers of the Great Spirit. This story and others like it have led me to believe that God makes Himself available universally and (though language cannot fully capture the experience) He is recognizable by any who know Him, regardless of culture and background. The worship experience of being in the presence of the Divine is the same; only the language and methods of practicing worship differ.

Experiences of mine, such as the Young Adult Friends gatherings in Richmond, Indiana, in May 2008 and at Guilford College in November 2008, have lent credence to this notion. Friends have been debating what the proper practice and terminology should be since 1827 (if not earlier). The most damaging effect of this debate is that we have become estranged from each other. Friends, we have been arguing over *semantics* for the last 180-some years. I therefore offer *some antics*, in the hopes that they will provide some grounds for reconciliation:

- God is to people as people are to musical instruments. The purpose of the instrument is to wait until it is picked up. If a player picks it up, the instrument's job is to sound in accordance with its structure and the input of the player. If a craftsman comes, its job is to receive repair.

- Whether it is picked up by the player or the craftsman, the important part of the instrument is the dark interior space where the sound resonates. It is this interior space that gives the instrument its own sound and personality; the player plays it because of this particular resonance, and the craftsman works on it to clean it and strengthen the broken parts so that it may be played more beautifully.

- Varnish is an integral part of the instrument. It prevents damage from the elements, and so lengthens the life of the instrument. I work on violins for a living, so I'm speaking from experience. The varnish must be thin, though, or it will stifle the sound. One should take care not to varnish oneself so thickly that one ceases to resound as the maker intended.

- Brokenness and suffering are undeniable conditions of human existence. We all know it, whether an outside force breaks us or whether we do it to ourselves. We are all broken. Acting from a motivation that stems from brokenness (sinning) only serves to worsen the condition. It breaks others. Brokenness is also a blessing. It is only from our broken state that we can be healed, and from our experience of being healed, we can teach healing.

- Separation is a disease whose symptom is brokenness. The action of brokenness is sin. Separation from what, you ask? The short answer is, yes. The long answer is the Word of God, but since God spoke all of creation including us into being, the answer remains, yes.

- It is possible to believe in the absence of creeds to the extent that the absence of creeds becomes a creed. Likewise, one can forget that one is speaking to a child of God when one is thumping the Bible at another.

- I have heard that the Bible is a crutch. A crutch provides support to a broken individual, and since the Bible does so admirably, there is no problem with this assertion. However, it is appalling to attempt to remove a crutch from someone who is using it, and it is alarming to beat someone else over the head with one's crutch. So please, Friends, use the Bible as it was intended, for one's support. Offer Scripture to those who ask for it, or if someone tries to move without it support them as they require, but please avoid violence to or with this venerable text.

- Christ is an action of the Divine. Specifically, Christ is the action of the Divine becoming active among us mortals.

- The Inner Light is the halo around Jesus' head. The Still Small Voice is Him whispering what we need to hear. We are saved because we know Him thusly. I offer the following Bible verses for consideration on this point: I Kings 19: 11–13; Psalm 43:3; Matt. 3:11; Mark 13:11; John 1:1–14; John 14:15–21; John 16:12–15; Acts 26:23; 2 Cor. 4:6; Eph. 5:14; 1 Peter 2:9; and 2 Peter 1:21. (NRSV)

The point is this: that we all—down to the lowest, most wretched, most corrupt of us—contain a spark of inspiration that was put there by the Divine creator of the universe that calls us into being, burns most fiercely when we truly live, and is fed by the fires of others. Not everyone tends it or even pays heed to it but it's there, and those who act in accordance with it are healed and transformed for the labor at hand. This is the central tenet of Quaker theology. Since we have this common faith, we are one faith and we need to act like it. Some of us labor for peace in the Middle East, in Iraq and Israel, in spite of five thousand years of bloody conflict. *Why can we not handle a mere 180 years of squabbling?*

There is a peculiar quality that defines a Quaker, but is so peculiar that I have not yet found the words for it, even ten years after I became aware of it. Perhaps every Quaker has a small echo of the divine space where the Light dwells, and where all words take their meaning. If this is the case, it would explain why no words can capture the fullness of this quality, but it is still a quality that all Quakers share.

This has been my experience with Friends: I was raised by two Quaker pastors (one birthright Friend from Iowa, one who converted during the Vietnam War and who currently frequents a Unitarian church, both still happily married to each other) in New England Yearly Meeting, a yearly meeting that has only eight programmed meetings in it; I have attended four yearly meetings in the United States of America (New England, Northwestern, Western, and Ohio Valley), two YouthQuakes (1997 and 2000), the 1999 FUM Triennial, and Vienna Meeting in Austria; I graduated from Earlham College with a Bachelor's in Philosophy; I worked with the programmed Christian Friends at Quaker Haven Camp for three summers; I moved to Louisville Friends Meeting in Ohio Valley Yearly Meeting, where I am witnessing an unprogrammed FGC meeting take programmed evangelical Quaker refugees from Burundi under its wing and provide them not only with the necessities of living, but with the physical necessities of worship as well.

And I can say with confidence that *We are One Faith*.

The state of the Society of Friends is currently that of a quarreling family: We have a lot in common, including an extensive history, and if you can get us all to sit down together we can work well with each other despite (or perhaps because of) our different experiences. We are a very loosely organized religion, full of mystics, artists, pastors, activists, teachers, craftsmen, parents, scholars, children, and performers, all of us and each of us following what God has revealed to us. Theologically, we run the gamut from hippie Buddhist Quakers to evangelical Christian Quakers; we draw inspiration from the Bible, from others' holy texts, and from our own history. We worship in silence and in song and sermon. But we all worship the same God, and this God has given us power to be healing hands in a world that is broken and torn. Sectarian bickering is paltry and embarrassing next to that, and we have suffered because we indulge in it.

There is a growing feeling among my generation that our debate over what truly makes a Quaker is pointless. It has only created rifts that isolate us from those with experience we need. Young adult Friends (roughly eighteen to thirty-five years old) are hungry for a living, relevant faith, and our searches have led us not only to examine our own branches of Quakerism, but the other branches as well. We are finding that other branches of our faith have useful insights that we have not been taught. Liberal Friends are looking into the Bible, both from curiosity as to what it actually says and as a tool to understanding Christian thought that has been sadly neglected at home. Programmed Friends have heard about how compelling unprogrammed worship can be, and are experimenting with it.

The Young Adult Friends gathering in May 2008 was intoxicating. Over a hundred of us learned about each others' faith and that we can, in fact, work together. And if we can, why not our elders? I found the November conference at Guilford College more sobering: Our religion needs this energy. Our meetings are getting older, more complacent, and may simply die out, either from lack of young people or from a slow death of the spirit. No other religion that came from Christ's teachings provides the variety of faith experience that is found within Quakerism, and my generation finds we can feed off the energy we find in other forms of Quakerism than the one into which we were born.

I realize this article flies in the face of the ongoing theological spat that is currently still active in the Society of Friends, and that many readers may feel that their identity as Friends depends on "winning" the argument. My overwhelming experience is that one's identity is strengthened as one is exposed to new insights. We Friends have never accepted the excuse that just because a position is historically untenable we shouldn't hold it anyway (abolition, anyone?), and I would not be living up to my heritage if I let this slip by. If I am acting against the trend of the past 180-some years of the Religious Society of Friends, so be it. I don't know if reunification is what God has planned. I certainly know those who have been wounded by Christianity find comfort in the Spirit with unprogrammed Friends, and I know that missions from the Christian yearly meetings have certainly brought comfort to desperate parts of the world; both these ministries need to be maintained. I only ask two things: Get to know a Friend or Friends from a different tradition and cherish those relationships.

I wonder if perhaps we are not like the Iroquois and Friends in *Fierce Feathers*. We're in the same room and not in the situation we've expected, but *the Spirit is here*. That one fact trumps everything else.

Howie Baker, 27
Louisville Friends Meeting, Ohio Valley Yearly Meeting
United States

Integration, photograph, Ben Watts, 25, Yearly Meeting of Aotearoa/New Zealand, New Zealand

Kingdom Life

Witness and Engagement
in the World

The Kingdom Life

Here is what I know about the kingdom life:

- It is to recognize the spirit of Christ infusing every moment and, in that awareness, to love and laugh and mourn and feel everything, held in the arms of God.

- It is to be aware of your own transformation, to see yourself reoriented toward greater faithfulness and courage and integrity.

- It is learning to love selflessly, which fulfills the self.

Kody Gabriel Hersh, 22
Miami Monthly Meeting, Southeastern Yearly Meeting (FGC-FUM)
United States

Imana Nibishaka: God Willing

During the summer of 2008 I traveled to Rwanda, thanks to support from the Clarence and Lilly Pickett Endowment and the Haverford College Center for Peace and Global Citizenship. I worked as an extended service volunteer with the African Great Lakes Initiative, visiting resettlement camps in eastern Rwanda to interview returned refugees and evaluate the impact of Alternatives to Violence Project workshops on the conflicts sparked by their displacement.

I knew that I wanted to work in Rwanda so that it would no longer just mean genocide to me; so that the images that came to mind would not be limited to what we read in books about machetes and suffering. Because of the time I was able to spend there, Rwanda is now the place with red earth that has permanently settled in my skin, the place where women smiled shyly back at me as I struggled to greet them in Kinyarwanda, and where the pineapple makes your mouth water. It is the place that smelled of dirt, ripe fruit and green plants, smoke from wood fires, sweat, sun, and in all moments, sweet, heavy, and pungent. For me, it will be the place of bustle and chaos in the outdoor market full of fruits, vegetables, meats, bags of dried fish, and beans of every shape and size. And always, the place where women wearing *pagnes* (a colorful rectangular strip of cloth worn in some African cultures as a short skirt or a loincloth) of the most beautiful patterns and colors blend into an ever-spinning and brilliant kaleidoscope set against the red dirt and the green of the banana trees.

As impossible as it is to write about a place or culture that is not your own, the very act of this writing matters; though the visitor may only understand a fraction of their surroundings, that fraction is an insight into the experience and for that, worthy. The potency of it, the assault on the senses, and the hopelessness of putting it into words is what I've been drawn to all of my life. After living in Zimbabwe as a child, I have felt a constant, persistent, and almost aching pull back to the continent.

In Rwanda, I learned about humility and forgiveness, just as I learned about anger and shame. In spite of everything I experienced, it was the faith I witnessed that moved me most deeply. In times of sorrow, it seems God is often the first casualty of grief. In Rwanda, I expected the question, "How could our God abandon us to such horrors?" Instead I found an understanding of the divine that threw my relatively untested faith into sharp contrast.

I arrived at the evangelical Friends church of Kigali on my first Sunday in Rwanda, and although I expected something different from the unprogrammed meeting I knew so well, I was wholly unprepared for the four hours of singing and dancing that followed. The Friends church service was the most joyous and soul-shaking, *worshipful* experience of my life.

I watched an older woman, dressed as though she had just come from her fields, stooped over from years of labor, as she shuffled up to the front near the altar, spread her arms, and began to dance. Her palms upturned, her face open and beaming, tears streaming down her cheeks, she looked up into the sky and I knew she was dancing with God.

It was in that church that I felt how distant my own experience of worship was from this glorious and visceral experience of God. We inherited our name, Quakers, from early Friends who were literally "quaking" with anticipation of the divine. Now, so often it seems, we settle into silence and we have settled into the absence of speaking, not the uncontainable joy in yearning to hear that still small voice from the center.

In a place where people have so little, faith in something beautiful, powerful, and loving is a solid rock of comfort in an ever-shifting world. In the moving words of author Zadie Smith, when one learns to "hold one's life lightly," perhaps the consequence is the need to hold onto something else more firmly. The God present in that church was a God of urgency, of passion and of fleeting momentousness; quite unlike the quiet God with plenty of time whom I had grown up imagining.

Now, as I've returned to my life in a world where I have been raised to hold my life tightly and God lightly, I know that the woman I watched dance until her faith turned her into Light will be with me forever.

Emily Higgs, 23
Unprogrammed, Unaffiliated
United States

Peace Poem

Peace, peace, peace, peace
Where are you peace?
I have searched for you in many places
But you are nowhere to be found
Where did you hide yourself peace?
Tell me to reach you peace,
Without you my life is a lie.

Many people are looking for you,
At home in schools at work, in organizations
And also in churches
Tell us where you are peace, we are confused
Of where to find you, where did we go
Wrong? Tell us to change, without you peace,
We are heading nowhere,
Even though you do well,
Without peace your life is a lie.

We who know what friendship is,
Let us make as many friends as mites,
We will never have peace where we
Are enemies?
Let us spread peace as seeds
To grow all over the World.
Our Christianity will not be complete,
Without you peace, even preaching
Will not be easy,
Truly without you peace our lives are big lies.

Peace is all we need
In everything we do
Jesus left us in peace
But also in pieces
We have to maintain peace
In order to stay/live happily
Without peace and holiness,
Not one still sees the Lord.

Charity begins at home,
Peace has to start from home,
To Church, community and then
Spread all over the world,
Peace is all we need in our daily lives,
Without peace and holiness,
No one shall see the Lord.

Our Country had been destroyed
Because there was no peace
Without peace in the world
There will be no truth at all
We thank our almighty Lord,
For granting us peace,
Despite of what happened
After election
Without peace and holiness
No one shall see the Lord
Watch out.

Wycliffe M. Musera, 23
East Africa Yearly Meeting of Friends (North) (FUM)
Kenya

God's Message Gets in One Deeply and Lives in Him

The Quaker church has a culture of worshipping, praying, and praising God in silence. God's message gets in one deeply and lives in him or her during his or her Christian life. Like Hanna, who prayed in silence and received a miracle, many in the Quaker church have received many miracles through such serious and deep-hearted [yearning] for God's Kingdom and intervention. Diligent seeking of the Lord has strengthened our faith and made us overcome our obstacles.

The [practice] of appointing the heads of the churches has been that of nomination. This, I believe, has lowered our faith in the church. I believe that leaders should be elected by members so that the right person is democratically chosen to spearhead the church to greater levels.

The culture of being insensitive to time has also derailed the church. Programs are set but sometimes are not followed to the letter, thus reducing faith in the church.

Many people believe that there is no salvation in the church, but I dispute that because I am saved and I'm a Quaker. I advise people that salvation is personal and comes by repenting and accepting Jesus as our personal saviour. This has built my faith.

On the side of technology, the Quaker church embraces technology, especially communication technology; the flavour in music and administering the word have been enhanced through technology. God's message has reached many through the use of technology (e.g. television, printing media technology, radio, and even over the Internet).

Despite the benefits of technology, it has also been devastating to our faith. Many have been misusing technology in the Quaker church, many have read and downloaded pornographic information from the Internet, many have also sent demoralizing information to the Internet to discourage Quakers.

Above all, culture and technology have done well and improved our faith in the Quaker church.

Wasike W. Noah, 19
Kenya

Culture and Technology Have Affected Our Faith as Quakers

Different aspects of culture and technology that are changing day by day are greatly affecting the Quaker faith in different ways, either directly or indirectly.

First, most different rites of passage are the ones that affect our faith negatively. For example, God commanded Abraham that all his descendants should be circumcised at the age of eight days old. But nowadays most Quakers circumcise their sons at puberty. Here they will organize a ceremony. They will eat and drink different forbidden brews like *changaa*, *busaa*, and so on. Once drunk, their faith in God is lowered because they will forget God and concentrate on ceremonies.

Different communities' understanding of God has also contributed to the loss of Quaker faith. This is so because each community has its own story of creation and understanding of God. For example, the Agikuyu community believes that their god is found on Mount Kirinyaga. If the Friends Church is founded in such an area, most of the members of the church will get confused. They will not be sure between Yahweh and Hgai (God of Agikuyu) who is the true God. Therefore their faith in God is greatly affected negatively.

Also, taboos between different communities have made most Quakers fail to learn God's word. This is because in most African communities, when a woman is pregnant, for example, she is not allowed to speak to her husband directly. She can only speak through an intermediary. This taboo is still carried out up to today. Most Quakers who belong to such communities also do it. In doing so their faith in God is lowered because such a woman will not share with her husband God's word. There is no way they will read the Bible in their house.

Wife inheritance has also affected most of our faith as Quakers. This is because in traditional African communities when a man dies, his immediate brother inherits his wife and property. This activity is carried out up to now and it has affected most Quakers' faith in God. This is so because, for example, even a pastor who belongs to such a community will be forced to inherit his brother's wife. If he fails he will be recognized as an outcast. Now, once he inherits his brother's wife his own wife will automatically pray to God wholeheartedly so her husband will come back. If God fails to answer such a prayer and the woman has no patience, she will not believe in God. She will even seek the witch doctors to assist her. By doing so her faith in God becomes less and less. So the action of wife inheritance may affect one's faith directly.

The idea of wealth and prestige has affected most Quakers' faith. Most African communities believe that when one owns a lot of cattle, wives, or children, he is rich. If a Quaker in such a community lacks these things, he will get confused. Instead of spreading God's word, he will be looking for wealth. He will even associate with witch doctors. Once he acquires property and becomes wealthy, he will not attend church services. He will value property more than God. So such a culture has affected the faith of most members of our church.

Apart from culture, most of Quakers' faith has been affected by technology. This is because nowadays there are a lot of electronic devices, for example, the computer. Most business organizations have employed many people due to the invention of the computer. They work from morning to evening. After work when one goes back home, he will be tired and will not even read or share God's word with his family. On Sundays the work still continues. This makes one end up taking one year or so without going to church or reading the Bible. This automatically affects his or her faith in God negatively.

Also, most youth don't visit the sick or read the word of God during their leisure. During this time they will watch pornographic films. Once they do so, they will also wish to imitate them. During any time they are free, they will be doing what they've watched. Since premature sex is against God, God will therefore get annoyed by such youths. He will even not answer their prayers when they pray to Him. If the youths pray without an answer, their faith drops. They start doubting if God really answers prayers. This has affected most Quaker youths for a long time.

Most industries and factories have been built as a result of technology. These factories release smoke into the air and also use water from rivers for cooling machine parts. This water is released back into the rivers. This leads to air and water pollution respectively. Release of smoke into the atmosphere leads to lung cancer, while water pollution causes typhoid if that water is drunk. Here it will be found that most people die of these diseases. Quakers have tried to advise manufacturers on better use and release of waste products. They've tried by all means to solve this problem, but they have not found a solution. This makes some of them lose faith in God. They don't believe God really values human life. So the activity of industry and factory building affects our faith as Quakers indirectly.

Indeed, culture and technology have affected our faith as Quakers. To find the solution to this we should trust God and have strong patience in Him. We should follow His teachings and avoid all earthly things. We should avoid different cultural practices and not be changed by technology.

Andrew Wafula Wakili
Kenya

Meeting Christ in Guatemala
In Memory of Andy Summers

In the spring of 2008, I took a college course called Cycles of Military and Economic Violence in Guatemala and Mexico. After eight weeks of background reading and preparation, we traveled to each country to witness conditions there firsthand, spending five weeks in Guatemala and three in Mexico. This essay is loosely based on an e-mail I sent to friends and family before leaving Guatemala.

Friends, I have met Christ, and Christ is in Guatemala. Please be patient with me, for I cannot explain in a few words what I mean by this.

My fellow students and I flew into Guatemala City on Palm Sunday, but our entry was not triumphal. Although it did not occur to me at the time, I realize looking back that we came more in the spirit of Good Friday than that of Palm Sunday. We came in mourning because the professor who was to have accompanied us, Andy Summers, had died three days before, just two weeks after being diagnosed with leukemia. Had he lived to travel with us, he would have turned sixty-nine during the journey. The last time I saw him, he was at the front of the classroom like any other day, smiling his joyous smile, brimming over with enthusiasm; the next day, he was in the hospital. As Andy wished, we went on without him. A former student who had taken the course two years before and planned to come along as Andy's assistant this time became his replacement.

What I saw during our few days in Guatemala City did little to take my mind off death. On Monday we visited the Forensic Anthropology Foundation of Guatemala. This agency is responsible for exhuming clandestine graves from the thirty-six-year civil war that ended in 1996, examining the remains, and returning them to their communities for dignified burial. We walked in through a hallway stacked to the ceiling with dusty boxes of human bones—overflow from the evidence room in the attic, which was full to capacity with cases awaiting investigation. The next day, we visited the city's main cemetery, which is adjacent to the municipal dump. We saw the ornate private mausoleums of Guatemala's wealthiest families and the unadorned alcoves where the bones of the poor come to rest (as long as their families continue to pay rent on the space). Then we walked to the edge of the cemetery and stood beneath trees filled with vultures, looking down over the edge of the ravine to where two giant bulldozers chugged along flattening a mountain of trash. Behind the bulldozers, dozens of men and women walked with their eyes on the ground, searching for something of value in the city's garbage heap. They too were victims of institutional violence, just like the skeletons in those boxes at the Forensic Anthropology Foundation.

By Good Friday, we had left the capital and traveled to Quetzaltenango, where we watched the *Semana Santa* procession. *Semana Santa*, Holy Week, is very important in Guatemala, but neither Palm Sunday nor Easter is particularly emphasized. What is emphasized is Good Friday. What matters for many Guatemalans, it seems, is not the Triumphal Entry, nor the Resurrection; what matters is the Crucifixion.

The procession in Quetzaltenango lasted all day and into the night, winding through the city center again and again. Hundreds of men and women carried floats adorned with life-sized statues depicting scenes from the Passion. They wore purple robes in the morning, changing into black at the hour of Jesus' death. There were little girls in angel costumes, a man with a twenty-foot pole to lift the power lines so the floats could pass, and a brass band that played the same, slow, bittersweet song all day long.

It was a beautiful procession, but it made me uncomfortable. Like many liberal Friends, I had never felt at ease with theologies that emphasized the suffering and death of Jesus. I had always thought it was his words and his example that really mattered—his *life*, not his death. After four more weeks in Guatemala, though, I began to understand the emphasis on the crucifixion. You see, my friends, the crucifixion happened in Guatemala. It continues to happen there every day and every night. If one is to have hope at all in such a society, it must be hope that is based on suffering and death—for there is suffering and death all around, and precious little resurrection to be seen.

I want to tell you a story now. It is a hard story to tell, and a hard story to hear, and it is true. I heard it from Maria, my teacher at the language school we attended in Quetzaltenango. One day in 1985, Maria's father, a village leader and a catechist in the church, called a community meeting to discuss the local school. He had noticed that the teachers, who had to travel every week over bad roads from the larger town where they lived, were arriving too late to hold classes on Monday, and often leaving for the weekend as early as Thursday afternoon. Maria's father stood up and asked, in a few simple words, that the teachers try a little harder to fulfill their obligation to the community so the children could have a better future. When he finished, one of the teachers (who happened to be the daughter of an army officer) leaned over and whispered, "If you go on talking like this, you are going to have problems."

Three nights later, a group of heavily armed men, dressed in black and wearing ski masks, kicked down the family's door and took Maria's father away. They also took her brother, who was studying in Mexico to be a priest but was home visiting that weekend by chance. Maria's other brothers, who were small at the time, still say of that night: *Cuando anochezó, éramos niños. Cuando amaneció, éramos adultos.* ("When the sun went down, we were children. When the sun rose, we were adults.")

Maria did not learn the rest of the story until 2005, when an uncle finally told her what a friend, torn apart by pain and remorse, had told him years before. This friend was in the army in 1985, and it was he who ordered the killing of Maria's father and brother after they had been in captivity a while. He said they were in a group of prisoners taken out one night and forced to dig a line of graves. When the graves were done, the men were made to lie down in them. Then, lying down, they were shot one by one. The man who ordered these killings left for the United States the day after confessing to the uncle and has never returned.

Maria's father and brother are two drops in a sea of innocent dead. At least forty-five thousand people were kidnapped and disappeared during Guatemala's civil war. Probably many more, perhaps over one hundred fifty thousand. That includes only those whose bodies were concealed—many more were assassinated in front of their families, or detained and killed and then dumped in the street as an example to others.

Jesus said, "Truly, I say to you, as you did it to one of the least of these my brethren, you did it to me" (Matt. 25:40 RSV). If that is true, then in Guatemala we beat Christ, raped Christ, and cut the baby Christ out of his living mother's womb with a machete—thousands upon thousands of times. I say we did this, for we are all our brothers' keepers; whatever takes place anywhere in the human family, we are all culpable. The impoverished Mayan conscripts of the Guatemalan army did nothing that we ourselves would not do against our own brothers, sisters, cousins, and friends if we, like them, knew we had no choice but to participate in senseless violence or fall victim to it. We are no better, no stronger in our convictions, no more compassionate and peace-loving than the

Guatemalan people. We, too, are capable of silent complicity in the face of injustice, capable of betraying our neighbors, capable of murder.

But now let me tell you another story. This, too, is a story of suffering, but whereas Maria's story fills me with horror, this one gives me hope. It is about Melvin, a ten-year-old boy living in a village outside Quetzaltenango. When I met Melvin his father had died about a year before, and his teenaged brother was working to support the family. Melvin helped out by going to the mountain for firewood two or three days a week, and on those days he missed school. Along with two other students from my group, I went with him once. We hiked for an hour to reach the part of the mountain where Melvin cuts wood, and he kept up a running stream of jokes and stories the whole way, swinging his machete carelessly. At one point he stopped and announced in a solemn voice, "Now we are going to play. You can only step on these rocks along the path. If you step on the ground in between, you lose." We all lost except for Melvin, who was as sure-footed as a mountain goat.

When we had gathered enough dry branches, Melvin cut most of them into short chunks which he loaded in his *Nicapal*, a sling supported by a strap across his forehead. He allowed us to carry only the few large branches he could not quickly cut up with his machete. Melvin carried the nicapal all the way down the mountain, stopping often to have us stuff large leaves under it to ease the pain of the load on his back. Two or three times, he tripped on the slippery path and fell flat on his chest, the wood tumbling over his head and landing farther down the slope. Each time, we begged him to let one of us carry the *nicapal*, but he refused: This was his job, and he would do it. What struck me most was that despite the obvious pain he was in, Melvin talked and laughed all the way down the mountain just as he had on the way up, cheerfully telling us about friends who had broken bones or gotten stitches, and daydreaming aloud about ice cream and cookies.

I walked back to the language school afterwards, overcome with reverence. Melvin bore the weight of the wood, the death of his father, and the abject poverty of his family all without complaining, with strength of spirit beyond my understanding. Amidst all that pain, he had not lost hope. It made me think of Andy, who had devoted his life to defending the forgotten, nameless poor in Latin America, who had witnessed so much suffering and injustice, and yet remained one of the happiest people I had ever known.

Then I thought about Christ. We tend to assume Jesus bore his cross to Calvary slowly, groaning in pain at every step. But what if the Savior of the World talked and joked with the soldiers as he was marched to his death? What if he ran recklessly like a little boy on a twisting mountain path, sometimes falling under the weight of the wood, but rising with a laugh to take up the burden once more, determined to carry it all the way in the service of his brothers and sisters? Would not such sacrificial suffering have the power to transform the world?

W. Geoffrey Black, 23
Menomonie Monthly Meeting, Northern Yearly Meeting (FGC)
United States

It Happens Every Day

While I sipped my tea in silence, I thought to myself, *It happens every day.*

On October 14, 2008, a group of six- to twelve-year-old Palestinian children returning home from school ran for their lives. Every morning and afternoon, these children had to walk past an Israeli settlement on their way to and from school. On October 14 two adult Israeli settlers waited for the children, threw stones at them and chased them toward their homes in the village of Tuba. Because these children have been attacked frequently, lately in this very location, the Israeli army is charged with escorting them each day. But that day, as usual, the Israeli soldiers drove away, abandoning the children while they were still in danger. "The children were very afraid when they arrived home," said one father.

It happens every day. Over the past year, I've lived in a small rural village in Palestine's southern West Bank called At-Tuwani. As a part of my work to support Palestinians struggling for peace and justice nonviolently, I've born witness to more attacks on these children than I've been able to keep track of. The children are not attacked daily, but every day they face more danger on their walk to school than I have faced my entire life. We've sat together, the children and I, and waited for the Israeli army to come for more hours that I care to recall. Sometimes we play together and manage to have a genuinely good time. One afternoon we held an impromptu photo shoot. The kids posed for me as they climbed trees, climbed on top of each other, giggled, and danced. The next day one of the older girls pulled on my hand and said to me, "I was so happy yesterday! Last night I woke up in the middle of the night because I had a bad dream about the settlers. But then I thought about all the fun we had and I fell back asleep." Those words broke my heart and I can't put it back together.

It happens every day. We all know the many ways, tiny and humongous, that our world is falling apart around us. Polar bears are losing their habitat. Millions of parents can't feed their children. We are surrounded by wars with no end in sight, petty meanness, decreased community, and children who are attacked on their way to school. It's so much to bear. Too much.

It happens every day, but that's not the end of the story. Lately as I sit in the presence of God, I keep thinking, "It is as bad as you think it is, but that's not all." To paraphrase an old slogan, if your heart isn't broken, you aren't paying attention. But if you aren't also filled with hope, you're missing half of the story. In at-Tuwani, every day Palestinians are resisting a military occupation that is trying to crush them and their culture. They are grazing their sheep, building new houses, organizing nonviolent demonstrations, and sending their children to school. In the fall, it will be time for the olive harvest and throughout Palestine, farmers will step out on to their land, sometimes risking arrest and attacks, to harvest a bounty of thousands of green-, blue-, and even purple-hued olives. Here in my own Pacific Northwest, I've been thinking about the salmon who every year come down the river, offer themselves up to the people, and then swim back to their headwaters to spawn and die. For thousands of years, despite ever-increasing odds against them, they've survived through this cycle. I can't help but think there is something they are trying to tell us.

It happens every day. Horror and hope. They stand together, side by side, on the knife's edge. And they offer us a choice—every day.

Joy Ellison, 26
West Hills Friends, Northwest Yearly Meeting (EFCI)
United States

A Gathering Storm

In 2003 the Chicago, Illinois, office of the American Friends Service Committee (AFSC), the Quaker peace and justice organization, created a memorial and witness to the human cost of the U.S. war in Iraq. The idea was simple: one pair of combat boots for every American soldier who died in Iraq. Shortly thereafter they added thousands of civilian shoes to reflect a small portion of the Iraqi civilians who have died in the war. Out of this idea came the exhibit *Eyes Wide Open: An Exhibition on the Human*

Cost of the Iraq War. By now it has traveled to more than one hundred cities in the United States, growing with the death toll.

Each pair of boots is labeled with the name, age, and home state of an American who has died in the war. Each pair of civilian shoes has a name and age: women's shoes for women and children's shoes for children.

As AFSC toured the exhibit through the hometowns of those who have died, family members and friends left mementos and other remnants with boots in honor of their loved one. Things like:

- A photo; smiling faces of friends clutched in embrace
- A smiling teenager perched atop a tank
- A love-worn teddy bear
- A personal note from a long-lost friend
- A bundle of letters from the U.S. government, formal, calm, direct: *Your son is dead.*
- A plaque from the state of Michigan commemorating service
- A single black rose.

As a staff person at the AFSC, I worked on the practical logistics of the exhibit four times.

As a photographer, I was compelled to document each of those times. It was the closest I have felt to the divine in years.

Eyes Wide Open Iraq, photograph, Chris Pifer, 28, Madison Monthly Meeting, Northern Yearly Meeting (FGC), United States

This photo is from May 11–14 2006; the *Eyes Wide Open* exhibit was on the National Mall in Washington, D.C. The Mall stretches for some fourteen blocks between the Capitol and the Washington Monument. By 2006, there were almost twenty-three hundred boots in the exhibit, filling two city blocks.

But my first true experience with this exhibit was Memorial Day weekend 2004. I was twenty-three, fresh from college, and new to life in Washington. The exhibit was in Upper Senate park; quite literally the lawn of the United States Capitol. At that time, there were 798 boots.

AFSC invited Ivan Medina, an Iraq War veteran, to be one of the speakers. After a full and strenuous day of work on the exhibit, I found myself talking with Ivan in my office into the early hours of the morning.

As a Quaker I strongly believe that there is commonality in human experience, that there is something fundamental in the experience of others which I can understand, relate to, and empathize with through the experiences of my own life. I found that my conversation with Ivan was affirming of that belief.

Ivan was twenty-three, just weeks younger than myself. He had an identical twin brother, was the son of Salvadoran immigrants; he grew up in New York. He ended up joining the military, and convinced his brother to join with him. He worked as a chaplain. They celebrated every single birthday together except their twenty-third. They both were in Baghdad, but didn't manage to connect. Two weeks later his twin brother died.

There is much I will never understand about Ivan's experience. But as he shared stories of pastoral care in a war zone, and of the human, civilian tragedy experienced by Iraqis, I caught the slightest glimpse of the destructive and disintegrating experience that war is for all involved. I suddenly had a concrete understanding of the reason I spent a year of my life in college organizing against the war, and why I spent five years in Washington working to shift federal budget priorities from war to human needs.

The *Eyes Wide Open* exhibit grew too large to tour and was broken up into smaller exhibits, with boots from a state or region touring locally to this day.

I no longer work for AFSC, but I still find myself almost moved to tears recalling these snippets of my life.

Chris Pifer, 28
Madison Monthly Meeting, Northern Yearly Meeting (FGC)
United States

Steady, Aim, Breathe, Fire

In the dark it was easy to sneak up behind him and soon his neck was broken and body limp. Still, David had to hide the body so no one would stumble upon it and set off alarms. Tall grass offered cover and the leeches in the swamp dissuaded any would-be adventurers. A patrol was coming, he had to move fast and spring forward underneath the shadow of a water tower, all without a sound. He made it, but just barely.

From here the rest was easy, he just had to slip the poison into the ventilation system and hack the security grid on the sewer tunnels. It took him only four tries, which was pretty good considering the difficulty was maxed-out for the game. His thumbs were sore, and with the level finally beaten, it was a good stopping point.

My brother has been involved in covert operations since the age of twelve, when he had his first kiss. Shortly after midnight, he left through his bedroom window (a stylistic choice, all the doors were left unlocked and unmonitored). After groping through the ramshackle remnants of moonlit farmland for two miles, he met his seventh-grade paramour, Bethanne. His adrenaline and testosterone fueled not one but two trysts that week. Unfortunately upon returning, Mom awoke to the sound of our washing machine removing grass stains and budding hormones from Bugle-Boy® jeans. Regardless of the punishment, it was worth the price to Dave, and personally, I could not have been prouder of my younger brother.

These days he rappels over the sides of buildings and through open windows to leave surprises for his puzzled peers to discover in their locked rooms. We even adventure together, but I make a lame co-partner. Unversed in proper hand-sign lingo, I resort to shadow puppets and lewd gestures in mockery. Our current escapade is rearranging public signs into amusing anagrams. Welcome Back Teachers = Come Beach Wrestle = Recheck Combat Weasel.

About four years ago he enlisted as an infantryman in the Army National Guard. It made sense, but certainly didn't make peace in our house. Mom and I are Quakers. On the other hand, David joined our father, uncles, grandfather, and great-grandfather in the heroic ranks of America's finest. Across such an ideological spectrum, the Dotson family dinner table has become its own war zone at times.

David graduated from a science and tech magnet school by the skin of his teeth. Others in his class went to work for the army, but typically in research and development or computing roles. Instead, as an infantryman, David learned the recoil rates of three different machine guns, proximity limits of laser mines, and how to simultaneously interrogate and befriend civilian populations.

"I know that I am gifted for this work. I know that I can handle its pressures better than most, and I know that this work is needed right now. It's that simple." As he exhaled, each word was a cloud of hookah smoke bellowing forth; he looked like a dragon with its mind made up. Steady-aim-breathe-fire.

I was dizzy from the hookah, the militarism, or both. Intellectually I understood; his reasoning was rational and virtuous, but my heart beat a loud protest. He claimed to be called to this work, he claimed it spoke to him spiritually. Still, I couldn't make it real. I couldn't find acceptance without approval. I didn't know the middle-ground between supporting him, my brother, while not affirming his role as soldier.

In the beginning, it was easy to handle David's enlistment in the guard. He lived the normal college-student lifestyle, save one weekend a month when he took the boots and camouflage out of the closet and returned at the end of the day either extremely bored, or completely exhausted (such is the way of the army). When I shared news of David's choice with others, they were more astounded than I. They looked at me as if I must feel crushed under an unbearable weight, yet I told them the news with a lightness that, in hindsight, clearly hinted at denial.

Somewhere, in the back of my mind, I knew the day would come.

He said, "I'm going over." And I knew: *He is bound for Iraq. He is no longer simply my brother, he is now Private First Class Dotson, and he will do what he is ordered to do. There is less room for him to be his independent self now, only the soldier he knows how to be.* My mind recalled all the stealth and violence of our video games, all the brimstone and glory of marine corps commercials. Had he romanticized it all?

The following week I stared at piles of shoes gathered in Iraq in the *Eyes Wide Open* exhibit, a witness put on by AFSC to give a tangible visual manifestation of the real human cost of war. Piled knee-deep, sandals, boots, and tatters of brand-name apparel represented the civilian casualties on a fifty-to-one scale. Next to them and in proper formation were platoons of fallen American soldiers' boots. Identical boots have lived in our closet the past two years, and I never truly grasped the consequences of filling them (or emptying them). Statistics of body counts and explosive pictures had hardened in my memory, but I never sat with their reality so concretely near. It shook me from the inside out, I breathed in deeply, trying to fill the hollow vacuum that drained me.

I know of only one Quaker who has risked as much and lost as much. Tom Fox. Where are his shoes? Who is filling them?

Devotion. I was overwhelmed by my brother's devotion. It was not my own devotion, it was not my means, but it was soul and fire and Truth, and nothing more mattered. I cannot judge another person's path, only hold them accountable to the Truth revealed for them.

Who holds Quakers accountable to risk as much?

Through my own hot tears, one thing was clear: I must also live out my understanding of peace and what it means to me, and risk everything. We both carry ministries against war. As different as they might be, I must believe that one God led us each to our own life's work. My brother's calling is a reaction to establish peace, while my heart calls for proactive measures against the conditions for war. We must both risk our entire lives for what we believe. We are the necessary balance of idealism and realism. In this imperfect world, we must steady our aims and breathe fire to ignite whatever future will have us.

A year-and-a-half passes (along with our grandmother, Saddam Hussein, and support for the occupation of Iraq).

He returns. Thank God.

He returns a hero in the eyes of so many. He returns a rich man by comparison to his friends with school loans and empty resumés.

He returns after an uneventful tour. It wasn't quite what he was looking for. I know he wished for the full experience, I know part of him wanted to face death directly and know what utter violence looks like. I know it must be hard to be lauded as a hero after a relatively tame experience. And he is a hero, but only for facing the fullness of the life he found in Al-Nasiriyah.

You try not to enter a situation with expectations, but you don't expect to spend most of your time in a small trailer. They keep the Iraqi translators there, far enough away from any useful information regarding the layout of the base. In that small trailer he learned Iraqi Arabic in chalk scrawled upon the plywood walls, yet again enveloped by layers of hookah smoke. He found direction there; he found companions. These were deep and true friendships. Men who were professors in another time showed my brother pictures of themselves with the two things they took pride in now: their children and their AK-47s. Is there anything more terribly simple than reproduction and self-defense? They were people who exhibited more concern for their community than for themselves, who, if they had something they wished to partake of, would first offer it to everyone else in the group before enjoying it themselves.

Trust is not easily gained. You don't expect the bathrooms to carry graffiti questioning your loyalty for spending so much time with the Iraqis. "Watch out for Dotson, he's al-Qaeda." Most were meant jokingly, but there is a kernel of truth to every jab of jest. You don't expect to be bored, yet [you are] on high alert for weeks on end, in one-hundred-fifteen-degree heat and twenty-four-hour shifts.

He learned why trust was so rarely gained. Sitting idly on a jersey barrier and drinking chai just outside the base, he started a discussion with an Iraqi. Dave described to the man his admiration for the Islamic relationship to death and fate (the inherent command in the name of the religion itself is surrender). The Iraqi man agreed and said it is something that the West would do well to better understand. Later that night, a rocket attack occurred, landing twenty-five feet from David's vehicle, directed there by information that same Iraqi man provided to "unfriend-lies." The rocket failed to properly explode. Thank God. In confronting his own mortality, David says he came away with a sense of resignation, a sense that he had come a little closer to surrendering to his own death, whenever it may come. We all have people praying for us.

I won't try to convey a year of life lived in a war zone in four hundred words. That is ludicrous. I will only tell you what I see in my brother, neither clearly nor steadily, but as though through a glass darkly.

I see someone still trying to integrate an alien experience into a land filled with habit, comfort, and convenience. I see someone who has seen the destructive power of individualism when it is worshipped, the perseverance of community-minded living through crisis, and still doesn't know how to assimilate the experience. I see someone who, before his tour, had stores of momentum and broad intention, and came back with focused intention and little momentum. I see someone who has always been my beautiful antagonist, pushing me to commit myself to my path as fiercely as he does. And too, I am afraid of seeing someone who may think he's still playing a game, who may think that the energy of stealth and force is something to draw meaning from. I see someone who has not actively saved a life or risked his own consciously, but is looked to as a hero and now speaks of volunteering for a tour in Afghanistan. I see someone who wants to stand in between worlds, to help them each see the other more clearly, but who is reluctant to commit himself on either shore and may be intimidated by his task, which he alone truly understands. In naming these visions, I mean to challenge David as I hope he would challenge me. Isn't this truest service we can provide one another? To hold up for one another the questions that our lives present us, the questions that cut not to the bone, but to the soul?

My brother said to me, "True freedom exists in realizing our uniqueness, our singularity. We cannot let ourselves be limited to the ideas and labels that were previously created. Not simply, 'Think outside the box,' since that precludes reacting to preconceived perspectives—instead, 'Forget there is a box.'" If that is our duty to ourselves, then for each other, we must name the growing edges that we stand on and find our next step regardless of labels and boxes.

I love my brother. I don't agree with what he does. Yet, I cherish the wrestling that I do with him, with what he does and why. Because of it, I am held accountable to truly devote myself and take on real risk and investment in my own beliefs. He keeps me grounded in the truth of where we are, so I can more clearly see where we can be, and perhaps the most important fact—we can only get there together.

> *Stephen Willis Dotson, 25*
> *Goose Creek Monthly Meeting, Baltimore Yearly Meeting*
> *(FGC-FUM)*
> *United States*

Walking Peacefully through a Violent World?

My life up to this point has been struggling and deciding what paths God has wanted me to take. I have struggled spiritually to find a comfortable spiritual home living amidst the extreme and brutal violence of my city, Philadelphia. Every day I see on the news all the violent acts that happened the night before. It can be very hard to stand up and be a person of faith anywhere, but especially in a place where there is so much negativity and turmoil. However bad it may be, the violence that occurs in my city has changed me spiritually into the person that I am today. Some key points in my life up to this point have been my interactions with violence and how I deal with it.

When I was young, my Mom didn't let me or any of my siblings play with any guns or weapons. We didn't have Mortal Kombat or any of the other popular violent games. She explained to me that people actually died from weapons in our city, and that they were nothing to play with. I still didn't understand at the time. My mom had created a figurative fence to guard me and my siblings from violence in our world. She did an excellent job of guarding us from the news and explained to us that there were people out there who intended to do harm to other people. However, whenever I went over to my friend's house, I did indulge in several hours of Mortal Kombat. I was very curious and wanted to play it, and didn't pay much attention to what my mom had said. One day, however, my thoughts radically changed. I came home from school on a normal day and glanced at the TV. On the screen was the picture of a six-year-old, African-American girl who had been shot and killed the night before. I realized that she was the same age as me. I realized at this moment how real violence was, and how quickly it could affect me. I thought about her family members, and how they must have felt. I also thought that it could have been a picture of one of my friends on the TV screen, or maybe even my picture. At this point, I felt the fence that my mom had worked so hard to keep up crash down.

I quickly decided that I wanted nothing to do with violence, and that I didn't want it ever affecting my family. I continued growing up and had no interactions with violence. I was attending a Quaker school and thought that I would be immune to violence because I was at a Quaker school. I felt very safe and everything seemed to be going on fine. People continued to die in Philadelphia due to gun violence, and, honestly, I wasn't that concerned. As long as my family and I were okay, everything was fine. At twelve years old I completed the seventh grade and was going to continue my education in another school. I realized at this point I wanted to become a Quaker, because I felt so strongly about being anti-violent. I also felt that if I was a Quaker, I would be immune to any violence that occurred, simply because I was a Quaker. Then the Iraq war started when I was fourteen. I saw the missiles the tanks shot and watched them blow up more than one building at a time. People began to talk about the draft, and I began attending conferences and meetings about being a conscientious objector. I was worried at that point about being drafted for the war when I was eighteen. At this point I knew that violence was real and alive in my world. Not only was the fence that previously guarded me from violence down, but I felt as though I could really see the brutal effects of violence and that its impact and influence was standing right in front of me looking me in the eye.

When I was sixteen, violence took a step forward and hit me hard. One rare day when I was not with my brother, he was jumped on the way home from school only a minute from our home, This was my first real instance with violence. I couldn't believe that this had happened. I thought that no violence would happen to me and that I wouldn't be affected because my family was good and went to church. I really felt angry at first and guilty that I wasn't with my brother to protect him. This was a random act, and he never saw these kids or did anything to them to deserve this. After this incident, I realized there has to be change to control this violence. I realized that just worrying about me and my safety was not the right thing to do. I realized that my brothers and sisters who were being beaten up, mugged, and gunned down needed help. If they were not okay, then I shouldn't feel okay. I decided I was going to give this up to God. I didn't know the answer to this problem, but I was hoping that God could help us out.

After this incident violence continued to make its presence known to me, and this time I was the victim. A friend and I were on the train riding home from school when two guys came up to us. After they tried to start a conversation, I knew that something was wrong. I knew that this was a bad situation and that I had to find some way of getting out of it. They asked for the time, and my friend pulled out his cell phone. At that moment, I knew that they were going to try and take his phone, either through intimidation or force. After a while the two guys left, and I told my friend how I felt and for him to be ready.

They came back a few minutes later, one with a hand in his jacket like he was holding a gun. I began asking God then to help me through this, and to give me the ability to do whatever I had to do to get out of this situation. They began talking and saying how easy it is to shoot someone. I stood there and began looking around for help. I saw a woman sitting across from us and I made eye contact with her. I tried really hard to show her this situation through my eyes, and hoped that she would do something. The train slowly rolled up to my train stop, two stops before my friend got off. I had to decide whether I would get off the train and run for it, or stay with my friend and help him. I remembered that even if I was okay, that was not enough. I had to try and help others who weren't okay. I stayed on the train with my friend. Meanwhile, the two guys were still standing there trying to intimidate us; one still had his hand in his jacket. We rolled up to the final stop. I was wondering what was going to happen next. I looked at the same lady who was sitting across from us. She got up, pushed my friend and me behind her and away from the two men, and told us sternly, "You two should leave now." We left the train and didn't go back. I was so relieved that nothing happened and that we were fine. I realized that there was no easy way to get away from violence. That it would always be out there, and that it would take a lot to end it. I needed to find a dependable way to find peace and connect with God in this hectic and violent world.

Now I am a little bit older and I can find peace in meetings for worship. I am still very active in anti-gun violence and anti-violence activism in Philadelphia. When I do feel overwhelmed by all the violence, I try to center myself and connect with God and find peace. I realize that there is peace in my home, peace in the streets, and peace in a noisy Quaker meeting. Yes, it's there. We just all have to find it. When we all do find it, no one will have to solve their problems with violence any more.

Richard George, 19
Frankford Friends Monthly Meeting, Philadelphia Yearly Meting (FGC)
United States

Sight of the Kingdom of God

While I was growing up in a suburb of Akron, Ohio, I can remember seeing someone who lived in poverty and moving to the other side of the street. I don't know who exactly taught me that a person living on the streets or begging for money had no value, but I learned it. I can remember my eyes beginning to well up with tears in compassion and quickly brushing their weight from my cheeks before I had a chance to acknowledge them. I had adapted to the thought that homeless people were only alcoholics and drug dealers who made bad choices. I do not remember the point in time where this view of poverty changed. Maybe it was not so much an exact moment, but rather a realizing of a responsibility I had as a moral human being and as a disciple of Christ. Whatever the reason, I started to see people as I think God would have always wanted them to be seen.

Poverty is not something I can actively avoid, as I found out early in my childhood. The Bible says in Deuteronomy 15:11 that there will always be the poor in the land. This is not the only place in the Bible that it discusses how to respond to the poor or the widow, or even the injustices of the day. The Bible is clear that it is not a choice and that if you love God you will love others. If the Bible is so matter of fact about this issue, then my response is absolutely necessary. I am not pretentious enough to assume the world depends on my response, but I think God does use the willing.

A couple years back I spent a few months in the Philippines participating in basic humanitarian work and assisting the church. I truly believe that the way I act now toward injustice and the poor was greatly affected by what I saw through the eyes of the unfortunate. I don't even know if it is a correct thing to call them unfortunate because I think they possess a lot of wisdom I could really use every day. The best experiences I had were when we were walking with the indigenous tribes, sleeping on floors, and eating whenever our bodies absolutely required it. I went there to teach them about the love and affection of Jesus and in the end I was the one who learned. Poverty in a third-world country is not necessarily handled the same way it is in America. You can't fix things with money; it doesn't clear your conscience. The truth that I really seemed to experience while I was over there was that more money will only cause more problems. Honestly, it probably is the same in America. When you give someone money and don't teach them how to act with money or what the proper things to buy are, their view of needs and wants becomes skewed. You have to buy food, you have to teach the people a trade and you have to send them back into their community with this knowledge. Coming back from this voyage I was left with a decision.

The Barrel is Empty but the World is Consumed, sculpture, William Hunt Tinsman, 17, Solebury Friends Meeting, Philadelphia Yearly Meeting (FGC), United States

What would my response be in America? This question haunted me day and night for a few weeks until I resolved that this change was inside of me and I had to let it out. How would the Inward Light guide me to experience this kind of attitude toward the poor living next door or down the street or even on the other side of town? The answer is simple. It drives me to love. It helps me to give. It reminds me that tomorrow I could be in their shoes. It teaches me humbleness and the beauty of simple living. Everything comes back to my heart. It comes back to the heart of the church and the heart of God. My experiences cause me to try to love with pure motives. Social injustice makes me angry. How could a person's social class, race, age, sex, or even choice of lifestyle decide what they are worth? We are all Children of God, created for Him and by Him. I don't think the Bible leaves us wandering in the dark about what we are to do regarding injustices and the poor. What did Jesus do? How can I be a part of this today? What am I doing to not only build the Kingdom but also to strengthen the one that exists today?

I've decided that I can throw money at the poor or I can build relationships. I can live among them or I can avoid them. I can welcome them into the Church or I can stand afar and speak volumes with my actions. It is a personal decision and it's one I am trying to make the right and Godly way every day. I am not saying it's easy. I am not saying that I make the right decision every time. I am just saying I'm trying. I am trying to let my faith interact with [the] Inner Light to change this world. It might just be with one cup of cold water, but I will be hopeful. I won't lose sight of the Kingdom of God.

Kristen M. Johnson, 25
Evangelical Friends Church—Eastern Region (EFCI)
United States

Las Cañadas Ecovillage

I recently came back from a Quaker Leadership Program trip to Las Cañadas Ecovillage in Mexico, where I spent a week eating food grown within a ten-minute walk of where I slept at night, washing my hands and my dishes with captured rainwater, and using composting toilets. My traveling companions were the other members of a work crew that had come to Las Cañadas to learn how this piece of land went from being a cloud forest to a cattle ranch, and how it is slowly becoming a cloud forest again.

During the days we worked in the fields with Don Adán, a toothless, sun-worn *campesino* with twinkling eyes and a ready laugh. I wondered how we must have appeared to him, this group of relatively affluent North Americans who traveled to southern Mexico to work with our hands and our bodies in the hot sun. What did Don Adán make of our eagerness to spread sheep manure compost over a field of corn and beans? We sang as we shoveled, and I thought about Don Adán and me, about the nature of work, and about what my college educations (both of them) have prepared me for in life.

My trip pulled into very sharp focus a question that has been on my mind in one form or another for the whole of this past year. *How shall I live?*

It is a very simple question, so simple as to be totally overwhelming. I am in the thrilling and terrifying position of being able to approach this question with openness and sincerity, with a field of possible answers that is nearly limitless.

That the question of how to live is so prominent in my life feels like the culmination of several years of building awareness. Along with many other people, I have recently become painfully aware of how dependent I am for my very existence on distant lands and distant people, and of how poorly my values are expressed through the relationships that sustain me. As for many others, this journey started for me with an awareness of how far most of our food travels to get to us and of how ecologically and socially destructive conventional agricultural practices are in many parts of the world. Several years ago, I began to make an effort to buy more of my food from local growers who use agricultural methods that are more in line with my values. Last year I planted my own garden. This year, as the prices of food and other commodities have steadily risen, I have watched my choices move increasingly into the mainstream.

Yogis like to talk about the pain that comes with the moment of realization that one is not living up to one's potential as a human being. This awareness necessarily precedes any positive change, but it is painful nonetheless. For me, the awareness of where my food comes from led to a whole series of other painful realizations about how my basic needs are met and about how little control or even knowledge I have with respect to these things. In thinking about how to live, I have been actively searching for communities that have achieved at least some autonomy with respect to their food supply, their water supply, their energy supply, and the treatment of their waste. It is this search that brought me to southern Mexico, to a cloud forest turned cattle ranch turned agricultural cooperative.

Now, as I contemplate this question of how to live, of how to move from painful awareness to real change, I feel that my heart is being pulled in two directions. On the one hand, I am a thoroughly urban person. I love being able to walk, ride my bike, and take public transportation to every place I need to go. I love corner markets and corner bars. I love neighborhoods and dog parks and community gardens. I love salsa clubs and coffee shops and twenty-four-hour diners. I am also convinced that if our species is to have a future on this planet, we must find a way to make cities work, since over half the world's population now lives in them.

On the other hand, I love the great outdoors. I love walking through woods, swimming in lakes, working in the sun. I love quiet. I love stars. In a rural area it seems possible that I might find or help create a community that handles its own food, water, energy, and waste needs; whereas in a city, this task is so daunting as to feel nearly impossible. I loved being at Las Cañadas, and yet, as much as I respect and admire the life in which I was immersed there, I can't shake the feeling that the question of how I myself shall live has an entirely different answer from the one that is expressed there.

I am searching for a lived praxis, a way of being in the world that reflects my values. I might call myself an environmentalist, but most environmental rhetoric feels hollow to me. My environmentalism is spiritual. It is based on the four Quaker pillars of Simplicity, Integrity, Peace, and Inner Light, not on a belief in Progress or a deep and abiding faith in Technology. Furthermore, I don't believe we can protect nature without protecting each other. My environmentalism is a search for the Good Life, a life of abundance and joy that requires exploitation of neither people nor planet. I suspect that my search will be a lifelong endeavor.

Laurie Pickard, 29

Monthly Meeting of Friends of Philadelphia (Arch Street),
Philadelphia Yearly Meeting (FGC)

United States

Author's note: This piece previously appeared on my blog, *Wanderphilia: A blog about my travels.*

Practicing Peace in a World of Impermanence

During the summer of 1993, my father and stepmother moved into an old, solid limestone house in Bloomington, Indiana. A physician by trade, my father is a gardener and homemaker at heart. My stepmother shares his passion for the garden so, together, they made the old house their home. Over the course of a decade, I admired the changes they made, most notably the garden beds of hostas, daylilies, roses, and English ivy that replaced what had been a yard of grass. The last patch of sod in the backyard was removed in the spring of 2004 and replaced with a bed of hostas shaded by well-established hemlock trees that lined the north and east edges of the property. Work accomplished! Now to sit back and enjoy, or so I thought.

To my surprise, my parents purchased another home that summer to downscale in preparation for my father's retirement and coinciding plans to winter in Sarasota, Florida. My first response was "What about the garden? What about all of your work?" My father replied that he was excited about the clean slate that lay before him at their new home—a new project that he was fit and energized for. It was I who struggled with letting go of my parents' beautiful creation. They have since proceeded to tear up more sod at their new home, to lay new paths, to design and build contraptions for ease and efficiency. They have a new work in progress.

My parents' story of ever-changing, creative accomplishments echoes the story of planet Earth. I relay this story because my response to their fresh start in 2004 echoes my response to Earth's present change. Attached to what *has been*, I have questioned and resisted this age of loss. As far as we know, Earth has gone through many changes, some quite extreme, much like the change Earth experiences now (the sixth great mass extinction of species). A once-diverse garden is being wiped clean. And, while there is no end or beginning to Earth's story (at least not in time we can comprehend), this present time may be likened to a fresh start for Earth, given how much of what *has been* is passed away or soon *will* be.

As a birthright Friend, I was raised to believe the light of God is in every person. As a young adult, I consciously joined a group of Friends who extend that sense of the light to all beings and, still more encompassing, to planet Earth. In my continuing revelation, I have come to believe that this planet *is* a living being of which we are part. Since this revelation, I have gone through major spiritual and emotional convulsions as I have witnessed human destruction of self and community—the extinction of species known and unknown to us. The pain of believing that all of the many cultures and species passing before us embody the sacred and that we are responsible for their destruction is too much for the human being to bear. We become martyrs or we turn away.

I claimed martyrdom for many years and have only been saved from my suffering by the teachings of Buddhism, particularly the natural law of impermanence. The law of impermanence teaches that the planet changes, as part of the ever-unfolding universe, through endless cycles of birth and death. When attached to form—such as a planet of flourishing diversity—we suffer when this form changes. Attachment to planet Earth's past and present form is particularly painful in this time of extraordinary loss. In accepting impermanence—the fleeting nature of form—I have found peace with loss. This is not to say that I do not lament the loss of beloved form (I would hardly be human if I did not grieve), but that I realize the divine essence, which gives rise to form, cannot be lost.

My husband and I have debated at length this matter of impermanence. We have discussed two potential responses. One response to impermanence may be to accept that all is fleeting and, so, care less for life—to be *careless* with life. The person taking this perspective will deny the sacred in life (*For how could life be sacred if it is to end?*) and see no sense in any effort to care for anyone (including him or herself) because death is certain. The second response to impermanence that we have discussed and vow to practice is one of extreme care for everyone *because* death is certain, making each moment with any and all a blessing. Given the Quaker tenet of that of God in everyone, this second response to impermanence is my only *true* response. Our faith demands that we be careful with all life because the Light is here within.

Thus, acceptance of impermanence, coupled with the Quaker tenet of nonviolence (also a Buddhist precept), forms the foundation of my spiritual practice today. One allows me nonattachment to a beloved, fleeting world, and the other allows me to love with every ounce of my being that which exists before me. I am free to speak and act on behalf of everyone even as I know that everyone, including this one planet, will change in continuous cycles of death and birth. I am free to grieve the loss of magnificent form, knowing that, though form is lost, the divine light carries on. My great task at this time is to honor and celebrate those who are passing before us with my tears, to speak and act with compassion on behalf of those who are now harmed, and to celebrate and welcome those who are being born into this story.

As my father rejoiced in a fresh start, may we rejoice in our daily works with a sense of renewed spirit. May planet Earth rejoice in change for eternity.

> Megan E. Drimal, 35
> Originally a member of Friends Memorial Church, Indiana Yearly Meeting (FUM), later Clear Creek Meeting and Bloomington Friends Meeting (both Ohio Valley Yearly Meeting, FGC). No current affiliation.
> United States

block out the sun, turn on all the lights

> *mankind you've done it*

this is not playing god
god would not be so silly

to kill something just to meet it

wanting a why
> is no excuse

to destroy the what

> *mankind you haven't done it*

can is not should
> made is not understood

you have not done it at all

god would not be so silly

block out the sun
turn on all the lights

> kit wilson-yang, Camp NeeKauNis
> Canadian Yearly Meeting (FGC-FUM)
> Canada

Reflections on Values, Community, and Vocation

Matt. 22:34-40; 23:1-12

I love *The Message*, Eugene Peterson's version of the Bible. Listen to this: "Do you want to stand out? Then step down. Be a servant." Jesus really sounds like he's calling his disciples, and anyone who is reading this, into accountability. But I get tripped up on the contradiction. How can anyone expect to change lives, move mountains, become great, if they are "stepping down"? After all, we go to college—spending $40,000 a year on our liberal arts education—as a means of getting ahead, not as a way of putting other people's needs in front of our own. And yet Jesus asks us to do this very thing over and over again: to feed the hungry, to clothe the naked, to help those less fortunate, to be a servant. Those are good ideas. But by stepping down and serving, can we really hope to stand out? At first consideration, it sounds like a stretch.

Aren't contradictions fun? I love how I've spent my whole life simultaneously trying to stand out and fit in. I spent my high school and college years proving my individuality in various ways (complete with weird clothes and pink hair), while at the same time staying within the confines of what was socially "acceptable" to my peers. After all, you have to stand out the right way. And yet, I think I went through my whole undergraduate experience at Whittier College without ever really advertising a part of myself that would have *really* made me stand out in a positive way: the proclamation of my Quaker beliefs.

It's true! A real, honest-to-goodness Quaker student at Whittier College! We are a rare breed, it feels like. And yet this wasn't always the case. I run out of fingers when I list all the people I am related to that attended this Quaker-founded liberal arts college: my mom, both sets of grandparents, various aunts and uncles and great-aunts and great-uncles, even great-grandparents. They all have cross-connections to Whittier First Friends Church and to the college the church founded. And I like to think that this isn't purely because, way back when, Whittier College was one of the only four-year colleges near Whittier. I like to think that my family chose to attend this college for other reasons. I did.

I have attended the college three different times, collecting first a B.A. in English and art and then an M.A. in education. I am consistently impressed with the small class sizes and the fact that my teachers treat me like an individual, rather than like one of many hundreds of students they see every day. But, as nice as that is, there's something more to my school. I like to think it has to do with Whittier's Quaker roots.

It's a funny thing, being one of the only Quakers on a college campus that was founded by Quakers. I have always gotten to hear about the dear, sweet values "of our founders, the Quakers" during speeches and lectures, as if these Quakers were a mythical group of people. These Quakers seem remarkably similar to leprechauns, only instead of granting wishes, they had the peculiar habit of sitting in silence and waiting for God to talk to them. People at Whittier College like the idea of Quakers; they say such nice things about us and our values of equality and peace and integrity. And yet, they like us without really knowing us personally.

It's not really a surprise to me that the campus doesn't know us Quakers intimately. Statistically, most Quakers are introverts. We are definitely not like those Pharisees mentioned in the scripture. Many of us have the distinctive habit of "standing down," of preferring not to tell others how to live their lives, particularly without living our own lives as examples. Maybe I love contradictions, but not when it comes to what I say, versus what I do. It seems weird to me to lecture someone on how they should be living when I'm still working on how I should live. And when someone is honestly living with integrity, it just feels right that they would keep quiet about it. Living with integrity is not flashy or attention-getting.

But hearing this passage from Matthew frustrates me because I feel like I am failing just a little. When George Fox saw this great vision of people to be gathered in God's name, I am sure he wasn't thinking "and these people will be gathered because Cassie lives a quiet life, walking her walk in the least hypocritical way possible." How can it be that my school doesn't know anything about Quakers, when I've spent so much time there over the course of six years? This habit I have of being a closet Quaker really is a problem. My stepping down is *not* leading me to stand out, as much as *The Message* Jesus claims it will. And this is because stepping down is not the point. I need to step down to serve.

Even though Whittier College doesn't seem to know Quakers personally, I feel like my own Quaker identity has grown a lot while bopping back and forth between my experience with the college and my experience outside of the college. One of my favorite parts about being a Quaker is the understanding that we are always growing and always changing. How does that famous Quaker saying go? "We are never fully arrived. We are always on the way." Both the college, as well as this church, seems to understand this concept especially well. After all, we don't attend church (or college) to stay the same. We attend to grow.

I really appreciate how my church embraces people of all faith walks, believing in the worth of each individual. If I asked each attendee what their personal beliefs are in connection to their relationship to God, each answer would be different. And that would be great. We can't learn from each other and grow as individuals if we don't start out as individuals with our own faiths and our own beliefs.

In the end of the scripture, *The Message* translation reads, "If you puff yourself up, you'll get the wind knocked out of you. But if you're content to simply be yourself, your life will count for plenty." I plan to do this now, as I work at Whittier Friends School, our church's elementary school. There I am constantly being a servant while aiming to live a good example.

All of us are going in varying directions. As we work through the process of being people here on this earth, we will all doubtlessly grow. And as this happens, we need to share this growth with others, because without doing so, we aren't serving each other. We are just hiding in our own silent little boxes, stepping down without standing out.

Cassie Leigh Wright, 27
Whittier First Friends Church, Western Association of the Religious Society of Friends (FUM)
United States

From Pendle Hill to Capitol Hill: Quakers Working with Congress

I attend Quaker meeting every Sunday. I call myself a Quaker. I see my religion as an important part of my life. However, since I am not a spiritual person—I draw no deep fulfillment from sitting in silence; I have had no personal experience of the Spirit; I do not believe in God—I sometimes wonder what the purpose of my religious practice is.

A few weeks ago, I had the opportunity to take a week off school to do a project pursuing some interest that my high school couldn't cover with its curriculum, and this project week gave me some answers to my wondering. I worked at the Friends Committee on National Legislation (FCNL), a Quaker-led group which lobbies the United States federal government to move toward a better expression of the Quaker values of simplicity, equality, peace, community, and integrity. Specifically, FCNL seeks "a world free of war and the threat of war; a society with equity and justice for all; a community where every person's potential can be fulfilled; and an earth restored," as they say in their mission statement.

I was working under interns Christine Haider and Stephen Donohoe, who manage FCNL's relationship with its nationwide membership of Quakers (and others) working for social justice. Most of the week, I was contacting the most active segment of this membership: those who came to FCNL's annual meeting in Washington, D.C., and committed to do grassroots action, whether fund-raising, organizing the local constituents of a member of Congress to lobby for an FCNL goal, or trying to bring others in their community into the FCNL base. This might have been a dull exercise at another organization, but I finished nearly every phone call astounded at the activity and dedication of Friends all over the United States. Some were beginning a study of the arrangement of the world economy in comparison to our Quaker values, examining its justice and equity, or lack thereof. Others were active in the electoral politics of their area; one woman I spoke to was the Democratic Party chair of her Colorado county, and many had worked on the campaign to elect Barack Obama to the presidency. One apologized for her lack of attention to FCNL issues for the last few months; because she had been busy pushing the Virginia state government to end the death penalty. These are just a few of more than one hundred stories I heard.

I also saw the other side of what FCNL does—what they call the Hill side, the direct lobbying of members of Congress. It's called that because the members meet and have their offices on Capitol Hill. I sat in on a staff meeting at the beginning of the week that examined FCNL's behind-the-scenes victories of the previous two weeks: the House of Representatives included a twelve-fold increase in funding for weatherization of low-income homes in the stimulus bill. FCNL staffers had pushed the increase because it would help many of America's poorest and most vulnerable people not to freeze in chilly winters, would put people to work doing useful jobs, and would help reduce climate change by reducing fossil fuel use. They were thrilled at such a large increase. Another victory was the new president's declaration against torture. Some might question the last as an FCNL victory: Hadn't Obama campaigned on ending torture? How could we take credit?

FCNL felt that it could, at least in part. As they saw it, their work (starting several years ago) to organize religious opposition to torture was what pushed the issue to the forefront of the nation's dialogue and created it as a campaign issue that Obama took hold of. This story opens another important issue around FCNL's lobbying work: To what extent does the political party or administration in power matter to FCNL's ability to win on its issues? If John McCain had won the election, it seems unlikely that a similar declaration would have come out of the White House, regardless of FCNL's actions. On the other hand, without the moral pressure FCNL and other faith groups helped build, would Obama have made ending torture such a priority? It is impossible to say, but it goes to show that no one group or person can claim complete responsibility for what happens in an institution as complex as the United States federal government.

During my week with FCNL, I learned more than I had known about how exactly lobbyists influence government. Many Americans think that it's accomplished through the simple tactic we often hear about indicted lobbyists using: bribery in one form or another. However, the vast majority of lobbyists influence Congress simply by informing them of the facts around an issue and possible solutions to problems. Congress often has a scarcity of useful information about the thousands of different complex issues that they have to decide on, so the best role lobbyists can play is to provide information to Congress about how to govern the nation in the public interest. Applying this tactic to the prevention of war, FCNL had me call the Foreign Policy staffers of members of the House Committee on Foreign Affairs—not to tell them how to vote, or to bribe or threaten them, but to invite them to a panel discussion on how to effectively prevent war through funding diplomacy and foreign aid. The information that members gained at the well-attended meeting will probably make it into future budgets, and the resultant diplomacy could prevent wars and save lives.

So how did my work at FCNL answer any questions about me and my religious practice? I got to see what I am part of. FCNL and I are both part of a stream of Friends activism that stretches back and (hopefully) forward in history, covering several continents and many issues. Some see Quakers' greatest activism in nineteenth-century abolitionism, or twentieth-century conscientious objection to war, but I increasingly think that it is occurring now. The Quakers in my community and around the world are courageously confronting the most serious issues that face humanity: nuclear weapons, war, torture, climate change, racism, inequality, capital punishment, genocide, and homophobia (to name a few), and we continue to have influence disproportionate to our tiny numbers.

If I do not believe in God, I do believe in our struggle. If I have had no personal experience of the Spirit, I have had a personal experience of that change that Friends can lovingly bring to human society. And although I find no great fulfillment in sitting in silence, I certainly don't dislike it—and I am sustained by the lives that speak, and have spoken for centuries, out of that silent tradition.

> *Russell Weiss-Irwin, 18*
> *Cambridge Friends Meeting, New England Yearly Meeting*
> *(FGC-FUM)*
> *United States*
>
> A version of this article was published by FCNL on their intern blog, "Of Peace and Politics," on February 20, 2009.

To Be Friends with Animals*

A spark from the One
In every creature.
You give us of your self,
All of us, without exception.
Give us likewise of your peace.

A concern that I have carried and been engaged with as a Quaker is care for our fellow creatures. Creation and nature also lie near my heart, but this text will focus on animals.

We Quakers say that God's Light is in every person. It's no great leap to think that the spark of God's essence or the inner Christ can also be found in other creatures. Maybe it can be found in all living things, or at least in all conscious life. Personally, it's hard for me to believe that only people have this inner spark. I believe that both humans and animals are shaped by God's hand and that we received the inner spark when God blew his spirit in us and gave us life.

Is there a difference between the inner Light of humans and that of animals? I believe that they are identical in their essence, but can vary in their function. I believe that animals didn't break their close relation to God in the Garden of Eden, like humans did, so the animals live in harmony with their inner godliness and so live morally. People, on the other hand, have turned from God and don't live in the same constant accord with the inner Light, but yearn to. Thus, the Light acts as a guide to community with God and to what is right and wrong. Even though people and animals have a spark of God's essence we are not the same as God. Only a part of us is in God's image. Otherwise, we are different than God—God is much more than that essence and transcends it.

I don't intend to argue tediously about whether humans or animals are nearer God, just that we have a small piece of the Great One.

Hear, Oh God,
Care for my suffering siblings,
Animals in nature and animals in captivity.
Help us people to see the consequences of our behavior.
Help animals to endure and to be freed.

As a pacifist, I want to avoid violence against a person because that would cause violence to God himself, that piece of God in the person. If animals also have that inner Light, our pacifism must extend to include animals. It follows that we don't have the right to kill them with intent—to eat them, to wear their skin, or to use them for research. Naturally I feel that way because I'm interested in minimizing animal suffering that comes from large-scale animal husbandry, but also because of the religious reason that I don't want to harm my fellow creatures that have Christ's Light. There are many links between my commitment to animals and my commitment to nature. One is that by not eating my fellow creatures I preserve God's nature; that preserves natural resources for producing the animals' own food.

It seems important for Quakers to attempt to practice a Christlike life, to try to live as He taught. Jesus broke many of the norms of His time; among others, He expanded the idea of "our neighbors" to include not just our own family or ethnic group, but also the stranger and "least of us." Who is the "least" and stranger that we should see as our neighbor? Yes, not just children and the poor—animals are also a good example. They are relatively powerless against people and cannot make their voices heard when we oppress them—who will take care of God's "least" creatures, our neighbors, in their oppression if not I who follow Jesus and am Quaker?

Highest on Earth,
lowest in heaven—,
we humans.
Lowest on earth,
highest in heaven—
you sparrows.
First on earth,
last in heaven—
my people.
Last on earth,
first in heaven—
my sparrows.

But what about the fact that they ate meat in the Bible? Even if the Holy Spirit is an important authority for me as a Quaker, so is the Bible. I think two things about the Bible on this subject. Before the fall from grace, Adam and Eve lived in harmony with the animals as vegetarians in the Garden of Eden. God told Adam and Eve in the first book of Moses: "I give you all of the fruit-bearing plants of the earth and all trees for their fruit, that you may eat from them." This relationship with animals and their food is an ideal that we should try to return to; it was the original balance of creation. As a Quaker, I am not satisfied to just believe in that; I must work toward it in my own life. I believe that even though the Bible speaks of other uses for animals during the time it was being written, the Holy Spirit inspires me to behave differently today. Possibly God finds it more important to lead us today to care for the animals than it was during biblical times. There are, after all, many more human stomachs to fill today than there were then with the population growth, and moreover animal husbandry is now done on a large scale. Those factors make it more important to not eat animals today than in biblical times. Today's animal production leads to much more animal suffering than in the past.

Bee, horse and shepherd—
We are Your children,
Jesus friend,
each other's siblings,
different but the same,
equally loved in Your eyes.

I'm glad that I'm not the first and only Quaker who is concerned about animals. On the contrary, this concern is broader in the Quaker community than in many other Christian communities. In the seventeenth century, Quakers had John Woolman, who preached that we should show mercy rather than cruelty to animals. He himself avoided using a whip to hurry horses. I'm proud to find myself in the same tradition as such a pioneer. Even if many Quakers, then and now, have been role models in their concern for animal welfare, there is still more work to do in the community. A concern for animals is still behind more classic Quaker ideas like the Peace Testimony. But, of course, there's no reason why we can't be engaged on several issues; the only constraint could be a lack of time. I would like to see the animal rights issue move from the periphery to the front of the agenda. The fact that I'm grateful to see it on the agenda at all is something that needs to change. Thoughtfulness about animals must become Quakerly through seeing what ideas the inner Light finds for consequences.

Slavery didn't end overnight with Quakers, though they were pioneers in that realm. Aren't there enough webs now that we no longer need animal-derived food on our dinner tables and at our communal meals? And not just, like today, as an alternative to vegetarian food? Apart from vegetarian eating, there are many other issues around animal welfare that the Quaker community should work more actively on. Today there are projects in many lands for building schools and peace and easing poverty. I would like to see more projects that deal with improving use of animals for transportation, banning farms where people misuse animals and projects for preserving biological diversity. When we collect money and support other organizations' projects, we can work with humanitarian organizations like Djurskyddet Sverige, Royal Society for the Prevention of Cruelty of Animals (RSPCA), and People for the Ethical Treatment of Animals (PETA). Working for human rights and animal rights can expand to include work for animal's rights.

Love me, Christ,
as you love the animals.

What can Quakers and others who share my concern for animal welfare do? One important thing to emphasize is that I as a Quaker want to work in a peace tradition with these questions. That means that I won't use force or threats against people to reach my goals. With love and activism, I'll spread my message. Those who contribute to the oppression of animals, on the other hand, are not my enemies but individuals who deserve respect even if I don't sympathize with their behavior.

I'll write letters to the editor [of newspapers] for the sake of animals. It's hard to know how much impact those letters have, but that's an easy way to work on behalf of animals. Furthermore, it's easy to be involved broadly on behalf of animal welfare issues—from circuses to animal research. Something that is also hard to measure in terms of impact is street demonstrations. When I began to work on behalf of animals, I went to many demonstrations on the street and at mink farms, but today I prefer more religiously grounded methods. For example, I participated in a Christmas prayer action with likeminded friends outside a slaughterhouse. Around Christmastime we prayed for animals at the slaughterhouse and lit candles—which wasn't completely without media attention, a nice secondary effect. I hold readings on eco- and animal-rights theology in various halls and, as a devotion, I usually pray that animals' sufferings should be eased.

Let the inner Light
that is in all creatures

light up
and help us understand
that the Light is in us all.

When, as a teenager, I began to have a concern for animals, it was primarily a philosophical and secular cause but, with time, it became more religiously motivated, motivated by a great love for animals. I believe that it is important that one's activism is not just based in practical convictions that peoples' use of animals is wrong. I believe that activism connected with God and love of creation leads to an activism that reaches to our innermost depths. The protection of animals must go hand in hand with the desire to follow God's will and wonder over his creation.

Since I met my wife, Louise, who is a zoologist with a focus on animal welfare and a great love of animals, I've gotten better grounding for my work. From having been an engaged city-dweller, I now live out in the country with nature and have many animals in the yard. Living near animals and nature leads to a natural fellowship with them and points to a deeply satisfying plan. The more I live in harmony with God's creation, the more I feel a mission to protect them.

Your creation
Is connected with you,
Is connected with each other,
Is connected with the beginning and the end.
Never separated from you,
not the greatest and also not the least.
Your creation

> *Andreas Hernander Brand, 29*
> *Sweden Yearly Meeting*
> *Sweden*
>
> Translated from the Swedish by Kori Heavner
>
> Three of the prayers used above were published in *Alla Varelser Ropar till dig: en djurvänlig bönbok* (*All the creatures are calling to you: an animal friendly book of prayer*), edited by Annika Spalde and Tobias Herrström, 2008.
>
> * Editor's note: The author of this piece expresses a perspective that there is that of God in animals, which may be familiar to some Friends while bizarre to others. Internationally, many contemporary Friends are vegetarian or vegan, while many also eat meat and some are even pastoralists who make their livelihood from animal husbandry. How might we engage in this conversation together?

Unspoken Truth

My shoulders are bare
My skirt handmade
We are walking down an unfamiliar street
Our sandals slap the pavement
To the same
Rhythm
In the same
Repetitive
Beat
My heart is alive
My head held high
Because we are on our way to celebrate Pride

When coming from the right
We hear him yell
"Do you know you are going to hell?"

And my jaw sets
I look past my dark sunglasses
Beyond the protection of my hair
To see a figure
In alabaster boots
Taking the shape of a man with too much to hide
Clinging to a worn-out
Misspelled sign

I can only sigh

But he speaks straight to me
With an aching grin
"You know there is no room in my God's heaven for rebellious women."

I want to scream

That is not what I learned
Sitting in a circle
Sitting in the silence
Sitting with my mother

That was not the message
Whispered to me
In soft sung lullabies before nap

Not the God with the son who loved me and
"All the little children of the world, red and yellow, black and white . . ."
Precious

I heard about a man who said
You treat me as you treat the lowest of men
Those people you call sinners
You are in no place to condemn
You will be judged as
You judge them

Barelegged babies
On handmade blankets
Taught me to be humble and cherish
What is precious

You frighten children
With threats of damnation
Worry them sick with the direst of consequences
Failing to mention
Simplicity–Integrity–Equality–Peace
And the greatest of all–Love

While I quietly hummed myself to sleep
With songs about candles
That would not go out
Would continue to shine
Despite how hard
You continue to try
To snuff it out
To snuff out me

I can see the blood on your hands
Up to your elbows
That you cannot scrub clean
With the best of intention

To cover your shame you build
Million dollar statues
Of a man who hated money
So maybe he won't see

Maybe it
Will be seen
From the highway

Divinity does not care
If girls hold hands
And boys hug each other tight
Because in all this mess
All love is good and comes with
Its very own inalienable rights

I propose it is not God
But you who sit
In fear and judge
And that is Truth

But the man in alabaster boots
Is not Power
And all he can hope to do
Is break my stride

And since I cannot find my words
I let my sandals slap their rhythm
Stronger than my voice
And carry me to Pride*

Micky Jo Myers, 25
Englewood Friends Meeting, Indiana Yearly Meeting (FUM)
United States

* Editor's note: Pride parades are annual events, which happen in
many cities in North America and the world, celebrating lesbian, gay,
bisexual, and transgender (LGBT) culture.

Friends Leaders Must Be Generous (excerpted)

The Friends, Quakers, believe in staying with peace. Without peace
they cannot survive. When the Quakers notice that there is no peace in
some of the places, they must make plans to resolve the dispute and make
people stay [in] peace.

They also believe in simplicity. This allows the Quakers to concentrate on the seeking of truth so that they may avoid being distracted.
This simplicity they may advocate in languages and behaviors. Truth

became their way of life for them. This truth would lead them to integrity; often it was a conviction that arose from worship.

The problem they have is that they lack justice [to] share powers equally. This may make the Quakers break up. When they get in power it is not easy for them to withdraw, yet there are youth who need this leadership. The Friends leaders must be generous.

> *Gerson Khayongo, 17*
> *East Africa Yearly Meeting of Friends (North) (FUM)*
> *Kenya*

Army for Quakers

I was born and raised Quaker, and at the age of sixteen decided that to truly understand my religion's strong opposition to military action and, more importantly, my own fears of the military, I needed to join and experience it for myself. I needed to face my fears to really overcome them. Once I had decided that I needed to do this, I asked myself a question: *What do you need to do to a person to make them kill another human being?* I also wanted to know who joins the military, and I wanted to dispel the classic stereotypes of the typical army dudes and wanted to really meet people. With questions in mind and a heart on a mission to conquer my fears, I set out.

How everything felt then and how it all feels now are very different. The application process was a joke and they helped me, and many others, cheat. The written test felt like a grade-six math test. The personal interview was filled with questions that all answered themselves, as the army wanted to hear it. The physical exam was the bare bones of fitness and when I didn't quite reach the minimum requirement, they just lied and wrote me in at the lowest possible mark. Looking back on it now, the most noteworthy part was that I left the application centre feeling like I had truly accomplished something and that I had made new friends. I was already one of the gang.

My basic training was twenty days on weekends over four months. I was the youngest in the course and the oldest was fifty-four. Most of the guys were between eighteen and thirty. There were thirty-two of us, all men. The weekends were hard, and right away I hated them. It was cold, uncomfortable, and harsh. It was the first evening when my sergeant asked, "We don't have any hippie vegetarians, do we?" From then on, I was singled out as the hippie vegetarian. Yet they were accommodating and brought me special vegetarian meals every day both at lunch and dinner. Also, I was not ostracized for my differences, quite the opposite. People went out of their way to bring me into the melting pot and make me see how foolish and unimportant my beliefs were.

I hated those weekends so much. Many times I considered dropping out and quitting or just taking off and disappearing. I stuck it out and saw it through. To this day, people ask me if I liked being in the army and the answer is always no. It was a valuable experience that I will always carry with me. I learned how to work as part of a unit and how to be efficient. The things we could get done in thirty minutes were truly amazing. But all to what end? Over and over they reminded us that everything we did was to help us destroy our enemies.

One evening, near the end of our course, our section (which was ten of us) sat down together and our sergeant asked each of us why we were there. Seven of the ten opened by saying "To play with guns!" and then went on to elaborate. This was a little nerve wracking as the following weekend we were to head out to the shooting range with live ammunition. Of the ten, five were becoming police officers; three were there because their father and their father's father were in the army. One needed a good steady job, and there was me with my wacky religion and self-discovery.

After our last weekend I dyed my hair bright green. When I began the process to quit, I got more than a few strange looks. My warrant officer refused to sign my papers until I did something about my hair. When I offered to go home, shave my head, and be back in thirty minutes, he understood how bad I wanted out and signed the form, "just to get me out of his sight!" Another old man, maybe in his seventies or older, grabbed my arm as I walked by and said, "If you were in my army, you'd be shot!" Good thing I was in the Canadian army and not his! I emerged from the Canadian army on July fifth, hair intact and free from bullet holes. It was a happy day.

I had all my stereotypes of the military reinforced rather than dispelled. My sergeant would yell at us until red in the face, my warrant officer referred to handkerchiefs as snot rags and sleeping bags as fart sacks. And although they trained us to be efficient machines, there was so much material waste of food and other supplies.

As for my big question, how do you train people to kill, I saw standard brainwash at work. Low sleep, low food, zero time alone. Also they create a false sense of community. I call it false because if you removed the one common goal, defeating the enemy, there would be nothing. You never truly meet these people you are with. And it works. It worked on me. I caught myself at the end of a long weekend thinking to myself in a disappointed tone, "Ah darn, now I have to go home and think for myself again."

As for my fears, I did not overcome them as I hoped I would, but came to understand them better. I am still terrified of the fact that I was able to give into that brainwash. I am still frightened of the efficiency with which my government seeks to destroy the enemy. And I now see that a group can never change from the inside because of one individual. To have enough power to make change, that person would have to have been a part of the system for so long that they too would buy into it.

I am changed for the experiences I had and am glad to have the stories to share. I learned of my fears and I challenge you to learn of yours.

Kelly Ackerman, 24
Prairie Monthly Meeting, Canadian Yearly Meeting (FGC-FUM)
Canada

Living as a Friend in Korea

Valuing Diversity

In my home country, South Korea, being a Christian is not a proud thing because they often take an unfriendly attitude toward other religions. It hasn't changed much until now. I was raised as a Presbyterian until twenty but gave up going to church. Christian people, including me, were the least-peaceful creatures to my eyes.

Quaker community came to me when I was thirty. Being among the silent meeting for worship has been revolutionary and radical, but requested my awakening all the time. I have met some Friends from diverse countries. In 2005, I was at the World Gathering of Young Friends in the United Kingdom. That was my first experience to see other young Friends abroad. At that time, severe tension in my body and mind was painful. I might have been overwhelmed with the corporate spirituality of the gathering. The first international gathering let me know I'm one of diverse Friends in the world.

After the gathering, I went to Pendle Hill in the United States. Living in a Quaker community was another gift. I feel still connected with the friends I met there. Again, I was able to feel that I'm part of the whole Religious Society of Friends. The word love has become a cliché these days, but the experience of Pendle Hill was love itself. We were from different cultures but respected each other. There was beauty of diversity there. I consider Pendle Hill friends as my family as much as my biological one. It's very clear that we are one.

Since I got back to my home country from Pendle Hill, I have gotten married and moved far from my meeting. Whenever my husband and I have a meeting for worship, just the two of us, we feel connected with all my Friends.

Respecting Minority

As a psychological counselor, I love my job and meet people with the heart and mind of a Friend. I respect them and try to find their own strength instead of labeling them. Being a child of deaf parents, I have a dream to enjoy a specialty in counseling for the deaf. Minority is beautiful.

When I was young, I didn't know how much the deaf need special caring. My father passed away fifteen years ago and my mother is getting old. I started to relearn sign language because I had forgotten most of what I knew.

Paying attention to alienated people is very Quakerly. Each person is unique, precious, a child of God. My life will be focused on that belief. The Quaker community is also very small compared with other major religious groups. Even though Quaker is part of Christianity, I feel Friends have a different way of living from other Christians and I love the Quaker way of life. In my country, people almost don't know who Quakers are and some Christians consider Quakers to be pagans. Despite their criticism, I love what Quakers say. Particularly this: *There's something sacred in all people. All people are equal before God.*

Caring for Nature

Before I became a Friend, I was ignorant of living with nature. I'm still not good at making friends with nature but trying to be a good friend to her. The friends I have met are people of nature. They love and take care of nature. I can't forget the beauty of my Friends' beautiful gardens. Quakers might have known that nature heals human beings.

My husband and I live in a semi-country neighborhood. We moved here from a noisy city recently. Trees, water, birds, various plants, fish, stars, and the moon. We bow to them when we encounter them to show our respect for them. Busy life snatches our right to live peacefully. At our wedding, we promised to balance between work and rest and take care of the earth through a simple life. I realized that there are many ways to help heal the earth. Nature heals us while we human beings hurt her.

As I'm connected with my Quaker friends all over the world, I'm united with nature because I'm part of her. True religion leads to respect for the earth and all life upon it.

Bokyom Jin
Seoul Meeting, Korea Yearly Meeting
South Korea

Social Commentary, oil painting, Amelia Carlie, 17, Orlando Monthly Meeting, Southeastern Yearly Meeting (FGC-FUM), United States

Tukadumishe Amani

Ningejua tangu kale, Kwamba kuna uchafuzi
Nisingekuja milele, mahali pa uchokozi
Mahuluku awe mpole, akapata uchongezi
Tukadumishe amani, maendeleo twapate.

Kabila na maumbile, uyaleta ubaguzi
Kuwa sisi tukombele, wachache kupata kazi
Ufukara teletele, dunia na ujambazi
Tukadumishe amani, maendeleo twapate.

Vilio na ukelele, uyayyma kwa shambulizi
Kwa bunduki na shiale, vinamaliza vizazi
Damu zamwagika tele, watu kuwa wakimbizi
Tukadumishe amani, maendeleo twapate.

Mola kwa maasi yale, shetani wake ongozi
Zikazuka myingi ndwele, ukimwi, pumu na tezi
Tuombe mungu jinale, atuletee ujazi
Tukadumishe amani, maendeleo twapate.

> *Lopeto Peter*
> *Lodwar Monthly Meeting, East Africa Yearly Meeting of Friends*
> *(North) (FUM)*
> *Kenya*

We Cling to Peace

I wish I'd known earlier there would be a fracas,
I wouldn't have come to this chaotic place at all.
The very soil, normally gentle, has become malicious,
Yet we cling to peace, we progress.

Tribe and stature bring discrimination
So that even we who are educated are without jobs.
So much poverty, a world of robbery,
Yet we cling to peace, we progress.

Crying and wailing follow the attacker,
Generations are finished by rifle and arrow.

Too much bloodshed, people displaced,
Yet we cling to peace, we progress.

God, for that rebellion, has left Satan in charge,
while diseases emerge and spread—AIDS, asthma, tumors.
We pray in His name, to bring us abundance,
While we cling to peace, we progress.

> *Lopeto Peter*
> *Lodwar Monthly Meeting, East Africa Yearly Meeting of Friends*
> *(North) (FUM)*
> *Kenya*
>
> Editor's note: Translated by Judith Ngoya and Eden Grace, Friends
> United Meeting Africa Ministries Office, Kisumu, Kenya

In Solidarity We Stand Together

We had been singing all day, all week, every round and call-and-answer song that anyone could dig up from the bottom of their mind.

Almost sixteen and I was still so shy, my voice all trembly and quiet when I thought anyone could hear, especially when it came to music. Singing, to me, had always been something I did in my room with the door shut when the rest of my family was out, and this was a revolution in itself—guitars and folk songs and fifteen people standing in a circle, each raising their voice in song.

In solidarity we stand together,
With the Mirrar people on their land . . .

It was the first time I heard a protest song outside of records from the Sixties.

I had always liked the social conscience of Quakers. I loved their work for peace, and that my local meeting held a group of adults who were hopeful and working for change instead of just expecting the youth to change the world for them.

But I had always felt that Quakers were a group of people who had been around in the time when nonviolent change belonged, and had managed to hold on to those ideas. I was living in a time that I didn't quite belong in and no one my age cared about changing the world.

These people did.

No more uranium, leave it in the ground . . .

Over those ten days my voice became bigger as night after night we sang round after round, song after song. Sitting in the bathrooms for hours bouncing harmony off concrete. Splashing in sunset waves with our voices raised until dark. I taught people how to play chords on the guitar. One evening we stood in a circle at the nearby marina, dressed in daggy clothes that we had been wearing all week and not caring one bit, and sang our songs for the world outside.

We are singing this song for Jabiluka . . .

It was not from another time. It was not from early Quakers, or the Sixties, or anywhere else.

It was from us. A group of people my age, from my time, believing that we could make a change.

A few weeks after camp was over, some of us from Young Friends camp arranged to meet at a protest rally about the Jabiluka uranium mine. I caught the train the long way to Fremantle with Amy-from-camp, twitchy, visions of violent chanting and batons from the news vivid in my mind.

When we got there, I found those images to be far from real, and after the quiet speeches we filed onto the streets for a peaceful march. Partway through, walking in my new little mob of Young Friends, a murmur filed through the group.

They needed somebody to lead the song.

Grace, who knew someone from the organising crew, looked at me, nodded, and called out to her friend, "Alexa can do it!" pointing to where I stood.

For a moment, all I could hear was my heartbeat.

Grace smiled, expectant, encouraging. Amy, who was to become my closest friend for the next ten years of my life, squeezed my hand. My voice shook and I trembled, but I took a deep breath.

In solidarity we stand together . . .

The crowd echoed my words.

With the Mirrar people on their land . . .

And as they did, my voice grew bigger.

No more uranium, leave it in the ground . . .
Kakadu is sacred, Kakadu is sacred . . .

And in that moment, barely sixteen, tucked up hand-in-hand with this group of my people, I knew the world could be bigger and my voice could be stronger than I had ever felt before.

Alexa Taylor
Australia Yearly Meeting
Australia

This piece was written for the 2009 Backhouse Lecture in Australia Yearly Meeting.

Another Culture that Transcends All Cultures

Culture affects my faith because, as a Burundian Quaker or Friend, the way I talk, I walk, I do, I wear, or relate to people has to match the way my society expects me to be. But the most important is that I know that there is another culture that transcends all cultures. That culture is the biblical culture. What I do has to be acceptable to God rather than acceptable to people. Christians all over the world are the same. Christ makes us all one family. Technology affects my faith because if I want to send a message to my Christian colleagues abroad, I use the Internet which is the quickest way to communicate; television programs affect my faith because my children copy different things they see on TV.

Personally I believe only in one God, the son Jesus, and the Holy Spirit, not in mysticism. I was born in a Christian family. I pray to God only because it is the only way to speak with Him. I know that God is the God who takes care of my life.

Joyce Mattimama, 40
Burundi Yearly Meeting
Burundi

The Temptation to Surrender

During the 2008 presidential race I was pretty vocal about my support of Barack Obama on my blog. Because of this I was called out by another Christian blogger for my endorsement. The problem, as he saw it, was that by endorsing a candidate it appeared as though I gave in to the dominate powers of the world. The answer that the blogger gave (in response to my own position) was that the most radical and Christ-like response a Christian can take is to resist the temptation to give into the ideologies of the world.

In other words, the implied message was "withhold your vote!" If voting is symptomatic of American citizens being drones within empire, then I can see how this is a good solution, especially when we look at how often the church finds itself wrapped up in the current political rhetoric and ideologies of the day. Of course, at another level, when we take this to its ultimate conclusions aren't we all, already, implicated in the empire at some level? Doesn't "withhold" in reality function more like "I surrender!" or "I give up!"?

In my view, withdrawal such as this (or coded language that passivity can be wrapped up in) is, in the end, giving into the dominant powers of the world. Modernity has created a small public space for dissenters, as long as you stay within those bounds of dissent you won't break any laws (or actually dissent from anything). My feeling as a Quaker is that surrender is the exact opposite of how we should respond faithfully in the world. So then, how might we think about this?

One Sunday, on a drive home from a friend's birthday party, my wife and I listened to Krista Tippett's interview with evangelical leaders Chuck Colson, Greg Boyd, and Shane Claiborne. They billed it as three generations of evangelical leaders and what they see as the role of Christians in the public sphere. It's a big question. It has always been a big question, and it goes all the way back to Jesus' own crucifixion. Wasn't Peter's attempt to draw his sword when Jesus was arrested an attempt to institute Christendom (through force)? Peter gave in to the temptation to surrender to the (violent) politics of this world. I don't really fault Peter for this. I think Peter is a lot like us Christians. He was really earnest and committed, and wanted to do right no matter what it would take. But, as we know, Peter's solution was not Jesus' way.

Theologian John Howard Yoder argues in his book, *For the Nations*, that the role of the church in relationship to culture and politics must be rooted in Jeremiah 29:7 (NRSV): "But seek the welfare of the city where

I have sent you into exile, and pray to the LORD on its behalf, for in its welfare you will find your welfare." When the book of Jeremiah was written, the Hebrew people were living in exile under the Babylonian empire, yet God called them to live in such a way that the very neighborhoods and cities would be better because of their presence.

In the same way, the church as an exiled people always rubs up against the powers of the world, yet it doesn't retreat from it, it constantly seeks the peace of the kingdom within those places. The Hebrew people remained distinctive during their time in exile by compiling the Hebrew canon and worshiping YHWH. But their distinctiveness did not preclude actively dialoguing with and seeking to transform their world; in fact, it is what freed them from the dominant ideologies of their world, enabling them to be creative in the culture with which they worked. According to John Yoder, this was the same distinctiveness/dialogue pattern that Jesus exemplified and the church is to embody.

So then what about Friends? What are our political options? Is it okay for an evangelical (Quaker) to endorse a political candidate? The answer follows this bifurcation: I think the answer is both yes and a no. This is why the Quaker position is still so radical and closely aligned with Yoder's distinctiveness/dialogue. The Friends Church has been activist-oriented from its very inception: Think of letter-writing campaigns to change unjust laws; the many Friends, including George Fox and James Nayler, who rejected war and violence; those who worked for prison reform and helped to end slavery; those involved with women's suffrage; and those who have paid the price for practicing peacemaking in Iraq. All of these things were political acts done by Christians who believed it wasn't enough to just vote or not vote, but who really believed that the church is itself a (counter) political institution in the world. Change comes through the way we live everyday, it comes by way of our communities "seeking the peace of the city" where we live.

The catch was that these Friends accepted that the only way to do kingdom ethics was through the kind of nonviolence and love of enemy practiced by Jesus. Take the example of Pennsylvania. Here was a state that was founded not simply on Quaker principles, but on what Quakers saw as kingdom politics. For three generations this experiment went on in a way that would end up shaping much of what is assumed within America today. During the French and Indian War, the Quakers allowed themselves to be voted out of the assembly. This form of surrender came not before, but after many political actions were taken, after all other avenues and possibilities for peaceful resolutions had been exhausted. When the only other option left was to resort to the rules of the world, the

Quakers then stepped down. The commitment to nonviolence does not manifest itself in withdrawal but utilizing creativity and imagination, seeking out every possible avenue for a resolution, and then being willing to humbly sacrifice oneself if violence is the only option left. This is a lot different than doing whatever it takes to make sure your platform or political position is upheld at all costs. This is why Yoder argues that Pennsylvania is a successful picture of nonviolent political involvement.

In this way I can see how not voting and those who vote on one or two issues are in a similar boat. Both are a form of surrender. The first is surrender by way of building on the lingering assumption of Christendom. The internal dialog sounds like this: *If I vote, it is equal to my believing that God will usher His kingdom in through this candidate. A vote is my being involved too deeply in the world; therefore, since this is obviously wrong, I should not vote.* The other is to surrender to political hegemony, which co-opts moral issues away from the kingdom of God (and the church) and ultimately reduces faith to voting blocks. The internal dialog might sound like this: *There are issues that are important, but abortion (or homosexuality, or the environment) is the most important issue, no one could even pretend to have faith unless they voted in this particular way.*

Rather than entertaining these positions, we can avoid the temptation to surrender by planting our hope firmly on our citizenship in the kingdom and the hope that God can work in all aspects of culture.

We are called to live out the kingdom in every area and moment of life, which means that even when we participate in empires we do it in a way that plays by God's rules, not the rules of the world. Let us take the risk of choosing sides and coming down on the issues not by how we vote, but by how we embody them in our church communities. Let us not be afraid to stand for the kingdom of God, even if it means we will get voted (or thrown) out of town (again).

C. Wess Daniels, 31
Camas Friends Church, Northwest Yearly Meeting (EFCI)
United States

A Continued Conversation

And Jesus said, "No, wait, pray this way."

To the inexplicably brilliant force that created the universe,
and who continually allows us glimpses
of herself when we least expect them:

> Wow. You are
> Holy
> You are so holy, even your name is holy.
> There is no way I can capture you inside
> A single word.

> I can only hope that we will let your Kingdom come.
> That when we see you—
> That when you are an old casino man,
> Or dandelion heads before a lawnmower,
> Or wedding rings melted into gold teeth—
> We scoop you up
> Stick you in our mouths
> And carry you along until your earthy, toothy will is done
> And we are loving each other
> > in a Kingdom of this world.

> But let's be real, God:
> Until then, we just need to eat. Consistently.
> Give us our Snak-Paks
> Our caffeine,
> Nicotine,
> And our hugs.
> Give us bungee cords and warm tea and humanitarian aid,
> And love us anyway when we inevitably abandon the tea on a
> > windowsill—
> We'll do our best to forgive Arthur,
> Who rushed it over without sugar.

> Also: please, for the love of all that is holy,
> Be kind and lead us away from things we have little traction in resisting.
> You know how we are.
> You know that I could not say no to a chocolate chip cookie
> If it meant saving every endangered species
> In North America

From extinction.
We're going to need your help,
We're going to need to see those dandelion heads
At just the right moment in order
To be successfully delivered from our own sweet evils.

But it's worth it, O Universe-thing,
Because this part doesn't need any revision:
   When we see
       the Kingdom   and the Power   and the Glory,
Peeking out from beneath tired, hardened hands,
They are you. Yours.
I mean,
    w

     o

      w.
We're open!

Cara Curtis, 22
Adelphi Monthly Meeting, Baltimore Yearly Meeting (FGC-FUM)
United States

Into the Darkness, photograph, Ben Watts, 25, Aotearoa/New Zealand Yearly Meeting, New Zealand

Deep Oceans of
Darkness and Light

Sufferings

Why Do Bad Things Happen to Good People?

Some time ago my wife and I, for an unknown reason, were watching a certain fundamentalist TV preacher. This person would show a clip from the news mentioning efforts for peace between Israel and Palestine and then he would cut to another clip showing that a few days later a storm hit the United States somewhere. He did this several times, commenting on a news clip about efforts for peace in Israel and then cutting to a natural disaster somewhere in the United States.

This TV preacher was trying to make the point that God was punishing the United States for seeking peace between the Israelis and the Palestinians. The storms, according to this person, were acts of Divine punishment.

This is retribution theology. Retribution theology says that when we disobey God, God causes some disaster to happen in order to punish us. So, God seeks retribution for things that displease God.

After the show my wife and I went to bed and immediately fell asleep. In the middle of the night we awoke to hear our dog running around in the living room. My wife drowsily went to correct him, but found that he was chasing something around in the dark. She called back to me: "Jon, there's something flying around in here!"

I hopped out of bed and went to investigate. I turned on the lights to see a bat flying around our living room! We caught our dog and shut ourselves in our bedroom and then tried to go back to sleep, deeply unnerved that there was a potentially rabid bat flying around in our apartment. We felt trapped. We had no way of catching the bat, so we decided to wait until morning when, hopefully, it would be asleep. When morning came I slowly and stealthily emerged out of the bedroom and began searching our apartment. Finally I saw a black, hairy figure hanging upside down in a decorative bird house in the kitchen. I quickly threw a towel over the bird house and carried it onto the porch and let the bat go.

As my wife and I were talking about what had happened, we jokingly thought that maybe God was punishing us for watching this fundamentalist TV personality. Perhaps God had sent a plague of bats upon us in retribution!

I say this jokingly because the same mixed-up theology the TV preacher was using to prove his point could just as easily be used against him! God does not expect us to look at every event in our lives (every calamity and every illness) as punishment for something we have done in the past.

At the beginning of John (chapter 9), Jesus and his disciples were walking along when they discovered a man who was blind from birth. According to popular ancient tradition, when a malady struck a person it was because that person had committed a sin and God was punishing the person. That's retribution theology. Since this man was blind *from birth*, the disciples wanted to know where the sin that caused the illness came from. They asked Jesus whether the man had sinned or whether his parents had sinned.

Ancient tradition held that a fetus could sin before it was born, and so the sin committed in the womb could have brought about God's punishment of blindness. The other possibility, according to Jesus' disciples, would be to place the sinfulness on the man's parents. Exodus 20:5 says that God punishes children for the "sin of the fathers." Could the parents' sin cause the son's blindness, the disciples wondered? The disciples saw only two possibilities as to why this man would be blind from birth: Either he sinned in the womb or one of his parents sinned. The disciples blamed this man and his parents for the blindness. They said he was blind because of sin.

The question that the disciples raised is a profound question and a very old question: Why do bad things happen to good people? The disciples blamed the blind man for his infirmity, they thought the man's blindness was a result of sin and God had willed the blindness as punishment.

It is a natural tendency for people to look for a cause or a greater purpose in the face of tragedy. Perhaps the disciples thought that a lack of calamity in their lives was proof that they were good people and their goodness was a guarantee protecting them from illness and premature death. Likewise, the thought is common today that if we are good people then we will be kept free from tragedy. However, the disciples' lives prove this assumption false. Certainly the disciples were good, faithful people, and yet most of the disciples died in exile or as martyrs. They were tortured and persecuted. Were these tragic deaths a punishment for sin? No, it was their faithfulness that led [to] them, not their shortcomings.

Part of retribution theology is the assumption that when tragedy strikes, God has willed it, God wants it to be so. Sometimes when tragedy does strike, we mistakenly describe the tragic event as God's will. This is not the case. God did not cause the man in our text to be born blind—he just was.

Ten days after his son, Alex, was killed in a car accident, Reverend William Sloane Coffin shared these thoughts with his church:

When a person dies, there are many things that can be said, and there is at least one thing that should never be said. The night after Alex died, I was sitting in the living room of my sister's house outside of Boston when the front door opened and in came a nice-looking, middle-aged woman, carrying about eighteen quiches. When she saw me she shook her head then headed for the kitchen, saying sadly over her shoulder, "I just don't understand the will of God." Instantly, I was up and in hot pursuit, swarming all over her. "I'll say you don't, lady!!" I said. (I knew the anger would do me good, and the instruction to her was long overdue.)

I continued, "Do you think it was the will of God that Alex never fixed that lousy windshield wiper of his, that he was probably driving too fast in such a storm, that he probably had had a couple of 'frosties' too many? Do you think it is God's will that there are no street lights along that stretch of road and no guard rails separating the road and Boston Harbor?"

In the clarity that could only come from experience, Dr. Coffin made a valuable point:

Nothing so infuriates me as the incapacity of seemingly intelligent people to get it through their heads that God doesn't go around this world with his fingers on triggers, his fist around knives, his hands on steering wheels. God is against all unnatural deaths. And Christ spent an inordinate amount of time delivering people from paralysis, insanity, leprosy, and muteness. . . . The one thing that should never be said when someone dies is, "It is the will of God." Never do we know enough to say that. My consolation lies in knowing that it was not the will of God that Alex die; that when the waves closed over the sinking car, God's was the first of all our hearts to break.

When the disciples pointed out the blind man to Jesus, they were motivated by a desire to know who was at fault for the blindness. They wanted to know who had sinned to bring this affliction down upon the blind man. But Jesus responded in verse 3, "neither this man nor his parents sinned . . . but this happened so that the work of God might be displayed in his life."

Jesus' remark was clear. Sin had nothing to do with this man's blindness. Causality had nothing to do with this man's blindness. No one sinned. God did not cause this blindness to happen; no one can be blamed. God is not vindictive. In fact, even here God can work. Even the eyes of a man blind from birth can be made clean and clear.

Jesus bent down, spat in the dirt, made some mud, and put it on the blind man's eyes. The blind man could have been offended, he could have been repulsed, but he wasn't. Obeying Jesus' orders, he went to the pool of Siloam and washed his eyes and went home seeing.

Jesus changed the nature of the discussion. Jesus shifted the disciples' focus from a retribution theology to a theology of grace by moving past questions of sin and, instead, simply reaching out and getting his own hands dirty.

Jesus does not give answers as to why people suffer, but maybe answers are not helpful in times of tragedy. Instead of answers, when Jesus healed the blind man he said in essence, "I am with you when you suffer and I can give you the strength to persevere."

Maybe the question of "why" can never be answered. Maybe we will never know why bad things happen to good people. But maybe we wouldn't feel better even if there was a "why."

The real question should be: When tragedy comes my way, do I have to go through it alone? Is it all up to me to bear the burden? And to this question there is an answer.

The French philosopher Simone Weil died at the young age of thirty-three after a life of illness. She suffered from severe headaches, the cause of which was never determined. She tells us that it was while she was suffering intensely from one of these headaches that in her words, "Christ himself came down and took possession of me."

The presence and care of Christ became known to Simone Weil while she was suffering. This leads us to a mysterious realization: The love of God is at work in both good times and in bad times. Jesus said that the blind man was not blind because of sin, and reframed the situation to show that God can work at any and all times. The blind man's infirmity became a way through which Jesus revealed Himself to the world.

The last several years have been tough ones. We have seen the anguish of war, economic collapse, unemployment, terrorism, and natural disasters—not to mention the deaths and illnesses of loved ones. All these things have taken their toll. But we have hope in knowing that God can handle our questions and that we have the companionship of one another. Even in grief and confusion we can point to the strength of Jesus Christ who willingly and lovingly carried His cross in a statement of solidarity with us, even when we dwell in the pit of despair. At that lowest and most painful point, Christ gives us dignity and value in spite of sickness of body and affliction of mind.

It is the dignity and value Christ gives to those who are suffering that empowers the community of Christ to stand up for the victimized, to mourn with those who mourn, and to use human hands in the name of Jesus.

It is because the real and eternal God became human and suffered a violent and degrading death that those of us who suffer from illness, violent crime, a death of a loved one, and emotional and spiritual afflictions find traces of redemption in our lowest moment and hospitality to dwell in the presence of Christ as we are—that even when things are at their darkest God is still at work.

Jon Kershner, 32
North Seattle Friends Church, Northwest Yearly Meeting (EFCI)
United States

This sermon was originally preached at Olympic View Friends Church in Tacoma, Washington.

Music of My heart

"My Dear Larissa," said the heart

Will you turn down your blurred thoughts
for a moment and listen?

I see you; a prisoner
under a soft cloak of insanity
that is your skin.
I watch your thoughts racing around
having panic attacks, and worrying about
your colorful imperfections.
Your hands are bound by voices renting time
in your mind and drowning the
music of silence.

I see the bitter black marks you hide
in your hair and in your eyes
to fit in with the people crowded
around life you think wouldn't understand—
the people hiding scars under
their finger nails and in their ears.

My quiet hands,
as big as time
are here to hold
your delicate breaths.

> *Larissa Keeler, 22*
> *Live Oak Friends Meeting, South Central Yearly Meeting (FGC)*
> *and Monterey and Peninsula Monthly Meeting, Pacific Yearly*
> *Meeting (Independent)*
> *United States*

The Road to Kitale

This is a true story as shared by John Lomuria, the Kenyan representative to the editorial board, to Angelina Conti, the Youth Book project coordinator.

May I share an experience of life [I had] when serving the purpose of God the creator in the Turkana District of Kenya? I have been on this road for years and have met several such incidents, but none has ever been more terrifying than this.

It was an evening of joy, when all my family knew that I was to go to Kitale to make a presentation on the Quaker Youth Book Project, but at the same time my heart knew the type of journey I was to cover to Kitale. This is the type of journey that [requires] prayer among other human efforts like armed escorts, in buses and speeding buses, to cover this horrible distance and come out safe to continue with the rest of the journey.

By seven in the evening we were set to move. My mind was imagining the number of people I would meet the next morning, how to convince them to write submissions.

My mum invited all family for prayers before I could walk out of my house. She did so briefly, and [it was] usual for her, and so I went. On our way, [with] almost half the distance to cover, we had just passed by the famous black spot Kakongu, a place named so by my tribe's men to mean "on the eye." Why so? I do not know. I heard [a sound] like "tar-tar-tar." Was it a tire that burst? No, it was real. The bandits had taken our bus captive. In the flash of an eye the buses stopped, and guns were all over the place, surrounding the bus. The passengers kept quiet awaiting the next move. "God," I said in my heart, "be ready to receive my soul."

The only words we could hear were "Lete besa," with the accent of Kiturkana in it, which means "Bring money." Then *"Toka nje"* ("Get out") was next, and passengers came out running like small children dropping Kenyan notes down as if giving offerings on the altar. Half of the bus was almost empty when the savior came flashing from afar—an escort car with ten police personnel officers. The bandits ran after they saw the car. I was terrified beyond measure, for I knew that if [the police] had delayed, they would have killed a few of us, as usual, as sacrifice to their spiritual beings. The police came and took cover as we reentered the bus. Nobody talked in the bus until we reached Kainuk, the next stopping point where passengers would relieve themselves. Everybody came out terrified and nobody bought anything that night, not even water.

Do you know what will happen next? At times I am not counting on what might happen next in Africa, and so I trust that God [has] plans for me before I start thinking on what I should do next.

This I realized later was a preparation for the culture shock that I experienced in Philadelphia while talking to my great Friend Lucy Duncan. I learned that advance plans can start immediately—an American woman [can] conceive something impossible in Africa, particularly in a desert like Turkana.

Are we prepared for the road to Heaven?

John Epur Lomuria, 32
Lodwar Monthly Meeting, East Africa Yearly Meeting of Friends
(North) (FUM)
Kenya

Naming Our Own Radical Faith

In the Gospel of Matthew, in the record of the Sermon on the Mount, Jesus teaches his disciples, saying, "Blessed are the merciful, for they shall obtain mercy" (Matt. 5:7, King James). Blessed, meaning ultimate well-being, spiritual joy, for those who share in the kingdom of God. Merciful, for those who seek peace in all their relationships through love, forgiveness and compassion.

So how do we live into that space of mercy, compassion, and forgiveness? Jesus, by example, showed us that to be truly merciful we must feed the hungry, give drink to the thirsty, clothe the naked, shelter the homeless, comfort the imprisoned, visit the sick, and bury the dead.

This call to become merciful, to be brought home into that space of forgiveness and compassion, is what leads us to faithfulness. Obedience to faith is our work in the world. Naming our own radical faith, a faith that is of the root, the core, the essence of who God calls us to be, is our life's work. My own faith became rooted in forgiveness and compassion in unexpected ways through serving the Religious Society of Friends.

In January 2006, I took on the responsibility of directing Arch Street Meeting House, the largest Quaker meeting house in the world, located in historic Philadelphia. About a year after I started working there, someone began breaking into the building on a regular basis. I was awakened continually by phone calls from the security vendor and basically wasn't sleeping through the night anymore, feeling terrorized by this person breaking into my house—or so it felt. My prayers were for patience and companionship in the darkness.

Finally, in the third week, I received a call from the security vendor telling me they had heard someone in the building. I arrived on site with the police, who caught the intruder and arrested him. The man was covered with dust and looked like he had been living on the street for some time. The police asked me to identify him and I could not, although later I learned that he sporadically attended worship.

What surprised me most about him (Scott) was that I instinctively knew him to be essentially good. I could see, even in that moment, that he was a child of God. And, even more, I inherently trusted him and knew that he was just as scared as I was.

Over the coming weeks I was in and out of the Philadelphia court system, speaking with prosecuting and defense lawyers, attending hearings as a witness, and awaiting sentencing for Scott. I remember at the second hearing sitting on the witness stand, looking across the room at this small, humble man behind the defense table, in an orange jumpsuit with handcuffs on his wrists, and being reminded of the conversation I had had with his mother just the day before as she pleaded with me to drop the charges against her son. I had tried to explain to her that I was not the one who had charged her son; it was the City of Philadelphia that had made the arrest and moved forward with the prosecution. Still, she saw me as both the enemy and her only hope.

During these weeks I was barely sleeping or working. I began therapy at the request of my boss, and I tried to regain a sense of safety and security while I was in the meeting house. But my body was not cooperating; the fear in my heart was not readily turning into love. It was turning into anger, rage, frustration, and hate. I felt put upon; I felt violated; I felt that I wanted Scott to experience everything I was experiencing. I wanted him to really understand the impact his actions had on my life. I did not feel ready to forgive him.

So how do we move into that space of mercy, compassion, and forgiveness? How do we do it when we are tired, anxious, upset, and angry? How do we turn fear into love? We begin where we are.

I had no idea, at that time, how to forgive Scott, but it was clear that punishing him was not the solution. So that's where I began. I wrote to the judge, and wrote to and spoke with the prosecuting attorney about my desire for Scott to be sentenced to a rehabilitation program, rather than to serve hard time. I was told by the prosecuting attorneys for the City of Philadelphia that I could make any request I wanted, but that the prosecution was ultimately out of my hands and in the hands of the city.

I knew from speaking with his mother that Scott had a history of alcohol abuse. She also shared with me the story of his first arrest. Many years ago, shortly after his uncle (her brother and Scott's role model) died unexpectedly, Scott lay down in the middle of the street near their home, hoping to be run over by a car, no longer having in him the desire to live. He was arrested for vagrancy and endangering the lives of others. Thus began an almost twenty-five-year period of being arrested for petty crimes, which, his mother said, often happened when Scott was upset.

Six weeks later Scott was sentenced by a Philadelphia judge to spend a year in a medium security prison, and, a few weeks later, my partner and I were approved to visit him.

I had no idea what to expect from the Pennsylvania prison system. I did not know that we would have to wait for nearly four hours to see Scott or that I would be searched repeatedly before entering the prison. I didn't expect that I would have to remove my underwire bra and strip down to my tank top because layers of clothing were not allowed. I had no idea that I would encounter cold concrete walls, wailing children waiting with their mothers to see their fathers or brothers, or the onslaught of guards everywhere. Pain is a powerful force. Anger, resentment, punishment, fear; all of these negative energies were enabling one another in the space of these waiting rooms.

I spent most of the four hours weeping in my partner's arms—weeping for my father and my brother, who had each served time in prison; weeping for the men, women, and children waiting to visit their loved ones; weeping for Scott; weeping for the horrible, corporate-run prison system that exists in the United States; weeping for my Quaker community, so torn apart around the issue of the homeless at the meeting house.

I wept because my mind, my heart, and my body were tired, and I was scared that I wouldn't know what to say to Scott. I was scared that I would hate him. I was scared that I would love him. I was scared that he would despise me for wreaking havoc on his life.

I remember entering the visiting room and being surprised by how small Scott was, possibly only my height, and slight. In my mind, over the past few weeks and especially the past few hours, he had grown tall and strong. Instead, in front of me sat a forty-one-year-old, fragile white man with dreams, hopes, and desires, as well as much pain and sadness.

Scott expressed remorse about his repeated break-ins at the meeting house and asked for my forgiveness. That was one of the first things he said: "Emma, will you please forgive me?" I started crying, he started crying, and then my partner started crying. We sat there and wept for a long time.

I thought: What's keeping me from being able to forgive this man sitting next to me? I realized that I needed to tell him my story. I needed to tell him both about my own father's experience with homelessness and serving time in jail and the effects of my father's actions on my life—the overwhelming sense of abandonment and despair I still carry in my heart from choices my father made almost two decades ago.

I also needed to tell Scott about the pain *his* actions had caused in my life. So I started talking. Scott listened, asked good questions, and was present. He didn't get defensive, he didn't try to make everything better, he just listened. I got really upset, I yelled. I said I felt hurt, angry, resentful, and violated. He really got it; he heard me. Once I felt truly heard, I felt the way open for forgiveness. Because Scott was able to meet me in my pain—to sit there and be fully present with me—I was able to forgive him in that moment.

Scott then shared his experience of being arrested, his feelings around serving a year-long sentence—the longest amount of time he has ever served in jail—and the effects of the prison system on his self-esteem and his capacity for growth. What amazed and astounded me in his sharing was that he had already forgiven me, even before I walked into the prison that day. He understood his time in jail as an opening for turning his life around. He wasn't angry; he wasn't upset; he wasn't complacent; and he wasn't feeling sorry for himself. I was moved and inspired by his presence.

I recognized that this was an opportunity for me to truly learn about forgiveness and compassion in a way that I had refused to do for years, especially with my own family. I also believed that God had brought Scott into our lives to invite our Quaker community into action and support for this man—to testify for our commitment to peace and equality.

In our first face-to-face visit, Scott expressed thanks to me for intervening in his life, for allowing him the opportunity to clean up his act and become a self-respecting person. Scott also shared, and continues to tell me, that knowing me has taught him about forgiveness and compassion.

I look at Scott and think how simple and easy it was ultimately to choose to love him and to stand by him; to let him know that I believe in him, and that I believe he can create whatever he wants for himself and his life. We all deserve to have someone stand beside us and believe in us, to offer us forgiveness and compassion, whether we are rich or poor, white or black, and if we are homeless or behind bars. We all deserve and need love and faith in our lives.

Gandhi challenged us to be the change we want to see in the world. A simple thought, really. You, as an individual, can radically alter the way society and the world function through your daily actions, through your moment-to-moment choices to forgive and to seek love.

I believe that living a radical faith is possible. I believe that if you ask for lessons of forgiveness and compassion and seek to live in obedience to faith, your own radical faith will be born.

In the Gospel of Matthew, Jesus says, "Ask, and it will be given to you; seek and you will find; knock and the door will be opened to you. For everyone who asks receives; he who seeks finds; and to him who knocks, the door will be opened" (Matt. 7:7–8, NIV).

We must be teachable. We must be willing to persistently and boldly pray to be taught. We must ask for what we are ready to learn, eagerly anticipating these gifts of wisdom. We must be ready, when the door opens, to receive the lessons God brings to us. For me, this lesson of forgiveness and compassion happened in the instant of looking into Scott's eyes for the first time and choosing to see him as a child of God rather than as an enemy.

Emma M. Churchman, 36

Monthly Meeting of Friends of Philadelphia (Arch Street),
Philadelphia Yearly Meeting (FGC) and Friends Meeting of
Washington, Baltimore Yearly Meeting (FGC-FUM)
United States

Restless

Ain't a damn thing can help me now.
There are no words still left in me,
no sassafras, no verdant green—
just this ache and a fear of birds
(tight beaks and those solid bright eyes).

I sing Mama's glory songs, but
even in darkness they're too weak
to find the way to Heaven's ears.

Hope is a hard thing to find, like
last winter's crocus bulbs in June.
Everywhere is so dark and torn
as the last of the finger-clouds
from a named storm quietly pass.

I could patch the holes in the walls
and prune the pink geraniums
but there is no home without you.

> *Rachel Anne Miller, 30*
> *Greenville Friends Meeting, North Carolina Yearly Meeting*
> *(Conservative) and Cambridge Friends Meeting, New England*
> *Yearly Meeting (FGC-FUM)*
> *United States*

The City of Remembrance

The summer after I graduated from high school I didn't do what
most of my friends did, which was get a job and hang around the local
river; instead, I embarked on a journey. Although this journey lasted only
a month, the experiences will last a lifetime.

I went to Europe on the Quaker Youth Pilgrimage with 28 other
youth, 14 from North America, 14 from Europe, and 4 leaders. I flew
to Newark with my best friend from Kamloops, the only other person
I knew on the trip, and nervously wrote in my journal the whole way.
I was sure everyone would be insanely religious, the type of people I
pitied at school because they couldn't think past their religion and

refused to be open-minded because it said so in the Bible. The people on the Pilgrimage were the opposite of that; like me, they were just average teenagers. But although I say average, what we grew to have, in terms of relationships, understandings, and friendships, was completely above average. The trip was filled with laughter and tears, anger and joy, peace and utter raucousness and everything in between. We all brought different things to the group and although we certainly did not all agree on how to define God, if He/She exists, or even what time bedtime should be, we respected each other and each other's beliefs.

We stayed in England, the birthplace of Quakerism, for a few weeks and explored 1652 country—climbing Pendle Hill, exploring Firbank Fell, and experiencing Quaker history. We then took a boat over to Amsterdam. We all were full of energy on the trip over, playing in the kids' ball pens and dancing madly on the five-foot dance floor. Our main theme in Amsterdam was going to be World War II. This related to Quakerism as some Quakers helped in hiding Jews. Also, it was important to Dutch Quakers for us to gain an understanding of what went on during World War II, so as to hopefully prevent an occurrence of a similar situation. I found the stories we heard and the sites we visited while in the Netherlands and Germany very moving. Thus, although I could write books about the many great adventures of the Quaker Youth Pilgrimage in 2004, I will focus on the experience hearing and seeing the effects of the Nazi regime.

Growing up I did not have a TV, and thus I read constantly, reading anything I could get my hands on, but I mostly enjoyed reading stories. In particular I devoured books about the Underground Railroad and books about World War II, especially the Kit Pearson series about war children coming to Canada from England, *The Diary of Anne Frank*, and *I Have Lived a Thousand Years*—a true story from an Auschwitz survivor who was thirteen. Thus, when I arrived in Amsterdam I was full of anticipation about going to the Anne Frank house.

The only thing that distinguished the Anne Frank House from other houses in the region was the long line of people snaking from the front entrance and around the corner. We had a large group and a reservation, so we waited only a few minutes before we were admitted into the house. After an introduction we left the museum section and headed up the steep narrow stairs to the area of the house where the Frank and Von Pels families lived for two years. The heat was stifling and the air in the room remained stagnant despite the fact that the windows were open with fans feebly blowing fresh air in. A thought skittered through my mind that at least we could open the windows and, after the tour, go outside. On the walls of Anne's room pictures from magazines of actors and actresses were still pasted to the walls. In her diary Anne said how the pictures made the room so cheerful:

> Our little room looked very bare at first with nothing on the walls; but thanks to Daddy who had brought my film-star collection and picture postcards on beforehand, and with the aid of a paste pot and brush, I have transformed the walls into one gigantic picture. This makes it look much more cheerful. (July 11, 1942)

To me the tiny black and white photos were lost amidst the gray wallpapered wall of the tiny room. The floors squeaked as I walked slowly about the room, the air stuck, hot in a lump, in my throat and my body felt immensely heavy. A quote on the wall from an Auschwitz survivor, Primo Levi, captured my thoughts:

> One single Anne Frank moves us more than the countless others who suffered just as she did but whose faces have remained in the shadows. Perhaps it is better that way. If we were capable of taking in all the suffering of all those people we would not be able to live. (1986)

The next few days were filled with laughter and fun, but with an air of seriousness as we were all affected in some way or another with the heavy content we were dealing with. Two older Quakers, who had been alive during World War II, came and spoke with us. One of the men was from the Netherlands and had gone into hiding with his mother as his father had been taken for resisting the Nazis. Luckily, they remained undiscovered throughout the war. He recounted how the day after the Netherlands was liberated his grandmother, who had been sending them food in hiding, arrived to see him and his mother. When they went to open the door to her carriage she was sitting there dead. She had starved to death, sending all her food to her daughter and grandson. The other Quaker man had been a photographer for the Nazis. He grew up in Germany, not as a Quaker, and was a member of the Nazi youth. Of course, like the majority of young people at the time, he was completely entranced with the idea of a powerful Germany, and believed the ideas he was taught at school. A seed of doubt was planted in his mind when he was fifteen, when his father took him out into the forest, and explained to him that perhaps the Nazis weren't always right. His father used an example of a recent hanging where the men hadn't been given a trial. Thus, however small, the seed was planted, and throughout the war, the idea that maybe his country was not always right began to grow. After the war he took many of his photographs to international papers to share the horrors, although they were mostly photos of the soldiers and training, not of concentration camps.

We traveled to Camp Westerbork the next day. Westerbork was a transit camp where over one hundred thousand Jews, Gypsies, and resistance fighters were taken and then shipped in cattle cars to concentration camps, most often Auschwitz, Sobibor, or Bergen-Belsen from 1942–1945. We looked around the museum and with pride I took a picture of the Canadian uniform in the display case. The Canadians had liberated most of the Netherlands, including Camp Westerbork.

We walked about 2 km to the actual location of the transit camp. As we walked the sun beat forcefully down upon us. We stopped to eat our packed lunch just outside the camp and were surrounded by swarms of wasps. They were everywhere. These were not normal wasps either. They seemed to have the preemptive strike technique, loved by leaders worldwide, perfected. One girl was stung on the tongue, another on the eyelid and many more of us managed to be stung. It wasn't just in that area either; the entire camp was hot, shadeless, and filled with wasps and horseflies. Some barracks had been partially reconstructed and in the center of the camp there was a monument to the thousands of Dutch Gypsies and Jews who were deported from Westerbork and never returned. One of the families deported was the Frank family—from a group of eight, only Otto Frank remained at the end of the war. The memorial was a city of bricks all of varying heights that stretched ten square meters. The red bricks had symbols in brass on the top, each representing a dead Dutch Jew, Gypsy, or resistance fighter. The Jews had a Star of David on their bricks, the Gypsies had flames, and the resistance fighters had blank bricks. The gypsies and resistance fighters were in one small section and the rest of the area was filled with skyscrapers, houses, and small apartment buildings with the Star of David on the top creating the miniature city of the dead. They created a map of the Netherlands, with small pathways to walk along, and the sheer number of them blew me away. Then I remembered, six million Jews were murdered in WWII. The memorial city at Westerbork was only for one hundred thousand, a mere 1.6 percent of the six million people killed.

We had meeting for worship by the partially ripped up train tracks where one hundred thousand people had been shoved into cattle cars, separated from their loved ones to go down the train tracks to their deaths. The heat was intense, and still the wasps buzzed around, ready to sting, and the horseflies hummed biting chunks out of our flesh as we stood in traditional silent Quaker Worship.

We walked back, parched, to the bus, and I was delighted to get into the air-conditioned bus and head back to the community center where we were staying. As a child I had read books about the Holocaust, and in Social Studies we briefly studied World War II. But all of it seemed distant, a story. I knew it was real, but to me it was as real as the Greek myths we also learned about. On that hot day in August the actuality of the horrible deeds people can commit finally sunk in. Back home, rereading Anne Frank's *Diary*, I was amazed at her optimism:

> It's difficult in times like these: ideals, dreams and cherished hopes rise within us, only to be crushed by grim reality. It's a wonder I haven't abandoned all my ideals, they seem so absurd and impractical. Yet I cling to them because I still believe, in spite of everything, that people are truly good at heart. (July 15, 1944)

These words also ring true for the Quaker ideal of Goodness, or God in everyone. As George Fox, the founder of Quakerism, said, "Walk gently over the world answering that of God in everyone."

Amy Jean Singleton-Polster, 24
Vancouver Island Monthly Meeting, Canadian Yearly Meeting
(FGC-FUM)
Canada

Ice Storm, photograph, Seth Barch, 27, Schuylkill Monthly Meeting, Philadelphia Yearly Meeting (FGC), United States

Through a Glass Darkly

I was in a strange, small room I wasn't familiar with and I was worried about accidentally brushing thighs with the woman next to me on the sofa. What if she thought I did it on purpose? Would I make her uncomfortable, a stranger inside her personal space? I didn't know anyone else there, but it was better than not going to meeting at all. On break from college, I had returned to a kind of chaos my family had never seen before: some of us not speaking to others; some of us speaking angrily all the time; and none of us speaking openly about what was going on. It was tense and suffocating and I was sad for all of us; all of us were sad for each other. And in the midst of all this I had gotten up early on a Sunday morning in the cold quiet and driven to the closest meeting I could find. It wasn't the one I had grown up in, and it was small enough that my unfamiliar presence was very noticeable. I smiled anxiously and hoped I wouldn't have to make small talk.

But then after we all sat down you could feel silence walk into the room like the last arrival to the group, and settle among us with ease and intimacy. In its presence, all my discomfort fell away and we were quiet together. The room, filled with armchairs and sofas, was the size of a large public restroom. The heat of our bodies filled the space quickly, and everyone felt a little drowsy. I don't know how much time passed before one man rose and cast his voice like a fishing line into the silence. He was older, and spoke with gravity and authority; clearly a weighty Friend. His story went like this:

> The early Quakers, in the 1700s, had a different meaning of the word *exorcise*. Now it means to cleanse or purify; we think of the old priest and the young priest, Hollywood movies about demons. But then, and for them, it meant to be challenged, or to have a hard thing in your life. He gave the example of a meeting for business he attended recently, where no one could agree and nothing could get done and everyone was hurt and angry. And someone stood and said, "Friends, we are exorcised."

Somehow in that trancelike half-asleep and half-holy state, that meant so much to me. My family was falling apart; I couldn't even talk to my father on the phone without my heart clenching, my teeth grinding. My best friend's mother was dying; my brother was constantly enraged or in tears; I was about to leave all of them to live in another country for six months; and I was so afraid of what might happen while I was gone, what I might hear about over the phone or in a curt e-mail and not be able to do anything about. To be honest, nothing was really making sense just then, but that word did. *We are exorcised, we are exorcised.* Because when you say it that way it doesn't sound so bad. It sounds like you are going through a painful process, sure, but in the end you will be rid of something awful and painful that was inside you.

At that point, I had been and still am trying pretty hard to tell the truth, in a real sense of the word, in the way we are called to. Not like "I'm probably going to stay out past curfew," but more like, "I have trouble trusting you because I'm afraid you'll hurt yourself." It's an incredibly difficult kind of honesty, and not just because it requires saying things that will cause pain to the people you love. It's hard because a lot of the time it seems pointless. There's no guarantee that voicing these kinds of truth will be more effective than sullen silences or careful avoidance of the subject. Sometimes it can be hard to see the grace in it; sometimes it just feels like cruelty.

But with this one phrase, with the idea of being exorcised but standing before the Light, suddenly I felt like maybe that really did mean something. Maybe things could get better. Like maybe this was going to be real bad for a while and there would be a lot of conversations and arguments that left me feeling like a bad daughter and a bad person, but maybe we could in fact be exorcised. Maybe when we say these things we are finally being honest with one another, and maybe in some small invisible way that is making us cleaner and better and saner and more able to love each other someday. Maybe it is within our power to exorcise ourselves.

Do you know that verse from the Bible about glasses, or mirrors, depending upon your translation? I looked it up, and it's I Corinthians 13:12: "Now we see each other through a glass darkly" (King James), or, alternately, "in a mirror dimly" (English Standard). Regardless of our relationship to scripture, I feel like we all understand that, on some visceral level. It's a scary and frustrating truth that there are some things we just can't quite make out, some things we just cant quite get across. That line, "through a glass darkly," has been used a thousand times, from Madeleine L'Engle to an episode of *Highlander*. What is not often quoted is the next part of the passage: "Then we shall see face to face. Now I know in part; then I shall know fully, even as I am fully known. We shall see each other face to face, and be fully known." That's what I was thinking about today in a tiny, cramped room full of old people in expensive sweaters that I didn't know. That we are exorcised now, and now we see each other as in a mirror dimly. But one day, we will see each other face to face.

Rachel Kincaid, 21
North Shore Friends Meeting, New England Yearly Meeting
(FGC-FUM)
United States

Fiel Siempre Fiel

Cuando decidí aceptar al Señor en mi corazón yo tenia una enfermedad, una enfermedad psicológica, tenía mucha ansiedad, depresión, hiperactividad y sobre todo miedo: todo esto ocasionaba que yo no pudiera descansar (dormir).

Yo pensaba que me iba a sanar rápidamente pero no fue así. Una noche mientras caminaba sentí en el corazón muy fuerte algo que decía SERA UN PROCESO.

He tenido que enfrentar muchas batallas conmigo misma pero he descubierto que Dios siempre estuvo ahí conmigo; al principio me sentía sola y sentía que el Señor no estaba conmigo pero no era así, El estaba a mi lado, Nunca me dejó, estuvo todo el tiempo cuando la ansiedad estaba por ganarme siempre había una palabra en la radio, la tele y hasta de una persona que no conocía. Y cuando tenía temor de que Dios se alejara de mi había una palabra que me ayudaba bastante "si somos infieles el permanece fiel porque somos parte de el mismo" (2 Tim. 2:13).

Ha pasado tiempo desde que me encuentro mucho mejor y realmente fue un proceso duro pero aprendí muchas cosas de todo aquello; aprendí a que puedo ser valiente y fuerte no importa que sea pequeña, débil, delgada o que nadie crea en mi, mientras El este ahí yo se que puedo salir adelante. Además se que El estará siempre conmigo a mi lado, El es fiel.

Esto es algo que deseo dedicarle; es una canción pero es mi vida misma:

> En paz me acostaré y así mismo dormiré,
> es que se que en ti Señor puedo vivir confiado.
> Quien me libra del temor,
> quien me quita la ansiedad,
> solamente tu Señor.
> Quien me da de su amor
> y me da de su perdón
> solo eres tu mi Señor.
> Quien me abraza con su amor
> y me da de su perdón solo eres tu señor
>
> — *Daniel Calvetti*

Las pruebas pueden doler mucho pero debemos confiar en tener la certeza que El siempre será fiel, esta ahí contigo ayudándote a derrotar aquella prueba o problema o le que te impida ser mejor. Dios es tan cierto como esta palabra mientras nosotros nos preocupamos en que tan lento crecemos, Dios se interesa en tan fuertes crecemos.

Maritza Cordero Quispe
Iglesia Nacional Evangélica "Los Amigos" de Bolivia (EFCI)
Bolivia

Faithful Always Faithful

When I decided to accept the Lord in my heart I was ill, mentally ill. I suffered from anxiety, depression, hyperactivity, and above all, fear: All this meant that I could not sleep.

I thought that I would be able to heal rapidly, but it did not happen like that. One night while I was walking I felt in my heart something very strong that said *it will be a process.*

I have had to face many battles with myself, but I discovered that God was always there with me; at first I felt alone and felt that God was not with me, but it was not so. He was at my side. He never left me. When anxiety was about to overcome me there was always a word on the radio, on TV, and even from an unknown person. And when I feared that God would distance himself from me there was a [Bible verse] that helped me a lot: "If we are unfaithful he remains faithful because we are part of him" (2 Tim. 2:13).

Some time has passed [and] I now feel better and really it was a difficult process, but I learned many things. I learned that I can be courageous and strong. It does not matter if I am small, weak, slim, or that no one believes in me; while he is there, I know that I can move ahead. Furthermore I know that He will always be at my side. He is faithful.

This is something that I would like to dedicate to you, it's a song [by musician Daniel Calvetti], but it reflects my own life:

> In peace I will go to bed and thus I will sleep
> I know that in you my Lord I can live confidently
> Who releases me from fear
> Who removes anxiety
> Only you my Lord
> Who gives me his love
> and gives me his forgiveness
> It is only you my Lord

Who embraces me with his love
and gives me his forgiveness it's only you Lord

Tests can be painful but we must trust in the certainty that He will
always be faithful, always there with you helping you to defeat that test
or problem or that which is preventing you from being better. God is as
true as this word: While we are worried about how slow we are growing,
God is interested in how strong we are growing.

Maritza Cordero Quispe
National Evangelical Friends Church of Bolivia (EFCI)
Bolivia

Prayer

You have always given me
just a little more than I can withstand,
leaving me broken, freshly injured.
You know that I carry
each failure like an aching wound.
These are not garments I can shed
to take on the new. I am red and
I am raw and I cannot
imagine surviving
another stripe.

But You have known me
from before I was anything at all.
Only You can heal me
Only You can make me whole.

Oh, Lord, let this be
something I can do.

Rachel Anne Miller, 30
Greenville Friends Meeting, North Carolina Yearly Meeting
Conservative and Cambridge Friends Meeting, New England Yearly
Meeting (FGC-FUM)
United States

Hope in the Night

I can hear God humming in the quiet room. I don't know the tune, but He's been at it for quite some time. I think He does it to remind me He's there in case I can't feel the hand that has been holding mine for what seems like eternity. His hand is there on the bed cover, intertwined with mine, my one connection with what is real in this world as I fade in and out of a raging fever and dark dreams. His other hand I can occasionally sense caressing my forehead with a cool cloth, softly and tenderly. I cannot seem to move my body or even open my eyes, but the paralysis does not scare me. I am now far past the point of feeling or fear. The ability to speak, pray, or even cry is well beyond me and I don't care. I just know He's there beside me in the silence, and for now that's enough.

Into this room, God invites another soul to enter, one I can hear when I can't understand Him. She takes her place on my other side, looks into my eyes, and quietly asks me to give into the pain and to let the fever take me. She helps me see at last what I couldn't bring myself to feel and as the anguish I buried for so long washes over me in waves, God climbs into bed beside me and holds me as I drown in my tears, weeping with me as I sob into His chest.

Slowly, day by day, we go deeper and deeper. As I cry out and acknowledge the pain, God holds it in His hands before my eyes. I feel like a caterpillar in a cocoon, completely taken apart, but I trust the process even though I don't understand it. Everything seems to be cast into darkness and I can't find the thread of hope the other soul emphatically tells me she's holding onto for me. Chokingly, I ask if there could possibly be life in the black water, light seems so far away, and passionately, she answers me, "There *is* life on the other side."

As we sort through the feelings that have been buried for so long, I realize how much I've held inside. Painful though it is, it feels really good to finally clean the darkness out and let it go. Knots start to come undone, dark closets are opened up and sorted out. Gentle though God is, I can tell He's really enjoying Himself in the process. I can now sit up and talk to God every day; He is still there holding my hand. I find I am okay with crying, and to my surprise I once again learn what laughing with my whole heart feels like. I start asking Him questions about what has been happening. I tell Him that to me it has felt like He's taken my life down to its bare foundation, to the cement above the dirt and rocks so He could get at everything that needed His touch. He acknowledges this is true and then one day, when He senses I am ready, God asks me,

"So what do you want to build?" I think about the qualities I want in my life: hope, joy, and fun. I want to live as a whole and integrated person.

We rebuild my life from the ground up and we plant a garden outside. This time there are a lot of windows to let in the light, tons of open space in the floor plan, and no more hidden closets. Clean air blows through the rooms and I find this cocoon is, after all, a refreshing place to be. One of God's greatest joys is opening up His hands to show me how the pain I gave to Him months before, the weights I let go of, have now been transformed into building blocks of great strength and integrity, adding beauty and love to my life.

To further help me in this process, God brings along other souls to my side to help teach me things I will need as I emerge from such an intense and raw experience. One new friend teaches me how to walk again by teaching me how to dance and another gives me the tools I need to see myself with greater clarity and understanding. People around me start to notice I am different, and I even surprise myself with changes I didn't notice had taken place, such as in my reactions to things said, words I am willing to say, or new choices I make.

The other soul God originally invited to walk by my side is still close by, speaking truth to my life and helping me know that everything I need is already within me; I have a deep strength of my own. From her, I learn that not only is it possible to live outside the box, but that there is no box in the first place; that I am free to explore God and that He invites me to do so. I learn about the power I hold and how to use it. These are truths that will stay with me and hold me fast as I move out of this time and into the life I told God I wanted.

In the few years since going through this process, I have thought a lot about what that particular dark night meant to me and how it transformed me into the person I am today. Though I was never actually physically sick, it is the best description I have for what it felt like. That time with God holding my hand in that room is more real to me than many other experiences I've had. Though it was incredibly painful, as transformation usually is, it is the time in my life when I have felt God's presence most intensely. Saint John of the Cross calls it "the dark night of the soul," a time when God blinds us to what He's doing in us because we would not otherwise wish to go through it, rather like blindfolding a person before walking them through a burning room of flames. But walk we did (He actually carried me most of the way) and I now can't imagine my life without that time we spent together in the fire. I have learned for myself that there *is* life on the other side; my friend was right, and that

I have the strength and tenacity I need in seeking how to really live that life with all the joys and struggles within it.

One of the things I find most interesting about the whole experience is that God and I are still building; I don't think that process is ever over, not for any of us. Other dark nights will come in different ways. New souls will, and still, come into my life with lessons to teach me, new building blocks of qualities God and I build into myself. I am grateful to all those souls who have walked this way with me thus far and who are still yet to come. They have each left a deep impression on my heart, and I can't thank God enough for orchestrating those friendships, to give me hands to hold along this journey we call life. The really fun thing for me, and a humbling honor, has been being able to return the favor and walk with others along journies of their own.

We all carry pain inside us that we need to work through, and I believe God helps us each do that in different ways. As every person is different, so is the process, but I am sure there are inherent truths underlying them all. We are each unspeakably valuable to God and anything we put our energy into, including our hurts and pain, He values and will not throw away. He takes our pain and transforms it into beauty and truth that changes us and helps us know Him and each other better.

God and I still take walks in our garden; the flowers we planted have been blooming for some time, and I still visit that room on occasion when I need to talk about something with God that is particularly tender and hard to discuss. For me, these places are holy ground. Even today, especially today, as things change, God's holding my hand is my constant. No matter what changes come, within or outside of me, or what about God I explore—no matter where I go and what life brings me—I know He's always there beside me, and so I reach out and grasp His hand often to better feel His presence and His love. Feeling His hand, remembering our time in my cocoon together with me lying there as a caterpillar taken apart, it is only now I realize that the tune God was humming all that time, was the healing chant for the soul of the butterfly to be free.

Sarah Katreen Hoggatt, 30
Freedom Friends Church (Independent)
United States

Yo Soy Una Persona Importante para Dios

Antes de asistir a la Iglesia pensaba que sólo era una persona que vino al mundo para estudiar, para trabajar, casarme, tener hijos, envejecer y luego morir; esa era la forma de cómo pensaba de mi vida. Un día mi tío me invitó a su Iglesia a la cual el y su familia asistía. Entonces comencé a ir a la Iglesia, y mi forma de pensar sobre mi vida empezó a cambiar, empezaron a cambiar las cosas cuando escuché de que el Señor tenía un propósito para mi vida no sólo estudiar, trabajar, casarme, tener hijos, envejecer y luego morir, sino de que El quería que yo estudie pero que estudie su Palabra, que trabaje pero en la Iglesia en su ministerio, al casarme me casaría en la Iglesia y luego cuando tenga hijos sería para dárselos al Señor para criarlos en el camino del Señor, pero el día que muera moriré en paz con El, se que cuando muera sabré de que yo iré al lado del Señor.

Las pruebas nos ayudan a crecer espiritualmente. Cuando empecé a ver la vida de esta forma empezaron a surgir muchas tragedias en mi familia, la separación de mis padres nos afectó a toda la familia, sentí como si Dios se pusiera en contra de mi, cuando mi padre se fue de la casa [y] mi madre tuvo que trabajar para poder mantenernos, en el tiempo de que ella trabajaba mi hermano mayor Roney comenzó a caer en el vicio del alcohol; nosotros vivíamos viendo el sufrimiento de mi madre Benjamina en todo momento ella trataba de que mi hermano deje el vicio pero todo lo que ella le decía era en vano; el no escuchaba; luego de tanto hablarle, recomendándole y tratar de que cambie todo era imposible. Ella se dio por vencida, en su trabajo ella empezó a sentirse enferma, el trabajo que ella realizaba era un poco pesado para ella. Parece de que su enfermedad y el problema de mi hermano hizo que ella sintiera un vació en su corazón como si ella no encontrara sentido en su vida, a veces ella se sentaba a solas y empezaba a llorar, a quejarse de la vida. Todos estos problemas no fueron motivo para que yo deje de asistir a la Iglesia. Yo le comente sobre estos problemas al pastor y el me dijo que oremos por mi madre para que ella sienta en su corazón la necesidad de conocer el amor del Señor. Entonces un día la invito el pastor a la Iglesia y es entonces que ella comenzó a asistir a la Iglesia una vez al mes, dos veces al mes, tres veces al mes y hasta que luego de mucho orar Dios hizo la obra en mi madre.

Luego de cada tormenta sale el sol. A pesar de todas estas dificultades Dios nunca nos abandona, hoy tengo 15 años y estoy muy agradecido por lo que Dios ha hecho en mi vida y en mi familia. Dios toco el corazón de mi madre y hoy ella forma parte de la Iglesia como anciana; hoy mi familia no es perfecta pero Dios lo ha mejorado ya que si antes había tormentas hoy sólo hay lluvias pasivas. Pero seguimos orando para que Dios toque el corazón de mis hermanos. De esta forma Dios ha obrado en mi vida y en mi familia. Yo estoy conociendo mas sobre la palabra de Dios y se que mi vida tendrá mas sentido de lo que pensaba. Espero que tú no pienses de lo que yo pensaba sino que pienses que Dios tiene un propósito, y una misión muy importante en tu vida.

Gabriel Flores Arauz, 16 años
Iglesia Nacional Evangélica "Los Amigos" de Bolivia
Bolivia

I Am an Important Person for God

Before I started attending church, I thought that I only came to this world in order to study, work, get married, have children, grow old and then die; this was how I thought about my life. One day my uncle invited me to his church, which he and his family attended. From then onwards I started going to church and my way of thinking about my life started to change. Things started to change when I heard that the Lord has a purpose for my life—not just study, work, marriage, children, old age, and then death. Rather, He wanted that I study, but that I study His Word, that I work, but in the church for its ministry. When getting married I will get married in the church and then when I have children it will be to give them to the Lord in order to raise them in the path of the Lord. But the day that I die I will be in peace with Him. I know that when I die, I will be at the Lord's side.

Trials and tribulations help us to grow spiritually. When I started to see life in this way, a lot of misfortunes started happening in my family. The separation of my parents affected everyone in my family. I felt that God had turned against me when my father left home and my mother had to work in order to support us. While she worked, my older brother Roney started to fall into the vice of alcohol abuse. We lived seeing the suffering of my mother Benjamina; at all times she tried to get my brother to leave his habit, but all her words were in vain, he did not listen. After trying to speak with him and trying to change him, she gave up. She started to feel sick, and the problem of my brother made her feel empty in her heart, as if there was no meaning in her life. Sometimes she would sit alone and would cry and complain about life. All these problems did not lead me to stop attending church. I spoke about these problems with my pastor and he said to pray for my mother, so that she could feel in her heart the need to know the love of the Lord. Then one day the pastor invited her to church and she started to attend first once a month, then twice a month, three times a month, until after much prayer God carried out His mission in my mother.

After the storm, the sun comes out again. Despite all these difficulties, God never abandoned us. I am now fifteen years old and I am very grateful for all that God has done in my life and that of my family. God touched the heart of my mother and today she is part of the church as an elder. Today my family is not perfect, but God has improved it. If before there were storms, now there are only light rains. But we continue to pray that God touches the heart of my brothers. In this way God has worked in my life and that of my family. I am learning more about the word of God and I know that my life will have more meaning than I thought earlier. I hope that you don't think what I used to think but rather that you think God has a purpose and a mission very important in your life.

> *Gabriel Flores Arauz, 16*
> *National Evangelical Friends Church of Bolivia (EFCI)*
> *Bolivia*

Outback Sunset, photograph, M. E. Hogan, 25, Athens Friends Meeting, Lake Erie Yearly Meeting (FGC), United States

Faith

Clouds form
Dust falls
And all is dispersed; into vapour and shadows and light

With absense
More pressure
New feelings emerge; new memories and old mix in flight

Tears at sunset
Faith at sunrise
Both fade into nothing as I close my eyes

Darkness engulfs me
And I am alone
But inside light shines that no-one has known

Bridget Holtom, 21
Hebden Bridge and Brighouse Meeting, Britain Yearly Meeting
United Kingdom

Petals, photograph, Marie-Helene Drouin, 35, Derby Local Meeting, Britain Yearly Meeting, United Kingdom

Stories of Convincement, Conversion, Salvation,
and Personal Transformation

Reflections on a Quaker Childhood

I eat leaves. Onlookers have been disturbed by the six-foot-two giant of a girl swooping down to pluck at the undergrowth with a casualness usually reserved for nose-picking or public spitting. In childhood, I came to know the subtle scents of the plants, their secret names, and through a perilous process of trial and error, which were good to eat. And eat I did, gorging myself on sultry hibiscus, indulging to excess in sweet lippia leaves, growing fat on the natural knowledge I gained with each discovery.

This natural knowledge was the basis of my childhood, an odd kind of youth of perpetual bare feet, bedtime stories from *National Geographic*, and tofu substitutes for every possible food. During the sullen summer months, I steeped in the swimming hole of Bull Run Creek instead of the chemical marinade of a conventional pool, whose chlorine depths were disappointingly free of beavers and water snakes. My frantic escapes from harassed wildlife provided more entertainment than any inflatable toy. Delivering lambs in the spring was more delightfully gory than any television show, and the bouncy newborns were more endearing than their static, stuffed imitations. Getting lost in the rollicking Blue Ridge foothills was encouraged, just as bee stings were celebrated as character building.

Left to my own juvenile devices in a vast organic playground, I discovered a necessity of self-reliance that did not exist in society: the world of prowling teachers, suspicious nurses, and attentive mothers. Alone but not without resources, my blossoming cuts were treated with the clear gelatin of jewel weed and then bound with stachys leaves, while clothes ripped in play were pinned with hawthorn spikes. Far from watchful eyes, my ten-foot fall from a rickety hunter's nest had to be dealt with in painful, bloody isolation.

There is something about the American South that nurtures legend, that cradles, spanks, and slaps it into infamy, and in such a tradition the fame of Randy Peyton's herd was born. Rumored to have three of the most unpredictably violent bulls in the county, the herd overwintered on Suicide Hill, prime sledding territory for reckless tobogganers such as me. Confident that no temperamental cows would harass a person of my backwoods skill, I had barely entered the pasture when I was deftly surrounded by a ring of meaty Anguses out for blood. Inspired by a recent infatuation with Jack London, I dove to the ground and packed snow in an arc above my head, burrowing an icy, camouflaged cocoon. The cattle remained still, motionless menaces. It was a charged standoff, my personal Cold War. A little past nightfall, the herd, bored with their fruitless vigil, moved on. Erupting from my wintery stronghold, I galloped home, frozen and utterly humbled. This benign rebuke of my childish hubris inspired in me a profound humility.

The authority of Mother Nature over her human children was a lesson thoroughly instilled in me by a band of murderous cows, by a provoked wasp horde, by a ruthless river current. But what I learned and understood in childhood is still unrecognized and disregarded by the vast majority of adults, who fill the wetlands and wonder why floodwaters ravage their homes, who poison the air and lament their diagnosis of lung cancer, who sit prostrate in front of the television like piglets suckling from a sow. It is this breed of adult that triggered in me a Peter Pan like dread of growing up.

Eighteen now, and confronting this looming threat of adulthood, I try to maintain my girlhood habits, my simple wonder at life. But the battering ram of "progress" makes casualties of so many wild, free things, tempting my spirit toward cynicism and despair, for the forces of industry and vice have felled so much that cannot be resurrected. However, with this new and strange maturity comes a snapping, striving sense of purpose that holds me hostage with its urgency, refusing me sleep, hunger, and peace. The need to protect wilderness is all-consuming and undeniable, like I am but an instrument of some greater design. Life and living things are so much more precious to me now because I understand their capacity to be lost. I am all too eager to fashion a new world, a better world, in which no child is taught that it is dirty to eat leaves.

Liv Henry, 19
Goose Creek Meeting, Baltimore Yearly Meeting (FGC-FUM)
United States

Why I Became a Quaker

What attracted me to the Quakers was the open-minded attitude toward spirituality. To build a faith out of experience rather than belief in creeds. My previous spiritual seeking had led me into exploring different eastern traditions and new-age spirituality. But I couldn't find a spiritual home in any of these traditions. My doubts prevented me from settling into a belief system.

I first heard about Friends when I was in a doubtful and agnostic period. I was surprised by the open-minded attitude and inspired by the idea of the Inner Light. It really spoke to me in my situation because I realized that even if I couldn't believe in anything else, I could still believe in my Inner Light. I had felt It inside me for many years and felt Its bliss when playing or listening to beautiful music or falling into spontaneous meditative peacefulness when being alone.

I soon went to an unprogrammed worship and experienced it as soothing and meaningful. I could probe into that sacred feeling for the first time without distorting it with confusing words. I also liked the people I met and soon became friends with some of them. At the same time as me, a couple of other young people found their way to our meeting. Earlier on very few young persons attended the meeting, but now this is beginning to change. I soon found out that most of us had found the Quakers through the Internet, in several cases through the www. beliefnet.com site. In a number of cases their Belief-O-Matic test gave the result that the person completing it had a spiritual profile most closely matching that of the Quakers.

My experience with secularization in Sweden is that often young people reject religion and spirituality because they identify these matters with blind faith in dogmas. The only real facts are the ones that can be investigated scientifically. There is a tendency to look upon religious people as naive. But I also see much spiritual longing and seeking among young people. There is a growing interest for meditation, yoga, and personal development.

In this situation I believe that the Friends have great potential. As a rich tradition on the Judeo-Christian ground, enhanced by the lives, actions and testimonies of at least a dozen generations of Friends, there is an abundant well of inspiration for the seeker here. There is room for finding words but also silence, introverted mysticism but also extroverted activism, belief in Jesus but also universalism. There is room for spiritual seeking, sharing and communion, without the pressure to agree upon a certain confession of faith.

I became a member of the Swedish Yearly Meeting in November 2007. Since then I have gone through different phases in my spiritual life. I have expanded my understanding of Christianity. I have been driven through pantheism and agnosticism. But all the time, despite the turmoil, I kept the faith in the Inner Light. It has always been a quiet spot inside of me, like the eye of the storm, where I can find peace of mind, and soul.

Kenneth Platter, 34
Sweden Yearly Meeting
Sweden

Looking for God

I don't remember the first time I watched someone and saw their Inner Light, but I remember the first time I found it in someone I didn't particularly like. Armando always kind of scared me. He was a "left back" with rumors of fights, drugs, and gangs hanging around him. He was also in my gym class.

One day our class was playing soccer, a sport better without all the out-of-bounds rules. Armando was the goalie for the other team, and I found myself alone with him on that end of the field after the ball chased everyone to the other end. I wondered aloud about how soccer works, and much to my surprise, I got an entire explanation of the game from Armando.

Something in the way he explained it to me made me think he could make a good father. It was like a flash away from his hardened outer appearance and into the kind of person he could have been and maybe still could be. It was a glimpse not of his potential, but the beauty he kept covered up.

For me, that's all God is really about, that touch of beauty in even the most ugly of things. Sure, I didn't become friends with Armando after that day in gym, but I could never strongly dislike him after that. Once I'd seen a person's Inner Light I could no longer hate them. Realizing this, I began to look for the Inner Light of anyone I didn't like or was mad at. Looking for that piece of beauty that is God in everyone cured my feelings of anger and hate.

Maggie Wanner, 17
Lake Forest Friends Meeting, Illinois Yearly Meeting (FGC)
United States

Testimony of a Nontheist Friend*

I identify as a Quaker. As I write this, I'm in the process of becoming an official member of the Religious Society of Friends. I believe deeply in Quakerism and in the Quaker community.

I also identify as a nontheist. I do not see any contradiction.

I see myself not only as a Quaker, but as a religious person. I hold deep spiritual beliefs that do not center on a figure that I would identify as God—especially not an anthropomorphic one. What exactly I do believe in and how and to what extent is a lot harder to pinpoint, and in any case vacillates on a daily basis.

Whatever I believe in, I generally consider it to be an inseparable part of the universe, rather than *apart* from it. As someone at FGC put it: natural rather than *super*natural.

I can no longer state with any certainty how my consciousness evolved; my childhood recollections are too hazy and probably subject to selective memory by now. I think what happened is that somewhere before I turned thirteen, I came around to the thought that a universe with an omnipotent, omniscient, omnipresent force creating and controlling it made less sense to me than a universe without.

It seems to me that the universe makes sense by itself, and so therefore there wasn't any need to believe in something extra to explain its existence. Besides, I take the view that if you *do* believe in something extra to explain the universe's existence, then you have to explain the something extra's existence as well.

Basically, I view the idea of God or any comparable entity, entities, force or forces as superfluous concepts which needlessly complicate our view of reality.

I know that we don't have all the answers (why does the universe work the way it does? What happens to us when we die?), and possibly we never will. However, this does not mean to me that we should just pick a plausible answer and call it the right one.

Some people, I know, find comfort in the certainty that comes with their belief in God, or some analogous concept. For myself, I have learned to appreciate the virtues of ambiguity. If I can't know the right answer, I'll settle for the answer "I don't know."

Of course, you can believe in something even while admitting that you can't actually *know* whether it's true or not. I certainly believe plenty of things I can't prove objectively. But I don't think I believe anything in particular about those great, unknowable questions to which God is supposed to be the Answer. I do believe that several possible answers are *not* the Answer, and that happens to include God by any other name.

How am I religious, then? How am I a Quaker? As my mom likes to point out, the root of the word "religion" means "binding together" and makes no mention of a deity or deities. This is how I view religion: a spiritual connection between two or more human beings, and between human beings and their environment. A connection very much like the connection between family members and between close friends: namely, love.

Religion, to me, is all about this connection to and love of other people and of the universe we live in. The different faiths and sects reflect the different ways human beings express this all-encompassing love, and how they think best to serve it. That is what being religious means to me.

What makes me a Quaker, in my mind, is my belief and participation in Quakerism. I believe in the testimonies of integrity, equality, simplicity, and peace (some of which I have a harder time following than others, just like everybody else). I believe there is "that of God in everyone" where "God" is understood to mean "goodness," "humanity," "morality," or something along those lines.

I participate in Quaker communities and in Quaker processes, which I have great respect for. Thus, I am, in my own consideration at least, thoroughly Quaker.

Lincoln Alpern, 22
Scarsdale Friends Meeting, New York Yearly Meeting (FGC-FUM)
United States

*Editor's note: Nontheism encompasses both atheism and agnosticism, but it is a broader term. For some people, it means a rejection of or questioning attitude toward God, however defined. For others, it is embracing a spiritual, metaphysical, supernatural, Divine concept which adherents believe to be God, but which they see as different from the archetypal image of God. "Nontheist" is usually a self-chosen moniker: If you call yourself a nontheist, you probably are one. The above piece is not intended as a definitive statement of what constitutes "nontheism." Rather, the intention is only to give the reader a general idea.

Un Ateo Arrepentido

Mi nombre es Raúl Choque, nací en mil novecientos setenta y cinco, en una localidad del altiplano de La Paz – Bolivia. El hogar donde vine al mundo era muy pobre, en casa había muy pocos objetos y entre estos una maleta de libros dejados por mis abuelos. Posteriormente, estos libros me llevarían a poseer el hábito de lectura.

Mis padres se convirtieron a la Iglesia evangélica Bautista, cuando yo tendría mis siete años y, dos años después, cambiaron por razones desconocidas por la Iglesia de Santidad Amigos. Fue de esa forma, como yo llegué a congregarme entre los Amigos Cuáqueros.

En mi adolescencia, llegue a una crisis en mi fe, a pesar de estar estudiando en un colegio evangélico, y de haber terminado de leer toda la Biblia a los catorce años. Mis preguntas y dudas eran generalmente sobre la existencia de Dios, la validez de los dogmas y el papel desempeñado por el cristianismo en la historia. Todos estos cuestionamientos me llevaron a dudar y al escepticismo, que finalmente llegue a ser ateo. En ese entonces, solo soñaba en ser un revolucionario así como Che Guevara o Tupac Katari, por mi condición Aymara, Carlos Marx se había convertido en mi ídolo. Mi odio por la Biblia y el Cristianismo en general era como un fuego inextinguible.

Mientras yo andaba orgulloso de ser ateo, interior y psicológicamente me encontraba muy mal: tenía frecuentes pesadillas y mi mamá me decía que dormía con los ojos abiertos. Por tanto tuve un problema en la cabeza, en la parte de la nuca sentía una especie de calor. Alguien me dijo que yo padecía este problema por el exceso de estudio, pero esto no era cierto, ya que yo podía asimilar normalmente lo que leía.

Andando así cierto día del año mil novecientos noventa y cuatro, caminando por una plaza céntrica de la ciudad de La Paz, por curiosidad me acerqué a una conglomeración de personas, donde en su interior, estaban unos supuestos astrólogos o mentalistas que tenían los ojos vendados y trataban de leer la suerte de las personas que los rodeaban. Esto me causó impresión, que al parecer estos mentalistas estaban diciendo lo cierto de las cosas; por ello, igual que otros transeúntes o curiosos, compré un sobre de carta que vendían por el derecho de consulta. Luego nos llevó a su consultorio, no muy lejos del lugar. Al llegar allí yo fui el primero en ingresar al consultorio. El mentalista me preguntó sobre mis problemas y yo se lo conté todo lo que me pasaba y, en seguida me puso en la palma de la mano un objeto que tenía la forma de una pirámide egipcia, luego, me dijo que tenía todo estos problemas porque estaba embrujado y que, el me haría una limpieza espiritual, por un costo módico, en ese mismo momento, si no llevaba dinero, podría dejar mi reloj como prenda. Todo esto lo que me dijo, me causó un gran impacto en mi vida, me sentí como entre la pared y la espada. Por un lado, aunque ateo, dije en mi conciencia aceptar la propuesta del mentalista, ¿A caso no sería como entregarse al enemigo, si por si acaso existiera? Pero, además ¿Qué me dirían mis padres cristianos al enterarse de esta mi decisión?. Todas estas razones hicieron que yo no cediera a esta tentación del enemigo. Del consultorio me fui de lágrimas y muy quebrantado el corazón: me decía a mi mismo ¡por qué soy tan infortunado! ¿Por qué a mí me tiene que pasar todo esto? A la noche para dormir, después de mucho tiempo, hice un lamento, no se si llamarlo oración, que fue algo así: "Señor Dios, no se si existes, si existes quisiera que me ayudes, a salir de esta situación tan difícil en el que me encuentro." Así me rompí a llorar por una media hora. Luego dormí y en sueños ví prendida una luz grande en una densa oscuridad y a la vez me peleé con una loca que dormía envuelto con mis frazadas y esta me dió un tremendo golpe con su espada en la nuca, y fue este dolor el que me despertó del sueño, pero el dolor era una cosa muy real.

En los siguientes días, acostumbraba antes de acostarme hacer lamentos y llantos por mi desdichada situación. En mis sueños constantemente peleaba con animales extraños, unas veces me vencían ellos y en otras yo los vencía. Algo raro ocurrió también en todo este lapso de tiempo: el hecho de que cuando yo tenía algo de fe, en mi nuca sentía poco calor, en cambio si dudaba, más calor lo sentía. Todo esto se repetía muchas y muchas veces ¡fue una cosa muy extraña! Pero, a la vez mi pregunta era ¿Quién o qué hacía todo aquello en mi vida? ¿Si Dios no existía, entonces a quien le interesaba mi fe? Por ahí empecé a pensar que algún milagro estaba ocurriendo con mi vida.

Al saber que el tener fe, le favorecía a mi salud desde entonces, trate de obtener la fe, por cualquier medio posible. Recuerdo que un día miércoles a fines del año mil novecientos noventa y cuatro me propuse leer un texto que contenía argumentos sobre la existencia de Dios y con la finalidad de dejar de dudar y así quedar definitivamente sano de mi enfermedad. Pero, lamentablemente, al terminar de leer el texto en la tarde, seguía con dudas entonces en ese momento me sería imposible creer completamente en Dios. Creo que voy a quedar, escéptico por el resto de mi vida, dije. Esa noche, como había culto de oración en la Iglesia, fui allí, no se más que por curiosidad o por charlar con algún amigo, que por devoción. Pero, lo extraordinario fue que recibí un flechazo de sermón durante la predica, no por que supiese el predicador mi situación, si no, mas bien, yo le atribuiría todo esto al Señor. El predicador mas o menos decía así: "*usted porque anda diciendo que no puede, no debes decir que no puedes, porque no vas a pelear tu, sino el Señor. Si usted se encuentra como Israel en el Mar Rojo, pesimista o falto de fe, pues no se rinda, el Señor nos promete que El peleará por nosotros y por ti (Éxodo 14:14). Lo único que tu debes hacer, es orar, caer de rodillas ante El y con esto de seguro usted será victorioso, póngalo en practica todo esto.*" Así tronaba en mí la voz del predicador. Estas palabras calaron tan hondo en mi vida que, al regresar a casa, en serio lo puse en practica en oración. Al empezar como siempre mis frases eran "no se si Dios existe y si existes ayúdame," así de manera monótona y con un corazón tan duro como el acero me quedaba buscando el favor Divino. Después, pasados unos diez a quince minutos de orar y repetir aquellas frases en mi interior sentía una especie de llovizna, como que algo me estuviera mojando. Luego seguía orando y pasados otro tanto sentía aun más quebrantamiento de corazón, la presencia del Señor; es decir ¡mi pobre corazón de acero se estaba derritiendo! Las dudas y la enfermedad se habían desaparecido de mi vida. ¡Qué lindo fue aquel momento! ¡Gracias al Señor lo digo aun hoy de lagrimas! Así como yo vencí al ateismo y a las dudas con el arma de oración, fui ganado por el Señor!

Por ello siento la fuerza de decirles a todos que el Dios que les escogió es un Dios real, pero muy real. Es un Dios verdadero. Nunca antes había pensado que Dios fuera tan cierto y tan verdadero! Y cuantas maravillas y milagros más me mostró el Señor hasta ahora.

Actualmente, con la fe que me dió el Señor me encuentro trabajando, estudiando y siempre ocupado en su obra. Además me siento muy Cuáquero. Leí que nuestros hermanos Cuáqueros han realizado una obra muy noble por el mundo, principalmente en lo social, pacifismo y espiritual. Pero también, quiero aprovechar en citar una de nuestras debilidades; que es la falta de comunicación y poca coordinación que aun existe entra los Amigos Cuáqueros de diferentes países. Este vacío lo debemos llenar nosotros, los jóvenes Amigos. Esto debe ser uno de nuestros objetivos y desafíos, con la ayuda del Señor podemos. ¡Trabajemos juntos!, ¡sintamos la identidad Cuáquera!, y ¡sigamos llevando la luz del Evangelio por el mundo! . . . Amen.

Raul Choque Mamani, 33
Iglesia Los Andes B, Iglesia Evangélica Misión Boliviana de
Santidad Amigos (EFCI)
Bolivia

A Repentant Atheist

My name is Raúl Choque, I was born in 1975, in a locality of the heights of La Paz, Bolivia. The home where I came into the world was very poor, there were very few objects in the house, and among them was a suitcase of books left by my grandparents. Subsequently, these books would lead me into the habit of reading.

My parents converted to the evangelical Baptist church when I was seven years old and, two years later, they switched for unknown reasons to the Holiness Friends Church. It was in this form that I came to congregate with the Quakers. In my adolescence, I had a crisis of faith, due to studying in an evangelical high school, and having finished reading the whole Bible at the age of fourteen. My questions and doubts were generally about the existence of God, the validity of the dogmas, and the role played by Christianity throughout history. All of these questions led me to doubt and skepticism, such that I ultimately became an atheist. At that point, I only dreamed of being a revolutionary like Che Guevara or Tupac Katari (an indigenous leader), because I am Aymara. Karl Marx had become my idol. My hatred of the Bible and Christianity in general was like an inextinguishable fire.

While I went around proud to be an atheist, inside and psychologically I was in a very bad place: I had frequent nightmares and my mom told me I slept with my eyes open. Because of all this I had a problem with my head. On the nape of my neck you could feel a type of heat. Someone told me that I suffered from this problem because of excessive studying, but this wasn't true, because I could assimilate what I was reading normally.

Going along that way, there was a day in 1994 when, walking through a central plaza in the city La Paz, out of curiosity I went to a large group of people; in their interior, there were several supposed astrologers or mind readers who had their eyes blindfolded as they tried to read the fortunes of the people around them. This made an impression on me, that apparently those mind readers were telling the truth about things; because of that, the same as other passersby and the curious, I bought a letter in an envelope that they were selling as entrance for a consultation. Later they took us to their office, not very far from that place. Upon arriving there, I was the first to enter their office. The mind reader asked me about my problems and I told him everything that was going on and, right after he placed in my hand an object that had the shape of an Egyptian pyramid, he told me that I had all these problems because I was bewitched and that he would do a spiritual cleansing for me, for a modest cost, at that very moment. If I didn't have money on me, I could leave my watch as collateral.

All that he told me had a great impact on my life, I felt like I was between a rock and a hard place (*entre la pared y la espada*). On the one hand, despite being an atheist, my conscience told me to accept the mind reader's proposal. Wouldn't it be like giving myself in to the enemy, if by some chance it were to exist? But, furthermore, what would my Christian parents say upon being informed of my decision? All of these reasons made me not yield to this temptation of the enemy. I left the office in tears and very heartbroken. I said to myself, why am I so unfortunate! Why does all this have to happen to me? At night when I went to sleep, after a long time, I recited a lament, I don't know if I should call it a prayer, that went something like this: "Lord God, I don't know if you exist, if you exist I would like you to help me, to leave this very difficult situation in which I find myself." After this I was able to stop crying for half an hour. Then I slept and in my dreams I saw a great light lit up in a dense darkness and at the same time I fought with a crazy woman who slept wrapped up in my blankets, and she gave me a tremendous blow with her sword to the nape of my neck, and it was this pain that woke me from the dream, but the pain was very real.

In the following days, I became accustomed to reciting laments and cries about my unfortunate situation before going to bed. In my dreams I was constantly fighting with strange animals, sometimes they beat me and other times I beat them. Something strange also happened in this whole lapse of time: the fact that when I felt a little faith, the nape of my neck felt little heat, on the other hand when I doubted, I felt more heat. All of this repeated many, many times—it was a very strange thing! But, at the same time my question was, who or what was doing all this in my life? If God didn't exist, then who was interested in my faith? At that point I began to think that some kind of miracle was occurring in my life.

After realizing that having faith improved my health, I tried to obtain faith by whatever means possible. I remember that one Wednesday at the end of 1994 I decided to read a text that had arguments about the existence of God with the purpose of stopping my doubt and thus definitively healing my illness. But, lamentably, upon finishing the text in the evening, I continued with doubts so in that moment it was impossible for me to completely believe in God. "I think that I'm going to remain skeptical for the rest of my life," I said.

That night, as there was a prayer worship in the church, I went there. I don't know if it was more out of curiosity or to talk to a friend, than out of devotion. But the extraordinary thing is that I received an arrow in my heart from the sermon during the preaching, not because the preacher knew of my situation; but, rather, I would attribute this to the Lord. The preacher more or less said this: *"You go about saying that you can't, you should not say that you can't, because it is not you who will be fighting, but the Lord. If you find yourself like Israel in the Red Sea, pessimistic or lacking faith, do not yield, the Lord promises us that He shall fight for us and for you (Exod. 14:14). The only thing that you need to do, is to pray to fall to your knees before Him and with this you will surely be victorious, put all of this into practice."*

Thus the voice of the preacher thundered in me. These words penetrated so deeply into my life that, upon returning home, I very seriously put prayer into practice. At first my words were, as always, "I don't know if God exists and, if you exist, help me." In that monotonous manner and with a heart as hard as steel I kept seeking Divine favor. Later, ten to fifteen minutes had passed in praying and repeating those phrases after I felt a kind of light rain inside me, as though something were wetting me. Then I continued praying and after awhile had passed, I felt even more breaking of my heart and the presence of the Lord. That is to say, my poor steel heart was melting! The doubts and the illness had begun to disappear from my life. How beautiful that moment was! Thanks to the Lord I say even today in tears! That is how I conquered atheism and the doubts with the weapon of prayer. I was won by the Lord!

Because of it I feel the strength to tell all that the God who chose you all is a real God, very real. It is a true God. Never before had I thought that God was so true and so real! And what marvels and miracles has the Lord shown me up until now.

Currently, with the faith that the Lord gave me I find myself working, studying, and always occupied with His ministry. Furthermore I feel very Quaker. I read that our Quaker brethren have carried out very noble work in the world, principally in social, peace, and spiritual issues. But also, I want to take advantage of the chance to note one of our weaknesses, which is the lack of communication and little coordination that still exists between the Quaker Friends in different countries. This is an emptiness that we must fill. This should be one of the objectives and challenges of us the young Friends, with the help of the Lord we can—we must—work together! We must feel the Quaker identity! And we must continue carrying the light of the Gospel to the world!

Amen.

Raul Choque Mamani, 33
Los Andes B Meeting, Bolivian Holiness Mission of Evangelical
Friends Church (EFCI)
Bolivia

Friends of the Truth

George Fox writes, "There is one, even Jesus Christ, who can speak to your condition." He felt he had found God on his own and his "heart did leap with joy."

I was born in a small village of Nepal and my family was very poor. My father is an alcoholic and has had this problem for as long as I remember. My father was always unemployed, so for his expenses he used to sell crops. So our family did not have enough food for the whole year and my mother used to go to her parents' house and bring food for us. She worked hard to feed us. He sold half of our land for his expenses. I have two older sisters and one younger brother. Both sisters were married at the age of fourteen, as we did not have enough food to feed the whole family. They are also poor and I am trying to support all their kids and family. One niece stays with us, and I have paid for her study.

During my childhood and teenage years I have experienced poverty, crying every day for food and because of my father's behavior. Somehow I managed to finish school. Then I started searching for a job to help my family and continue my study. I did work such as cleaning jobs in restaurants, office boy, and delivery man. From my income I was buying food for my family and paying my college fees. With difficulty I was able to finish college. Then I started searching for better jobs. I tried many places but did not get a job. There was no one to help me, to give me a reference for a job. I did not have any support from relatives or to show me the way. I was in a really bad condition.

During those days I used to keep searching and visited many places looking for a job. At that time I met a friend who took me to Friends Church. I was having lots of difficulty, but there I found peace. I kept on attending the service every week. Finally I found worshipping the Creator is better than worshipping created things like stones, rivers, trees, cows, etc. After that I was feeling happy even though I was having hardships. I found there is One who can speak to my condition.

After that I was abandoned by my family, friends, and society. I endured lots of persecution mentally and, sometimes, physically for being a Christian. They used to say I was a cow eater and I became a Christian only so I could get a dollar and go to the USA. In the Hindu religion a cow is a goddess. So my days were so bad, but as I walked in the Light I was able to handle all the circumstances and keep walking in the faith that God has a plan for me, which was to make my future bright.

I kept looking for a job but did not get any. I found out to get a job in Nepal I must have technical knowledge so I shared my feelings with my church. After a year, one missionary from the United States helped me to join a computer course. I started learning basic computers. After I finished the basic course I started teaching computer in a small computer institute and as a home tutor. I was then able to buy enough food for my family and save some money for further computer study. I worked for three years and then after saving some money I went to Bangalore, India, for further computer studies. I returned from India by God's grace (it is very hard to get information technology jobs, too, because there are many IT experts available), and I got a nice job in a newspaper company. I am able to support my family, friends, and church.

Now things are different. As the Bible says, there is [a] time for everything. Those who used to hate me and not want to see my face come to me and ask for suggestions for their kids, businesses, and many other things. My presence for them is now prestige for them because I work for a big company and hold a senior post. So now I am able to tell them easily about the love of God. Sometimes I wonder why we always share with them. Let them come to us by seeing our life and listen to us. Let our lives speak why we are different than others, and let them ask and we will tell why we believe.

But I remember when George Fox found this truth, he wanted to share it with others. He began to travel about England, talking to people. His main message was that religion wasn't just a matter of going to church, repeating prayers, singing hymns, or reading books about God, though all these might be helpful. True religion was a personal experience, a personal adventure. It was the spirit of God within us meeting the greater spirit of God outside ourselves.

Pradip Lamichhane
Nepal Yearly Meeting
Nepal

just me and my smugness

"i must like quakerism because in the silence it's just me and my smugness."

i wrote that on october 2, 2006, in some musings on why i was interested in quakerism after having been intrigued by and then eventually annoyed by unitarian universalism. i was a little bitter about the whole situation at the time, feeling like unitarian universalists had let me down somehow. in my perspective, they just did not challenge themselves enough.

the quakers i saw when i finally started coming to san francisco monthly meeting seemed to be challenging themselves. i heard difficult questions being asked, and that excited me. there was activism going on and there was something pulsing that i couldn't find in unitarian universalism. and people welcomed me. i was odd and quirky and shy but i felt

welcomed and kind of already loved right away. i like supportive attention, and i really felt that, with these people, i could grow.

the meetings were sort of terrible. i didn't know who or what god
was, i didn't know what i was supposed to do, and all i had were me and
my thoughts. my thoughts were pretty incriminating. i spent so much
time searching around for god, asking for some sort of acknowledgment
that i was doing something right, feeling more alone than i had before i'd
come. but then someone would speak out of the silence and i would be
amazed that people were saying these loving, amazing, challenging things.

i went to the social hour and tried to talk to people. i went to the
thursday evening study group and tried to figure out how to listen. i
read our seekers' packets and everything that the keyword *quaker* brought
up in the local library. and i started going to therapy and codependents
anonymous. i told my truth and i listened to others and i blinked and i
breathed and eventually the silence of quaker meeting made sense. yes,
there was my smugness and my anger and my ugly ugly insides, but there
was a gentle voice, too. a voice that knew that yes i did these things and
yes i thought these things, but i was human and i was loved and the universe could hold me. the universe could hold me and was holding me. it
can and it does.

quakerism doesn't mean that i don't have ugly thoughts anymore.
that i'm not sometimes grumpy or have sour opinions of other people.
but for me it has meant that i can listen to the gentle parts of myself,
and to the truth of those who i have sour opinions of. the universe can
hold me and the universe can hold them and we're all in this together.
i'm more gentle with unitarian universalists now as well. maybe i'll go
back and visit sometime. they've done some amazing things, too. but i'm
pretty sure my home is in quakerism.

> *cubbie storm, 30*
> *San Francisco Monthly Meeting, Pacific Yearly Meeting (Independent)*
> *United States*

My Relationship with God

Some years back, I was not saved. I was living a life that no one could
understand. I was one of the girls who was more stubborn and, when
it came to the word of God, I was unable to attend any church services
although my parents were all fully Christians of the Quaker church. I

continued with my stubbornness and unfaithfulness until it reached a time when I attended a crusade last year, when one of the pastors preached about the way you could know God and the way to live your life with God. Without wasting time, I humbled myself in front of the crowd and I was given some words of prayer. Meanwhile the pastor held his hands on my head to show that I have received the word of God in my heart. He told me that from today onward I would be humble, intelligent, and faithful in all situations that I am going to live in.

Surely from that day when I gave my life to God, I have experienced more good things in my life than a few years back. I see that the power of God is controlling my life. Even now I am able to spread the gospel of God to all people in the world, to be able to know more about God and to worship him in all ways because he is the only God who answers prayers whenever one asks.

I also obtain courage to stand in front of those who do not know God, and they all get saved as long as I say a word of prayer from God. Surely to know God is more and more good than to live without Jesus Christ in your life.

From the time I got saved I have assisted the churches in different places, although I am still a schoolgirl. I have found out that to know God is another wonderful thing because in my primary education and even in secondary school I was very weak in class. I was always among the last students in secondary school from Form One, but when I got saved all things went on well, even in my academics. I moved from poor performance and became a hero. Many of my fellow students and teachers were very surprised to see me appearing as "top student" and wondering how I moved to that position.

I called all the students to assemble and told them all things that God had done for me to be able to move up to where I am now. They were all happy, as many of them were urging me to pray for them to get saved so that they can know God and God will help them in their life situation. Where I am now, I want to act as a role model to my church, school, village, and the whole world by being a Christian who knows more about God. I am ready to save other people and to convert other people from different countries to be able to know God. I am praying to God to give me wisdom and ability to pray for other people in the whole world of Africa.

Eddah Robai, 16
Kenya

Faith Is the Breakthrough of Everything

After passing so many challenges, I realized that without God everything is useless. So I decided to go to church and receive Christ as my personal saviour so that I can get direction on what to do.

I got saved while in form two in Gaseta Mixed Secondary School. When I got converted I passed many challenges, and after every challenge I realised that God wanted me to be strong. Reading the word, attending Bible studies at school and visiting different preachers made me grow in my faith.

Now in my faith with Christ, my faith has grown and I have high hopes that if you believe in Christ Jesus, one day [you] shall see God. My faith in God is very strong, because in my lifestyle I have always been faithful knowing that one day my faith in God shall protect me and keep me in a safe place. Through faith you can do everything through Christ, who strengthens his people. Faith, according to me, is the breakthrough of everything. With faith you can succeed in everything you do, so my faith in God has grown out of my experience, and has made me strong in prayers. Because without faith you can't pray.

Our God is a faithful God. When I communicate with Him through prayers, He has answered me. I have been successful in life because of prayers. In school and high school I used to be the last girl in class, but after my prayers, church prayers, and my parent's and sisters' prayers, at last in my KCSE I passed my exams. Really, with God everything is possible. Through prayers and your faith in God you can be a successful person in life.

Catila N. Brenda, 23
Kenya

Dios Guia Mi Vida

Vengo de una familia no cristiana, pero Dios puso en mí la necesidad de asistir a una Iglesia, pues me mostró una vida diferente a la que tenía y desde entonces siento en mi el deseo de buscar al Señor.

Empecé la vida cristiana a los 12 años, hoy tengo 23 años; y en todo este tiempo hubo veces en los que me aleje del Señor, pero aun así me he dado cuenta de que mi Señor no me ha abandonado.

Sea vuestras costumbres sin avaricia, contentos con lo que tenéis ahora; porque el dijo: no te desamparé, ni te dejaré (Heb. 13:5, RSV).

De manera que podemos decir confiadamente: "El Señor es mi ayudador; no temeré lo que me pueda hacer el hombre" (Heb. 13:6–7, RSV).

Después de tantos tropiezos en mi vida mundana, o no cristiana, el Señor me llamó de nuevo a su camino; y yo, muy emocionada y feliz de saber y poder ver el amor de Dios por mi, volví corriendo y sedienta de su palabra. Hasta hoy siento al conocer lo que Dios hace por mi. Porque es ahora cuanto más puedo ver el cuidado de Dios para guiar mi vida y las oportunidades que El me da para crecer en mi fe y para trabajar por amor a El en mi Iglesia. En los problemas aún cuando yo se que estoy mal y no puedo corregirme, es El, El que me corrige con su palabra, en este caso y en estos tiempos mas utilizando a mi maestra de discipulado; y por medio de un libro que por leer compré en la calle lo cual fue de gran apoyo en mi vida.

Ahora sirvo en mi Iglesia, soy maestra de niños, miembro del ministerio del alabanza y secretaria de concilio; me gusta trabajar para el Señor porque yo se que lo que hago en la Iglesia es de agrado para mi Señor y me gusta hacer de todo lo que se pueda.

Agradezco al Señor por el amor y paciencia que tiene para conmigo y eso me hace feliz. No se imaginan como quisiera saber hacer de todo, para que con todo lo que sepa pueda servir al Señor. "¡¡¡Dios es grande en amor!!! Y yo feliz.

Erika Paula Miranda Gutierrez, 23
Congregación Cristiana Amigos, Iglesia Nacional Evangélica "Los Amigos" de Bolivia
Bolivia

God Guides My Life

I come from a family that is not Christian, but God put in me the need to attend a church, because he showed me a different life from the one I had, and since then I have felt in me the desire to seek the Lord.

I began the Christian life at age twelve, today I am twenty-three years old; and in all these years there have been times when I withdrew from the Lord, but even so I have realized that my Lord has not abandoned me.

Keep your life free from love of money, and be content with what you have; for he has said, "I will never fail you nor forsake you." (Heb. 13:5, RSV)

Therefore, we can confidently say: "The Lord is my helper, I will not be afraid; what can anyone do to me?" (Heb. 13: 6–7, RSV)

After so many lapses in my worldly, non-Christian life, the Lord called me again to his path; and I, excited and happy to know and see God's love for me, returned running and thirsty for his word. Even today I feel touched to know what God does for me. Because now more than ever, I can see God's care in guiding my life and the opportunities He gives me to grow in my faith and to work for love of Him in my meeting. When I have problems, even when I know that I am wrong and cannot change my ways, it is He who changes me with his word, in this case and in these times, mainly via my teacher of discipleship, and by means of a book that I bought in the street to read that has been of great help in my life.

Now I serve in my meeting, I am a teacher of children, a member of the ministry of praise and secretary of the council. I enjoy working for the Lord because I know that what I do in the meeting is pleasing to my Lord and I like to do all that I can.

I thank the Lord for the love and patience he has for me and this makes me happy. You cannot imagine how I would like to know how to do everything, so that with everything I knew I could serve the Lord. "God is great in love!!!" And I am happy.

> *Erika Paula Miranda Gutierrez, 23*
> *Christian Friends Congregation, National Evangelical Friends*
> *Church of Bolivia (EFCI)*
> *Bolivia*

My Relationship with God

I was saved in 2003 when one of my brothers in Christ came [to] our home and visited me. He tried to tell me the difficulties that one could face during his or her life in the world.

Before being saved I was involved in too many things that no one was happy with, things like theft. I used to steal to the extent of even stealing one of my neighbor's chickens. Later on he was to [be]witch me till death. When my brother explained to me what God does, that was the very first thing I had to tell him. If God could really forgive me, I could ask for forgiveness. He encouraged me through giving me examples of the prodigal son in the Bible who was forgiven by his father, and he also gave me an example of God himself, who gave his only son to die for all of us on the cross.

Things were not so easy the way you [might] think. It came to this thing that my brother said, to visit at the church I had to think twice before telling him anything. After awhile I asked him if he would introduce me at the church. This was easy for him. So he told me to believe, and he prayed with me and even taught me how to pray, since I was totally a good pagan.

The day came. I went to church as usual with some [shyness], since my friends behind me [were] laughing at me and even barking at me for the choice I made.

It came time for praying and worshipping. This was hard to me, and I could try to peer at my friends. They were praying very hard and some of them talking in tongues, so I had to believe myself when a pastor came and prayed for me. I had to confess myself to God and asked him if he could really save me and make me his daughter.

After awhile I saw things changing in my life, and this was due [to] regular church youth meetings. This was unbelievable to my parents, who had given up on me.

Within a short period I had to visit seminars at different churches, and this was the very time I could face very many problems that could even make me backslide. Through prayers I overcame them.

I had to put my faith in God and believe in Him though my parents were not saved. I used to pray each and every time so that my parents would be saved, but this was nonsense if I would try to explain to them. But a time came when God really wanted me to show that the God I serve is a Living God. I went down on my knees and prayed so bitterly and this was the time when my parents came to me and told me I could take them to church. I had to thank God with all my faith and strength since through me many of my people got saved. And through all that I have overcome, prayers have been my savior and I will continue believing in Him.

Linate Munyane, 19
Elgon Religious Society of Friends (FUM)
Kenya

Brokenness and Touching God's Divine Presence

"Out of our brokenness make us a blessing." (Judith L. Brutz, 1990)

"Rise radiant in the sacrament of pain." (Thomas Kelly, 1939)

I have been thinking and praying lately on the idea of brokenness. When I was at the 2007 young adult Friends conference in Burlington, New Jersey, a Friend spoke in meeting and said that the Religious Society of Friends was broken and it was we who had broken it. Later, several Friends encouraged me to view the idea of brokenness not merely as negative, that if something is broken we must work to fix it. Rather, perhaps it was a more positive sensitizing and opening to God.

As I was praying on brokenness in meeting for worship recently, several things came to me. The first was a variation on a line from a prayer I had just written: "Let us know suffering so we might find your strength Oh God and ours." I also continuously kept returning to the image of fire and burning as representing the Holy Spirit. The idea of hearing God, and being open to the Spirit only after knowing great suffering and pain, is an idea with very biblical roots. I was reminded of images of the Holy Spirit as tongues of fire in Acts, the idea of being baptized in fire as representing the Holy Spirit, the line from Thomas when Jesus says, "I have cast fire upon the world" (Gospel of Thomas, Saying 10), and in Paul when he says, "Where the Spirit of the Lord is, there is freedom" (2 Corinthians 3:17, NRSV).

Also during meeting, I was reminded of a story told by a Friend at the Young Adult Friends conference about a group of early Friends who gathered one Sunday for worship only to discover that their meeting house had been burnt to the ground during the night by a hostile mob. Instead of going home, these Friends chose to worship standing on top of the burnt rubble of their meeting house.

After much prayer, I have come to see brokenness as being broken open to God, as having one's walls torn down to experience God's love and grace, and as being torn from the roots to find freedom in the Lord. What does it mean that the Religious Society of Friends is broken, and that it is we who have broken it? I now believe that we have broken ourselves open to the power and grace of the Lord. That we have struggled and suffered and cried out for guidance and have been torn open to Her divine will. We have lit ourselves afire with the power of the Spirit and we are made free. I believe that when the smoke clears we will find ourselves standing among the rubble of that burning, made new in the simplicity of what we truly are: a group of people bound together by the expectant waiting and witness of the Lord. And we will know our strength. And we will know God's.

> *Anna Obermayer, 23*
> *Binghamton Community Friends, New York Yearly Meeting*
> *(FUM-FGC)*
> *United States*
>
> Editor's note: A version of this piece appeared on Anna's blog, *Raised in the Light.*

Meet God in Desperation

Growing up in my home meeting I was filled with emptiness. My curiosity was answered with questions. I found answers in Taoism, Buddhism, Bushido, Spirit Animals, and Punk Rock. Through these I was given the power of stillness, the strength of sensitivity, deep inward knowledge that connected me to the world beyond myself, and a desire to be an agent of transformation. I lost my finitude in the infinite, finding communion with all that is. I did not find friends in my meeting. I was a seeker but not a Quaker. I was certainly not a Christian. I was not taught about the history, theology, or practice of the Religious Society of Friends, but I was given the space to begin an exploration of the world of spiritual reality that would, eventually, lead me home.

I was confronted with my first unmediated experience of Quakerism and Christ during the summer after my second year of seminary. I had grown up in the Friends Meeting of New Orleans. I attended Earlham College, majoring in religion, and went on to the Earlham School of Religion. I enjoyed thinking about the "big questions" and reflecting on my role in the world. I was an observer of religion but not a participant in religion. Through school I was beginning to know about religion but I had no *experience* of relationship, divine communion. The nature of this relationship with spirituality was called to account on my first day as a chaplain intern at a hospital in New Orleans. Another chaplain's mother was ill and I told him, in a liberal, unprogrammed Friends way, that he would "be in my thoughts." He snapped at me, "Say a prayer, will you?"

I was shocked into realizing what would be expected of me as a minister. Hurricane Katrina and the subsequent flood were still at the forefront of everyone's mind. I was going to be building relationships with suffering and grieving people of faith, people who had an experience of God, people who needed something that was from God and that they expected me to share with them. After nearly ten years of interest in spirituality, I had no idea what I could say to anyone about God. I spent a lot of time in my first month of chaplaincy lurking in hallways, peering furtively into patients' rooms, believing that there was nothing that I could offer.

This self-doubt and insecurity is something that had built up in me over the course of my life. In myriad relationships I was told, in word or deed, that I could not trust the love of other people. I could not trust that I would be accepted, not judged. I could not trust that I was accepted even by the people with whom I related most closely. As a person who felt rejected, I found that aligning myself with God gave me immediate acceptance in the eyes of most people. I was only rejected by people who did not accept God, in which case they were not rejecting me. As I discovered that my ministry was valued, my self-confidence flourished. I put together a little chaplain's toolbox of useful hymns, passages, prayers, and behaviors and I felt great. I was not just working well, but I was doing good work.

Then I met Ms. Mildred. Mildred was depressed, she was in pain. She was stuck in the hospital; away from her pets, friends dead and dying, no family, feeling rejected by her church. She was depressed and she wanted me to make her feel better. I talked and listened. I prayed. I asked what Bible passages and hymns she liked. I visited her for three days and each time she sent me away, telling me that I was not helping. She expected me to say something that would make her feel better. I was rejected by a person craving salvation. In this case, a patient desperately wanted God, comfort, love, and I was unable to present God to her.

Ms. Mildred and I were alike in our despair. Her sense of rejection and her depression mirrored my own. This woman sat alone in her dark room longing for care and comfort but totally unable to accept it when it was offered. I saw myself in her, abandoned and afraid, running after friends and family looking for acceptance and love, never being able to accept acceptance when it was given. I did not realize any of this until later, but we were united in grief and fear of abandonment. What I knew then was that she was despairing and I was desperate to find a way to help her. Like Jacob wrestling in the dark, in desperation I met God face to face.

I left Ms. Mildred's room for the third time and I sat by a window looking out over the lake that had so recently flooded the city I loved. I stared out of the window for a few moments in silence, the blue sky stretched to the horizon. Even from the ninth floor I could not see the far shore. I closed my eyes and I prayed. I prayed more earnestly than I ever had before. I prayed for myself and for Ms. Mildred, asking over and over again, "What can I say to this woman? What can I say?" I rocked back and forth in the darkness behind my eyelids, repeating, "What can I say? What can I tell this woman?" I felt my chest caving in. I felt my body vibrating. A golden light flashed in the darkness and a message came into my mind that I knew with direct certainty was of God, mediated by Christ: You are loved.

I stood up. I walked back to Ms. Mildred's room and lurked in the hallway, peering into her room. I paced up and down. I knew what I had to say. And I bounced and shook and almost turned away. But I walked into her room and stood at the foot of her bed. The lights were low and she asked me what I wanted. I told her that I had a message for her. She told me she was trying to sleep. I stood awkwardly at the end of her bed with my fists clenched looking down at her through eyes glistening with tears. I said, "Ms. Mildred your friends care about you. The nurses and doctors here care about you. I care about you, and God loves you." My eyes were running with living water, my fists unclenched. My chest felt full, full of wonderful terrible love and I was broken open. "Fine," she mumbled, "I want to sleep." I ran from the room. I ran home. I shaved my beard and my head and was naked and vulnerable and washed away in a flood of feelings that I had held behind a dam for twenty-five years. This was my convincement, my baptism in the Spirit; the expression of God's ultimate desire for me to know that I am cared for and accepted and that I am to share love with all creation.

I started drinking. My experience with Ms. Mildred and with God broke open a persona that I had taken up diligently each day of my life, the image of a person who does not need to be loved by other people or by God. I had been a wild and wooly ass of a man, my hand against everyone, believing everyone was against me. In the moment of revelation this comforting armor that kept everyone at a distance was taken away from me. I found I needed to numb myself to the well of emotions. I replaced Spirit with spirits and ran full tilt from love in my life. I sought to turn myself into the ugly, stupid, insensitive jerk I had always known myself to be. It was easier than caring for people and definitely easier than being cared for. I was comfortable in my armor. God had lifted the trap door on the basement I was living in and invited me up into the light. I said, "No thanks. I'm fine down here."

This lasted for almost two years. I graduated with my Master of Divinity degree and moved home to begin a residency year as a chaplain in the same hospital. I believed in the experience of divine love that I had received, though I was behaving in a way that was contrary to it. I sought membership in my home meeting. They were shocked that I did not already consider myself to be a member, and we went through a quick process of clearness. In this process the question that I was asked that stumped me was "How can the meeting support and care for you, especially in your work as a chaplain?" My answer was that I didn't know, I was still unwilling to accept acceptance. I went back to the bar to celebrate. Instead of being full of love, I was full of anger. I had moved to New Orleans with my girlfriend of four years, we broke up soon after because I was depressed and angry, and drunk. The moment of Grace that I had received was not enough to save this wretch.

In June of 2008 I attended a gathering of Young Adult Friends at Earlham College. It was with this group that I shared the deepest experience of communion with God in worship that I have ever experienced among Friends. Since it happened I have jokingly told people that I "got saved" in worship there. Out of a period of silence I responded to an "altar-call" offered by a speaker who asked over and over, "What are you waiting for?" in terms of responding to God. I bounced off my bench as soon as she sat down and stood silently for a few moments before telling this story: Earlier in the day I had been walking down the road and thinking of the Old Testament and all of the stories of the people of Israel falling into idolatry and being taken into slavery. I was asking myself what idols I follow, what drags me into slavery. The answer sounded clear as a bell in my mind: only myself. I understood immediately that I drag myself into slavery by my willful rejection of God's message, my unwillingness to believe in the Truth that had been revealed to me. I had chosen instead the worldly truth of my inadequacy. I testified to the power of God's Love and stated that I would make that the Truth of my life in the future.

As a young, angry person I struggled with my grief and this led me into a ministry of service to those who are grieving: the sick and dying and their families. In this work my own grief was revealed to me as the foundation for my behavior that was contrary to God's Truth, the Truth that we are all loved and called to love. In this revelation I have been prepared and transformed. I am led into a new ministry by the possibility of transformed and transforming relationship with the people around me. I have not found these relationships in my home meeting, but I want to encourage them throughout our religious society. I want to form around myself a transformed and transforming community of people living continually into a deeper and more authentic expression of God's love for the world. This has been, and must be, the work of Quakers. Friends in the past have believed in the perfectibility of humanity through grace and experience and diligence. They believed in the present possibility of God's Paradise on Earth and lived radical, peculiar lives that made this their reality. I'll be home again soon seeking this reality for myself, for Friends, for New Orleans, and for our world.

> Mac Lemann, 28
> Friends Meeting of New Orleans, South Central Yearly Meeting
> (FGC)
> United States

Mi Conversion

Quisiera compartir mi testimonio de conversión de como conocí al Señor Jesucristo. Desde niña fue inculcada al camino de Dios porque toda mi familia es cristiana y mi Padre es Pastor de una Iglesia Santidad Amigos. Yo siempre era muy fiel a Dios por lo tanto a mi no me agradaba llegar tarde a la Iglesia; y a mis 14 años sentí ese amor de Dios en mi corazón, lo cual era algo que jamás lo habia sentido antes en dentro de mi. Sin embargo pasaron los años, llegué a la secundaria en el colegio y yo empecé a alejarme de Dios aun sabiendo todo lo malo que sería si me alejaba de El. Me volví roquera, era fanática de la música rock pesada pero a mi hermana le molestaba esa música porque yo vivía en un solo cuarto con ella. Para mi la vida no tenía sentido en Dios puesto que ya me había olvidado de El; incluso pensábamos ir a bailar al cementerio, lo cual no se dió afortunadamente; mis amigos eran neto roqueros y yo me sentía bien con ellos porque ellos me demostraron que la vida era un vaivén que no había amor en nadie y que el amor es un fanatismo de locos. Pero esa vida mía era algo terrorífico dentro de mi familia: mientras mi madre oraba de rodillas por mi, yo lo espiaba por la ventana y mi corazón no sentía absolutamente nada; por otro lo lado mi padre estaba predicando la palabra de Dios y yo esclavizado por el diablo Satanás. Además yo solía ir a los cumpleaños de mis amigos en ese entonces, pero yo pienso que Dios jamás me había dejado por que en esas fiestas jamás bebí las bebidas alcohólicas porque siempre tuve en mi conciencia de que eso era malo.

En una oportunidad mi padre se enteró de que hay encuentro de jóvenes Amigos en una Iglesia de Santidad Amigos, y me dijo que yo deberia ir allí y el me dió dinero para mis pasajes del viaje, cosa que jamás había hecho antes cuando yo tenia que salir con mi amigos de viaje. En realidad yo me senti casi obligada a ir a la Iglesia donde se reunían los jóvenes Amigos.

Cuando entre a la Iglesia era muy distinto, mire a mi alrededor y eran gente joven que estaban congregándose; y yo dije: "Que aburrido estar aquí." Porque ellos eran muy diferentes a mis amigos pero mas tarde escuche la predica de un predicador su nombre es hermano Virgilio; el mensaje de Dios llego hasta el fondo de mi corazón como un puñal; el decía: "Cuantos de ustedes están esclavizados por el diablo incluso haciendo llorar a sus padres." Esas palabras eran suficiente para quebrantar mi corazón desde ese momento no me recuerdo como llegue de rodillas al altar y por mi mejilla no paraban de bajar mis lagrimas; y le pedi a Dios que me perdone y que yo quería reconciliarme con mi Señor. Entonces en eso momento me sentí libre del pecado. Ahora ya no me gusta la música rock y ya deje a esos mis amigos que me estaban influyendo mal.

Ahora estoy feliz, una hija responsable en mi familia, una persona de bien en la sociedad y trabajo en la Iglesia. Desde mi conversion comense a trabajar como maestra de clase dominical de los niños y jóvenes Amigos, compartiendo mi experiencia y la palabra de Dios. Comprendo que sin Dios yo no haría nada en esta vida.

Rebeca Tintaya V.
Iglesia de Evangélica Misión Boliviana de Santidad (EFCI)
Bolivia

My Conversion

I would like to share my testimony of my conversion about how I met Jesus Christ. Since my childhood I have thought about God because all my family is Christian and my father is a pastor of a meeting, Santidad Amigos (Holiness Friends). I was always very faithful to God, so I didn't like to arrive late to the meeting; and when I was fourteen years old, I felt God's love in my heart, which was something that I had never felt so deeply before. However, the years passed, I was in high school, and I began to move away from God even knowing how much worse that could be to live separated from Him. I became a rocker. I was a fanatic of hard rock music, but this music annoyed my sister, since we had the same bedroom. Life did not have a sense of God anymore for me since I had already forgotten Him. We were even thinking of going to dance at the cemetery, which, fortunately, did not happen; my friends were hard-core rockers, and I felt good staying with them because they showed me that life was like a seesaw and that there was no pure love, and that love is a fanaticism of lunatics. Nevertheless, that life of mine was something terrible within my family: While my mom prayed on her knees for me, I was watching her through the window and my heart felt absolutely nothing. On the other side, my father was preaching the word of God and I was enslaved by Satan, the devil. Moreover, at that time I used to go to my friends' birthday parties, but I think that God had never left me because in those parties I never drank alcoholic drinks. I always felt in my conscience that it was bad.

Once, my father found out that there was a meeting of young Friends in a meeting, Santidad Amigos (Holiness Friends). He told me that I should go there and he gave me the money for my trip, which he had never done before when I had to go on a trip with my friends. Actually, I felt as if I were obligated to go to the church where the young Friends were having a meeting.

When I entered that meeting house, it was an unusual place, and there were young people who were gathering there; and I said, "How boring it is to be here!" They were very different from my friends. But later I heard the sermon of a preacher named brother Virgilio; the message of God reached into depths of my heart like a dagger. He said, "How many of you are enslaved by the devil even making your parents cry." Those words were enough to break my heart, and from that moment I don't remember how I got to the altar on my knees, and my tears did not stop rolling down my cheeks. I asked God to be forgiven and that I wanted to reconcile myself with my Lord. In that moment I felt free from sin. Now I don't like rock music anymore, and I have left those friends who had a bad influence in my life.

Now I am happy, a responsible daughter in my family, a good person in society, and I work in the meeting as a Sunday School teacher of the children and young Friends, sharing my experience and the word of God. I understand that without God I would not do anything in this life.

Rebeca Tintaya V.
Bolivian Holiness Mission of Evangelical Friends Church (EFCI)
Bolivia

Today I Choose You

Today I choose you—
Like the soldier lays down arms
And goes home to his own country
To live in peace.

Today I choose you—
Like a child turns to her mother,
Relying in all ways upon her father,
With no thought of departing.

Today I choose you—
Like the field hand goes home
After long labor on another's land
To his own house and kin.

Today I choose you—
Like the slave breaks his shackles
And goes in search of his family,
Never resting till they're found.

Today I choose you—
As the traveler from the desert
Drinks down the cool river water
And stills a long thirst.

Today I choose you—
As the sheep follow shepherds,
And as the foals follows mares,
And as summer follows spring.

Today I choose you—
You, who have more names
Than all the stars in all the heavens
And as many faces.

Today I choose you—
Though I have chosen otherwise,
And rent my body, mind, and soul,
Today I come back.

Today I choose you—
Humbly I come, begging crusts,

And asking no forgiveness,
But you lead me to the feast.

Today I choose you—
I shelter behind the Immutable Stone,
And beg the blessing of the Immanent Wind,
That I may make you my home forever.

Today I choose you—
Though I did not yesterday,
And may not on the morrow,
In this hour I am yours.

Today I choose you—
As the Moon chooses Earth,
As the Earth chooses Sun,
As you have chosen us.

Paul Christiansen, 26

Eastside Friends Meeting, North Pacific Yearly Meeting (Independent)

United States

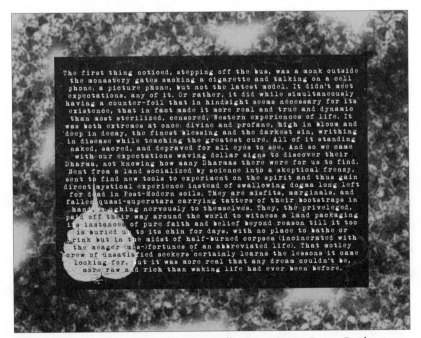

The first thing noticed, stepping off the bus, was a monk outside the monastery gates smoking a cigarette and talking on a cell phone, a picture phone, but not the latest model. It didn't meet expectations, any of it. Or rather, it did while simultaneously having a counter-foil that in hindsight seems necessary for its existence, that in fact made it more real and true and dynamic than most sterilized, censored, Western experiences of life. It was both extremes at once: divine and profane, high in bloom and deep in decay, the finest blessing and the darkest sin, writhing in disease while teaching the greatest cure. All of it standing naked, sacred, and depraved for all eyes to see. And so we came with our expectations waving dollar signs to discover their Dharma, not knowing how many Dharmas there were for us to find. Sent from a land socialized by science into a skeptical frenzy, sent to find new tools to experiment on the spirit and thus gain direct mystical experience instead of swallowing dogma long left for dead in Post-Modern soils. They are misfits, marginals, and fallen quasi-superstars carrying tatters of their bootstraps in hand, laughing nervously to themselves. They, the priveleged, paid off their way around the world to witness a land packaging its instances of pure faith and belief beyond reason till it too is buried up to its chin for days, with no place to bathe or drink but in the midst of half-burned corpses (incinerated with the meager (mis-)fortunes of an abbreviated life). That motley crew of unsatisfied seekers certainly learns the lessons it came looking for, but it was more real that any dream couldn't be, more raw and rich than waking life had ever been before.

The First Thing, digital collage, Stephen Willis Dotson, 25, Goose Creek
Monthly Meeting, Baltimore Yearly Meeting (FGC-FUM), United States

In Him I Am Edified and Fulfilled

I joined the Quaker church at the age of ten years. Both my parents were Anglicans, but they had backslid. It was through their conversion that I joined the Quakers. My elder sister (who had joined the church five years earlier) witnessed to me; then I had faith in Christ. Imagine, at that age I had not been dedicated to God through any church! Therefore I joined the Quaker church as a child member and continued to grow in faith.

At the age of sixteen years I became an associate member and gave my life to Jesus Christ. This time I was in secondary school and I became zealous for God. My faith in God grew because I committed myself to prayer, reading the word of God and serving as a Sunday School teacher for young children.

Through the spiritual exercise of prayer, Bible study, preaching the word, and attending youth seminars and conferences I kept on growing in faith.

I wish to say that my walk with Christ in the Quaker church has been spiritual and fulfilling. As a youth I managed to keep myself pure until the age of twenty-six years, when I was married in a holy wedding. By this time I had graduated with a bachelor's degree in education. After my marriage I became a full member of the Quaker church. All along from my teenage [years] I have served as a pastor. Right now, I pastor a monthly meeting. My gifts in the body of Christ are pastoring, teaching, and intercessions. All in all I have known the truth, Christ Jesus who is my Lord and Saviour, and I serve him diligently. In him I am edified and fulfilled.

Isaac Wekesa Makokha, 36
Elgon East Yearly Meeting (FUM)
Kenya

Forgiveness and Divine Love

Five years ago, at the closing worship of North Carolina Yearly Meeting (Conservative)'s sessions, something big happened to me. Something that changed my life.

I've experienced the Divine in palpable ways since I was a small child. Sometimes I experienced it visually, but most often aurally. There is a voice that comes to me and guides my path, and I was in my teens before I realized that the clarity with which I hear that still small voice is a gift.

This experience five years ago in an old meeting house, in the middle of nowhere, was the most powerful of all my mystical experiences. To this day, when I am in need of comfort, I can call upon the memory of that day and feel substantially calmer. Whatever is causing me distress pales in comparison to the life-changing moment of realizing God's Love and Forgiveness in a palpable, undeniable way.

I was sitting in the meeting house, facing my fears about leaving North Carolina. I was worried that I was leaving behind a calling. I was worried about leaving behind my responsibility to my family. I was worried about moving to a new city without having found a job yet. I was worried that I was running away. Overwhelmed by my fear and shame, I started to cry.

Through my tears I stopped blaming God for my failures. I stopped believing that He had given me unachievable tasks, and I asked for His forgiveness. I felt a huge sense of relief at being able to forgive God and being able to take responsibility for my own weakness. I was truly humbled in that moment and found a certain amount of comfort in that humility.

Then, in that moment of humility, I felt a large hand on my forehead and heard, in that voice I know so well, "You are forgiven."

So, what does that mean? Have I been saved? What is salvation, anyway? Heaven? Hell? Sin? I don't know what it means in the grand scheme of things. I don't know how to express to other people how life-changing that moment was—with or without going into the nitty-gritty of all the things that have changed about me and my life since that moment. I certainly don't know if this change in me has any bearing on anyone else.

Without dabbling in semantics, what it does mean is that I have a different relationship with God. I have trouble putting it into words, but somehow there's no room for doubt that God loves me now. Not even in my darkest moments do I get close to the bitterness I used to carry around with regard to my relationship with God.

I used to feel as though God asked too much of me. I used to think that other people, people who didn't hear the still small voice that I heard, had it easier. They could choose to believe, or not. Now I feel blessed to have bypassed that choice. I don't have to wonder. I know that God exists, that God loves me, and that He has a plan for my life. No matter how badly I screw up, He's still on my side. I feel loved.

Rachel Anne Miller, 30

Greenville Friends Meeting, North Carolina Yearly Meeting
(Conservative) and Cambridge Friends Meeting, New England
Yearly Meeting (FGC-FUM)
United States

My Conversion

While I was in Standard Four in primary school, I received a dream which said to me that "I would be God's pastor." Therefore, I could not understand it immediately, since I was immature in the things of God.

My father died in the same year in the month of December when I was still in Standard Four. But the same vision continued to come into my mind just as when I slept during the evening time. Learning became a problem to me, because my mother was not able to provide for my school fees, and even for the family. But I found favor in the eyes of the Lord God, whereby the teachers did not send me home for school fees. Instead they encouraged me to be hardworking.

God gave me wisdom in doing my class work. At five o'clock in the morning, I used to go to the nearby river to fetch sand in order to get a little money to purchase some exercise books, pens, and clothing. The payment for one wheelbarrow [of sand] was 150 Kenyan shillings. I did this work very early in mornings before classes and also in the evenings after classes every day.

I did my Kenya Certificate of Primary Education (KCPE) and obtained good grades. But I lacked school fees to continue with the Kenya Secondary Education. However, the Lord God gave me more wisdom, where I was to repeat the primary school. God was faithful to me. He made me to pass the primary exams of Standard Eight. By the grace of our Lord Jesus, I obtained bursary money from the government to continue with studies. The bursary money was incomplete. Again I had to find some ways of getting money. Therefore I began plaiting ropes to support my everyday needs, and one was sold and earned 150 Ksh. This money enabled me to get some exercise books and pens. And the little money that remained, I used to pay for school fees, because I could plait five ropes in a day during evening time when I was free. After finishing my Form Four Level, I passed my Kenya Certificate of Secondary Education (KCSE) exams with the grade of a C-. Getting the original certificate was quite difficult because I had not paid the school fees.

However, the Lord of hosts did a great miracle on the balance of my school fees. When I went to school to get my certificate, the school accountant was very surprised to find my school balances having been cleared. Full of amazement, he asked me, "Who paid your school fee balance?" Immediately, full of courage, I told him, "It's my heavenly Father who has paid that balance for me." Indeed, I remembered that the Lord is the Father of orphans. He, therefore, gave me my original certificate plus the school-leaving certificate.

In 1999 I committed my life to Christ Jesus. And this is the way I met the Lord Jesus as my personal savior. It was in August 1999, when the team of Nakura Friends Evangelistic Ministry came to Teso District to evangelize the people. When the servant of God preached the good news to me, I felt myself being touched with the message of Christ Jesus. I found myself surrendering to the Lord because of my sins. A servant of God led me to salvation by confessing my sins to Christ Jesus.

I was directed to read the word of God daily, especially the gospel books. The Holy Spirit who is my light is revealed to me day by day in the secret things of Lord. And the Spirit led me to be reading at least a verse of the scripture every day. By doing that the light from within made me also to testify about Christ to my friends, especially those who haven't met with Christ. Also, the spirit made me visit the sick from the district hospital every Saturday at the evening houses. I encouraged the sick people through the word of God, to put their faith in Christ Jesus.

While in the ministry of Christ, I became involved in the Church's ministrations. I participated in youth's ministry very well. I was selected to be the village meeting youth leader in 2001. In the same year, I heard a voice from God saying to me that I "would become a pastor of the Lord in the United States preaching the good news of the Lord Jesus."

In October 2002, I was appointed to be a village pastor in Kocholia Village Meeting in Teso district, under Busia Quarterly Meeting of Friends Church. And in the same year, by the power of God, we managed to purchase a plot worth sixty thousand Ksh where Kocholia Friends

Church building is being constructed. It is still incomplete due to lack of finances. The population of the church members is still small, approximately fifty members.

Finally, the vision of proclaiming the gospel to the United States keeps on coming to my mind season after season and I don't know what to do. But I trust God to enlighten me. I thank my God, I am now in the third-year diploma class [at Friends Theological College]. God bless you. Amen.

Pastor Peter Ikapolon, 32
Kocholia Village Meeting, Elgon Religious Society of Friends (FUM)
Kenya

How I Became a Quaker

I have probably been saved more times than anyone else you have ever met. By "saved" I mean "accepted Jesus Christ into my heart as my personal Lord and Savior." I think the first time was when I was about six. I talked to my parents about wanting to have Jesus in my heart and we all prayed about it. It was great.

The only problem was that people at our church were constantly prophesying the return of Jesus. These were the end times and we all had to be prepared. At six, I had finally realized a lifelong dream of being cast as a mouse in the local production of the *Nutcracker*, and I was pretty worried that Jesus was going to come back before I could be in it. So I prayed a lot that he would just wait awhile before his triumphant return. Then someone at church mentioned no one could predict the day or hour of Jesus' return. So I started predicting all the time; I figured this would keep him from showing up. I got to be in the *Nutcracker*, but I felt vaguely guilty for postponing the rapture.

Maybe that is part of the reason I started getting saved all the time. I was worried that I wasn't quite saved enough, so I would double check by accepting Jesus into my heart whenever it occurred to me. And every time there was an altar call at church or a youth event, I would go up and get saved again. I really liked the feeling of confessing that I was a sinner and being made pure, although I think the analogy of being "washed as white as snow" didn't quite have the same significance for someone born and raised in Alaska.

I was very involved in the youth group in middle school, partly because the youth pastor's daughter was one of my best friends and partly because I had a crush on a guy in the youth group. (We ended up going on one extremely awkward date and I heard that he got married a few years ago.) It was also because I loved how into God everyone was. We would sing and testify, and people would cry [because] they were so filled with love.

Then I went to high school and fell apart (in terms of my faith, at least, otherwise, high school was pretty great). Usually, I say something fairly benign about my crisis of faith, such as I stopped believing in Hell or I just met people who were different from me. While those things are true, the whole truth is much simpler: Gay people made me want to stop being a Christian.

I do not mean that any individual gay person convinced me to stop going to church. I especially do not mean that gay people made me gay and that caused me to stop being a Christian. Although I am still straight, once I had a few gay friends I found it impossible to believe their attractions to people of the same sex was a sin.

The last straw for me was a discussion section I read in my teen study Bible. It was in the Old Testament, a half-page description that tried to make biblical rules more accessible to teenagers. The gist was that although God does not expect us to follow all of the silly rules in the Old Testament, the Bible is very clear that homosexuality is wrong and engaging in homosexual practices is a sin. I had been raised to believe that every word of the Bible was the literal word of God and the hypocrisy overwhelmed me. I put the Bible down and I did not seriously engage in reading it again until my mid-twenties.

About the same time, the state of Alaska was going through its marriage initiative, ensuring that marriage could legally occur only between a man and a woman. It was very disturbing to me to see nice Christian people from my church acting downright gleeful at the prospect of keeping others from sharing the benefits they enjoyed in marriage. It was pretty clear that this was not a community I wanted to be a part of. I kept going to church, but I was very uncomfortable with the mix of politics and religion there.

Fortunately, I left for college the next year. It was pretty easy to not go to church in Santa Cruz; it seemed like the primary religion there was surfing. I don't think I ever really stopped believing in God, but I definitely didn't give God a lot of thought. I was pretty distracted by school and jobs, boyfriends and breakups, and trying to figure out what to do with my life. When I studied abroad in Chile, I started going to mass every once in a while. I think it helped that the services were Catholic (I didn't have many bad associations with Catholics) and in another language. I even had a great conversation with a woman there who assured me it was okay if I didn't know if I believed in God, as long as I believed in Mary. I still went to church with my parents when I was home, but we pretty much had a "don't ask, don't tell" policy regarding my churchgoing habits at school.

When I returned to California, my attitude toward the church went back to the way it had been before. But then I went to law school and I seriously needed a church. Law school was a pretty toxic environment for me and I found myself praying again. I knew I needed to go at least once a week to a place where people were focused on God instead of grades, competition, and the Socratic Method. My roommate, Jessica, felt similarly, so we started checking out local churches. Neither of us had much interest in the denominations we grew up in so it was all pretty new to us. We were like two Goldilocks churchgoers. We liked the music at the Episcopalian church and the proximity of the Lutheran church, but none of them was quite right.

One Sunday close to finals, we stumbled into Freedom Friends Church. Honestly, I don't remember a lot from our first visit. I was pretty wrapped up in my anxiety about law school at that point. I think there were probably about five people there, including Jessica and me. I remember Peggy, the pastor, being a very good hostess and checking to see if the room was the right temperature, and I remember discussing the relative merits of different brands of travel guitars with Alivia, the clerk, but that's about it. They both seemed very Midwestern and that was comforting (I had good experiences with a Midwestern boss in college).

I just kept going back. Jessica had decided law school was not for her, so I was on my own, and I felt like Freedom Friends was a place where I could breathe. Then I started talking during silent worship and I felt like I couldn't stop. Speaking in front of groups (even small groups) is not my favorite thing, and I never intended to say anything in worship. But week after week, I felt led to speak and gently held by the Friends there.

After I had been going to Freedom Friends for about eight months, Peggy decided to hold a Quakerism 101 class. I don't think many of the regular attenders at that point had any previous experience with Quakers, so we all needed some education. I missed most of the classes, but I made it to the last one, where we read *Freedom Friends Church's Faith and Practice* aloud.

Before we started, Peggy said (I think as a joke) that she was going to have an altar call at the end of the class. I had a very strong negative reaction to that; I had been to enough altar calls and I wasn't interested in any more. But as we read through the *Faith and Practice*, it dawned on me this was a community I wanted to be a part of. I fiercely believed in the things I was reading and I really wanted to be a member. I did not hear the term *convinced Friend* (a term Quakers use to distinguish converts from birthright Friends, who are born into the Religious Society of Friends) until years later, but in that moment, I was convinced. That afternoon I wrote an e-mail requesting membership. A little while later I met with a clearness committee, and in a few weeks I officially became a member.

After leaving my parents' church, I never thought that I would find a church where I could fully be myself. In Freedom Friends Church, I felt that I had found my way home. I am also grateful that my story does not end with my decision to become a member. I know that my faith community will hold and support me as I continue to learn and grow.

Ashley M. Wilcox, 28
Freedom Friends Church (Independent) and University Friends
Meeting, North Pacific Yearly Meeting (Independent)
United States

Children's Church Program in Bolivia, photograph, Emma Condori Mamani, 31, Misión Boliviana de Santidad (INELA), Bolivia

Breaking Bread
Fellowship with God and Others

Pouring Tea

One cup of chai rich
with milk and honey, the spices
just licking up against the lip
of memory, poured thick
from a teapot of deepest blue—

A year ago, when we
were first together,
the four of us, in our
old craftsman house, the windows
of the kitchen just opening
out to meet the world,
we served our tea
in cups, a different
teabag for each personality.
One rooibos, one Good Earth®,
and two lingering on the verge
of different flavors 'til the water boiled.

Now we have our tea
from a pot: one vessel full
with loose leaf tea, unencumbered
by the confines of separated cloth.
One vessel, but many lives
swirling around the boiled pot
'til they are poured
into our separate entities,
four cups reaching out
to accept their living grace.

> *Brianna Richardson, 23*
> *Bellingham Friends Meeting, North Pacific Yearly Meeting*
> *(Independent)*
> *United States*

A Quaker Marriage

When Ben asked me to marry him, I didn't say "Yes." Instead I paused and replied, "We'll try." He gazed at me and asked, "We'll try? What do you mean?" I explained that I didn't want to say yes until we had met with a clearness committee, and until we knew that they had approved us for marriage. Ben asked again if I felt that I wanted to be his wife. Then I responded, "Yes, of course." Ben gave me a big hug, and I felt so much joy that I was a bit dizzy. We both knew it felt right to get married.

Ben wasn't Quaker, but he understood that Quakerism had shaped my ideas about relationships and marriage. He knew that Quaker principles and attending weekly meeting for worship together were important to me. He knew that he didn't need to kneel down on one knee and present me with a thousand-dollar ring. In fact, he knew that I didn't like the symbol of wedding rings at all. Neither did he.

We first talked about Quaker marriage when we began dating as Peace Corps volunteers in rural Ukraine. We saw a Ukrainian wedding together and discussed Ukrainian wedding traditions. I told him about traditional Quaker weddings and how unusual they were. Ben was surprised and interested.

I attended few unprogrammed Quaker weddings while I was growing up, and I did not understand much about the traditions. I knew there was silence, a certificate, and vows were exchanged between the couple rather than repeated after a minister. However, beyond those customs, I did not know of the many other differences from traditional Protestant weddings.

In fact, the Society of Friends has struggled with the topic of marriage since its inception. George Fox strove to help early Friends develop unique marriage practices by organizing men and women's meetings to handle Quaker business in an orderly fashion. In his *Journal*, Fox writes, "After we had visited Friends in the city, I was moved to exhort them to bring all their marriages to the men's and women's meetings, ... that care might be taken to prevent such disorders that had been committed by some" (Fox 1: 73).*

However, it was not easy to develop new, ideal marriage practices. Early Friends focused on the importance of gaining approval from Quaker women's meetings and men's meetings and consent from all family members. Yet, Quakers were prohibited from marrying non-Quakers. Even Fox himself married Margaret Fell without the approval of her son from her first marriage.

Nevertheless, the basic Quaker wedding was established. Once the men's and women's meetings gave their approval of the marriage, the couple would call a meeting for worship with as many witnesses and as much publicity as possible. During the silent worship, both bride and groom would rise and exchange vows. Similarly to early Christians, Friends united through God directly rather than through the assistance of a priest, and they did not exchange rings because this was a pagan symbol of inequality.

In the eighteenth century, Quakers were divided because many meetings refused to allow marriages between people of different faiths. Thousands of Friends were disowned by their meetings during this period. Friends continue to discuss the topic of marriage—although now Friends are concerned by the issue of same-sex marriages. Quaker weddings can take almost any form today. They can include wedding rings, bridesmaids, receptions, and ministers.

When Ben and I began the process of planning our marriage, we knew we wanted our wedding to come from our own principles. The first thing we did was to ask each of our family members, including our parents and grandparents, to write a letter to our meeting explaining whether they approved and how they felt about our marriage. Once we had collected these letters, we wrote a letter ourselves to our meeting requesting to be married under their care.

It was difficult to balance twentieth-century mores with traditional Quaker values. It took a while before our clearness committee was approved at business meeting. We attend a very small meeting, and we ended up having to choose a date and reserve a room for the wedding before our clearness committee even met.

When the clearness committee met, it was during a single evening. We had a casual dinner together. Then we worshipped in the living room, and out of that silent worship we were asked many questions about our past struggles in previous relationships and with each other. We discussed our plans for our future family together. Then we briefly split apart— women and men separately—for more questions. At the end of the night we began talking about Quaker wedding practices, certificates of marriage, and previous marriages in the meeting.

We tried to be as thoughtful and organized as possible as we approached our wedding. Many of our decisions were shaped by our principles of simplicity, integrity, and community. Yet there were also other things that were important to us—our experiences of Ukrainian weddings and my Italian heritage. A wedding is an event that many people have ideas about, and most of all we found it important to make our community of loved ones feel like their thoughts were important to us.

In some instances, we were flexible and made changes. Our wedding committee from Fresh Pond Meeting had many good suggestions about how to hold the meeting for worship. We chose not to have any recording or photography during the meeting for worship. We arranged for child care with their help, and thought of many other small tasks that people in the meeting could fill. My father wanted to walk me to my seat, and even though I didn't agree with the symbol of the father "giving away the bride," I respected my father's wishes.

We did everything a little bit at a time, and refused to give up all the creativity and hard work, which we felt were an integral part of our marriage. We chose not to have any bridesmaids or groomsmen, but rather we thought of all the ways the people who were closest to us could offer their gifts to help with our wedding. With the help of a printer from our meeting, we designed our own simple invitations. We wrote our own vows—carefully thinking about what we honestly could say to one another. At last we also decided to make our Quaker wedding certificate. Rather than hire a florist, a group of us gathered together the day before the wedding to arrange flowers, some of which were wildflowers picked by a woman from our meeting.

In the end, all the energy we spent carefully planning, listening, being flexible, and asking for help paid off. We were both able to feel comfortable and joyous, and we felt everyone around us was celebrating with us. It was fun, and surprisingly beautiful!

All along, we thought of our Quaker wedding as an instrument that would allow us to establish our relationship with God and our wider community of friends and family. We believe in God, but we know he is not a person. We were not sure that the actual moment of our marriage would feel like God was marrying us. What would that feel like? Could it do something that would change our relationship and make it new?

However, when the wedding day came, the experience of the meeting for worship was incredible. Ben and I entered the room with our family members around us, and a large group of friends and family circled around us. I remember the feeling of warmth and calmness, like we were floating in the room. Everything went just as we'd expected, but the emotions and movements I felt within me were much stronger than those I felt during a usual meeting for worship. God was really there with me. All the messages we heard seemed to fit together more perfectly than any meeting Ben or I have ever been to. For us, they were exactly the messages we needed to hear—speaking directly to us in a startling way.

No Greater Love, etching, Erin McKibben, 18, Portland Friends Church, Indiana Yearly Meeting (FUM), United States

We were occupied the rest of the evening, but later that night when I continued to think about the worship, I could not sleep. In fact, I was so spiritually moved that I didn't sleep much for three nights afterwards. I was lying awake thinking and writing in my journal about the amazing experience of our marriage. The memory brings joyful tears to my eyes, even though I have not cried many sentimental tears before. Nothing had prepared me to feel so spiritually moved. I really did feel something new, even though nothing had changed between us. It's still difficult to explain to anyone else, but I feel so grateful for my Quaker community and their influence.

We can't imagine being married in any other way. Some people continue to ask us why we do not wear rings, and I always use this opportunity to tell them a little bit about early Quakers and our Quaker wedding. I still feel that some people who know us do not approve of our decision not to wear rings. However, no one makes us feel that they don't approve of our marriage. Ben and I made our marriage our own, respecting our own values and those of our community. Because of this we feel closer than ever to each other, our meeting, our friends, our families, and God.

Elizabeth Baltaro, 29
Fresh Pond Monthly Meeting, New England Yearly Meeting
(FGC-FUM)
United States

*Fox, George. *A Journal or Historical Account of the Life, Travels, Sufferings, Christian Experiences, and Labor of Love in the Work of the Ministry, of that Ancient Eminent, and Faithful Servant of Jesus Christ, George Fox.* New York: AMS Press Inc., 1975. Vols. 1 and 2 of *The Works of George Fox.* 7 vols. 1975.

Knowing Where You're Going

Buses carry their destinations
boldly, literally upfront;
but their passengers
each bear a secret destination.
If they have a number
it is on the heart not the forehead
and the route will lead
to realms unmapped and glowing.
They come together, though,
as they escape the city
under the bus's bright banner
which gives them seeming unity.

> *Rhiannon Grant, 24*
>
> *Nottingham and Derby Area Meeting, Britain Yearly Meeting*
>
> *United Kingdom*
>
> Editor's note: This piece first appeared in *Watford Friends Sharing,* a volume of work by Friends in Watford Meeting, Britain Yearly Meeting, in March 2007.

A Good Samaritan

Dear Friends and friends,

I wanted to share with you all an act of kindness that I witnessed on my way into work this morning.

A woman, quite elderly, boarded the train at Sevenoaks and sat on one of the seats behind me. As the train pulled out, she looked in her bag and realised that she had left behind her purse, including her tickets, credit cards, and all her money. She was headed for Ipswich and had no means of contacting her adult children, who were working, or anyone else who could help her.

The woman sitting next to her, a complete stranger, immediately offered to give her what little money she had with her. Since this would not have been enough money to pay for the woman's ticket, she then insisted on getting off with the older woman at Waterloo, taking her to the cash point, and giving her another £20 or however much she needed to complete her trip. She wouldn't even hear of giving the other woman her address (the older woman, at first reluctant to accept the offer, then asked for the younger woman's address so that she could return the money by post). The women spent the rest of the journey talking and the older one, who would otherwise have been very worried about how she would complete her journey, was comforted and reassured.

Why did the "Good Samaritan" do this? Because she knew it was the right thing to do, and because it was what she would want someone else to do for her own aging mother, if ever she was in a similar situation.

I also feel that this act of kindness lifted the mood of the giver as much as that of the one who received. It certainly lifted mine!

Life isn't so bad.

Peter Parr, 33
Sussex East Area Meeting and Young Friends General Meeting,
Britain Yearly Meeting
United Kingdom

Mi Experiencia Personal con Dios

La verdad antes que yo asistí a la Iglesia veía los problemas de familia aún mas grave de lo que eran, mi forma de ser era insoportable, me enojaba de nada, les faltaba el respeto a mis padres, y no tenía mucho gozo en mi vida.

Un día mi hermana Erika me convenció de asistir a la Iglesia. Después de asistir por primera vez sentí algo diferente dentro de mi; y mi comportamiento tuvo un cambio tremendo. Empecé a compartir mas con mis hermanos y sentí el gozo que antes no sentía, con la llegada de Dios a mi corazón me di cuenta que los problemas tienen solución si estamos sujetos de El. Dios al ingresar a mi corazón me transformó en una nueva criatura como dice en la Biblia en 2da de Corintios 5:17 (Spanish Modern): "De modo que si alguno está en Cristo, nueva criatura es, las cosas viejas pasaron; he aquí todas son hechas nuevas."

También tuve muchas experiencias de protección, pero una en especial. Un día que tuve una reunión con los integrantes de un campamento al que asistí, me subí al micro equivocado y cuando me di cuenta me bajé pero no conocía aquel lugar y ya no tenía para mi pasaje, entonces no sabía que hacer y me llené de miedo. Después Dios me dio a conocer el número de celular de mi hermana; luego la llamé pero ya había oscurecido, mi hermana se preocupo y estaba lejos de donde yo me encontraba, tardó algo de una hora en llegar al lugar donde yo estaba; cuando yo la ví llegar sentí un alivio inmenso y no me cansó de darle gracias a Dios por haberme dado a conocer el número de mi hermana porque la verdad yo no me lo sabía; y de ahí en adelante mi fe aumentó aún más porque viví una experiencia propia del cuidado que Dios tiene para con nosotros.

Sara Miranda Gutiérrez, 18
Congregación Cristiana Los Amigos, Iglesia Nacional Evangélica
"Los Amigos" de Bolivia
Bolivia

My Personal Experience with God

Before I went to church for the first time, I would always get all worked up over small problems with my family. My lifestyle was out of control, I would get angry about nothing, I had no respect for my parents, and I didn't enjoy life at all.

One day my sister, Erika, convinced me to go to church. After I went just one time, I felt something different inside myself and my behavior changed dramatically. I started to enjoy spending time with my brothers and sisters, and I started to feel a joy that I'd never felt before. With the arrival of God in my heart, I realized that there is a solution to every problem if we trust in Him. Once God came into my heart, he transformed me into a new person, as the Bible says in 2 Corinthians 5:17 (NIV): "Therefore, whoever is in Christ is a new creation: the old things passed away; behold, new things have come."

I have had many experiences where God has protected me, but one in particular is special. One day, I had a meeting with the members of a camp that I attended. I got on the wrong bus and when I realized what I'd done, I got off the bus. I didn't know where I was and I didn't have any money to buy a new bus ticket. I didn't know what to do and I was so scared. But then God allowed me to know my sister's cell phone number.

So I called her, but it was already dark. My sister was worried and she was really far from where I was. It took her almost an hour to get to the place where I was. When I saw her arrive, I felt so relieved. I kept thanking God for allowing me to know my sister's number because the truth is that I had never known it before. Since then, my faith has grown even more because I experienced for myself the care that God has for us.

Sara Miranda Gutiérrez, 18

Christian Friends Congregation, National Evangelical Friends Church of Bolivia (EFCI)

Bolivia

Practicing Hospitality

I attend Keystone Fellowship Meeting, a small meeting in south-central Pennsylvania, and my meeting is affiliated with Ohio Yearly Meeting (Conservative) in Barnesville, Ohio. Besides the fact that some of us are plain (or simply dressed), one of the more visually noticeable things about our meeting is that we don't always meet in a meeting house. We could if we wanted to, and we do meet there once a month. The rest of the time we worship in each other's homes, like some early Friends did. Worshipping and fellowshipping in homes is also the practice of our spiritual and geographic neighbors, the Old Order Amish.

Hosting meeting can be a bit of an undertaking. It requires planning, since our meeting for worship is always followed by a sit-down meal. When my family prepares for this, the work starts a week in advance, with menu planning and grocery shopping. Hosting also most often means cleaning. We put away books; my mother clears her papers off the dining room table; I vacuum; my father rearranges the furniture to accommodate meeting members in the living room. We get out the plates and flatware and set them on the counter.

There are only ten to fifteen of us in our meeting, and cooking is not usually a monumental task. I enjoy cooking and love preparing meals, and I look forward to when meeting is held at our house. I love sitting in worship while the smell of our meal wafts out of the kitchen into the living room, especially when I have helped to make it. Some Friends might offer vocal ministry during meeting, but I offer food afterwards. I like to think the love and joy I had while preparing it makes the food really special.

Once our meeting hosted a gathering of Conservative Friends, and we prepared meals for sixty or so Friends, three times a day, for almost a whole weekend. That was a deeply spiritual experience. It was a lot of work, but it was meaningful to make food for Friends who so deeply wanted to visit and worship with each other. Food was a medium through which this could happen, and so preparing food was service I offered deeply from my heart.

Practicing hospitality is a meeting-wide spiritual discipline for Keystone Meeting. Because we live at a distance from each other (for some of us, it is a two-hour drive to get to meeting, depending on where members are located), we regularly spend a few hours with each other when we meet. Worship and sharing a meal are very important aspects of our time together, and they do require time and energy, but going to each other's homes deepens the fellowship. For example, one of the families in our meeting is hosting three high school-age students from Korea. These guys like to play and tease, and they consider it great fun to untie the apron strings of the women who help in the kitchen. My mother usually laughs and teases them right back. I enjoy singing with them at the piano, and I think their energy and playfulness add spark to our fellowship.

Holding meeting in homes means that we are inevitably involved in each other's lives, and sometimes personal concerns become corporate meeting concerns. After my grandmother died, I moved back home from graduate school and from living in another state. My sister came home from college, and our family couldn't host meeting because our house was full of belongings. Other meeting members graciously offered to host instead. One family even let me store my furniture in their garage for the summer. Most of the meeting came to my grandmother's memorial service, too.

I don't know what the practice of hospitality means to other Keystone Meeting members personally, but I do know what it means for me. Besides the opportunities for creative expression and heart-felt service, I find the practice of hospitality is really a discipline of making room, of opening to something much greater than I am. In the Scriptures, I read about Christ wanting to be within us and to engage us in fellowship: "Behold, I stand at the door and knock; if anyone hears my voice and opens the door, I will come in to him and will sup with him, and he with me" (Rev. 3:20, American Standard). As I help my parents tidy the house and move the furniture for worship, I am also preparing myself for a time of deeper fellowship with Christ. I sometimes find it helpful for me to avoid books or movies on the day of meeting. I also feel strongly about preparing spiritual space so the rest of Keystone Meeting can come into an atmosphere that is calm and conducive to listening. I want Christ to feel at home among us. When I sense in my heart during meeting for worship that Christ can sit down and eat with me, that is a deep fellowship I would never trade for anything.

One day during the summer, meeting was held in the county east of us. It took my family an hour to drive there. We arrived, and our hosts were busy arranging chairs for a backyard meeting for worship. "We've got an extra chair," one host said. "Is there anyone else coming?"

"Elijah," my sister and I said at exactly the same time, thinking of the Jewish practice of keeping an empty chair at the table during Passover. There were a few chuckles.

One thoughtful Friend said quietly, "If Elijah comes, I will be happy to give him my seat," and then we settled into silence. The food in the kitchen waited; behind us, the picnic table waited; and so did Christ, who had found the empty chair.

Eileen R. Kinch, 28
Keystone Fellowship Meeting, Ohio Yearly Meeting (Conservative)
United States

Holy Healing

God, I'm listening.
Looking for meaning
in the peeling paint,
and the very faint
pip, pip, pip.
Of rain cascading
from the Heavens.
Or is it the earth?
This endless cycle
of change and rebirth.
How the rain heals,
restores and reveals,
Washing away my doubts, Lord,
You cleanse my soul.

Crystal Waitekus, 29
Virginia Beach Friends Meeting, North Carolina Yearly Meeting
(Conservative)
United States

Stone Love

Stone
appearing steadfast
is smoothed away
by water.

Love
the smoothing
remains, eternal.

> *Megan E. Drimal, 35*
> *Originally a member of Friends Memorial Church, Indiana Yearly*
> *Meeting (FUM), later Clear Creek Meeting and Bloomington*
> *Friends Meeting, both Ohio Valley Yearly Meeting (FGC).*
> *No current affiliation.*
> *United States*

Dear God

The following is a letter I wrote at the age of twenty-two and stumbled upon again two years later. Rereading it at that time inspired me to add an account of the events that helped me to discover God as a young adult.

Sometime in 2006

Dear God,
      Thank you for making me young and pretty and not terribly fat. Thank you for letting me get older and for allowing me to become a better person since I got the hell out of Iowa. Thank you for giving me the potential to age with my natural teeth intact. Thank you for keeping me out of meth's destructive path although I have chosen a rural life for myself in the past few years. Thank you for my lovely baby. Thank you for keeping me fertile through thick and thin. Now I must admit I deserved it, for my baby is truly the prettiest. Thank you for the patience I do have and for my capacity to wish for more. Thank you for making me idealistic and principled. Thank you for keeping me smart even when it seemed I had no use for my strong opinions. Thank you for making me friendly, professional, and relentlessly appropriate. Thank you for my husband and for his kindness. Thank you for his values, his intellect,

and his sculpted butt and legs. He could lift a cow with the right body mechanics. Thank you for the immaculate timing which brought us together and for those precipitating coincidences which sparked our affection. Thank you for giving me a forgiving heart to let at least the big things out, at least eventually. Thank you for my rigidly selective passion, which guards me from getting my feelings casually hurt. Thank you for all the times I have had enough heat and enough to eat. Thank you for my encounters with justice. Thank you for the occasions where I proved people wrong: got my diplomas, had a natural childbirth, held a job, and quit smoking. Thank you for the closeness I have earned with my other family, for rewarding my decision to stop holding grudges, to stop withholding letters and phone calls, to stop blaming.

November 9, 2008

I wrote this letter around the time I started believing in God. The surprising thing about finding this letter today, as I rummaged through mediocre college essays in search of a writing sample to submit with my graduate school application, is that I don't feel convinced of some of the things I mentioned in it and I doubt I felt convinced of them when I wrote this in quick, sloppy handwriting on a loose sheet of notebook paper two years ago.

Thankfulness, however, was not an issue. I thanked God for the things I almost had or that were good enough. This is significant. "Young and pretty" are words I would never use in earnest to describe myself, for example; neither are, "friendly," "professional," and "appropriate." But I know I had similar, somewhat fleeting qualities and I was thankful for them on that occasion.

I was as genuine in offering thanks for those things as I was in offering thanks for those gifts that overwhelmed my heart and are undeniable: my son, my husband, heat, and food, my natural teeth. I also feel the presence of God when I read this letter today, having come to love God in the past two years. I think this letter is a striking metaphor for the way I understand and love God today. It contains giant leaps, inconsistencies, and impossibilities I don't need corrected. It makes me laugh.

Since childhood, I wondered what it would take to convince me of the existence of God. I spent many years angry and defensive in my atheism. My mom told me she stopped being a Lutheran because the church lies to people. I misunderstood her simplistic explanation at my young age (was I six?) and thought I was privy to a great secret. If only I could make it obvious to everyone; why were they so stupid? Why did they insist, and cling, and embrace oppressive rhetoric? In my adolescence, I became aware of other possibilities—New Age ideas—and dismissed them too. These followers were not hateful, but they were still ridiculous.

Secretly, I hoped that magic existed in the universe. As an adult, I concluded that if I were to have a revelation, it would reasonably coincide with the most spectacular life event I could experience—childbirth. If I were to believe in God, it would happen then or not at all. It was a minor hypothesis I maintained throughout my pregnancy with my son, Victor. I was not invested at all in the conclusion I would find, but I was genuinely curious.

When Victor was born, I cried out loud, making audible those profound, confusing tears I started experiencing and trying to hide as a teenager listening to sermons in a Unitarian church (about tables or pets or genitals, as Unitarian sermons go). Unlike those odd stealth cries seeded in ego and loneliness, I embraced those tears for Victor and felt and somehow knew where they came from. But I did not think it was God, and within minutes of my son's birth, I acknowledged that I still could not detect magic in the universe, and I was minorly disappointed. But I was in love! I was happier than I ever had been and my thoughts turned away from God for several months while I basked in the radiance of a spectacular new human being with my blood still pumping in his veins.

It was when his radiance did not wear off that I knew it was not his newness or even my distractible narcissism that made him glow. When I still welled with tears at the new things he did and at the non-things he did (sleeping, eating, pooping), I began to suspect God.

We walked into a Quaker meeting in Missoula, Montana, one fall morning in 2006. Thus began my honeymoon. I watched the sun dance on the floor through big, bright windows, I felt my body vibrate, I let someone I didn't know but trusted automatically for some unknown reason watch my baby in the adjoining room. And when the quiet worship was over, a woman shared a joy with the meeting that it was nice to see a baby today and to remember how brilliantly the Light shines in a child of that age.

I began to realize that the phenomenon was apparent to others, and I began to see light elsewhere too. I got chills when the Quakers talked about the place of children in the community of Jesus: front and center. I found a book of readings about children, and found I loved the prayers most, found them the most loving, the most expressive of what I wanted for all children—something greater than the material world and feelings I could name. I was finding a way to be a part of this unavoidable aspect of my culture: spirituality, even religiosity, even Christianity.

I don't think about scientific incongruencies when I think about God now. I don't think about why not. I think about children, and when I wait restlessly for one long hour in a silent meeting for God to speak to me, I realize every time anew that God enters at the end of the hour when the children rejoin the circle. Also, I think about speaking the language of the Religious Right when I argue against them. I say with confidence they don't understand God's love when they say that God would withhold it from anyone.

I do understand God's love, though I can't describe God other than the chills I get and the tears. And when I say "God bless you" to my son, I find it silly, but I mean it without understanding, or needing to understand, all that it means.

> Mallary Allen, 26
> Southern Illinois Society of Friends, Illinois Yearly Meeting (FGC)
> United States

Bird Shadows

My God is the god in the next room,
cooking unseen feasts and humming;

the ache of the moment before the rain
when you're sure the whole June
cloud is ready to burst through
though you haven't felt a single drop;

the photographer's ironic smile
after her darkroom discovery
that in the background of a misfire
she has captured two lovers gazing
longingly at each other's meals;

the dandelion blade that insists
adamantly that it must reside directly
in the middle of your neighbor's
blacktopped suburban driveway;

the sight of the shadow of a bird flitting
by the sill near the bed of an aging Grace,
who can no longer move but counts herself

lucky because at least she can still see.

This is my God:

expectant and grinning

wild and near.

L. Callid Keefe-Perry, 27
Rochester Monthly Meeting, New York Yearly Meeting (FGC-FUM)
United States

An Experience of the Divine

A while ago I had a revelation.

I didn't know it was coming (well, there's a surprise). I wasn't pre-pared for it. I was no Joan of Arc or George Fox. I'd thought things like that didn't happen in this day and age, in nice, safe Britain. They'd been confined to the Bible, the beginnings of Quaker history and the odd, "crazy" preacher.

I'd never really understood people of the strongest faith. Those who endure horrific experiences and, when asked if it had tested their belief in the Divine, say "No, my faith was strengthened." I could not understand that. Then I read a quotation from a young priest who had been broken by his imprisonment during the Russian revolution. It made me under-stand that when all else is gone, there is only God left: "Nothing is left of me, they have burnt out every single thing, love only survives."*

I was in a strange state of mind when I read this—unhappy (though I didn't know it) and exploring for a better sense of the Divine. I was brought up as a Quaker, with a belief in God. As I got older, what the adults told me was backed up by the feeling I sometimes got that there really was something there—most often experienced in meeting for worship, or on top of mountains, or among trees. It was all a bit hazy, though, and I envied those early Quakers and Bible characters the strength of their faith.

About six months ago I moved away from home, away from my friends and family. I felt their role taken up in part by the Quaker meet-ing in my new town; I will always think of the wider Quaker community as an extended family where I can feel at home. Meeting for worship there was more profound than I had experienced before, and I sometimes felt a very deep connection with the Divine.

It was to try and deepen this newfound relationship with God that I'd been reading a book about prayer, where I found the quotation. After reading those words I went for a walk. It was dark by the time I got to a rock on the brow of the hill and sat down facing the sea. I felt very alone as I closed my eyes and tried to empty my mind. I didn't succeed, but I had no distraction but my thoughts. I could see nothing, I could hear nothing but the wind, and there was no one with me but God.

Suddenly I knew what God was and that God knew me. This was a direct experience of the Divine. It was like meeting someone face-to-face after previously only speaking to them on the telephone. It was both awe-inspiring and terrifying—as the rabbit must feel when blinded by the headlights. I get the same feelings thinking about it even now.

It hasn't happened again. I get the impression that it's a once-in-a-lifetime experience. But now I know, whether I'm sitting in meeting for worship trying to centre down, or just on my own in a busy street, that God is here. It's a life-changing bit of knowledge. It doesn't matter if I can't connect with the Divine every single week, and really it doesn't matter what else happens. God is here.

Jenny McCarthy, 21
York Area Meeting, Britain Yearly Meeting
United Kingdom

*Quotation is from Living Prayer by Archbishop Anthony Bloom, Libra 1966, p. 17

Our Father

I ride out seeking you, my God,
In the mist-cloaked evening.
Our Father, who art
In the bay, and the wind,
And the rain-soaked pavement.
Hallowed be thy street lamps,
Light of the world.
The darkness has not overcome them.

When I was a child,
I sang to flowers,
And did not concern myself with you.
I wonder
If I was not more faithful then.

We each bring things to your table,
"Burnt offerings" a not inaccurate label.
I have nothing to offer that is not
At least slightly
Singed.
But as I ride through this pale summer night,
I realize
The daily bread is given,
Deliverance is bidden,
Our trespasses forgiven,
As we forgive those

Who close their windows to the night
And simply
Sleep.

There is nothing left to see here.
What I seek has already
Been found.

> *Kody Gabriel Hersh, 22*
> *Miami Monthly Meeting, Southeastern Yearly Meeting (FGC-FUM)*
> *United States*

How Does God Find and Touch You?

Every year my family and I go to Tofino, a beach fishing town on Vancouver Island. As a day trip we always go for the hike to Scooner Cove, a huge beach where having fun is involuntary. Because it is relatively empty, the walk through the woods is nearly silent. As I walk along the path and observe the unearthly beauty I start to fall behind my family, who continue on ahead. This is when I usually have a chat with God.

I feel warm when I talk with him. I tell him about problems I've had and feel like someone (other than my family) cares. This walk that my family takes is a time where I meditate deeper than in a regular meeting house.

It seems I feel closer to God on walks in beautiful places with no one else around. And afterward I feel enlightened and I find myself thinking about what I can do.

> *Flynn, 14*
> *Vancouver Monthly Meeting, Canadian Yearly Meeting (FGC-FUM)*
> *United States*

Daily Moments of Solace

I find daily moments of solace treading earth
It is as if I am asleep and dreaming
Although, I am not
I am awake and cheerfully walking her circumference
I want to develop peace in her
I want to dirty my hands
Dig them deeply into Mother Earth
To plant seeds of harmony inside her
So, she may give birth to it from her ground, it is hallowed
I want to plant, grow and reap love
If we surrender to reconciliation, we are by it swallowed
These are the efforts and labors of the righteous
If we do not regard the Light it fades from our collective vision into a blur
These messages find their way to me, a young Friend, like Truth by way
of the air
By way of the Spirit
I find daily moments of solace treading earth
It is as if I am asleep and dreaming
Although, I am not
I am awake and cheerfully walking her circumference

> *John C. Lawson-Myers, 26*
> *Englewood Friends Meeting, Indiana Yearly Meeting (FUM)*
> *United States*

Members One of Another

> Therefore, putting away falsehood, let every one speak the truth with
> his neighbor, for we are members one of another.
>
> — Ephesians 4:25, RSV

"I'm not a member."

Throughout my journey with Friends I have said that sentence many
times and many different ways (apologetically, insecurely, matter-of-
factly, as an aside or by means of explanation) but very rarely with any
sense of empowerment. The reactions to this revelation vary (surprise,
bafflement, consternation, concern) probably because I *seem* so committed to the Society.

I have been active in Friends communities, mostly in youth programs, during much of the past twelve years. I have held clerkship positions, worked at several Quaker organizations, attended a historically Quaker college, traveled nationally and internationally for work related to Friends, served as project coordinator for *Spirit Rising*, teach now at a Friends school, and am increasingly asked to serve as an elder and companion in ministry.

But I am not a member anywhere. Let me explain.

When people ask me if I was raised Quaker, my answer is "Sort of." That is, though my father is a member of a meeting he no longer attends; my parents did not really raise me Quaker or make me a member of that meeting. I had to be bribed with sweets to go to worship on Sundays for most of my childhood. First Day School classes never interested me and it was hard to feel welcomed in meeting among Friends who were bothered by noisy children.

My parents *did* encourage me to seek spiritually, however, and eventually my search led me back to Friends when I was about fifteen. I joined the high school program of Philadelphia Yearly Meeting and fell in love with a community life that was deeply nourishing and affirming and entirely unlike my public high school. We learned together, served together, cooked together, cleaned together, did art, sang songs, and stayed up too late. Walking with young Friends transformed my life, reshaped me emotionally and spiritually, and offered me many life opportunities that I would not have had otherwise.

It was my first glimpse of the beloved community of God, and my first profound experience of belonging.

Despite that profound reintroduction to Quakerism, I have not applied for membership because I have not yet felt led to do so. I take membership seriously and want to get the green light from God, and believe that I will. Also key is that, for much of my young adulthood, I have been or have felt transient. I haven't yet found a meeting I wanted to put roots into. In many ways I am part of that lost generation we often talk about. I do not consistently show up for meeting on Sundays, though my Quakerism is a key part of my identity. I believe that this waiting, often in the face of pressure and the conveniences of membership, has been an act of faith, if an awkward one.

I was also just waiting to be asked.

Two autumns ago, a Friend called me to see if I was interested in serving on a standing committee of the yearly meeting as a representative of my quarterly meeting. In my yearly meeting, standing committees oversee most of the working groups, programs and projects of the yearly meeting. You must be a member of a monthly meeting to be on a standing committee.

I explained to this Friend that I was not a member of a monthly meeting and it was my understanding that I couldn't serve because of that. I had my "haven't felt led yet" speech prepared.

There was a long thoughtful pause, then he blurted: "You should be a member!"

I did not know this Friend, in fact I do not even remember his name. But I remember experiencing his statement not as chastisement, or encouragement born of self-interest, but rather as a loving and good-natured, if slightly flabbergasted, stating of the truth.

He wanted me on his standing committee, that's true, but it was also beyond him that I wasn't a member anywhere. His simple sentence made me feel appreciated and needed, as if he were saying, "How could you not be a member? You are such a treasure!"

And he didn't even know me.

The thing is, Friends, we are *all* treasures. Every one of us.

I have been thinking a lot recently about the power of invitation. One of the most profound invitations we can extend to each other is the invitation toward belonging. The kind of invitation that says: *"You are wanted. We are incomplete without you."*

That kind of invitation is tantalizing and scary, the kind you don't want to say no to, the kind of invitation God offers us when we are called to God's work. The Friend who called me that day extended such an invitation to me.

Imagine if Friends of all ages spoke to each other this way, all the time. Imagine if that were the language of our monthly meetings and churches.

How would we be transformed?

I often ask myself what it means to hold membership. Is it about giving annually to the meeting, serving on committees, attending business meeting?

When I was a teenager and now that I am a young adult, membership has often been held up to me as a way to access money and sit on committees. My father's meeting encouraged me to become a member when I decided to attend a Quaker college. The clerk of the meeting said that there was support they could only offer me if I was a member. I was pretty sure this meant some financial support for college. And money felt like the wrong reason to make a commitment to a faith community where I had struggled with belonging, and which I was moving away from.

And truthfully, service on committees at the monthly, quarterly, or yearly meeting level has never been very appealing. I have often experienced a sense of cooptation, of older Friends wanting to include me because they needed a token, youthful presence on their committee, or because I am organized and articulate "for a young person." Other Friends have made comments about wanting to "harness" youthful energy, which makes me feel like a battery and not a valued member of the community.

What's more, I've often felt the need from exhausted older Friends to pass me the torch. Both the exhaustion and the torch concern me deeply. Sometimes the "torch" is established peace work or service on publications committees. Usually there is little conversation about the *flame*, the heart and spirit of the work, or what other ways I could be trusted to keep the work alive.

I find that I if I do not want the torch, question how things have "always" been done, or suggest new ways to carry the flame, I am often dismissed as a flaky young person who is not really ready to make a commitment.

I struggled with cultural differences too. I am a white United States American, but even though many unprogrammed Friends are convinced these days, and so come from a wide variety of cultural, ethnic, and increasingly diverse racial backgrounds, I often found myself bumping up against unexamined WASPy, middle class, liberal political norms and beliefs that are assumed to be synonymous with Quakerism. Was there space for me, the highly educated granddaughter of working class, Catholic, Italian and Irish immigrants? Did Friends want to hear my stories of immigrant assimilation and culture loss, urban-to-suburban migration, the pressure of class mobility? Did they want to see beyond my degree from a fancy college and hear me talk about a learning disability? Was it possible to get beyond comments that my name is pretty and questions about where I went to school?

None of this is really a good motivator toward membership.

I know that I have caught glimpses of deeply nourishing community in various places, particularly among groups of sometimes geographically disparate teenage and young adult Friends. I saw it at Pendle Hill when I was a student there, and see that we are building it now at the Sierra Friends Center, where I work and live. Before I moved to California I lived in West Philadelphia, a neighborhood with a high concentration of young Quakers. We walked to each other's houses, cooked together, comforted each other when we got dumped, worshipped together, ranted together. We were awkward and flawed and sometimes dysfunctional, but our lives were stitched together somehow. I think that's membership. That's community.

Membership is about belonging, about choosing to connect your life (and acknowledging that you are connected) with the lives of the people around you. It is about entering into a deeper relationship with a covenantal community of seekers, of joyfully taking up responsibility and connection that transcend connections based on blood or law, social privilege or power. It is imperfect. It is always changing. It is intergenerational. In it we forge a new way of life together, choosing to nurture each other and allowing ourselves to be tender and transformed.

Once in a fit of spiritual crisis, while I was wondering if I truly belonged among Friends, if the lack of a call to membership was indicative that I had stayed too long in a community I was only meant to pass through, I asked God if I was really supposed to be a Quaker.

"Should I move on?" I asked. "Am I kidding myself? Do I belong somewhere else? What am I? If not a Friend, then *what am I?*"

I was desperate and a little hysterical, but the still small voice was swift and clear. In the true trickster nature of the Spirit, it offered me no specific clarity about denominational affiliation. Instead, the response was simply: *"You are mine."*

It was not about possession or exclusion, not about obedience or hierarchy. I understood in that moment that the same could be said for *everyone* and *everything* else.

Instead, the lesson was about understanding myself as a child of God, for whom connection and conviviality are a birthright. And that as a child of God I am in relationship with everyone around me, no matter who or how I draw near to a specific community of seekers. Who I walk with in my faith is not the most important thing. It is most important that I walk. I will be accompanied. I was being reminded of the true root from which faith, and so eventually denominational affiliation, grows: connection.

Sometimes we need reminding.

I have stopped worrying about membership so much, and I find that whether or not Friends or Friends organizations worry about it is often a good indicator of their nature. I believe that one day the call will come, but in the meantime I probably need to learn important lessons about belonging, relationship, and worthiness.

So am I a Friend? Yes. Am I a member of a meeting? No, not yet. Do I *hold membership?* Yes. Indeed I do.

Angelina Conti, 27
Unaffiliated, Unprogrammed
Long relationship with Philadelphia Yearly Meeting (FGC)
United States

By My Encounter with Him

My experience in my relationship with God as a Quaker highly challenged my faith positively. First, I have been able to pick up the challenge of knowing God personally—that is to say, not knowing God from what my pastor tells me [but] by my encounter with Him.

Second, I have realised that fellowship with other members gives me encouragement to grow stronger in God. This gives me the desire to serve in the church because [I] am able to bond with other members and, in the process, get to account our salvation walk to each other.

Third, I find it very convenient when praying because there are no set formulas when it comes to communicating to God. [I] am able to express myself without trying to sound technical (something that I think is essential in our walk with God). At the place of prayer God is able to deal with my character and that leads to wholesome transformation.

Last, I would say being a Quaker or Pentecostal or any other denomination is not what really matters in the Kingdom. Rather, it's what you do with it. Take it as an opportunity to thrive and most importantly to help or in other terms to witness to others. We all have one destination—Heaven.

God Bless!

Nancy Ghangahoa, 18
Kenya

La Juventud Cristiana: Etapa de Decisiones y Experiencias Valiosas

En este mundo amplio y diverso en culturas, religiones, políticas y a causa de ello una sociedad diferente entre otras. En la cual nos encontramos nosotros los jóvenes cristianos Cuáqueros viviendo en un amor fraternal y como también en experiencias espirituales y sociales valiosas para la Iglesia de Cristo.

La experiencia de uno es muy importante por que esas mismas se convierten en el cimiento de su vida y las decisiones hechas en momentos decisivos ya es parte de otra experiencia viéndose también a lo lejos la madurez, la inteligencia en la vida y la sabiduría en lo espiritual.

Yo decidí seguir a Cristo en muchas ocasiones pero el problema era continuar firmemente en esa decisión y en muchas ocasiones caminaba empujado; y entre tantas repetidas veces tuve muchas experiencias hermosas que empezaba con un decaimiento como si ya no hubiera esperanza para mi, pero ahí está la Iglesia donde el hermano (a) que me animaba. Viendo a Los niños y a mis hermanos jóvenes animados y vivos espiritualmente yo me arrodillé y oré reconociendo que soy un pecador y confiando en el Señor Jesucristo y su obra en la cruz por mi eso fue el momento hermoso de mi vida, con las lagrimas de arrepentimiento que salían del corazón recibía el perdón de mis pecados así confirmando ser un hijo de Dios.

Viendo mis experiencias y la necesidad de la Iglesia para mi vida, en medio de los jóvenes conocí a Cristo como mi Salvador; reconozco que había vuelto a desanimarme pero la semilla del amor de Dios en mi corazón ya estaba y me levanté confiando en Jesús y en Dios todo poderoso.

Y la experiencia de un grupo de jóvenes donde se puede participar también es de mucha importancia ya que la influencia del uno con el otro es de gran manera. Yo aprendí de eso es que es tenerlo siempre en oración cada decisión que tomamos. Y la influencia de nuestras decisiones y experiencias personales y grupales debería ser un ánimo ya anticipado para el futuro de uno mismo y hasta para el futuro de los niños.

Y esta es mi gran experiencia en base a una decisión de confiar en Cristo como mi Salvador y se que me espera más experiencias. Dios nos guarde en su Santo Amor hermanos y hermanas.

Wilder Amado Condori Pillco, 20

Iglesia Nueva Marka, Iglesia Nacional Evangélica "Los Amigos"
de Bolivia

Bolivia

Christian Youth: A Time for Decisions and Precious Experiences

In this wide world of diverse cultures, religions, and politics, and because of this, we are a society that is different from the rest. It is in this world that we young Christian Quakers find ourselves living in brotherly love as well as in spiritual and social experiences, precious to the Church of Christ.

The individual experience is very important because it becomes the foundation of one's life. The decisions made in decisive moments are already part of another experience, a resemblance of maturity, intelligence in one's life and wisdom in spiritual matters.

I decided to follow Christ on many occasions, but the problem was how to firmly continue in my resolve on the many occasions in which I was pushed along on the walk; repeatedly throughout, I had so many beautiful experiences that I started to become disconsolate, as though there were no longer any hope for me, but the church was there for me, along with the brothers and sisters who encouraged me. Seeing the children and my young, cheerful brothers and sisters, spiritually alive, I got down on my knees and I prayed in the realization that I am a sinner. Trusting in the Lord Jesus Christ and his work on the cross was, for me, the most beautiful moment of my life, and with tears of repentance that flowed from my heart I received forgiveness for my sins and was thus affirmed as a child of God.

Examining my experiences and the need for the church in my life, through the agency of young people I met Christ as my Savior; I realized that I had again lost hope but the seed of God's love in my heart was already planted, and I got up, trusting in Jesus and almighty God.

The experience of a group of young people where one can participate is of utmost importance, since the influence of one person on the other is great. What I learned from this is to always hold every decision that we make in prayer. And the influence of our personal and group decisions and experiences should be an expectation and an encouragement for one's future and even for the future of the children.

And so this is my great experience based on a decision to trust Christ as my Savior and I know that more experiences await me.

May God keep us in his Holy Love, brothers and sisters.

Wilder Amado Condori Pillco, 20
Nueva Marka Meeting, National Evangelical Friends Church
of Bolivia
Bolivia

My Nana's Meeting House

My nana's village meeting house has big windows looking out onto a green, tree-filled cemetery. She has a plaque in a stone wall there next to my grandpa.

The year my nana died, I went and stayed in her house. I spent slow, winter evenings sorting out photos, crockery, books, linen, papers . . . cooking with the food from her freezer. I walked to the meeting house, which was full of people who had known her better than me in a way, and yet who lovingly and willingly carried out the business of hosting her memorial meeting.

My nana's village meeting house is the same one she went to as a little girl. It is part of the Quaker school my great-grandfather taught in and my mother attended. I come from a long line of Quakers. She used to talk to me about "Daddy" who was a conscientious objector in the First World War and who was nearly executed and my great-grandmother who was a suffragette and used to leave her purple sash in a secret box under the hedge. Nana went on the big anti-war marches in the years just before she died. She wrote to Tony Blair on Father's Day about all the soldiers' fathers. She followed events in Palestine with unwavering concern. She also talked incessantly to everyone she ever met, and it surprises me that she sat through silent meeting week after week after week.

Being in my nana's house, in her village and in her meeting house gives me a sense of being whole. Being a Quaker was such an embedded part of her identity that it can't help but also be mine. It's not only the stories and the places, it's also the way I have learned to behave, the innumerable small ways a child learns what her mother learned what her mother taught her.

We decorated my nana's meeting house before everyone came to the memorial meeting. There was holly and ivy and a Christmas tree, and we filled the meeting house with chairs and set out a hundred teacups next door. It made me excited to think of all the people coming to my nana's last party; to think how excited she would have been and how much she loved them.

In the meeting I was burning with what I wanted to say, but it was never quite the right time and others kept speaking. I laughed and cried with their ministry and by the end of the meeting I had nothing to say. The meeting had spoken for me. I felt a little sad for my nana that her one granddaughter didn't speak, but I also felt a broad sense of peace and a little wonder: that this Quaker process had worked. Much more than being sad, I was grateful; recognising this as one of the rich gifts my nana gave me.

I may never visit her old home again, but I will go and sit in her meeting house and there, more than anywhere, I will know that there is a cheeky, passionate, concerned, self-righteous Quaker inside me that I inherited from my nana. And I will be quiet.

Ailsa Wild, 31
Northern Suburbs Meeting, Australia Yearly Meeting
Australia

I suppose our most overt concession to religiosity was Christmas In The Fields... a tradition, a Bible story, small girls in angel wings made from coat hangers & masking tape, mesh & glitter, cotton balls glued to large cardboard sheep, carols sung, who gets to be Mary & hold the baby, if it was real - a new addition that year or the one before, warm & squirming & not really a person yet, or at least certainly not as much as a seven year old ... or the year we set the story in the present, angels on TV & the first time I heard of Motel 6, though I was old enough to be a sternly disapproving Aunt Herodette in too much makeup & someone else's stole (which Seth would later, at a New Year's party, pronounce "fuzzy dead thing" & have us in cheese-puff & sparkling cider-fueled hysterics, weak & teary-eyed with hilarity).

...or the time we had it at the Jones' & I got to ride a horse bareback - an experience more damp & cold than I had originally pictured - but how cool to have real hay in a real stable, real animals putting our babydoll Jesus to shame and the barn filling up with the warm full evocative sand of so many people all being quiet.

Christmas in the Fields, drawing, Alice Rutherford, 27, Schuylkill Monthly Meeting, Philadelphia Yearly Meeting (FGC), United States

The Most Important Thing

It was a warm night in December at the Baptist Church of San Pedro Sula. I was nervous, the children also; and they were very restless: "Sister Ruth, when will we go out? Sister Ruth, Is it good this way? Sister Ruth, help me with this . . ." They asked these, among many other things. Suddenly the director of the Christmas worship announced the participation of the Smiles children group. As the directress of the group, I stood up and I made them enter to sing as we had rehearsed it. People wondered: "What will they do today? Will it be a drama? Will it be a serenade? Or will be it only songs?" The music began, and suddenly an angelical melody was heard. No! They were not angels! They were twenty-five children among the ages of nine to eleven years old that were singing!

That was a very special period in my life. I dedicated all my time to the service of the Lord, I learned to work with children, and I formed a group called Smiles. I rehearsed them to sing, to make dramas and serenades, and they ended up being so good that they had invitations from other churches, and at Christmas it was the busiest time for them and me; they didn't only have to participate in our own church but cover the other invitations.

I gave to these same children the Sunday classes, classes of Basic English, organized camps, biblical studies twice a week, and I visited them when I could because I was studying in the high school.

Two years later after the group Smiles was formed, I read the Bible for my biblical studies, but I didn't have enough time to pray. The group Smiles was succeeding, and my ego also; but my spiritual health began to decay. The group Smiles was famous among some Baptists churches of the epoch, so I filled with pride and I forgot that it was God who had given me the capacity and the gift to direct it, and I neglected my intimate relationship with God.

It was a day in June that was a sad and dark day. My desperation for the many activities was such so that I only thought to leave the church. I didn't have the value to say no, nor to stop a little what I had begun, and I decided to escape, to run away [so I would not have] to give any explanations. I went to another city, and I left the many children's lives destroyed because of deception: their world came down, and I killed their illusions. And I took time away from the church for a while. The sense of guilt of having abandoned those children didn't move away from me.

I fought against God's will for a year and a half. And one day in December, I was invited to a camp of the Youth of the Friends Church: the Peniel Camp. There God touched my life again.

In January of the following year some young Friends from Guatemala that I knew in Peniel invited me to a university encounter (meeting) in their country. Being in that encounter, God led me to meditate on the Martha and Mary passage. When I finished meditating, I reached the following conclusion: It is good to work for the God's ministry, to dedicate time to the service in the meeting, but it is very important to take care of our spiritual health, and that includes a deep life of prayer and reading of the Bible.

Some years ago I went to visit the children in San Pedro Sula; I was very happy when I saw them, and they were also.

Smiles no longer exists. The children now are older. Many of them serve in their churches, and others that were in the group are no longer there. But I am sure about one thing: The Word that was sowed in their hearts, God will make it grow.

I always keep in my mind and heart the passage about Martha and Mary (Luke 10:28–42). Through the experience that I lived, Martha and Mary gave me a lesson, in order not to fall in the same error. I haven't stopped participating in the activities of the church, but one thing I do is that I try to have a balance between the work of the church and my personal relationship with God; I think that it is not the only important thing, but *the most important thing*.

Ruth Bueso de Coronado
Guatemala

When Did You Get "Mom Spit?"

"When did you get mom spit? Was it during the pregnancy, at the moment of birth, or sometime else?"

This question, recently asked by a Friend, raises so many questions for me about my identity as a mom. When did I become a mom? When did I stop feeling like an imposter and start owning my new identity as a mom? And how does that experience compare to my other identity labels? After all, I am more than a mom. I am Quaker. I am lesbian. And I am a mom.

I discovered Quakerism in my early twenties, and joined my first meeting shortly before finishing my graduate program and leaving town. I intended to move back within a year or two, but life intervened. A decade later, a whole continent still separates me from the meeting of my Quaker youth.

I suppose I was the quintessential young adult Friend: passionate about my newly adopted Quaker faith and very transitory. My membership in my home meeting meant so much to me, even when it became clear that I would be absent from the meeting for longer than I had been active.

When I first moved back East and started to root myself with my current meeting, I felt deeply frustrated that my early attempts at involvement were rebuffed until I transferred my membership. "Wasn't it more important that I was there and trying to be active?" I wondered. Why was there a perceived difference between being a member of the Religious Society of Friends and being a member at this particular meeting? (I still struggle with my meeting's more rigid attitudes toward membership, but that's another story.)

"Quaker" remains a core part of my identity, a core part of my life. I am a Quaker, I work for Quakers, I learn from Quakers, and I strive to be a better Quaker. From the very beginning, I wanted to claim that label of Quaker and own it.

But when did I cease to be a young adult Friend? When others stopped treating me as a transient and relied on me for leadership? When I realized that I had more in common with older adults in my meeting than I did with the younger adults coming up behind me? When I became a mom and focused my attention on "the next generation of Quakers"? Or am I still a young adult Friend—learning how to grow in my life and in my faith, figuring out who I am and who I want to be?

Like my early claiming of Quaker as my identity, once I came to grips with my same-sex attraction, I embraced my identity as a lesbian. Even when I was occasionally interested in a guy, I knew that my best and truest relationships were with other women. It's no surprise that I am married to a woman. While fifteen years of being "out" have dulled the vibrancy somewhat, I still find it to be a handy name to describe who I am and who I love.

The "mom" thing is another story, though. I remember returning to work when my son was three months old and finding an envelope addressed to "mom." At that time, it seemed like everyone was calling me "mom" and it was pretty jarring. I felt like a fraud— I loved my baby, I loved being a mother, but it still felt odd to be called a "mom." A mom was something that I had, not something that I was. It made it sound like I knew what I was doing, and I was just winging it!

At some point during that first year, I started to feel more comfortable in my mom skin. I stopped feeling the urge to look behind me when someone said, "Hey, mom!" I never lost the sense of wonder at the miraculous little person I had brought forth, but I did stop wondering how on earth I was expected to fill my mother's—or any mother's—shoes.

Sure enough, I got my mom spit. One day, that smudge of lunch just wouldn't rub off. A lick of the thumb, a quick swipe, and mom spit solved the problem. Somehow, miraculously, the new label fit. I am Quaker. I am lesbian. And I am a mom.

Carrie Glasby, 34
Central Philadelphia Monthly Meeting, Philadelphia Yearly Meeting
(FGC)
United States

The Speeding Up of My Heart and the Trembling of My Fingertips

It was the last night of camp, my second Young Friends camp and my first time ever to leave Western Australia. I was farther from home than I had ever been, but it didn't feel that way, tucked up on cozy old couches under the wooden beams of Pete and Ailsa's home in Candelo. Hands rested on legs and legs sprawled over knees, all of us squashed in the one room together, cradling heads on each other's shoulders.

It was the deepest silence I had felt before in a meeting for worship.

There were so many things woven into that silence. A week of jumping off cliffs, terrified, into the river; of digging a pit toilet and clearing the bushland near our tents to protect them from fires; of singing silly songs while drying the dishes; of playing guitar, playing the dictionary game, the animal game, and up-the-river-down-the-river-in-the-river—struggling with the idea that we could each belong, belong in this place, belong to each other. Of whispering in our tents, giggling and fumbling our way through honest conversations as night drew closer in. It was woven out of friendship so different from what I knew from school back home, where even among friends people would tease and others would storm off, hurt. From our week of testing the waters gently to see if it was safe, there we were, tucked up in a room together, holding each other in silence.

People spoke, their voices soft, as though something held tight had been let down and the part behind it was not so loud or so bold, not so easy to let through. They didn't speak of spiritual thoughts or big deep reflections, just quiet, honest bits of themselves. I remember one girl saying things she knew would make her cry, and I wondered at her courage. I wondered if I might cry myself.

I don't know if I actually spoke. If I did I have no idea what I said. But I remember it seeming impossibly hard to open that door to bits of myself that had already been so tightly shut. I remember the speeding up of my heart and the trembling of my fingertips as I decided it might be worth a try, to pry it open even a little. And I remember my quiet sense of surprise that the world didn't end when I did.

Alexa Taylor

Australia Yearly Meeting

Australia

Editor's note: This piece was written for the 2009 Backhouse Lecture in Australia Yearly Meeting.

Testimony of Simplicity, photograph, John C. Lawson-Meyers, 26, Englewood
Friends Meeting, Indiana Yearly Meeting (FUM), United States

Green Ripple, photograph, Marie-Helene Drouin, 35, Derby Local Meeting,
Britain Yearly Meeting, United Kingdom

World Gathering of Young Friends climbing Pendle Hill, 2005, photograph, Sadie Forsyth, 27, Putney Friends Meeting, New England Yearly Meeting (FGC-FUM), United States.

> Editor's note: Over 300 young adult Quakers from around the world climbed Pendle Hill together while attending the World Gathering of Young Friends in Lancaster, England in 2005. This was said to have been the largest group of Quakers ever to make that trek together, to visit the place where George Fox had his vision of a "great people to be gathered."

Troubling the Water

Calls for Transformation and Renewal

Spiritual Independence

A recent conversation on a train to a pilgrimage site in Varanasi, India, made me think about why I chose to become a Quaker and to reflect on the nature of my spirituality in general. One of my train companions asserted that religion, rather than foster mutual understanding, only serves to divide people, create separate identities, and (all too often) ignite conflict and bloodshed between communities. As any reading of history will quickly reveal how religion has been a critical factor in promoting hatred, domination, and oppression (particularly of women and minority groups), I was forced to agree with her.

Despite this bloody history, she, like me, has still chosen a spiritual path. Her particular path has led her to take *naamdan*, or spiritual initiation, from a certain Indian saint or guru. She now follows his guidelines for living and was energetically trying to convince another fellow passenger to adopt her path and take *naamdan* from this guru. "He will show you the way to spiritual peace," she emphatically claimed.

Her discourse highlighted for me what I find so disturbing in the religious world: the need for different religious groups, whether major world religions or small spiritual communities, to stake out boundaries beyond which their members are not allowed to "spiritually trespass." Most religious groups, for example, would not permit their followers to simultaneously belong to multiple faiths or spiritual communities. In this system spirituality is manufactured and defined from above, rather than evolving from the individual. I intensely dislike the control and manipulation I see in so many religious groups; this is particularly true with Indian gurus, where unquestioning obedience is the norm.

Given my distaste for and critique of so many features of common organized religious life, why choose Quakerism? After all, Quakers also represent an organized religious group that will necessarily need to erect and defend certain boundaries in order to survive in today's highly competitive religious marketplace. I was drawn to the Religious Society of Friends because I sensed that here I could build a spiritual home without the ubiquitous spiritual control; a place where I could be free to develop my own spiritual blueprint for living, on my own time. No dogma, no list of do's and don'ts but rather something much more radical: encouragement to trust one's own inner voice for guidance. In short, a spiritual home where my spiritual independence would not pose a threat or represent a problem. Of course, the form of Quaker worship that most spoke to me was silence. What led me to explore and embrace Quakerism was the feeling of spiritual independence instead of spiritual suffocation and guilt that I had experienced in another faith tradition. My embracing of Quakerism was a gradual process that did not entail my having to give up active participation in Asian religious culture, which I find very culturally rewarding and stimulating.

I have never understood why so many people (such as the woman I met on the pilgrimage train to Varanasi) expend so much energy on encouraging others to follow their particular faith path. My mission is not to spread the Quaker message; instead it is to live fully, applying my spiritual principles in my daily life. I do not assume that others will find happiness if they discover Quakerism. Perhaps they would, but perhaps it is not the community or spiritual path for them. The basic values of Quakerism are found in many other religious traditions. The difference is the unique Quaker community that seeks to apply these values in our lives.

I do not expect the Quaker community to satisfy all of my spiritual needs or lead me to absolute spiritual truth. I believe that it is healthier to nourish oneself from a variety of spiritual sources. One's spiritual diet should be as varied and balanced as one's physical diet. Would you eat only protein or only carbohydrates and consider yourself well nourished?

At times I have also had misgivings about the broader Quaker family when I read about the homophobic stances of some branches of Quakerism active in the Americas. Though I would like to think that my community is more progressive and fully supports the principle of human rights for all, I realize that Quakerism is not immune to deeply rooted social prejudices. Religious groups are fundamentally social and cultural institutions, and as such will reflect broader social inequities that permeate society.

Despite these misgivings and my continued mistrust of organized religion as well as religious authority, I am glad that Quakerism is part of my life. I have grown through my involvement in different Quaker activities, and feel grateful when I move to a place that has a Quaker meeting nearby—something not to be taken for granted in continental Europe!

I would like to see more spiritual promiscuity as opposed to just interfaith dialogue in the religious world, and especially on the part of Quakers. I hope that in doing so these rigid religious and cultural boundaries may be weakened and we can all be challenged, if only briefly, to move out of our cultural and religious comfort zones.

Kathryn Lum, 34
Bologna Friends
Italy

La Comunidad de los Cuáqueros como Iglesia y el Futuro

Bueno creo que voy a ser realista, porque en el año 1999 y 2000 los jóvenes de la Iglesia Ballivián I de Santidad Amigos nos levantamos con una visión de fortalecernos y fortalecer a la comunidad Cuáquera, pero nadie quería hacerse cargo de nosotros, les pedíamos que nos enseñen acerca de la Palabra de Dios, pero nada. Solamente nos hablaban que no esto y lo otro si, parecía ser pura religiosidad donde se hacían críticas pero para solucionar problemas desaparecían nuestros hermanos mayores de la Iglesia. Así esta situación fue una experiencia muy triste en esos años, Por ejemplo en un culto especial de jóvenes Amigos habían como 150 a 200 jóvenes quienes querían darlo todo por esa visión que nació en nosotros, pero gracias a Dios nos estuvimos discipulando entre nosotros los jóvenes hermanos; lo cual también fue para levantarnos espiritualmente ya que por medio de esa situación Dios nos enseñó a ser mas fuertes y valientes para seguirle y servirle. Ahora con una nueva generación hay otras cosas muy excelentes que en ese tiempo y estamos muy bendecidos y agradecidos por su Palabra de Dios que es nuestro escudo, alimento, fuerza y poder en contra de nuestros enemigos en la vida espiritual.

Sabemos que su Verdad nos ha protegido, toda la confianza en El vertimos, por su sangre preciosa fuimos y somos lavados, por su gracia también somos perdonados, su victoria nos dió la vida eterna y nuestras vidas están seguras en las manos de nuestro Señor Jesucristo. Le decimos: porque la vida que ahora vivimos en la carne, la vivimos en la fe del Hijo de Dios, el cual nos amó y por nosotros fue entregado para que vivamos libre de la conciencia del pecado y estar delante de nuestro Padre Dios Bueno, sin culpa o conciencia de pecado gracias a su Hijo Jesucristo, quien es también parte y autor maravilloso de la vida, que nos sostiene cada día y El hace que regresemos a su corazón de nuestro Padre Dios en el día de nuestra redención.

El es tan bueno, nuestro Dios eterno y por eso y muchas razones le amamos y bendecimos el momento en que le conocimos, cada latido de nuestro corazón siempre estará expresando adoración. Entonces UNA Iglesia DE CRISTO SIN JUVENTUD SERIA UNA Iglesia SIN PULMONES, la juventud es tan esencial en la sociedad religiosa de Amigos.

Oscar Cordero
Iglesia Evangélica Misión Boliviana de Santidad Amigos (EFCI)
Bolivia

The Quaker Community as a Church and Its Future

Well, I think I will be realistic, because in the years 1999 and 2000 the youth of the Bolivian de Santidad Amigos church got together for the purpose of strengthening ourselves and strengthening the Quaker community, but none of the elders wanted to take responsibility for us. We asked that they teach us the Word of God, but nothing, they only spoke about this "no," and that "yes." It seemed that they were espousing a pure doctrine; they would criticize, but when it came to solving problems, our elder church brothers disappeared. This situation was a very sad experience for me in those years. Then there was a special worship for young Friends; there were 150 to 200 youth present who wanted to commit to this vision that had come to Light among us, and thanks to God we were disciplined as young Friends. We began to raise ourselves spiritually and understood that it was through this situation that God taught us to be stronger and more courageous in order to be able to follow and serve Him. Now with a new generation, there are new excellent things that were not there before and we are very blessed and grateful for the Word of God that is our shield, nourishment, strength, and power against our enemies in our spiritual life.

We know that His Truth has protected us. We place all our trust in Him, because of His wonderful blood we are here and we are washed; thanks to His grace we are also forgiven. His victory has given us eternal life and our lives are secure in the hands of our Lord Jesus Christ. We say to Him that the life we now lead in the flesh, we lead in faith in the Son of God, who loves us and for us was given so that we could live free from the consciousness of sin. We live without guilt or awareness of sin thanks to his Son Jesus Christ, who is also part of the marvellous creator of life. He maintains us each day and assists us in returning to the heart of our Father God on the day of our redemption.

He is so good, our eternal God and for this and many other reasons we love Him and bless the moment in which we came to know Him. Each beat of our heart now expresses adoration. Because of this I say *A church of Christ without youth is a church without lungs*; youth are essential to the Religious Society of Friends.

Oscar Cordero
Bolivian Holiness Mission of Evangelical Friends Church (EFCI)
Bolivia

The State of Youth in the Religious Society of Friends and Their Hope for the Future

I'm forty-one. I do not fall inside the age range, but it is the joy of my heart to contribute to this project. I love the Religious Society of Friends, and this is why I am a member. So long as I am still alive, I feel it good to work together with you people to achieve the goal and reach the destiny God has for us all. On my side, the Religious Society of Friends is like a river that started from somewhere. What can happen if the source of a river is destroyed? As long as we divide the river into smaller streams, let us not *touch* the source which holds what God imparted in it. As a young adult in this Society, I have experienced a lot, but I am going to talk about the struggle, leadership problem, and lack of self-control.

It has not been so easy to survive in the Religious Society of Friends as a young adult, but I have. Some places still face this problem. I thank God for those places that have understood the youth and can live and work together with them in harmony. I like history because it helps us to understand ourselves. Even the Bible itself is [the most] wonderful historical book we have ever seen. It holds many historical events. We believe in it because it tells us how we came into being. Therefore, I don't refuse the idea that before us we had people who contributed to our survival in this Society. They received the word of God earlier and came forward to form this Society.

Now, because of the period of time in which they were living, certain beliefs and traditions were used so as to make the people understand what they were doing. As a young adult, I have found out that those beliefs and traditions became strong foundations on which some of the members have built their faith rather than on God, and they believe they should not be destroyed. My question is whether these beliefs and traditions take us to heaven? I strongly believe that there are no specific methods of worshipping God. Throughout the Bible, I see many people worshipping God in many different ways; even some of these people were instructed by God himself on how to approach Him.

It is my surprise that some of our meetings cannot allow the youth to worship God in their own way. I don't mean all the ways youth use to worship God are right, but provided they worship God in the right way according to the Bible, they should not be hindered. Because of this hindrance, many youth are leaving the Religious Society of Friends for other societies. I feel it's painful because we can't know what God had imparted in these youth for us as a Society unless we work with them. We should know that today is not tomorrow; as time goes by the word of God is being understood deeply. The more we continue reading the word of God, the more we understand it and the more we change. Therefore, let us expect change to the people (including the youth) and finally accept one another with the love of God.

Leadership problems are the worst disease that I have ever come across in this Society of ours. The kind of criteria used in some places to elect leaders is terrible. I have been observing the leadership election in the Religious Society of Friends for many years, and I cannot differentiate between the world election and the Friends election. I have found out that most leaders come from the same generations, others from higher education, others from their wealth, others from retirement and so on. Is this the kind of criteria the Bible used to choose leaders? I don't deny the fact that people with these qualities can also be strong leaders, but the most important quality is the gift God has imparted in someone. Do these people have the gift of leadership?

It is my humble request to all the youth in the Religious Society of Friends to be very careful when it comes to leadership. It is my prayer that we open up our spiritual eyes and ears to study the word of God, understand it properly so that whatever we do as far as leadership is concerned should have its roots in the Bible. We should also understand what it really means to be a leader and remember that it is a gift from God. I suggest as a young adult that we should organize for seminars all over and educate our youth about leadership so that we can prepare them in advance for the forthcoming leaders to be fit for the work ahead of us.

I have also found it a problem to survive in the Religious Society of Friends because of a lack of self-control. It has been a problem to be patient, especially when things are not going on well in the meetings. I have been too fast to react, and sometimes I have created problems. It has taken me time to learn to be patient even when I am rebuked. It is my advice for all youth to learn to be patient sometimes and wait upon the Lord. God is faithful and His own appointed time is the best. Remember, there is time for everything. When we are given opportunities by God, let us make use of them, but if not, let us also keep quiet for God's will to be done. When God says "Yes," not many will say "No."

I believe my writing is not in vain. God has a reason for it. If we as youth can work at all upon our struggles, leadership problems, and self-control, our lives will never remain the same. Even our Religious Society of Friends will never remain the same. Remember, we are the next leaders.

If we obey the voice of God, all that we do shall bring glory and honour to God our Father.

May God bless all those who believed in this project. Amen.

Pastor Sarah K. Makanga, 41
Lukhokho Friends Church, Lugari Yearly Meeting (FUM)
Kenya

There Is No Success without a Successor

The direction in which the Quaker church is moving is to ensure that all things are perfect. By this I mean that most of the Quaker leaders want to educate their children so that when they retire their children will take over. The other thing that the Quakers are looking forward to is fighting against tribalism. [Now that] new technology is at hand, the Quakers are looking forward to eradicating corruption. Also, the Quakers want to stand with the Quaker traditions and rules. They also want to see that no person or Quaker breaks the Quaker tradition and rules.

Also they want the Quaker church to have many young people. They want to make [an] effort to ensure that the youth, who wander without a religion, get a religion. They also want to ensure that young people take part in church leadership. They want to ensure that there is enough balance. The Quakers also want to start their own schools. These schools are to help the rural area people.

They also want to help those people who don't know God to know about Him. They also want to start their own projects. These projects are tasks such as water projects. The Quaker church also wants to ensure that there is peace everywhere. They also want to be known for their peace making in the world. The Quakers also want to work as a team with others. They don't want to separate themselves as Quakers alone.

The Quakers also want [to continue] projects [that they have already] started, such as hospitals. The Quakers are also looking forward to living in harmony with one another. The Quakers are also looking forward to supporting women's leadership. To build the Quaker church, they also want to fight against poverty. The Quakers want to ensure that there is no poverty. They also want to develop young leaders who will lead in the future. They also want to raise potential leaders. The Quakers also want to look for people with skills, so that they can use them to develop different things. The different skills and gifts in the people will help them get income, which will help in the building of the church. The Quakers also want to give youth the chance to explore and know their potential. They also want them to have the confidence that they need. When they give them the opportunity they also expect the best from them, by this I mean they should:

B Believe in them

E Encourage them

S Share with them

T Trust them

The Quaker church also wants to encourage youth to continue going to church and not to give up. They also want to encourage the Sunday School children to continue coming to church and continue learning more about Jesus. This is made clear in Mark 10:14, NIV: "Let the little children come to me and do not hinder them, for the Kingdom of God belongs to such as these." The Quakers also want to fight against terrorism. They want to ensure that there is no terror anywhere. They also want to fight against hunger. They want to make their efforts so that at least every [person] has a little to eat. They also want to help the landless get home and food.

All this is what the Quakers are looking forward to, to ensure it is done, because there is no success without a successor.

Domitilla A. Khayongo, 15
East Africa Yearly Meeting (North) (FUM)
Kenya

Reap Good Fruit

We are moving nowhere unless we change our beliefs and [assume] a leading role. I am not pleased to say this because it is my church. Our dear members, why can we struggle on every Sabbath day wasting our time; on the last day we will be ashamed! Oh my dear, that is very unfair. I think we are going to make corrections in our community, so that at least we could reap good fruit after struggling this entire journey to heaven.

Our ways of praising and worshipping are supposed to change and develop a strong way of performing it. We need to worship and praise God like those people who had strength; when the devil heard them worshipping, he just ran away. It does not delay because it might be destroyed by the power of the Holy Spirit. The issue of singing the book songs alone must stop. They have to mix all of them to make the meeting enjoyable.

Pasilksa Elimah
Kenya

Toward Damascus

Friends are heirs to a radical tradition of faith. Our history proclaims that the Gifts of the Spirit are still available and continue to be poured onto the flesh of men, women, and children all across this wounded Earth. We stand in a prophetic stream and are reminded by Friends both past and present that Elijah's mantle is ours to wear as well. Though foul winds may tear the land to pieces; though the very earth may shake; and even as great fires break out upon the ground, we wait to find the voice of God not among the things of the world, but later, in the small stillness. Or do we?

It has been my experience that many Friends like the idea of Quakerism more than they like the discipline that being Friendly might impose. And it does indeed impose discipline. How else could a faith tradition without dogma maintain its egalitarianism, except with rigorous self-searching and a constant appeal for accountability and honest reflection? When we abandon a serious practice of internal examination and do not make time to allow the Light to seek out our frailer parts, we become more susceptible to human failings and the temptations of shallow comfort. When we live in our meetings without any meaningful system of accountability, discernment, or love-guided testing, we invite a *laissez-faire* attitude of "anything goes" and risk the loss of our unique identity and purpose. When all that holds us together are secular commitments and a memory of our past, our present forms may become hollow. It is my sense that many of us stand on the brink of something greater and yet hold back from giving over completely. It is my hope that this article will serve as a vehicle to examine some of the obstacles that stand in the way of going the other half: reclaiming a transforming faith that is spiritually engaged with the world.

While the origins of our faith tradition are without creed and dogma, they are neither ambivalent nor wishy-washy. Early Friends believed that the surest signpost we had to show us the way was Spirit, and that we would be Led to right action if we sought out that which Spirit was lifting up. For example, the testimonies are called that because they were testament to our experience of being moved by the Spirit of God to live our lives in new ways. They didn't emerge as the result of secular brainstorming sessions, but rose up in the hearts and minds of Friends as they prayerfully sought out the work set before them by the Divine, testing their sense with a discerning worship community. Discernment was every bit as important as the doing of good, and individuals took seriously their call to hold each other accountable to faithful living.

Unfortunately, I think that many of us, me included, tend to work so hard at doing a good deed that we sometimes find it hard to make the time to listen for the good deed toward which we are *led*. We make the same kinds of mistakes that the prophet Elijah made. The story of his journey in 1 Kings 19 is where Friends can find mention of the "still, small voice" that is often referenced in Quaker literature. Besides being a great tale, it is worth recounting for the ways it can speak to our own condition.

Elijah on Mount Horeb

As the chapter begins we find Jezebel, the Phoenician wife of King Ahab, angry and threatening to kill Elijah. This is quite a change of pace. Not long before, he had prayed down fire from the heavens to ignite an altar as proof of the power of God. Now he was fleeing in fear! He runs to Beersheba and goes out into the wilderness, eventually falling asleep, feeling bad about himself. He is woken by an angel who gives him food and water several times. He is told he must eat and drink because there is a great journey that he must take to Mount Horeb.

There he finds lodging in a cave where he rests until the word of God comes to him and asks, "What doest thou here, Elijah?" His response is fascinating. Elijah, the great prophet, a sanctified man of faith who has been fed by angels, does not answer "Whatever you want, Lord." Instead, he continues to feel sorry for himself, answering that he is jealous of God and that "I, even I only, am left, and they seek my life, to take it away." He is referring to his belief that he is the only faithful prophet that remains and that even that isn't enough to stop Jezebel's men as they hunt him. God instructs Elijah to stand outside of the cave where an earth-tearing torrential wind rises, an earthquake rocks the mountain, and fire comes to him. We are not privy to Elijah's inner response to all this, but we do read that God was not in the wind, quake, or flame. It is only after they pass that Elijah hears a "still small voice." He is asked again why he is there and responds the same way as before, still concerned for his own safety and believing he is the only faithful servant left. Then, at the point where Elijah probably most wants to be comforted and told everything will be all right, he is told by God to go to Damascus.

There he is told he will find Hazael, Jehu, and Elisha. He is to anoint the first two as kings of Syria and Israel, and the third as a prophet who will join him. Upon entering the city he finds things just as expected, ends up placing his mantle on Elisha, and charges him with service as well. God's work continues to be done and Elisha's community eventually moves deeper into faithfulness. What's more, Elijah finds out that there are, in fact, 7,000 other faithful followers in Israel: He wasn't as alone as he had thought.

On the one hand, Elijah was a follower and prophet that prayed down fire and was faithful with God's Word. On the other, he was a man chased and frightened. It must have felt to Elijah that everything was falling apart, and acting from fear and worry, he found himself hiding and repeating things that were hollow and untrue. Yet in spite of this, he did not confuse the hubbub with his true Work. When it had all settled, he gave more credence to his faith and found a path to Damascus through the ruin. Following the word of God brought him into further relationship with other faithful people, and because of them he was able to serve more fully, less afraid than before. I believe this is our future as well, and see the Religious Society of Friends in this story in two major places.

Ears to Hear

Friends have had a powerful and tangible impact on the world. In some ways it seems as if our ancestors prayed their own fires down and the expectation for us seems large indeed. It begets a question though: Why have we contemporarily, at least in North America, slipped into relative obscurity? I would offer that perhaps we are more worried about getting important things done than listening for what needs to be done. We are concerned about the winds, fires, and earthquakes, and we work so loudly to fix the damage that we cannot always hear the Guide over the noise of the construction there outside the cave.

Recall the scripture that helped us to eventually accept being named Friends. In John's Gospel Jesus speaks: "No longer do I call you servants; for the servant knoweth not what his lord doeth: but I have called you friends; for all things that I heard from my Father I have made known unto you" (John 15:15, King James). Friends are Friends of the Spirit: a people that listens for the still, small voice and does the work it speaks of, knowing it is God's work. I believe that a measure of the power of our forebears came not just from their energy, intelligence, and effort, but from the ordering of those skills under the gifts and guidance of that small, still voice.

I know that there is much in the world that warrants attention and do not advocate that Friends remove themselves from work in the world. That is not our way. What I do suggest is that Friends earnestly ask themselves why it is that we do what we do. Are we acting out of worldly fear and drive or from some inward prompting? When Elijah stood on that mountain all the world around him was breaking into pieces, and yet he listened. And responded. It is upon us, too, to do the same, taking the time to engage in communal discernment even when we do feel pressed to move by wind, fire, and despair. When we speak and act from a leading, there seems to be more power in the word and service.

Desperation and Isolation

We can feel as if we are all alone, discouraged and disaffected. I vividly remember a message given at a humid Friends General Conference worship that essentially said, "With the world so messed up, it is good that at least Friends are here to do the right thing." On more than one occasion I have, myself, wondered why no one other than me seemed to be getting "it." Standing in the cave, it is easy to fall to the temptation of assuming we are all alone.

In particular I often experience Friends—especially liberal, unprogrammed Friends—as estranged not only from American society at large, but from other brothers and sisters in the Christian tradition. Politically and socially, many Friends find themselves outside of the norm. Where are the other pacifists? The war protesters? The defenders of the earth!?! The activists!?!?

When Elijah does this kind of complaining straight into the voice of God on the mountain, he is asked to go to Damascus. Being a faithful servant, he goes and discovers that he is, in fact, not alone at all. After he encounters Elisha they travel together for some time, and he is able to share the weight of his service with another. In spite of ourselves and our isolation, I think we are being called to Damascus as well.

Way Opens

Friends, we are not alone. There is a great, faithful wave rising across the globe and seeking a more just world in which to live. If we are not aware of its movement it may be because we remain on Mount Horeb repairing our cave. While we continue to repair our shelter, tend the memories of our past, and resist going "the other half," we deny the opportunity to live up to our namesake and allow ourselves to be guided by the same still, small voice that led Elijah out of seclusion. Our task now is the same as his was then: to break down the false gods of materialism and violent nationalism, to listen for the ministry we have been given, and to seek out others of faith, joining with all ears that hear and eyes that see.

If we are to live up to the name we gave ourselves, to become Friends in name *and* spirit, then we will invite each other into conversation, share in deep worship, and seek a way forward as guided. If we do not at least engage each other at a deeply searching spiritual level, I'm not exactly sure what we *can do* as a Religious Society. I have a great hope for the Religious Society of Friends. It is born of a desire for a rejuvenating and deepening practice of listening discernment and communal discipline. It is by asking to be bound more closely to each other in love that we will become a Gathered people. It is when we are Gathered and allow ourselves to be Led that we will be met.

Do we practice listening past the distraction of the winds and fires? Are our actions guided by the Inner Teacher? When will we again be Gathered, leaving the Mount for Damascus? What might we find there? Are we willing to go?

L. Callid Keefe-Perry, 27
Rochester Monthly Meeting, New York Yearly Meeting (FGC-FUM)
United States

A Strong Feeling of One Another

When we try to see through the problems the church is facing, we can realize that there are many obstacles that lead to this impending danger of the Quaker church. One thing in common is the emergence of many churches that praise God through many ways that are [too numerous] to talk about. For instance, use of advanced technological know-how, singing in high pitches that attract people from the Quaker church to go and "collaborate" themselves with the other members of the different churches. This stimulates the sense of the Quaker church that the methods of worshipping the almighty God are unpleasant to some members, thus they withdraw from the Quaker church.

Lack of transparency and accountability to the church resources has led to a negative attitude among Quaker converts. This is due to mismanagement of church resources unknowingly, without witnesses, for projects that will benefit the Quaker converts. If this is taken seriously from the perspective of our own hearts, if we check it thoroughly and then come up with a solution that is effective, then the Quaker church will be the best church ever.

For there to be a strong feeling of one another is more important to the other and [if we] give allegiance from the work he or she does, then the prosperity and achievements in which the Quaker church moves will be of great value. Let everyone realize that ability may get you to the top, but it takes both character and ability to be contented at the top; and let us keep in mind that the achievement of an organization is the result of the combined effort of each individual. Through this, the movement of the church will be vivid and straight always. This is the moment to show other churches that the Quaker church is stronger both in converting the faiths and worshipping the almighty.

Simiyu Kalamu Timothy, 19
Lugulu Friends Church, Elgon Religious Society of Friends (FUM)
Kenya

Friends Living the Resurrection

From John 11:1-44:

Now a man named Lazarus was sick. He was from Bethany, the village of Mary and her sister Martha. This Mary, whose brother Lazarus now lay sick, was the same one who poured perfume on the Lord and wiped his feet with her hair. So the sisters sent word to Jesus, "Lord, the one you love is sick."

When he heard this, Jesus said, "This sickness will not end in death. No, it is for God's glory so that God's Son may be glorified through it." Jesus loved Martha and her sister and Lazarus. Yet when he heard that Lazarus was sick, he stayed where he was two more days.

Then he said to his disciples, "Let us go back to Judea."

"But Rabbi," they said, "a short while ago the Jews tried to stone you, and yet you are going back there?"

Jesus answered, "Are there not twelve hours of daylight? A man who walks by day will not stumble, for he sees by this world's light. It is when he walks by night that he stumbles, for he has no light."

After he had said this, he went on to tell them, "Our friend Lazarus has fallen asleep; but I am going there to wake him up."

His disciples replied, "Lord, if he sleeps, he will get better." Jesus had been speaking of his death, but his disciples thought he meant natural sleep.

So then he told them plainly, "Lazarus is dead, and for your sake I am glad I was not there, so that you may believe. But let us go to him."

Then Thomas said to the rest of the disciples, "Let us also go, that we may die with him."

On his arrival, Jesus found that Lazarus had already been in the tomb for four days. Bethany was less than two miles from Jerusalem, and many Jews had come to Martha and Mary to comfort them in the loss of their brother. When Martha heard that Jesus was coming, she went out to meet him, but Mary stayed at home.

"Lord," Martha said to Jesus, "If you had been here, my brother would not have died. But I know that even now God will give you whatever you ask."

Jesus said to her, "Your brother will rise again."

Martha answered, "I know he will rise again in the resurrection at the last day."

Jesus said to her, "I am the resurrection and the life. He who believes in me will live, even though he dies; and whoever lives and believes in me will never die. Do you believe this?"

"Yes, Lord," she told him, "I believe that you are the Christ, the Son of God, who was to come into the world."

And after she had said this, she went back and called her sister Mary aside. "The Teacher is here," she said, "and is asking for you." When Mary heard this, she got up quickly and went to him. Now Jesus had not yet entered the village, but was still at the place where Martha had met him. When the Jews who had been with Mary in the house, comforting her, noticed how quickly she got up and went out, they followed her, supposing she was going to the tomb to mourn there.

When Mary reached the place where Jesus was and saw him, she fell at his feet and said, "Lord, if you had been here, my brother would not have died."

When Jesus saw her weeping, and the Jews who had come along with her also weeping, he was deeply moved in spirit and troubled.

"Where have you laid him?" he asked.

"Come and see, Lord," they replied.

Jesus wept.

Then the Jews said, "See how he loved him!"

But some of them said, "Could not he who opened the eyes of the blind man have kept this man from dying?"

Jesus, once more deeply moved, came to the tomb. It was a cave with a stone laid across the entrance. "Take away the stone," he said.

"But, Lord," said Martha, the sister of the dead man, "by this time there is a bad odor, for he has been there four days."

Then Jesus said, "Did I not tell you that if you believed, you would see the glory of God?"

So they took away the stone. Then Jesus looked up and said, "Father, I thank you that you have heard me. I know that you always hear me, but I said this for the benefit of the people standing here, that they may believe that you sent me."

When he had said this, Jesus called in a loud voice, "Lazarus, come out!" The dead man came out, his hands and feet wrapped with strips of linen, and a cloth around his face.

Jesus said to them, "Take off the grave clothes and let him go."

Message

"A call to spiritual awakening" is what our planning committee decided to name this event. Why? Because revival sounded dated, and renewal sounded a little boring. Yet, aren't they all, on a fundamental level, synonymous? To be awakened do you not need to be revived? To be revived do you not start anew? Regardless of whatever vocabulary you used to get yourself here, why did you really come?

Did you come for an awakening? Did you come because the Spirit moved you? Did you come simply because you come to all the other yearly meeting activities, so might as well come to this one? Did you come because you have witnessed the momentum the yearly meeting has been gathering, and wanted to continue to be a part of a good thing?

I am here because I said "yes" to all of these questions months and months ago when the select few of us began to plan this event. I am here because I believe the Resurrection and the Life is at work in our yearly meeting today. I am here because I want to be like Thomas and journey with Him boldly. I am here because I want to be faithful like Martha and Mary were to Him. I am here because I want to witness Christ at the tomb telling our yearly meeting to come out. I am here because I want to see our yearly meeting take off its grave clothes and begin to live again.

For the past several months, many of you have heard those on the committee and me tell you that this event was going to be just about worship. No business. No controversy. Just communion. Just fellowship. Simply witnessing the Holy Spirit at work.

Witnessing the Holy Spirit healing the tension, the bitterness, the unrest, and using someone who is too young to know any better to talk about it.

For the last eleven years I have served in this yearly meeting in some capacity. During those eleven years I have listened to weighty Friends discussing how our yearly meeting has been dwindling in numbers. I have heard the theories on how we can once again make an attempt to return the yearly meeting to its past glory. However, what I personally have heard too little of is doing it for God's glory.

I have listened to Friends comparing Quakerism to the other branches of Christianity. And a part of me wants to ask, "Why should we care?" George Fox compared Friends to the Church of England, but only enough to incite folks to return to a form of primitive Christianity. William Penn established Pennsylvania as a haven for people to have the freedom to worship God in their own unique way. John Woolman traveled the Eastern Seaboard to preach the Truth that all men, all women, white or black, were equal in the Light. Our legacy is simple. We believe in the Resurrection and the Life through the Light and Truth of the Christ. Why be anything other than that? Why not let that be the call we hear to exit the tomb?

Why not? Because spiritual death is difficult to overcome. And Death, besides Jesus, is the other main character in this passage. This passage is an intriguing story, because it has a powerful protagonist and an almost equal antagonist. We see Death almost dominating the entire passage. Death terrifies the Disciples; it is why they do not want to go to Bethany. Death saddens Martha and Mary. Death imprisons Lazarus. It imposes on every human being in the passage because it is more than they are. It is beyond their control. It is beyond their comprehension. It can only be defeated by something that is greater, something that is also beyond human control or comprehension. It can only be slain by its direct opposite.

As amongst these men and women found in John 11, the fear of death has reared its head at our yearly meeting. For some of us, we are like those Disciples; we fear that if we get too close to it by preaching the Truths that are in our hearts, it will strike us and maim us in some way. For some of us, we are like the sisters; we are so overcome with the sadness of what used to be our yearly meeting, and is no longer, that we sit at home, feel sorry for ourselves, and no longer try. And for some us, we are in the tomb. We are spiritually dead. We are the products of political correctness, or self-righteousness. Or we are in the tomb, and we feel the yearly meeting is dead, let it be dead.

Yet, the silver lining is that while death is greater than the yearly meeting, Christ is greater than death. And as these people, we are now in a position to witness Life bringing Resurrection. There has been momentum building for several years now. We have been like the Disciples, encouraged by the bravery of a few like Thomas, to compel the rest of us to travel with God to this point in time. We have been like Martha and Mary, who have desperately thrown themselves to the ground to offer up to God a lament. And some of us are like the Jews who just happened to be at the right place at the right time to see this.

This has all been a part of God's plan for us. Like those in this passage, He had to allow death to affect us in some way so He could announce to us what He is and what He can do for us. We had to be afraid of death so we could be desperate. We had to be desperate so we could begin to believe. We had to believe so we could have faith. We had to have faith to have resurrection. We have to have resurrection to have life. Life to be renewed, life to be revived, life to have spiritual awakening.

Now in saying that, let me ask you this: How do you feel at this moment? Are you feeling anxious? Are you feeling upset? Are you feeling uncomfortable? Are you feeling restrained? Is your heart speeding up? Is your mind turning circles? Do you have a knot in your stomach? Does the back of your neck burn?

The antagonist has arrived. He walked into this meeting room while I read this passage and you did not even see him come in. He walks around the pews and what you feel is the result of his growl. And if you do not believe that I can feel it, then you are mistaken. Of all the people in this meeting room, Death dislikes me the most right now. And even though he is more than me, the One greater than he also resides here.

The Resurrection and the Life resides in me. The Resurrection and the Life has given me this opportunity and the inspiration for this message. And I believe, and have the faith, that if the Resurrection and the Life has called me to this moment, He will not forsake me.

If the Resurrection and the Life compelled you to be here, for whatever reason, then He will also not forsake you in this moment. If you take hold of Him, Death will have no choice other than to flee. If we do as our ancestors did and begin to attain a spiritual life that is in total communion with the Light, then death and its darkness can no longer dominate us.

What is interesting about the climax of this great story is that Jesus never asks God to resurrect Lazarus. What does He say at the tomb to God: "Father, I thank you that you have heard me. I knew that you always hear me, but I said this for the benefit of the people standing here, that they may believe you sent me." What does that mean? It means that Jesus has been, during all this time, in communion with God. And in so doing all Jesus, the Resurrection and the Life, has to do is say, "Lazarus, come out."

All these years our numbers have been dwindling, Christ has been present and in communion with God. All these years monthly meetings have been disillusioned. All this time, we as individuals have been left wanting. Now the Holy Spirit has arrived, to say:

"Come out." "Come out." "Come out."

Come out, it's time to stop worrying about dying. Come out, it's time to start anew. Come out, it's time to quit feeling self pity. Come out, it's time to be who we once were again. Come out, it's time to start living the Resurrection.

North Carolina Yearly Meeting, it's time to start living the Resurrection. It's time to start reaching out to our monthly meetings that feel like they have been forgotten. It's time to start respecting our female ministers as much as our male ministers. It's time for younger Friends to seek the wisdom of older Friends. It's time, too, for older Friends to start being energized by younger Friends. It's time for center right Friends to start listening to center left Friends about social justice. It's time for center left Friends to start listening to center right Friends about evangelism. It's time for Friends to start writing again. It's time for Friends to start living up to their names again.

Yet, there is no committee that can do this for us. There is no recorded minister or clerk who can do this for us. We have to walk out of the tomb first as individuals.

When we first take off our own grave clothes given to us by death, we allow that new life of the Resurrection to shine for all to see. We have to have constant communion so that the Light may remove each piece of imperfect linen.

Then it will not matter if we are a member of a large meeting or a small meeting. It will not matter which quarterly meeting we are from. It will not matter if we are old or young. Because what is present for all to see is a vision of a man or woman, clothed in the protagonist of Life. And though death will ultimately take dominion of that body, it cannot nor will not growl again and shake that spirit.

And it is spirits like these that can add numbers to our yearly meeting. It is spirits like these that can be peacemakers and heal the tensions of past business meetings. It is spirits like these that Christ lived and died so that we could become.

Friends, we are at the tomb. It's time to wake up, be what we once were and more, and be this new kind of wonderful together.

Michael J. Fulp, Jr., 27
Prosperity Friends Meeting, North Carolina Yearly Meeting (FUM)
United States

The Sweat Lodge and Meeting for Worship

After participating in my first sweat lodge at the 2001 FGC Gathering, I remember feeling very vulnerable and very connected to nature. I had never felt this way before and it was an amazing experience. For the rest of the evening, I just wanted to sit outside and cry, because I felt life was so precious and I felt so connected to it. The whole experience is something I won't ever forget. For over a decade and half George Price led the Quaker Sweat Lodges at Friends General Conference Gatherings, which allowed hundreds of people to have this experience. These sweat lodges were popular among the participants from the High School and the Adult Young Friends programs.

In 2004, the Long Range Planning Committee of the Friends General Conference received a complaint from a representative of a Massachusetts tribe about the use of the sweat lodge by non-Native Americans. They responded by canceling the Quaker Sweat Lodge Experience workshop, led by George Price, Cullen Carns-Hilliker, and Breeze Richardson. Since then, they have set up an ad hoc committee, which has held meetings between those who support the Quaker sweat lodge and those who do not.* I am writing outside of this process and I don't want this article to be seen as representing one side or the other in this debate.

With my work on the Pine Ridge Reservation, where the Oglala Lakota people live, I met traditional elders who think no white person should ever participate in a sweat lodge ceremony, because it is one of the seven sacred ceremonies in the Lakota religion. At the same time, I met Lakota people who wanted to share their religion with non-Lakota people and would invite me to ceremonies.

Through my work on Pine Ridge, I began seeing similarities between the sweat lodge and meeting for worship. In the fall of 2002 I wrote an article exploring these similarities and others between the Lakota religion and Quakerism for an American Friends Service Committee (AFSC)

Central Region newsletter. In the article I talked about how both religions believe in the capability of people to have a direct relationship to God and in the promotion of equality. They both place an emphasis on caring for the environment and on service, helping their fellow neighbors. Even the ceremonies of both religions often take place using circular formations.

Thinking about these similarities raises some questions for me: If meeting for worship and the sweat lodge ceremony have so much in common, why do I not leave the room every First Day feeling as vulnerable as after my first sweat lodge? Why do a lot of my fellow young adult Friends spend hundreds of dollars and travel hundreds of miles to gather with other young adult Friends across the country at Quaker gatherings yet don't travel a couple miles down the road to visit the local monthly meeting on First Day?

To me, these two questions are very much related. Most of my friends feel estranged from their home meetings either because they have moved away or they are the only young people there. In my experience, many meetings for worship are dull and boring (other YAFs have shared similar stories with me). I strive in meeting for worship to be baptized with the Holy Spirit, which early Friends were seeking and experiencing when they began meeting in seventeenth-century England.

Yet, between hearing messages about daily news and left-wing politics, I feel disconnected from developing a deeper spiritual relationship with God and with my monthly meeting community. Sometimes I feel like I leave meeting for worship without a feeling of having ever been in a state of worship because the meeting hasn't felt gathered at all. Young adult Friends seek out gatherings of YAFs and other ceremonies like the sweat lodge to experience this missing element. I have seen this hunger for something more at these gatherings. Older Friends have told me of their hunger for something more too. If the sweat lodge and meeting for worship have so much in common, why do I feel like I have a less spiritual experience within my own religion? Why should I leave my religious tradition for another to experience the loving embrace of the Holy Spirit?

For the Lakota people, the sweat lodge ceremony represents a rebirth. The physical structure of the sweat lodge represents a womb and, during the ceremony, rocks are continually added to keep the temperature inside hot, like it would be inside the womb. What is our rebirth ceremony in the Friends tradition? I argue that meeting for worship can serve as a place for us to become re-immersed in the Holy Spirit, to become reenergized to continue our daily witness out in the world.

One difference between the sweat lodge ceremony and Quaker meeting for worship is time constraints. The ceremony for the Lakota ends when it ends, but in our meetings for worship we have them structured to start and finish at a precise hour, without even checking in with God about his schedule. Early Friends would wait in silence for hours until the meeting broke. Some gatherings of Friends are trying to bring back this tradition of waiting, like the Friends of Jesus Christ in Chicago, Illinois. How can we fool ourselves by trying to think that we can schedule God?

Instead of just debating whether it is appropriate for Friends to use Native American traditions, we need to look at why the sweat lodge experience is attractive to Friends. The overall urgent question is not, "Should the Quaker Sweat Lodge be allowed to continue at the Friends General Conference Gatherings?" but "How do we restructure our meeting for worship to be a holy divine experience where we spiritually cleanse ourselves as a community each week?" If we answer that question, we will be able to start rebuilding our meetings as our spiritual communities.

Greg Woods, 25
Columbia (Missouri) Monthly Meeting, Illinois Yearly Meeting (FGC)
United States

*Ad Hoc Committee for Quaker Sweat Lodge Discernment. "Final Report to the Executive Committee." Available online at www. fgcquaker.org. I recommend reading this report if you want to learn more about this process.

**Woods, Greg. "Similarities between the Lakota Religion and Quakerism." http://webarchive.afsc.org/central/2002/fa0209.htm.

The Way

If I offer you an ocean of peace,
an endless sky,
an attainable horizon,
then, will you be satiated?

Will your thirst for life
be quenched?

Will you see that you are alive
and, for this, you are free?

Or, will you stand in your place
to ponder your feet
soaked with tears,
frozen in your ancestor's fear?

You who fly, yet do not see the earth.
You who float, yet do not listen to water.
What have I to show
that has not been revealed always?

All of these gifts before you.
A small task, to lift your eyes.

>   *Megan E. Drimal, 35*
>
>   *Originally a member of Friends Memorial Church, Indiana Yearly*
>   *Meeting (FUM), later Clear Creek Meeting and Bloomington Friends*
>   *Meeting, both Ohio Valley Yearly Meeting (FGC). No current affiliation.*
>   *United States*

Editorial Hands, photograph, Lucy Duncan, Philadelphia Yearly Meeting (FGC),
United States

Dispatches from the Lamb's War (e-mail message, Oct. 28, 2008)

Dear Friend,

In response to your query:

Is the Peace Testimony a relevant part of Quaker life today?

I'd like to offer the following thoughts, which have arisen from prayerful consideration and my experience until now:

My understanding is that "The Peace Testimony" is only a way that Friends have in recent decades come to describe something much more deeply rooted in Friends religious experience—namely, our testimony to our experience of the work in our own hearts of the Inward Christ, the Inner Light, our Teacher and Guide (by whatever name). Lloyd Lee Wilson, in his book *Essays on the Quaker Vision of Gospel Order*, includes an essay with the title "On Remembering Why They Are Called Testimonies." His words speak much more deeply to this than I have here.

When we confront injustice, when we engage in Spirit-led service, when we speak prophetically to the condition of the world we live in and witness to the world we know is possible (and already here among us), when we are instruments of the Spirit for reconciliation, healing, and mutual understanding, we are testifying to the Truth through our experience of that Life and Love and Power that takes away the occasion for all war. That is remaking the world in far more effective ways than we can through our anger, grief, passion, and social action—no matter how well-intentioned.

I have no doubt that this Spirit leads us into prophetic witness and that this often means that we are involved politically as part of political movements, seeking to influence political decisions, or even supporting (to some extent) the work or agendas of political parties. But we go astray when we mistake the cause, or the ideology, or the party, or the idol of "effectiveness" for the real issue—our own journey toward and into the Spirit that is supremely effective.

I am saddened when the words Friends speak in meeting do not arise, at least as far as my Inward Witness discerns, from the promptings of the Spirit among us, for the sustenance, uplifting, and encouragement of the meeting as a whole on our individual and corporate journeys. But even these kinds of messages are opportunities to listen more deeply to the ways that I can center down more deeply, listen for God's voice, and follow my experience of Divine Wisdom wherever She leads.

A Friend who has been a mentor and elder to me on my own journey once shared with me the counsel "Get thee to God, before you get thee to the World."

Not "Don't get thee to the World." But ground yourself (myself) in the Presence of the Spirit in whom we live, and move, and have our being, to truly seek, through our speech and actions, to bring all into the more perfect, more whole expression of what early Friends (and Conservative Friends, and others today) call Gospel Order—a universe, including social, political, and economic relationships—that model what God intends for all of us. A world in living relationships of Love, Truth, and Justice. The key, as I've come to understand it, is that if we are pursuing our own vision of justice or peace through our own ego, anger, and confusion, we're less likely to truly be midwives for the inbreaking of Divine Love into our world. But if we honestly and patiently allow ourselves to be led, as imperfectly as we can understand those leadings, and if we follow faithfully, we can be (often in spite of ourselves) the radical agents of Love in our wounded world.

The Peace Testimony, then, is the outward sign of an inward transformation. As the Spirit does its work within us, our outward service and witness will reflect the qualities of the Inward Teacher and the fruits of the Spirit: love, joy, peace, patience, kindness, generosity, faithfulness, gentleness, and self-control (Gal. 5:22-23). Our actions may make people uncomfortable, and may challenge them more than they'd like to be challenged. They may make people angry. But if we are faithful, our actions should not wound people. And they should not demean That of God in those with whom we disagree, though we may disagree mightily. If we're doing that (wounding or demeaning), even out of justified frustration, outrage, and confusion, we're not Testifying as clearly as we might. If we do this faithfully, it won't be merely about vigils, rallies, banners, and bumper stickers. These are, in the words of an early Friend, a "Silly Poor Gospel," if this takes the place of radical, Spirit-led, and loving testimony in and among our brothers and sisters and neighbors. I don't want to limit an expression of all-encompassing Divine Love to an Obama for President bumper sticker or a Bush Lied, People Died sign. Walter Brueggemann, in his book *The Prophetic Imagination*, gives a useful description of what a prophetic witness might look like, beyond a simple challenge to or condemnation of the powers that be. A key element is a call to a future more in keeping with the promise of the Spirit—a world of love, justice, reconciliation, and healing.

My own experience of activism, in its secular forms, is that it is often something that pulls people away from a focus on and faithfulness to the leadings of the Spirit. The Catholic mystic and prophet Thomas Merton, in what has been called his "Letter to a Young Activist," might seem to agree (I carry that letter in my Bible and read it often, when I'm in deep need of reminders about this).

Altruism and a dedication to "saving the world" have in my own experience sprung more from anger (outrage) and sorrow (grief) than from Love. When I or others start from a place of activism (which I take to mean the imperative to "do something," to make our opposition to injustice known, to fight against the hatred and pain and suffering and ignorance and fear that seems to run unchallenged through much of our world), we tread on dangerous ground. We can make it very difficult for the Spirit to lead us, and we can do damage to ourselves and others in many ways. This certainly has happened in meetings with which I've been connected and in my own life. In our struggle for "positive social change," we can alienate others, in fact making it more difficult for them to respond to leadings that might invite them into partnership with us and with God in nurturing a renewed world.

The answer isn't to withdraw into spiritual, contemplative enclaves in which the pain of our selves and our neighbors can be ignored. It isn't to convince ourselves that we should avoid conflict in the name of not upsetting anyone, or to protect ourselves from the very real spectre of burnout or the pain of our perceived powerlessness or failure. Instead, the answer is to center down, to (in the words of George Fox) stand still in the Light until we have a clear sense that, because we are loved and are steeped in the love of God and our community, we can act out of Love, in testimony to our experience of the movement of the Spirit in our hearts and in the world. This doesn't mean we have to wait to be perfect to act in the world—far from it. But if we can give up control and surrender in small and large ways to first knowing God's heart and then being God's hands in a broken world, my experience is that we may find ourselves—and the service into which we're called—transformed. We do need to be prepared. And that's worth waiting (in the Light) for, though it will have to happen in God's time, not according to our timeline. And this searching, and this waiting, and this seeking, and this listening, is profoundly relevant.

These are some of my experiences, as these issues continue to be opened to me, through a glass, darkly. I might be completely wrong, but if I am, please take these words in the Spirit in which they are intended, with humility and in friendship.

I'm grateful to you, Friend, for inviting this sharing.

I hope and pray that some of what I've shared above speaks to your condition, despite the length.

In faith, stumbling in the dark,
Noah

> *Noah Baker Merrill, 30*
> *Putney Friends Meeting, New England Yearly Meeting (FGC-FUM)*
> *United States*

Sin Llevar la Gracia de Dios al Libertinaje

En estos tiempos se puede observar muchas cosas que llaman mucho la atención. Aun nosotros como Cuáqueros nos sorprendemos de los avances de la ciencia, medicina, tecnología y muchas cosas más. Pero lo que más llama la atención es el actuar de las personas porque parece que conforme avanzan y evolucionan las cosas así también se engrandece la maldad del hombre. Quien escribe este pequeño ensayo vive en un país como muchos llaman tercermundista pero viviendo aquí puedo ver muchas cosas que ocurren en mi propio país y en el mundo entero. Yo soy cristiano Cuáquero, como muchos con defectos que me propuse cambiar y en todo este tiempo he visto con mucha tristeza que la mayoría de las personas tiene el pensamiento de que lo principal es que uno se sienta bien sin importar que tenga que hacer o aceptar. Muchas veces los cristianos no entendemos aquella frase que dijo nuestro Señor "Aquel que quiera venir en pos de mi tome su cruz niéguese a sí mismo y sígame." Muchas veces para sentirnos bien hacemos y aceptamos cosas malas que van en contra de los buenos principios que recibimos de parte de nuestro Dios y muchas veces por causa de la modernidad y la presión que ejerce la sociedad no nos damos cuenta de la venda que tapa nuestros ojos de que lo malo poco a poco se fue convirtiendo en justo y quien sabe talvez más adelante se convierta en bueno. Sabemos que nuestro Dios es un Dios de amor y misericordia pero no tratemos de entender eso conforme a nuestros pensamientos humanos porque muchas veces nosotros entendemos conforme a nuestra conveniencia. Para todo aquel que lea esto quiero pedirle que haga un pequeño estudio de toda su vida de cómo esta viviendo, actuando y pensando. Si ve que ha encontrado algo que talvez no va de acuerdo con lo que nos enseñó nuestro Señor Jesús y Dios quítese la venda de sus ojos y trate de corregir tal error, porque al corregir estos errores iremos mas allá, pero debemos saber que nuestro Señor está aun mucho mas allá y para llegar allí debemos sacrificar muchas cosas. Ahora la pregunta es ¿estás dispuesto a sacrificar esos errores malos? Muchas veces será difícil hacer esto pero debemos dar el primer paso y avancemos poco a poco y pidamos a nuestro Dios que El nos ayude a lograr esto, El nos conoce, sabe de nuestras debilidades y también sabe como ayudarnos si nos ponemos en sus manos.

> *Edwin Ruben Quispe Arratia*
> *Iglesia Amigos Central Obrajes Bella Vista*
> *Junta Annual de la Iglesia Evangélica Amigos Central de Bolivia*
> *(EFCI)*
> *Bolivia*

Without Leading God's Grace to the Liberal Way

One can currently observe many things that frequently grab our attention. As Quakers, we are surprised at the advances in science, medicine, and technology, among many other things. But what gets our attention the most is how people behave. It seems as things keep going and are developing, men's wickedness grows more. I, who write this short writing, live in a country that is well known by many people as a developing country. But while living here, I can see many things that happen in my country as well as all over the world. I am Quaker Christian but, like many others, I have defects that I decided to change. However, so far, I have seen with a lot of sadness that most people have the thought that the main thing is that one can feel well without caring what they have to do or accept. Many times, we Christians don't understand the phrase that our Lord said: "That the one who wants to come after me, he should take up his cross, refuse himself and follow me" (Luke 9:23). So many times, we make and accept bad things in order to feel well even though they go against the good principles that we receive from our God, and most of the time it is because of the modern life or the pressures of the society that exist. We don't realize that a bandage covers our eyes so we begin accepting little by little that the bad is fair and maybe it could even become good. We know that our God loves us a lot and He has mercy on us, but we must not rely on our human thinking because we understand things only through our own perspective. To all of you who are going to read this, I would like to ask that you do a small reflection on your life and how you have been living, behaving, and thinking so that you can see what is not according to what our Lord and God has taught us. Then take the bandage from your eyes and try to correct that mistake, since if we correct these mistakes, we will reach further. We know that our Lord is farther yet and that while reaching where He is, we need to stop doing things that seem to us easy and good to do. Now there is a question, are you ready to give up those bad mistakes? It will not be easy to do this, but we should try the first step and continue little by little, and above all, we should ask God for help so that we can get it. He knows all about us, including which are our weaknesses, and He knows how He is going to help us if we trust in Him.

Edwin Ruben Quispe Arratia
Amigo Central de Obrajes Bella Vista Church
Central Evangelical Friends Church of Bolivia (Yearly Meeting)
(EFCI)
Bolivia

One Meeting

The sun is breaking through the trees as we make our way up the narrow path to the door. My mom, just ahead of me, carries a worn pillow under her arm and my dad clappers along behind in his maroon clogs. As we near the house, the yellow Lab gets up from his perch and comes to greet us with great enthusiasm. His whole body vibrates with the joy of the morning and having company!

The door opens and the mother steps out with a big smile creasing her face.

"Hello! Isn't it a beautiful day!? Come in!"

We step into the house and I wonder if the mother's adult children will be here today. I hope so. As we take our shoes and coats off, the father comes down the hall in his overalls; his lips are drawn up in a diminutive smile.

"Hi!" he says as he passes on to the kitchen.

Down the hall I can see the warm sunlight seeping into the living room, where we will meet, and making patterns on the old wooden floorboards. I notice, as we come into the room, that the mother has placed a bunch of flowers from their fields in the middle of the dark chest to the side of, and slightly behind, one of the chairs.

An interesting place for flowers, I think to myself. (There was an unspoken rule that flowers were not Quakerly and should not be placed in meeting.)

I sit down in the chair next to the flowers and watch as the room slowly fills with attendees. One of the first to arrive is the grandmother who lives next door. She gives a friendly nod to the three of us with a few short words of greeting. The adult children come and sit with each other on the couch by the window. A faint shuffle of feet is heard coming down the hall and an elderly couple, supporting each other with their frail arms, slowly makes their way to the circle.

The seats are soon filled and a fragile silence envelops us all.

I can hear the chickadee in the branches of the great maple tree outside the window. The sun warms my knees and my hands folded in my lap, but still I feel a certain chill in my bones.

I should have remembered that they always keep it so cold in here. I think to myself. *Now don't be so negative . . . clear your mind.*

I take a deep breath and focus my eyes on the coffee table in front of me.

In and out. In and out.

My thoughts drift back to a year ago, when I started to meet with these Friends. I had heard about Quakerism and its ideas through my mom, who worked with the American Friends Service Committee as a young person, and in many ways I already considered myself a Universalist Quaker without giving it that name, but until recently we had never lived near a Friends group or meeting. When we moved to this area I was excited to be able to go to a Quaker worship group for the first time. It was wonderful meeting these new people and starting to learn more about silent worship. Now, a year later, I don't feel that excitement anymore. The experience proved to be different from what I expected.

My awareness slips back to the feeling in the room. The chill won't go away! Then I realize that it is not just the temperature, it is the climate of suppressed emotions.

There is an underlying control that I feel in the room; an invisible, taut net has been flung over our heads. It bashes the possibility of a gathered meeting, as it affirms the unspoken rule of "no popcorn." No one is to speak in meeting. If you do, or a new guest does, you are subtly told by the birthright Friends that it was not called for or acceptable in our gathering.

I glance up to look at the mother sitting very still in her chair. Her eyes are closed and her chin is lifted ever so slightly. Her shoulders are relaxed back and her hands are gracefully folded in her lap.

What must she be thinking?

Over this past year subtle energies and dynamics have come to my awareness in this group. I have begun to feel the heaviness of the family's two-hundred-year Quaker history. I can feel a level of hidden control constraining people, preventing them from saying or discussing certain things about and around Quakerism. For instance, when my mother brought up an interesting Pendle Hill Pamphlet that she had been reading and asked if anyone wanted to discuss it with her, there was a strange silence. She felt like she had trespassed into forbidden territory.

Various people in this group seem to have ambiguous feelings about Quakerism.

My eye is drawn to the mother as she gives a soft sigh, opens her eyes with a discreet smile, and adjusts her position. The sun has moved on in its journey and is no longer showing its bright face in the room, but the warmth on my lap is still there. The clock in the hall is making a soft ticking sound, marking out every second of time.

I recall last week's gathering and how my dad asked about the social situation of the group. He mentioned how some of us would like to get to know the other attendees better, and we hoped we might have some social events outside the one hour of silence.

We have sat with this group for over a year, it seems like we should have some kind of relationship with them. They seem distant, holding themselves apart.

When this was brought up, everyone was all smiles but said they were just so busy with their lives. I felt a barrier spring up between us. This feeling is still with me today.

My thoughts rattle on in my head at an amazing speed.

Why does there seem to be a reluctance on the family's part to get to know us? Why is there a control that covers what feels to me like fear? I feel like there is some kind of unspoken conflict underneath the surface.

I sigh and try to bring my thoughts back to the present. Someone's stomach grumbles across the room, and I can't help wondering if they had breakfast or not.

My eyes glance down to my wrist, but the watch there is partially covered by my sleeve. I dare not move it.

This is only an hour; can't I have a clear, patient mind for just an hour? Come on! Breathe evenly, focus on the breath…

My efforts are interrupted by the father getting up to put more wood in the stove by the kitchen.

I decide to exercise positive thinking and slowly look from one attender to the other, offering up prayers of hope for all of them.

Let everything work out well for the engaged couple and may their wedding day be sunny. May the grandmother stay healthy and always be able to stay in her old farmhouse. May the father find rest and peace in his busy farm life and teaching job. May the dog always have juicy bones available. May my father find a job soon.

My eyes close and I imagine a circle of warm light enveloping us all.

A hand softly nudges me and I open my eyes to see that the meeting is coming to a close; everyone holds hands, smiling. I slowly get up from my chair. The young people are already at the door, rushing off to an auction.

The parents and grandmother, with radiant faces, start to gently usher us out to the car.

I am quite thirsty, but know that we will not be offered any drinks, snacks, or even chitchat after a meeting at this house.

We call our good-byes back toward the house and a thought crosses my mind:

Is this Friendly worship? Do I really know these Friends? What am I doing in this meeting? Is this what Friends meeting is about?

Kathleen Burckhardt, 18

Saanich Peninsula Monthly Meeting, Canadian Yearly Meeting (FUM-FGC)

Canada

Author's Note: This reflects my first experiences sitting with a group of Friends over a year-and-a-half period. Luckily I have found a "Friendly" meeting since then. In my three-year encounter with Quakerism I have seen some of both the bright and the shadow side. Despite this, I now consider myself a Friend.

Let Us Achieve the Height

From my point of view, I think the Quaker church has moved a milestone compared to other emerging churches. As young persons we were used to singing only hymn songs, but it reached a time where some of our fellow youths started moving out to join other churches because they looked at Friends church as being boring.

The other thing is that the division that [is there] in the Quaker church is very hard, [because] all of us are supposed to serve one God and we are all equal before the eyes of the Lord. Like in the case of North and East* we continue like this, I think in ten years to come we won't have a stable Friends church.

Sometimes when I am in the church, I am surprised when the old men don't want us to sing praise songs, that it is against the Friends tradition. This really annoys us, especially youth, this moving out of the church to look for another one that can accommodate you. Because if you associate with people who can't recognize your vision and mission you feel so helpless and disappointed.

Other times, I try to figure out the future of our church will be like twenty to thirty years to come. The Friends church will be of no difference with other emerging churches because the culture of the church won't be there anymore. This will be affected by technological advancement and emerging culture among the youth.

Finally, I will urge my fellow Quakers around the world: Let's join hands to [heal] the divisions that are there, and also to get more converts coming to Friends church [and] not only depending on biological inheritance.** Let us achieve the height which our founder Ford*** wasn't able to reach [and] by that Friends church shall stand forever. Amen.

Everet Nate, 21
Kitale Monthly Meeting, Elgon East Yearly Meeting (FUM)
Kenya

*Division among Kenyan Friends is a significant problem, much of it caused by inter-ethnic rivalries and poor leadership. In 1973, some key Bukusu leaders declared their own Yearly Meeting, separating themselves from East Africa Yearly Meeting, which they perceived to be dominated by Maragolis. The Bukusu people were of a divided opinion on this move, with some choosing to join the new "Elgon Religious Society of Friends" and others wishing to remain within East Africa YM. Conflict—sometimes violent, and sometimes resulting in lawsuits over property—ensued in many villages. As the situation evolved, there arose two Yearly Meetings with their headquarters in the same town of Kitale, and these are the two the author references in his essay: Elgon East YM and EAYM North. Much progress has been made in recent years toward reconciliation, but in many local situations the spirit of conflict persists, and there remains a public perception that Friends are a fractious and in-fighting group.

**In Kenya, the Friends are considered to be the church of the Luhya people (which is not actually a tribe, but a federation of 18 distinct but related ethnic/linguistic groups). The close association between ethnicity and ecclesial identity among all the mission-originated churches in Kenya has led to a deeply compromised experience of the universal nature of the body of Christ.

***Jefferson Ford was one of the first Quaker missionaries in Africa, sent by Five Years Meeting, now Friends United Meeting. He pioneered the work among the Bukusu people on the slopes of Mt Elgon, and founded the mission station at Lugulu.

All notes for this piece written by Eden Grace.

Speak for Ourselves

When I was a teenager, it was hard for me to feel appreciated by adults for what I could bring to the business sessions. They had seen me grow and still saw me as the little kid who came to yearly meeting with my parents. My parents were still coming to yearly meeting, so there was no understanding that I was coming for myself and not with them. At sixteen, I felt like I was supposed to be supporting the greater yearly meeting in their process, but when I would stand up to speak, I was seen as a child who did not have things to bring to the community.

In my case, it was adults who did not see me weekly at meeting who were able to respond to my plea for help. I needed the kind of support where I could talk about the gifts that I had been given, and these adults were able to help me find my role in my meeting and in the yearly meeting. These adults were able to see that I was being led to be in the adult world because I had something to bring to both the adults and my own age group as someone who was willing to be a "messenger." I did not want to be a formal messenger from or to the high school group, but was willing to keep the teens informed about what was happening in their name.

I want to tell older adult Friends that it is important to support those younger Friends who want to go to worship or business meeting, because they may bring some point of view that is not being heard in the meeting. The younger voice or presence will add to the depth of the discussion. For me in my yearly meeting, I needed to support the adults who were making decisions that affected my generation, though that generation was not in the room. Standing up for what we want as young people is important because we are able to speak for ourselves and not let others say what we should or should not do.

Rebecca Sullivan, 21
Santa Cruz Monthly Meeting, Pacific Yearly Meeting (Independent)
Friendship Meeting, North Carolina Yearly Meeting (Conservative)
United States

First and Foremost We Are Brethren

First and foremost we are brethren. As Christians and especially as Quakers we need to pray hard for guidance, salvation, good leadership from God for the mission and vision of the church to be accomplished. I say this because, when I stand and look around, most of the Quaker churches are facing hard situations to accomplish the mission of God.

From the book of Matthew 5:16, the Bible says let your light so shine before men that they may see your good works and glorify your Father which is in Heaven. Our deeds in the church today should offer leadership. In my church my fellow brethren have migrated to other churches because the leaders are not transparent or open. And so as time goes by, we are seeing that the number of attendance is reducing. Why? Because of selfishness and greed in the church.

In this generation, we are facing some challenges—especially the youth. We can see that now Protestant churches are very many and they have come up with different ways of praising and worshipping God. Some are good and some are not good. In the Quaker church we are not allowed to do some of the things and so we are told to use or sing songs from hymn books and so on. The youth are finding it difficult to abide by the constitution of the church. How we wish that we worshipped God through praise songs, clapping hands, musical instrumentations, dancing to the Lord, etc. I've said this because some of the youths have migrated to other churches and we shall come to a time where we shall have no youths in the church.

Lastly I want to urge the leaders to assist us in the Christian ministry so that we spread the word of God and accomplish his ministry. If [we are] given much time to sit down to talk about the Quaker issues, then it will relieve some of my fellow youth's problems.

God Bless You. "Stand firm in one Spirit" (Phil 1:27).

Dennis Murunga Nalyanga
Lugulu Quarter, Elgon Religious Society of Friends (FUM)
Kenya

Reclamation

I have been having trouble with labels lately. I've never been completely comfortable with the political labels people give me. I am a registered Democrat and my political views are pretty liberal, but my personal style, profession, and habits are much more on the conservative side.

I have also run into label issues within the Quaker world. Because I am a member of a semi-programmed, Christ-centered church but regularly attend an unprogrammed, liberal meeting, I suppose I embody "convergent," but I don't really feel comfortable with that label either. And because I come from a Christian background, the language I use is very biblical, which frankly makes some Quakers uncomfortable.

Most of my friends are not Quakers, and the previous paragraph probably would not mean a lot to them. When I talk to friends about being a Quaker, I spend a lot of time trying to define terms and explaining what the differences are between Quaker groups and why they matter. People seem to think that because we are Quakers, we must be pretty peaceful. That has not been my experience.

Over the past few months, I have been inviting a lot of friends to Quaker meetings. When I do this, I routinely tell my friends, "I'm not trying to convert you." To me, conversion and evangelism have pretty negative connotations and I don't want anyone to think that I am trying to coerce them into doing or believing anything. I don't think I have The Way to God or Truth; I just feel like I have found a path that is working for me, and I want to share that with the people who are important to me.

One of the things that initially drew me to the Quaker faith is how involved in social justice Friends are. I felt like this was a religion that did not conflict with my politics, but instead added a faith component to my political convictions. I feel strongly about Quaker values of equality, peace, simplicity, and service. I believe that being part of a community that shares those values helps me to live with integrity.

So I want to reclaim the words *convert* and *evangelist*. My new definition for *convert* is a person who is willing to change his or her life and follow the direction of the Spirit, and I define *evangelist* as a person who is willing to talk about his or her beliefs openly and honestly. With this in mind, I hope that all of my friends can be converts and evangelists because we can sure do a lot of good in the world if we are.

Ashley M. Wilcox, 28

Freedom Friends Church (Independent) and University Friends Meeting, North Pacific Yearly Meeting (Independent)

United States

Editor's note: A version of this piece appears in *Writing Cheerfully on the Web: A Quaker Blog Reader*, edited by Liz Oppenheimer, 2009.

To Better Places of Life

I am a Kenyan citizen, a youth aged twenty-two years. The Quaker church [is] my spiritual guide in my day-in-and-day-out life.

As a Christian believer I have always had a strong conviction that each Friend must discover truth for himself. Thus Friends, being like the majority of Christian denominations, believe in the reality of God, Christ, and the Holy Spirit. Thus the Quakers look upon God as Hero, Creator and Giver of Life. We know that God loves, that God longs for justice, peace, and spiritual growth among all of humanity. Through this we can illustrate that Quakers will always seek for justice when there is injustice and cry for peace in the countries in which war has torn apart the people. It also promotes humanity in the countries [that] have been overpowered by the leaders. The church is making the world a better place for everybody to live in.

The Quaker church moves from worse to better places of life. The church has had an effect in many parts of the world since the time it came to the establishment. It has influenced commerce, science, social justice, politics, and many other aspects of life in the world. The Quaker church has witnessed [much] work done by the volunteers in the church to promote development in some countries that are developing.

The Quaker Church is living a life of simplicity whereby they are all equal after God. Thus this indicates that the church is moving from the tradition of gender inequality to gender equality, where both men and women are given same responsibilities [in] families. Also women are being delegated to some issues in countries and even others are being given the same job opportunities as men. Some women like Wangari Maathaai and others are being awarded with Nobel prizes . This shows or symbolizes that they are both equal before God, that no one is superior to the other.

The Quaker church is using Christianity to promote peace and justice among the war-torn countries, such as Israel, Rwanda, Burundi, and Pakistan. Through they're spearheading in these countries, it has also promoted democracy among the citizens of various countries and condemning the dictatorship type of governance. This implies that the church is eradicating the sense of minority and educating the people to have majority governance. This indicates that the Quakers are promoting people's faith to have solidarity in peacekeeping.

The church has always made a move of educating the congregation and even the Christians-at-large by opening some learning institutions such as schools, colleges and even universities which are being sponsored by the Quaker church. They are making every place to be better, or civilizing the natives of the countries. Through this they are sometimes provided job opportunities such as Bible teachers, pastors, and even counselors who are trained from the Bible Schools.

To some extent, the Quakers are living exemplary lives in their homes. Thus they have a religious response toward terrorism, which is the biggest problem facing the world. Thus the Quakers are spending dollars and dollars educating the youths to avoid being used by the terrorist. As a church member, it pains when we lose relatives, friends, or even citizens in the catastrophes like bomb blasts. Thus the Quakers are pleasing to the eastern/Arab countries to avoid having the grudge with the Western countries. Through these the world would have the safest place to preach the word of God.

As Christians, the Quakers are being advocated to be examples in the leadership. But today the Quaker church is being faced with one problem. The church is headed by people who are famously known for one or two things, which causes the congregation not to believe in what is being preached but rather in what is being said by the church leader. Due to this the Quakers are being moved from the Godly way of church leadership to being ruled politically.

With the invention and innovations of machines through technology, the Quakers have abandoned the belief of not dancing in Church and [are] being forced to use the instruments by the youths as to retain them. Nowadays pianos and keyboards are the main attraction of church congregations.

Politics are also being practiced in church today due to the influence of some leaders, thus making it difficult for one to differentiate between Christianity and politics and why they are kept together in church. In my own county some political leaders attend the congregations in churches where they normally campaign their parties. The candidates even corrupt the church by giving bribes or money to the people. The church has moved from its positions [to some extent] and even engages in things that are against the law of the church. The Quaker church has witnessed some of the church members rallying Christian meeting to promote God's love and relationship.

The Quaker church has moved from worst part that it was failing when it started preaching the gospel; but for now it is better, because the people are being transformed and obeying God's commandments. Even around the world, the church is looking forward in progress of achieving its goals by organizing meetings of the church at various intervals to maintain the relationship in the world. It is a great advancement done by the Quakers so that the people can live in harmony with one another.

Timothy Umunzi Mutanyi, 23
East Africa Yearly Meeting (North) (FUM)
Kenya

Tokenism

As a young person within the Religious Society of Friends, I have experienced much ageism and tokenism. My involvement in leadership capacities for Quaker organizations has grown in the last several years. I have worked professionally for four different Quaker organizations, and served on countless committees and boards. I find I am often looked to as the voice of young people, almost as a consultant, as one of few, if not the only young person, present. This is tiresome. It doesn't leave much room for me to think or talk about other topics when I am constantly looked to for the youth perspective. I know I'm not alone in this experience. I know of many enthusiastic young Quakers who have been alienated and are tempted to give up on their religious community based on this tokenism and perceived invisibility.

And while I want to help Friends think well about young people, what I really want is for the voices of *all* young people to be sought, welcomed, and valued. I want a vital, inclusive, multigenerational Religious Society that actually reflects our vision of the Beloved Society we wish to model and realize in the wider world. And of course, that would require a deep examination of all of our "isms," as age is not the only thing that sets us apart.

I have also experienced competition and divisiveness among young Quakers who have felt invisible for so long that the process of claiming voice and place is painful. But I have also experienced deep communion in worship and fellowship with these same Friends who are hungering for a deep faith community that will love and challenge them to grow.

When young Quakers come together at weekend or week-long events, there is a palpable, powerful energy. They have a tenacity to speak truth directly, and go deep together quickly. Often, looking back, Friends share that these gatherings are some of their most memorable and transformative experiences within our faith community—and that it is there that they can most truly be themselves.

Young Friends, like the young people in so many movements, secular and religious alike, have long been the visionaries for Quakerism. They have birthed many of our ministries and organizations and continually call us to take greater risks for faithfulness. I see young Quakers now in the forefront of a movement calling us to reach across our different sects and old wounds, to become a restored community and to deepen our own journeys and understanding of the Divine through this convergence of different experiences.

My deepest hope is that young Quakers will continue to push us to review and renew our understandings, and that they will come to know that they are not alone—that Friends of every age are hungering to share their stories, build community, and grow deeper into a life of faithfulness.

Sadie Forsythe, 27
Putney Friends Meeting, New England Yearly Meeting (FGC-FUM)
United States

Psalm 151*

extend your ear, Mother of the circle, of all creation
behold your peculiar people, now madly talking around your blessed
    revelation
how immaculate our process, how simple, how pure
if only, yes then, wait minute that, are you sure?
that this is what you intended when you sent your Spirit out?
some days I'm just not so sure what it's all about

see how we go along, picking and choosing with such care
but consider the cross, the prison cell; is this not our history to share?
Peace—check, Simplicity—yes, well relatively, Integrity—sounds good to me
but when does all this just shroud us in the blanket of liberal complacency

all of this sounds good on paper, so let's minute that: umpteen dash one
what else could we do, well out of time today, let's be silent now we're done
and yes the quiet is good sometimes, but so is preaching from the trees
forgive me if all this minuting seems a little like a tease

what do we have left if we lose our tongue to preach?
look out—it's First Day School, these beautiful young faces, and us with
    little to teach
maybe we could begin by speaking of the living water that springs from
    a rock

but if we did that we might have to relinquish a worship-style governed
     by a clock
our young people may well demand some changes to our style and pace
perhaps more dangerously, they often call us to be faithful, face to face
is this why we separate ourselves, telling them that they're not ready?
better to keep them out if we hope to keep this little boat steady

and I keep thinking about that boat and this here storming
all these wars and injustices swarming
and there He comes, walking out across the water, the raging storm all around
but we look away, hoping for something that makes sense by way of dry
     ground
surrounded now we try desperately to cover our head
but He calls out: get up and get out of this boat, leave your fear and your
     dread
He called then, as he calls now: step away from the boat
then again, perhaps He'd understand our position better if we minuted
     that we can't float

it's just too much to take in, that She will provide,
so we just keep to the clock, and keep on sitting here side by side
but I kept on reading, this time skipping a few chapters back
and here's another story of God's people complaining of what they lack
a captured people scared to be faithful, the story reads the same
then and now, Pharaoh's slaves—frightened, divided, and tame

but the message is clear—She will give us the manna we need
plenty to go around, if we choose this feed
but how would we know, that yes, now we had enough
when all our consideration revolves around our stuff
locked into that liberal narrative that says you can straddle both sides of
     the line
loving your brothers and sisters on one side, and on the other keeping all
     that is mine
you could look at all this and say it is our luxury or privilege to choose
or you could see that it is those with everything that have everything to lose

this is the eye of the needle standing before us
and from every corner, the rebellious house sings its chorus
in our language, our mind-think, our TV
"not now, not this, not me"
but the blood is on our hands—this is our stain
you cannot be neutral on a moving train

but oh, when we hop off—the possibilities we might see
perhaps then we would hear the Truth in Her child's decree
Listen

no longer are you servants, passive and incomplete
now called Friends, from this moment from this seat
stand up, quake as you rise
the Power lies inside of you, Love is the prize
bearing, believing, hoping, enduring—all
this is the still, small voice of Her child's call

so, stand out, speak up, step off the curb
away from the way of life that has built 'burb after 'burb
let us begin as that change without the burden of guilt or doubt
she is calling to us again, Pharaoh's slaves—exodus out!
out into the desert, out into her care
faith is a choice and I for one am dog-tired of despair

so I pray
here I am Lord, there are some of us yet, willing to risk it all, to suffer,
  and take a chance,
willing to hear, willing to be transformed, willing to do the time, willing
  to advance
in the name of the Covenant, in the name of Beloved Community, in your
  blessed name,
these feet were made for walking, get up and walk, cured by Truth, behold
  the lame,
how freed from Cain's mark, released from our task of domination and toil,
the desert may bloom, a new harvest bursting forth from rich soil.

I raise this prayer up to God and up through each of you
it is up to us now, in our hands, to know what to do
Jesus dared to call us his Friends in John's gospel 15:15
will we take on this responsibility and be baptized in the prophetic stream?
the servant pleads "not now, not this, not me"
but we are Friends, now and forever—let's get free!

> *Zachary Moon, 28*
> *Strawberry Creek Monthly Meeting, Pacific Yearly Meeting (Independent)*
> *United States*
> *Editorial note: This poem was created to be a performance piece. It is
> intended to be spoken aloud, not read. An earlier version of this piece
> appeared in Friends Journal in April 2009. Reprinted by permission of
> Friends Publishing Corporation. For more information go to
> www.friendsjournal.org.

You Say You Love Me (God's Lament)

You say you love Me
But you walk on by
When I'm cold and hungry,
And I cry out for your help.

You say you love Me
But your neighbour starves
Needlessly
Because you do not share.

You say you love Me
And yet you destroy
The world that I gave you
To tend.

You say you love Me
But you kill one another
And worse
You do it in My name.

You say I am the Way
But my Way you do not follow.
You say I am the Truth
But Truth you do not hear.

You say I am loving
And still you imagine
I would send you to hell
For believing "wrong" things.

One day
You will realise
What it truly means
To love.

Peter Parr, 33
Sussex East Area Meeting and Young Friends General Meeting,
Britain Yearly Meeting
United Kingdom

Does God Feel Hungry?

My biggest question to all Quakers around the world is, "Does God feel hungry?"

"Love your neighbor as you love yourself" (Mark 12:31, NIV) are the true words of Jesus to his disciples.

As we all know, Africa is one of the worst climatically hit continents in the whole world. Kenya is one of the countries in this continent. Turkana, where I am from, is one of the districts in this country where poverty is the order of the day, but people live in this desert and preach the good news to mankind. You can guess how challenging it is to do this.

Poverty affects your normal life style and basics of life like clothing, shelter, food, education, and other basic needs and rights.

Being born in such harsh conditions, I learned to go without a dress to the age of twenty years. I was forced to eat one meal a day (evening) when food was available, otherwise going without food was not unusual. I learned to sleep outside in the open because there was no house to sleep in. I went to school at a late age of thirteen years because schools were scarce and far from where I lived. I was given the condition that for me to marry, I was supposed to go on a raid to the neighboring community, which meant that I was to use a gun to fight, kill, and get animals from them; something I refused to do, for I knew killing is against humanity. This has cost me not marrying properly other than cohabiting with my fiancée. I trekked for long distances to get water because there were no vehicles, all with heat over thirty-nine degrees Celsius. I learned to trust God and did all those things with his help.

All the crawling animals found in this land are hostile, too, and poisonous, but the Living God is keeping me and his people safe.

The good thing that God did for this land was give water. Though not easily available, it can be gotten after drilling with powerful machines that impel through the hard dry soils to reach life underground.

My question to you therefore is, "When you hear people on television talk of people dying of hunger, does God see that?" To me, yes, God does. He says in his holy book that Man was created in his own image and wherever this human is, he is definitely there. It's the reason why Jesus was narrating the story of the Good Samaritan in the New Testament. He challenged them that there is going to be a day when each and every one of us is going to be asked what you did in the world. Jesus says he will refuse to let some of us in to see his Father. Why? Because, he says, "You saw me hungry and you did not give me food. I was naked and you did not clothe me" (Matt. 25:42–43).That is an eye-opener that God lives in us, and when we feel hungry, he does also. Let's think about this. Have you ever lost a dollar from your pocket without your knowledge? If yes, do you think it's safely laying somewhere or someone picked it up? This is how I think God feeds the unattended. Before God gives it away, remember to give to your brother and tithe, otherwise he says I will put holes in your pockets and you will not realize how the money fell out of your pocket.

Each and every one of us has a duty and responsibility to help cushion the conditions that terrorize human life. Otherwise, if life was based on our liking, we all would refer to the good life of abundance.

Having grown up in these conditions, I am persuaded to trust and believe in a superior being that can hold lives in such a land as dry, hot, barren, and vast Kenya. God is his name: the provider where there is lack, security where there is fear, hope where there is despair, love where there is hatred. Poverty does not therefore stop me from obeying my God.

The Bible clearly indicates when Jesus encounters Satan after being hungry, "The Devil said to Him, 'If you are the son of God, command this stone to become bread.' Jesus answered, 'It's written: man shall not live by bread alone, but by every word of God'" (Luke 4:3–4, World English).

This is a significant learning experience in life that we should appreciate and learn from. Problems are associated with hunger, and Satan knows that. He makes good use of it by tempting people.

In searching deserts where lack of food and water is a problem, "churches" are mushrooming like weeds all over the fields, but the same God says, "Test every spirit because not all who call the name of Jesus will enter his light." The spirit we accepted is going to lead us not into temptations as in the Lord's Prayer but will deliver us from evil. That is God's plan. This is a challenge to us Quakers.

We have advocated for peace for centuries; we have provided schools, hospitals, and churches for the poor. We must realize the root cause of fights and wars in the world, particularly Africa.

Spiritually

Instead of the physical poverty, many of the developed country youth face the poverty of the inner being/Holy Spirit. They do not realize the presence of the Creator-God. They attach their existence to science, which has more origin in another greater being that I am very much convinced is not God.

The Devil was sent to tempt Jesus. He said "If you bow down to me, I will give you every thing you desire in this world." Jesus said, "It is written you shall worship God alone." Yes, that was the right answer because you can have everything in the world but then you lack happiness of the spirit which is God-given.

Believing in God as per my understanding is simply in two dimensions (Exodus 20:13). One, you ought to relate with the super-being, God, through Jesus Christ and, secondly, relate with other human beings—mankind, period.

A picture of a young innocent African boy I took in one of the new mission sites in Turkana indicates how innocent our souls were before we sinned against God.

The world today sees Quakers like billboards; we therefore need to clothe ourselves with Love plus all the fruits of the Holy Spirit as is written in Galatians 5:22-23. Otherwise, we will be behaving like a movement other than a "church" of Christ.

Let's take care of the unreached.

John Epur Lomuria, 32
Lodwar Monthly Meeting, East Africa Yearly Meeting (North) (FUM)
Kenya

Expanding Horizons
The Integral Movement, the Great Story, and the New Quakerism

A religion old or new, that stressed the magnificence of the universe as revealed by modern science, might be able to draw forth reserves of reverence and awe hardly tapped by the conventional faiths. Sooner or later, such a religion will emerge.

— Carl Sagan, *Pale Blue Dot* (1994)

The Religious Society of Friends is at a critical turning point. The problems of modernity—from catastrophic global climate change and mass extinctions, to human rights abuses across the globe, and the specter of true weapons of mass destruction—threaten the very existence of life on this planet as we know it. Throughout Friends history we have responded differently to the multitude of challenges that we have faced, at the personal, sociopolitical, and global scale, always coming back to the deep center of Friends testimonies and those few principles that hold the now-fractured Society together. The challenges we now face are questioning in many ways the fundamental assumptions and structures that we have held so dear for so long. The question we ask ourselves now is, "Where do we go from here?"

During the last half-century, a number of different approaches to dealing with the question of modernity within religious and spiritual life have been posited, both through rational discourse and through trans-rational, mystical insight and contemplation. These approaches all attempt to integrate the three fields of inquiry through which we organize and explain our world: the scientific, the spiritual, and the philosophical. Not surprisingly, many of these movements go by the name of "integral theory" or as the "integral movement," though by no means are they a monolithic front! I will address some of the main concepts within the integral movement, how I have experienced them, and show how Friends can learn from them and maybe even begin to answer the question(s) of our times.

The integral movement can be divided, very roughly, into three different "schools": those based around psychologist and philosopher Ken Wilber and his Integral Institute (and adeptly expressed on a visual level by his cohort, artist Alex Grey); those based around "geologian" Thomas Berry and cosmologist Brian Swimme and the California Institute of Integral Studies, where Swimme is based (termed there as the "Great Story" or "New Story"); and those based around philosopher and scientist Ervin László and his emergent Global Shift University. Though their techniques differ slightly in their details and they are sometimes at odds with each other, their basic aim is the same: to integrate scientific, spiritual, and (post-)modern philosophical thought into one emergent and holistic whole, what Ken Wilber refers to as "kosmology." Other related thinkers include physicist David Bohm, mathematical philosopher Arkady Plotnitsky, Turkish English scholar Serpil Oppermann, and French psychoanalytic philosophers Gilles Deleuze and Félix Guattari.

As a physicist, growing up in a liberal (viz., FGC-affiliated) Quaker household, I thought the eternal conflict between science and religion never was much of an issue. The Spinozian *"Deus sive Natura"* style pan(en)theism (later expanded-upon by Guattari and Norwegian eco-philosopher Arne Næss) was the rule, and I had no problem reconciling traditional Quaker theology and modern physics and cosmology; the Great Story affiliated phrase "Thank God for evolution!" is apt here. In high school, especially at Olney Friends School, I became increasingly influenced by Daoism/Zen Buddhism, and I saw these as natural extensions of Quakerism, with the same awe and wonderment of nature and the universe, and similar meditation styles. As Albert Einstein said, "I believe in Spinoza's God who reveals Himself in the orderly harmony of what exists, not in a God who concerns himself with fates and actions of human beings." However, it was not until the summer before my junior year of college (just before I attended the World Gathering of Young Friends in England) that I had the blinding mystical experience that would fully integrate the disparate realms of physics, philosophy, and spirituality.

In my experience, I came to see that, through the laws of quantum mechanics (laws from Pauli and Heisenberg), we are all equal, "we are all stardust" as the saying goes, and therefore the Friends Equality Testimony is written into the very fabric of the universe at the most fundamental level. I have learned since that, according to both leading quantum physicists (Fotini Markopoulou-Kalamara and Seth Lloyd) and to bleeding-edge philosophers (Deleuze and Guattari) alike, the quantum structure of spacetime itself acts as an emergent structure, calculating the equations of life, the universe, and everything on a very real fractal, rhizome-like quantum fabric; as Swimme has said, the "cosmological powers of the Universe are coursing through us moment by moment. To become aware of these powers is to touch the source of Life." Everything is sacred, since we are all the same, and we are all manifestations of the universal energy, of the Dao, of the Light, of God, and this sacredness manifests itself to us through what religious scholar Mircea Eliade calls *hierophany*, from the Greek roots ἱερός, meaning "sacred," and φαίνειν, meaning "to bring to light [i.e., Light]." Thus, in a very real way, the traditional Quaker term of Light can be seen to be surprisingly literal! As Einstein also said, a "human being is a part of a whole, called by us 'universe,' a part limited in time and space. He experiences himself, his thoughts, and feelings as something separated from the rest . . . a kind of optical delusion of his consciousness. This delusion is a kind of prison for us, restricting us to our personal desires and to affection for a few persons nearest to us. Our task must be to free ourselves from this prison by widening our circle of compassion to embrace all living creatures and the whole of nature in its beauty."

The traditional cosmogonies were also integrated, with the traditional pre-universal void, termed Χάος (Chaos) in Greek (another term revived by Deleuze and Guattari) and *śūnyatā* in Sanskrit, being identified with the contemporary quantum Hartle-Hawking state for *creatio ex nihilo* (creation from nothing, from the void). Thus, science, philosophy, and spirituality were finally completely and beautifully integrated for me, and I glimpsed the kind of "reverence and awe" that Carl Sagan referred to.

Although this trans-religious movement might seem to be leaving traditional Quakerism behind, in many ways it actually returns to many of the same principles present in Fox, et al.'s early Quakerism that have been forgotten and ignored in times since. In recent years, this has become more and more apparent, both through the work of Friends and non-Friends alike, and it is to this *Great Work*, as Thomas Berry calls it, that I have dedicated my life and work, especially as it relates to two of the most pressing of our many very modern issues, those of global ecological collapse, and of gender and sexuality equality. Three of the most influential Friends to have done work in meshing Quakers with the integral movement are noted South African mathematical cosmologist and anti-apartheid activist George F. R. Ellis, and American scientific theologians Mary C. Coelho and Philip Clayton, who chaired the New Story Study Group at Friends Meeting at Cambridge, Massachusetts, and who co-authored the seminal treatment of integral theory and Quakerism, *Quakers and the New Story*, in 2007.

To take the Equality Testimony seriously, though, is to extend it from the cosmic and the global to the personal and the political. From my involvement in the LGBTQ community, and especially the Quaker LGBTQ community, I have seen the issue of gender and sexuality equality as equally important as the ecological issues mentioned earlier. If we are all equal, the LGBTQ community should be treated with the same dignity and respect as anyone else, with special note to the transgressive power we have to help make this point. As one of the worship-sharing groups at the 2009 Friends for LGBTQ Concerns Midwinter Gathering sensed, this sort of radical transformation may not only be useful, but also vital to the future existence of Quakerism as a whole, and certainly liberal (viz. FGC) Quakerism specifically; if Quakerism is to survive into the twenty-first century and beyond, this is a necessary step we must take. This action must not be just theoretical, nor even just spiritual. We must faithfully integrate the two together, and then into our everyday lives if we are to continue to enact the kind of radical social change that Friends have been known for the past four hundred years, even, especially, in a society that may not share our values. The next few years will be critical for this, as many Friends within the Society are getting older, and the number of Young Friends continues to decrease. This is our challenge.

M. E. Hogan, 25
Athens Monthly Meeting, Lake Erie Yearly Meeting (FGC)
United States

Awaking the Slumbering Light

On one of my travels to an unfamiliar city, I made a point to visit the largest meeting in the immediate area. I was sure I'd find a strong sense of community dispersed among the hard wooden benches, bursting at the seams with history and tradition. Fellow Friends had promised me that the place would be home to a large number of Quaker youth. So it was that I arrived early for First Hour, took my seat, and surveyed the crowd, pleasantly noting a smattering of people my own age. When worship concluded, I eagerly took the opportunity to seek out conversation with as many of them as I could. That was my intention, of course, but the reality was jarring. Most young Quakers made no effort to meet and greet over refreshments afterward. Instead, they headed quickly for the exits, as though they had more important things to accomplish. This seemed somehow to defeat the purpose of what had been proclaimed upon the conclusion of First Hour, namely coffee, fellowship, and conversation. Despite an announcement to the contrary, none of these things were present and I wondered why.

In search of some explanation, I eventually was introduced to the clerk in charge of young adult affairs. She was a well-meaning, but woefully unprepared, woman without the vision and drive to be much in the way of an effective leader. In her hands, the position was nothing less than a ceremonial post, marked by vague promises and vaguer answers to the vaguest of queries. Her response to my question of why a young adult group had not been established was not particularly comforting. "It used to frustrate me that I couldn't establish any kind of lasting group, but I've realized there's nothing I can do about it."

She had been raised Mormon, then had converted to Quakerism. In her experience, the Church of Latter Day Saints did a much better job of providing an outlet for its youth. In this respect, right-wing religious groups are far more effective at providing their youth a kind of needed community. By contrast, more left-leaning faiths have continually dropped the ball. I've informally surveyed a wide variety of more liberal denominations over the years and found that each is struggling to the resolve the same issue. The buzzwords, project titles, recitations, and nomenclature may differ, but the end result is the same: Why can't we keep our young adults actively involved?

Friends actively participate until high school graduation arrives, then a distressing number of them all but abandon meeting and meeting functions. Some return when they approach middle age or begin having a family, but some never come back to the fold. Partially this is a result of the fact that few of us insist that our children hold the same religious persuasion as we do, but part of it too is that there is often a deficit of specific means to keep Young Friends in meeting. In an ideal setting, meeting would be a way for Young Friends to meet for a sense of community, common purpose, and even to find relationship partners who are assured of sharing the same basic virtues and core values in common.

Before someone devises an unnecessarily complex method of tending to this matter, might I suggest a simpler solution? This deficiency needs no study groups, long-winded sessions, consensus-building exercises, worksheets, handouts, or a book discussion group at Second Hour. This approach often creates no tangible results. The way to fix this problem lies within us. It starts with opening up and acting welcoming.

We seem to have forgotten how to speak, listen, trust, or even communicate with each other in any way whatsoever. Worshipping silently means that active listening and active revelation are free to blossom. What it does not mean is that silence should be arid and devoid of substance. Silence does not imply nothingness. I realize that we live in a world where our attention and our time are increasingly divided and fragmented. The insularity of our daily lives limits our contact with more than a few friends or acquaintances. And inevitably, we are slowly forgetting how to communicate with one another while believing that somehow worship is an individual action requiring no real need for fellowship.

Young Friends themselves have recognized what I've recognized. Some of us are too stubborn to give up and show up Sunday after Sunday, knowing that we might be the only person under the age of forty in attendance. Some of us wish for true community. Each of us wishes for the same thing: "If only there were more people here my age." If we cannot first begin to be unguarded and less afraid of others, we will never thrive; and we will repel not just Young Friends but those for whom Quakerism could be a spiritual home long sought for but never realized.

Ours is a rich faith, but ours is also a graying faith. It need not be. If I didn't believe the Light could be greatly beneficial to those who as yet have no clue of its existence or the scope of its potential, I would not encourage its spread and growth. Yet, we cannot keep doing the same thing the same way and expect a different result. Sleepwalking our way along out of complacency is what created this problem and we are the only ones who can solve it—through our deeds, not necessarily through our words.

Kevin Camp, 29

Birmingham Friends Meeting, Southern Appalachia Yearly Meeting and Association (FGC)

United States

Author and Artist Biographies

Kelly Ackerman (24) is currently living in Toronto, Ontario, Canada. He is a member of Prairie Monthly Meeting and Canadian Yearly Meeting.

Mallary Allen (26) lives with her husband and son in Carbondale, Illinois, where they attend the Southern Illinois Society of Friends Meeting. She worked in human services before returning to school in 2009.

Lincoln Alpern (22) has just completed his third year of college. At home, he attends Scarsdale Monthly Meeting, Purchase Quarterly Meeting, New York Yearly Meeting.

Gabriel Flores Arauz (16) is a member of Florida Friends Church, National Evangelical Friends Church (INELA) of Bolivia.

Efrain Cuellar Avalos (21) is a part of Christian Friends Congregation of INELA-Bolivia.

José Luis Cuellar Avalos (22) is a member of Christian Friends Congregation of INELA-Bolivia.

Howie Baker (27) was raised in New England Yearly Meeting by two midwestern pastors, and so was raised in both FUM and FGC Quakerism simultaneously. Howie doesn't know whether to call himself programmed or unprogrammed, and until recently refused to call himself Christian; but since God speaks to him no less through sermons and hymns than through silent worship, and since God has been speaking to him regardless of how comfortable he was with Christianity, he figures it really doesn't matter.

Noah Baker Merrill (30) is a member of Putney Friends Meeting, New England Yearly Meeting. His meeting has minuted its recognition of his call to a ministry of "waking hearts" among Friends, among the people of Iraq, and elsewhere.

Elizabeth Baltaro (29) has been a participant in Friends meeting since she was a few days old. She was born in Rome, Italy, and for the first two years of her life attended a small Quaker worship group there. She has since lived in seven U.S. States and Ukraine. In all of her journeys, she has learned the value of many types of spiritual communities and religious services, but Quaker meeting remains her home. She is currently a graduate student living near Boston, Massachusetts, with her husband and enjoys reflective writing in her free time.

Seth Barch (27) is a member of Schuylkill Monthly Meeting, Philadelphia Yearly Meeting. He is a metal worker, jewelry maker, and photographer.

W. Geoffrey Black (23) will graduate in May 2010 from Warren Wilson College (near Asheville, North Carolina) with a major in Religious Studies and minors in Spanish and Latin American Studies. Following graduation, he hopes to return to west-central Wisconsin, where he grew up, and start a small vegetable farm.

Andreas Hernander Brand (29) is a Christian Quaker and works as a teacher in religion and philosophy. He is a member of Sweden Yearly Meeting.

Julian Brelsford (27) is passionate about bringing the "love your neighbor" mentality we see in many religions into the world and into relationships among all people, especially in countries that have the most or least material resources. He has a particular interest in relationships between Haiti and the United States of America. He grew up in Alaska and Alaska Friends Conference (FGC).

Catila N. Brenda (23) lives in Kitale, Kenya.

Kathleen Burckhardt (18) is a third-culture kid who was born in Switzerland and lived in Ireland and the United States. She now lives on Vancouver Island in Canada with her parents and a llama, six sheep, and two dogs. She is a recent classical home school graduate who enjoys writing in her loft, cooking up a storm, dancing into the night, and reading historical fiction.

Ruth Calle (24) lives in El Alto, Bolivia, with her family. She is a teacher and a member of Santidad Amigos.

Kevin Camp (29) grew up a southern liberal in an overwhelmingly conservative state, which shaped much of his identity spiritually, politically, morally, and creatively. He took a long, winding, circuitous route to Quakerism, but found a spiritual home there after years of frustrating searching.

Amelia Carlie (18) attends Orlando Monthly Meeting, Southeastern Yearly Meeting (FGC-FUM) in Florida. Her oil painting is about the choice between peace and war.

M. Chadkirk (18) is a committed Young Friend to whom writing has always been second nature and yet who seeks to have a career in economics. She was pleased to be able to write this piece because belief—the presence of it, lack of it, or questioning regarding it—has always been a thread throughout her life.

Paul Christiansen (26) loves writing, Quakers, teaching, the Pacific Northwest, women, and basil pesto. Sometimes this gets him into trouble.

Emma M. Churchman (36) is a sojourning member at Monthly Meeting of Friends of Philadelphia and a member of Friends Meeting of Washington.

Angelina Conti (see editorial board biographies).

Oscar Cordero is a member of Bolivian Holiness Mission of Evangelical Friends Church

Ruth Bueso de Coronado is a Friend in Guatemala.

Susanna Corson-Finnerty (28) has been interested in artistic photography since she participated in the Philadelphia Yearly Meeting Quaker workcamp project in China in 2006. Her work has been shown in Philadelphia and surrounding areas and online worldwide.

Cara Curtis (see editorial board biographies).

C. Wess Daniels (see editorial board biographies).

Henry Loza Diaz is a member of Christian Friends Congregation of INELA-Bolivia.

Max Dixon-Murdock (12) lives in Vancouver, British Columbia, and attends Vancouver Monthly Meeting. Quakerism has been a big part of his ongoing spiritual explorations.

Stephen Willis Dotson (25) became a Friend through his relationship to Goose Creek Monthly Meeting and Baltimore Yearly Meeting's camping program (which he has served in various roles for the last nine years). He is a Guilford College and Quaker Leadership Scholars Program graduate, is involved in the World Student Christian Federation, Quakers Uniting in Publications (QUIP), and interfaith endeavors in Sri Lanka and India.

Megan E. Drimal (née Hollingsworth) (35) recently received her MS in Environmental Studies at the University of Montana, for which she explored human grief for the global loss of species and cultures. Megan and her husband, Charles Wolf Drimal, are starting an institute that will integrate contemplative practices with wilderness travel and permaculture in the Northern Rockies.

Marie-Helene Drouin (35) lives in Nottingham in the United Kingdom and attends Derby Local Meeting, Britain Yearly Meeting.

Pasilksa Elimah lives in Kenya.

Joy Ellison (26) is a Quaker writer and activist who supports Palestinian nonviolent resistance in the village of Tuwani and blogs at www.inpalestine.blogspot.com.

Sadie Forsythe (27) is a member of New England Yearly Meeting and currently serves as the Young Adult Friends Coordinator for Philadelphia Yearly Meeting.

Flynn (14) attends Vancouver Monthly Meeting of Canadian Yearly Meeting. This piece was written at a writing workshop for young people at that meeting.

Carly Beth Frintner is a member of Moorestown Monthly Meeting, Philadelphia Yearly Meeting.

Michael J. Fulp. Jr. (27) is currently the senior pastor of Prosperity Friends Meeting in High Falls, North Carolina. He is a fifth-generation, birthright Friend from Forbush Friends Meeting in East Bend, North Carolina, and a recorded minister in North Carolina Yearly Meeting (FUM). He is a graduate of Guilford College and Carolina Evangelical Divinity School.

Richard George (19) was born and raised in Philadelphia, Pennsylvania. After becoming a Quaker at the age of thirteen, Richard's mission in his spiritual life became to try and help urban kids in Philadelphia and anywhere else to find stable spirituality and end gun violence. Richard is currently a student at Temple University in Philadelphia and also enjoys sports, music, and theater.

Nancy Ghangahoa (18) lives in Kitale, Kenya.

Rebecca "Bex" Brinton Gilbert (22) lives on a small farm in West Chester, Pennsylvania, and is currently a senior at Williams College in Massachusetts. She is majoring in geosciences with a concentration in maritime studies. "Phish Food" was the essay submitted in her college application to Williams.

Carrie Glasby (34) lives in Philadelphia, Pennsylvania, with her wife Kathleen, son Tim, and daughter Alma. She is a member of Central Philadelphia Monthly Meeting (Philadelphia Yearly Meeting) and serves as Development Manager for Friends General Conference. She believes that mom spit can fix a multitude of ills, though it probably won't solve global warming.

Rhiannon Grant (24) was born near London, England, and first attended meeting for worship on Christmas Day, when she was exactly a week old. Since then, she has been involved with various groups of Friends, including Britain Yearly Meeting (where she wrote her first Quaker poem in 1998), the Quaker meeting for worship on the campus of University of Nottingham, and outreach in the form of Nottingham Quaker Quest.

Erika Paula Miranda Gutierrez (23) is a member of Christian Friends Congregation of INELA-Bolivia.

Sara Miranda Gutiérrez (18) is a member of Christian Friends Congregation of INELA-Bolivia.

Harriet Hart (see editorial board biographies).

Liv (Olivia) Henry (19) is a Friend from Loudoun County, Virginia. A recent graduate of George School, she is currently an Environmental Journalism major at Western Washington University in Bellingham, Washington.

Kody Gabriel Hersh (22) was raised Quaker in Miami Monthly Meeting, Southeastern Yearly Meeting (FGC-FUM), and is now living in Philadelphia, working on a book about Quakerism for teenagers. He has stumbled into a deeply loving relationship with Christ through his journey as a transgender person, social radical, musician, Quaker history geek, and hoping-to-be-faithful Friend.

Emily Higgs (23) graduated from Haverford College in 2008 and worked as a program assistant at the Quaker United Nations Office in New York from 2008-2009. She is a trained Alternatives to Violence Project (AVP) facilitator and has volunteered with Friends in both South Africa and Rwanda to support their peace-building efforts. Emily was also a part of the joyful Catoctin Quaker Camp community for many years as a camper and counselor.

M. E. Hogan (25) is a cosmologist, DJ-producer, ecofeminist-LGBTQ activist, and birthright Friend currently working on a master's degree in quantum cosmology at the University of Massachusetts-Dartmouth and is a member of the Athens Friends Meeting, Lake Erie Yearly Meeting, in Athens, Ohio. S/he is involved with many Quaker organizations, including Quaker Earthcare Witness, Friends for LGBTQ Concerns, and the World Gathering of Young Friends, and is a graduate of Olney Friends School and Earlham College.

Sarah Katreen Hoggatt (see editorial board biographies).

Bridget Holtom (21) lives in a small community in Hebden Bridge. Having a close circle of Quaker friends and a truly supportive family and twin sister has definitely moulded the individual she is today. She loves to travel, volunteer, and make music, and is off to the beautiful city of Edinburgh to study geography at university next year.

Julia Hood (25) graduated from Guilford College in 2006 with a degree in art (sculpture) and psychology with a minor in dance. She is currently pursuing a master's in the History of Decorative Arts at the Corcoran College of Art and Design and The Smithsonian Associates.

Tonje Smidt Hundevadt (21) comes from Norway and lives in Oslo. She is a twenty-one-year-old girl, and loves to read and write.

Pastor Peter Ikapolon (32) received salvation in 1999. He is a third-year diploma student in Friends Theological College.

Evelyn Jadin (see editorial board biographies).

Bokyom Jin is a member of Seoul Meeting in Korea Yearly Meeting and lives in South Korea.

Jacob Johansen lives in Bend, Oregon, where he works as a boot maker.

Kristen M. Johnson (25) attends Sevenoseven, a young adult ministry in Cleveland, Ohio. She graduated in 2008 with a BA in Bible and theology and a minor in world missions. She currently resides in Tallmadge, Ohio.

Rob Jones (28) is a radical educator and food activist based in the Triangle region of North Carolina. He organizes Crop Mob, a group of young, landless, and wannabe farmers.

Jaya Karsemeyer (29) is an educator who occasionally appears in movies. She lives in Toronto, Ontario, Canada, after working at Olney Friends School in Barnesville, Ohio, for the last year. She likes the way we talk to each other with our bodies, our language, and through computers. Dance is a deal-breaker.

L. Callid Keefe-Perry (27) travels in the ministry under a minute endorsed by New York Yearly Meeting and gives great acknowledgment to the power that language has to transform lives and dreams; at various times he identifies himself as a storyteller, minister, and poet. Occupationally he is a public school teacher and vocationally he is interested in theopoetics and the practices of early Friends, including issues of transformative discipline within monthly meetings.

Larissa Keeler (22) grew up in a small Quaker meeting in Monterey, California, and kept coming back because of the power of the community she felt at Quaker camps and larger Quaker gatherings she attended. Quakerism continues to be an important part of her life, even if it is not a specific daily practice. She works for Outward Bound in the North Cascades.

Jon Kershner (32) served for three years as pastor of a programmed Friends meeting in Tacoma, Washington, where this sermon was delivered. Currently he is pursuing a PhD in Theology, studying John Woolman's abolitionist theology. He lives in Seattle with his wife, Jessica.

Domitilla A. Khayongo (15) is a Friend in East Africa Yearly Meeting (North) in Kenya, which is affiliated with Friends United Meeting (FUM).

Gerson Khayongo (17) is a Friend in East Africa Yearly Meeting, affiliated with Friends United Meeting (FUM).

Rachel Kincaid (21) is a creative writing student at Brandeis University. Her creative efforts are supported by the Bernard and Lillian Bard Scholarship.

Eileen R. Kinch (28) identifies as a Conservative Friend and is a graduate of Earlham School of Religion. A freelance writer and editor, she lives in Lancaster County, Pennsylvania.

Pradip Lamichhane is a Friend in Nepal Yearly Meeting, and lives in Nepal.

Mathew Amoyi Lanogwa is a member of Kitale Village Monthly Meeting in Kenya.

John C. Lawson-Myers (26) is a convinced Friend, a feminist, LGBTQ equality advocate, Wilmington College Quaker Leader Scholar Program (QLSP) participant and social work student. He and his wife, Micky, currently reside in Dayton, Ohio, and attend a semi-programmed meeting.

Mac Lemann (28) graduated from the Earlham School of Religion aspiring to be a chaplain and a firefighter in order to fulfill his call as a minister to people in crisis. Since realizing that Friends are a people in crisis, he has turned his energy and resources over to the process of seeking God's will and living into the reality of God's Paradise on Earth.

Alissa LeMond (17) lives in Indiana. She loves watching TV and playing sports. Her favorite thing to do is hang out with her youth group at church. She has been writing poems since the seventh grade.

Damaris Mercedes Guardado Lemus (29) is an active member of Evangelical Friends Chruch in San Salvador, El Salvador.

Keith Lepinski (31) lives in Appleton, Wisconsin. He has attended the FGC Gathering for eight years and occasionally attends meeting in Madison, Wisconsin.

Hannah C. Logan-Morris (29) lives in Greensboro, North Carolina, with her wife Anne, where they both worship at Friendship Friends Meeting. Hannah is an elementary school teacher working toward her Master's at the University of North Carolina, Greensboro. She spends her free time writing both fiction and nonfiction. Her work has also been published in the anthology *Leaving Home, Becoming Home*, edited by Linda Bryant, InnerLight Publishing.

John Epur Lomuria (see editorial board biographies).

Kathryn Lum (34) is a globe-trotting anthropologist who currently divides her time between fieldwork in India, Spain, and Italy on caste and gender issues within the Punjabi community.

Pastor Sarah Makenga (41) is a student at Friends Theological College in Kenya. She has been a widow for ten years and has two children. She has experience as a pastor.

Isaac Wekesa Makokha (36) is a member of Elgon East Yearly Meeting in Kenya.

Emma Condori Mamani (see editorial board biographies).

Fanny Mamani is a member of Junta Anual de Santidad Amigos and lives in La Paz, Bolivia.

Raul Choque Mamani (33) currently works as a professor of Religion and Christian Education in a school of the Quaker Friends in La Paz, Bolivia.

Joyce Mattimama (40) lives in Bujumbura, Burundi, and is a member of Burundi Yearly Meeting.

Aimee McAdams (31) has been a Quaker since she was thirteen, growing up in Northwest Yearly Meeting. She was involved in the 2005 World Gathering of Young Friends and is a co-clerk of the FWCC Young Adult Committee. She now attends Twin Cities Friends Meeting in St. Paul and spends her time baking, sewing, blogging, gardening, and tending chickens.

Jenny McCarthy (21) has grown up within the Religious Society of Friends and is a member of York Area Meeting of Britain Yearly Meeting. Some things she likes are books, plants, and mountains.

Keava McKeogh (16) was born in Truro, Cornwall, but lives in New Zealand and attends Waikato-Hauraki Meeting. She loves to sing, dance, read, write, and spend time with family and friends.

Erin McKibben attends Portland Friends Church of Indiana Yearly Meeting (FUM) and is currently a senior at Jay County High School, with plans to attend Grace College in the fall.

Katrina McQuail (see editorial board biographies).

Heather C. Meehan (16) is a birthright member of the Religious Society of Friends. She spends her time reading, writing, and maintaining her blog at www. thedaisyedition.blogspot.com.

David R. Mercadante (29) is the pastoral minister of Archdale Friends Meeting in Archdale, North Carolina. He is a graduate of Wake Forest University Divinity School and has served in Friends ministry most of his adult life. He is married to Emily and the proud father of a baby girl, Lucy.

Rachel Anne Miller (see editorial board biographies).

Zachary Moon (28) travels among Friends teaching on a range of topics including the Bible, Quaker theology and practice, and community organizing. In May 2010 he received a master's of divinity from Chicago Theological Seminary.

Linate Munyane (19) is a member of Elgon Religious Society of Friends in Kenya.

Wycliffe M. Musera (23) lives in Lodwar, Kenya, where he is an ASCS teacher. He is a member of East Africa Yearly Meeting (North).

Timothy Umunzi Mutanyi (23) is a member of East Africa Yearly Meeting (North) in Kenya.

Micky Jo Myers (25) is a convinced Quaker, a married bisexual, and a pro-choice advocate. Micky and her husband, John, currently reside in Dayton, Ohio.

Dennis Murunga Nalyanga attends Kitale Technical Training Institute and is a member of Lugulu Quarter, Elgon Religious Society of Friends.

Elyne Juma Namuma (19) lives in Kenya.

Everet Nate (21) is the fourth born in a family of six children. He sat for his primary education in 2001, then his secondary level in 2006. At the moment he is at home doing manual jobs because his parents are unable to support him at college.

Wasike W. Noah (19) lives in Kitale, Kenya.

Anna Obermayer (23) is a young adult Friend from New York Yearly Meeting and a 2009 graduate of Earlham College in Richmond, Indiana. The article was taken from her Quaker theology blog, *Raised in the Light*.

Joe Oram (22) attends meeting at Warwick Friends Meeting, Britain Yearly Meeting.

Peter Parr (33) discovered Quakers in 2006, after searching for an open-minded faith community. His own faith is grounded in personal experience. He has always enjoyed writing and is currently working on a first novel.

Lopeto Peter is a member of Lodwar Monthly Meeting, East Africa Yearly Meeting of Friends (North) (FUM), Kenya.

Liani Phylis was a student at Kwanza Secondary School in Kenya when her piece was written.

Laurie Pickard (29) is a Peace Corps Volunteer in the agriculture program in Nicaragua. Her piece was taken from her blog, *Wanderphilia: A blog about my travels.*

Wilder Amado Condori Pillco (20) is a member of Iglesia Nueva Marka, Bolivian Holiness Mission of Evangelical Friends Church.

Chris Pifer (28) grew up in Madison Monthly Meeting in Madison, Wisconsin. He spent five years working on economic justice and civil liberties issues in Washington, D.C., for the American Friends Service Committee. He now works as the web and online giving manager for Friends General Conference.

Kenneth Platter (34) lives near Stockholm, Sweden, where he works in an optical store. In his free time he likes to create music, watch movies, go to worship, and meet friends.

Maritza Cordero Quispe is a member of the National Evangelical Friends Church in Bolivia.

Jorge Luis Pena Reyes is a member of Friends Church in Puerto Padre, Cuba Yearly Meeting (FUM) in Cuba.

Brianna Richardson (23) grew up in Bellingham Friends Meeting in Bellingham, Washington. She recently completed a degree in music at the University of Puget Sound in Tacoma, Washington, where she was actively involved in a writers guild with other students.

Eddah Robai (16) lives in Kenya.

Edwin Ruben Quispe Arratia is a member of Iglesia Amigos Central Obrajes Bella Vista of Central Evangelical Friends Church of Bolivia.

Alice Rutherford (27) grew up in Schuylkill Monthly Meeting, Philadelphia Yearly Meeting, and works as a graphic designer in Los Angeles.

Nathan Sebens (25) currently lives in Richmond, Indiana, where he is a student at the Earlham School of Religion and the Choir Director at West Richmond Friends. Nathan is a theater junkie, and enjoys spending time in any sort of musical setting.

Amy Jean Singleton-Polster (24) is a professional studier, aka a medical student, which generally keeps her busy. However, in her spare time she is a member of Canadian Young Friends Yearly Meeting, a Quaker Youth Pilgrimage alumnus of 2004 and one of the Three Quakerteers. This piece was first published in July 2006 in *The Canadian Friend* and later in the October 2006 issue.

Helen Sladen (22) lives in Nottingham, England. Her photos represent how God shows how amazing God is. They show how great the power held is, as things of beauty are produced every day.

Tai Amri Spann-Wilson (30) is an African American Quaker from southern New Jersey. He received his BA in writing and poetics from the Jack Kerouac School of Disembodied Poetics at Naropa University in Boulder, Colorado and is currently working on his masters of divinity at Pacific School of Religion in Berkeley, California.

Stephanie Speicher (26) is currently playing a prolonged game of checkers with the Divine, the winner of which will determine if Stephanie should throw caution to the wind to move to the Northwest on a whim leading. Stephanie swears she didn't just hear "king me."

Pastor Leonard Sshivage (36) lives in Kitale, where he serves Kitale Village Meeting as pastor. He is a graduate of Friends Theological College and is a member of East Africa Yearly Meeting (North).

Chad Stephenson (38) is a member of San Francisco Monthly Meeting, a liberal, unprogrammed meeting. He has been a jazz fan since playing saxophone in his high school and city bands way back in the '80s.

Emily Stewart (28) grew up in Durham Monthly Meeting, which is dually affiliated with North Carolina Yearly Meeting (Conservative) and Piedmont Friends Fellowship (FGC). She currently serves as the Youth Ministries Coordinator for Friends General Conference.

cubbie storm (30) is a goofy and serious transguy who works in special education and independent bookselling. He is still figuring out god and says "the universe" when he means god and "god" when he means the universe. You can read his blog at: peculiarqueer.wordpress.com.

Rebecca Sullivan (21) is majoring in peace and conflict Studies at Guilford College, where she is an active member of the Quaker Leadership Scholars Program, and is struggling to find her calling in the Quaker world. Since deciding at the age of sixteen that Quakerism was for her, she has struggled to be recognized as more than her parents' shadow. She has started traveling with other Friends in the ministry searching for her role as an elder in the Religious Society of Friends.

Kate Symank (23) recently graduated with a writing degree from Trinity Western University in British Columbia. She loves to travel and to vacation at the beach and is saving up to buy a pet kinkajou.

Alexa Taylor lives in Australia.

Abraham Quispe Ticona is a Friend in Bolivia.

Simiyu Kalamu Timothy (19) is a member of Lugulu Friends Church in Kenya.

William Hunt Tinsman (17) is a member of Solebury Friends Meeting, Philadelphia Yearly Meeting. He thinks his work speaks for itself.

Rebeca Tintaya V. is a Friend in the Bolivian Holiness Mission of Evangelical Friends Church. She lives in La Paz, Bolivia.

Crystal Waitekus (29) is a member of Virginia Beach Friends Meeting and a graduate of Guilford College. She currently lives and works on Capitol Hill in Washington, D.C.

Andrew Wafula Wakili is a Kenyan Friend.

Maggie Wanner (17) is a suburban Illinois high school student who enjoys playing the tuba and playing in the dirt outside. She spends a few weeks of every summer at Camp Woodbrooke in Wisconsin, which is Quaker owned. While her current religious feelings are shifting away from organized religion, she is proud to have been raised with Quaker values.

Joanna Waters (20) grew up near Doncaster, South Yorkshire, in the United Kingdom. Both her parents were Quakers, so Friends have been a source of growth and support throughout her life, in particular through losing both of her parents and then moving home. Quaker youth events have been a very important part of her spiritual life, and the friends met there continue to be so.

Ben Watts (25) has been involved with Friends in New Zealand his entire life. He works as a graphic designer.

Sara Waxman (27) is a teaching artist, stage manager, and member of Chestnut Hill Monthly Meeting in Philadelphia (Philadelphia Yearly Meeting). Her poetry is inspired by the space between her art and spirituality.

Russell Weiss-Irwin (18) is from Medford, Massachusetts, and a senior at the Commonwealth School in Boston. He bikes cheerfully through Boston, seeking to answer the humanity in everyone.

Evan Welkin (25) grew up in Olympia Monthly Meeting in Washington State, a body of the unaffiliated North Pacific Yearly Meeting. After graduating from Guilford College in 2006, he has pursued other motorcycles, other pilgrimages, and the same journey for God's grace and messengers in his life.

Ashley M. Wilcox (28) is a member of Freedom Friends Church in Salem, Oregon, and a sojourning member of University Friends Meeting in Seattle, Washington. She blogs at http://questforadequacy.blogspot.com

Ailsa Wild (31) was born in England and moved to Australia when she was five, where she was brought up on a community farm in Southern New South Wales. She moved to Melbourne when she was eighteen, where she performs, teaches, and directs circus for young people.

Liz Wine (27) worked as a school-based therapist at an elementary school before moving to Rwanda with Evangelical Friends Mission for two years to teach in a school for the children of missionaries. She is a Kansas native and enjoys working with children and laughing and spending time with her friends and family.

Greg Woods (25), is a member of Columbia (Missouri) Monthly Meeting (FGC). He graduated from Earlham College in 2007 with a degree in liberal arts, majoring in peace and global studies. When he isn't working as the Coordinator of Washington Quaker Workcamps at the William Penn House in Washington, D.C, he can be found attending demolition derbies and monster truck rallies.

Cassie Leigh Wright (27) feels privileged to have been born a Quaker so that she was able to grow up a very open-minded individual with an ability to appreciate and love herself and others. She is excited to carry these Quakerly traits forward with her to her upcoming marriage, career as a teacher, and someday experience as a mother. Her piece was originally shared verbally with the congregation of Whittier First Friends Church on Homecoming Sunday of 2007, when Whittier College is invited to worship with its founders in celebration of their historical ties.

kit wilson-yang has primarily written songs and music, but over many years has been compiling poems and unreadable private writings that kit is beginning to be excited about. Making art is like breathing and allows kit to process the world, especially when the presence of the spirit is not obvious. While growing up, kit attended Hamilton Monthly Meeting in Canadian Yearly Meeting and is/was a frequent visitor to Camp NeeKauNis.

Gayle Yeomans (30) is a music-art-and-literature-loving thirty-year-old currently working in an accountant's office in her hometown of Stafford. She is in a long-term relationship with a wonderful guy called Chris, and feels lucky to have a loving and supportive family.

Editorial Board Biographies

Angelina Conti (27) came to Quakerism through the youth programs of Philadelphia Yearly Meeting (FGC), is a graduate of Haverford College, and worked for two years at Friends General Conference. She is a teacher at the Woolman Semester in Nevada City, California, and a freelance writer and editor. Though she is enjoying her time as an itinerant Quaker, she intends to one day put down roots (and a big garden) in her beloved Philadelphia.

Cara Curtis (22) grew up in the schools and camps of Baltimore Yearly Meeting (FGC-FUM) and considers Adelphi Monthly Meeting her spiritual home. A senior religion major at Haverford College, Cara will graduate in May 2010 and hopes to subsequently find some sort of (vaguely) gainful employment. Chocolate chip cookies are her ultimate comfort food.

C. Wess Daniels (31) is a PhD student at Fuller Theological Seminary and pastor of Camas Friends Church in Camas, Washington. Wess and his wife, Emily, are originally from Ohio but love living in the Northwest and being a part of Northwest Yearly Meeting (EFCI). His academic work focuses on what he is most passionate about: issues such as the church in contemporary culture, missiology, and renewal in Quaker meetings. He has spoken and written on convergent Friends many times and thinks all these cross-pollinating friendships are the subversive work of the Holy Spirit. He writes regularly on his website *Gathering in Light*.

Harriet Hart (22) has been active in Britain Yearly Meeting's youth programs as both a participant and leader for many years, and has served as a writing workshop and peer group facilitator at Junior Yearly Meeting. She is a frequent contributor to *The Friend*, and in 2006 she participated in the Quaker Youth Pilgrimage in the Midwest of the United States. Having grown up in Yorkshire not far from the original Pendle Hill, she is now a Resident Student at the *other* Pendle Hill, in Wallingford, Pennsylvania.

Sarah Katreen Hoggatt (30) lives in Salem, Oregon, and is a member of Freedom Friends Church, an independent, semi-programmed, semi-pastoral, liberal and Christ-centered Friends church. A freelance writer, editor, photographer, spiritual director, and self-publisher, she has identified writing and public speaking as her passions in ministry and has developed Spirit Water Publications as an outlet for Christian writing. She is a graduate of George Fox Evangelical Seminary in Portland, Oregon, and is also active with ecumenical Christian organizations in Salem and Portland. Her other interests include hiking, theatre, dancing, and singing along with the radio. You can find more of her writing and a link to her blog at www.SpiritWaterPublications.com.

Evelyn Jadin (25) is a member of Jamestown Friends Meeting in North Carolina Yearly Meeting (FUM), where she served as Youth Minister from 2007 to 2009. She is a graduate of Guilford College, the Quaker Leadership Scholars Program there, and the Baltimore Yearly Meeting camping program. She is currently a master's in divinity student at the Earlham School of Religion in Richmond, Indiana.

John Epur Lomuria (32) is presiding clerk of Lodwar Monthly Meeting and reading clerk of the young people's program of East Africa Yearly Meeting of Friends (North) (FUM). He is treasurer of the Turkana Friends Mission of Friends United Meeting, has served on FWCC nominating committees, and has written and edited several articles for *Quaker Life Magazine*. He is the incoming clerk of the Young Quaker Christian Association (Africa), and participated in the World Gathering of Young Friends in Mombasa in 2005.

Emma Condori Mamani (31) is from La Paz, Bolivia, where she worked as a teacher in Quaker schools. She is a member of Santidad Amigos, the largest evangelical Quaker yearly meeting in Bolivia, and has worked with the Bolivian Quaker Education Organization, which supports and works with the several different yearly meetings in Bolivia. She is currently a master's of divinity student at the Earlham School of Religion in Richmond, Indiana.

Katrina McQuail (26) was raised on an organic, mixed-livestock farm in rural Ontario, Canada, and is a member of Kitchener Area Monthly Meeting of Canadian Yearly Meeting (FGC-FUM). She spent her formative years attending Camp NeeKauNis. She has served as an editor of the Canadian Young Friends publication the *Sporadical* and has been published in a number of Quaker publications. She is an unprogrammed Friend who went to Earlham College, attends Friends General Conference Gathering and tries to serve the Quaker community widely. She attended the World Gathering of Young Friends in 2005, which opened her eyes to the wide spectrum of Quakerism.

Rachel Anne Miller (30) lives in Somerville, Massachusetts, where she attends Cambridge Friends Meeting, New England Yearly Meeting (FGC-FUM). She holds membership in Greenville Friends Meeting in North Carolina Yearly Meeting (Conservative).